CASE CLOSED
VOLUME 28

Gosho Aoyama

Case Briefing:

Subject:
Occupation:
Special Skills:
Equipment:

Jimmy Kudo, a.k.a. Conan Edogawa
High School Student/Detective
Analytical thinking and deductive reasoning, Soccer
Bow Tie Voice Transmitter, Super Sneakers,
Homing Glasses, Stretchy Suspenders

The subject is hot on the trail of a pair of suspicious men in black when he is attacked from behind and administered a strange substance which physically transforms him into a first grader. When the subject confides in the eccentric inventor Dr. Agasa, they decide to keep the subject's true identity a secret for the safety of everyone around him. Assuming the new identity of first-grader Conan Edogawa, the subject continues to assist the police force on their most baffling cases. The only problem is that most crime-solving professionals won't take a little kid's advice!

Table of Contents

CONFIDEN

CASE CLOSED
Volume 28 • VIZ Media Edition
GOSHO AOYAMA

Translation
Tetsuichiro Miyaki

Touch-up & Lettering
Freeman Wong

Cover & Graphic Design
Andrea Rice

Editor
Shaenon K. Garrity

Editor in Chief, Books **Alvin Lu**
Editor in Chief, Magazines **Marc Weidenbaum**
VP, Publishing Licensing **Rika Inouye**
VP, Sales & Product Marketing **Gonzalo Ferreyra**
VP, Creative **Linda Espinosa**
Publisher **Hyoe Narita**

store.viz.com

RATED
PARENTAL ADVISORY
CASE CLOSED is rated T+ for Older Teen and
is recommended for ages 16 and up. This volume contains realistic and graphic violence.
FOR OLDER TEEN
ratings.viz.com

www.viz.com

Printed in the U.S.A.
Published by VIZ Media, LLC
P.O. Box 77010
San Francisco, CA 94107

10 9 8 7 6 5 4 3 2 1
First printing, March 2009

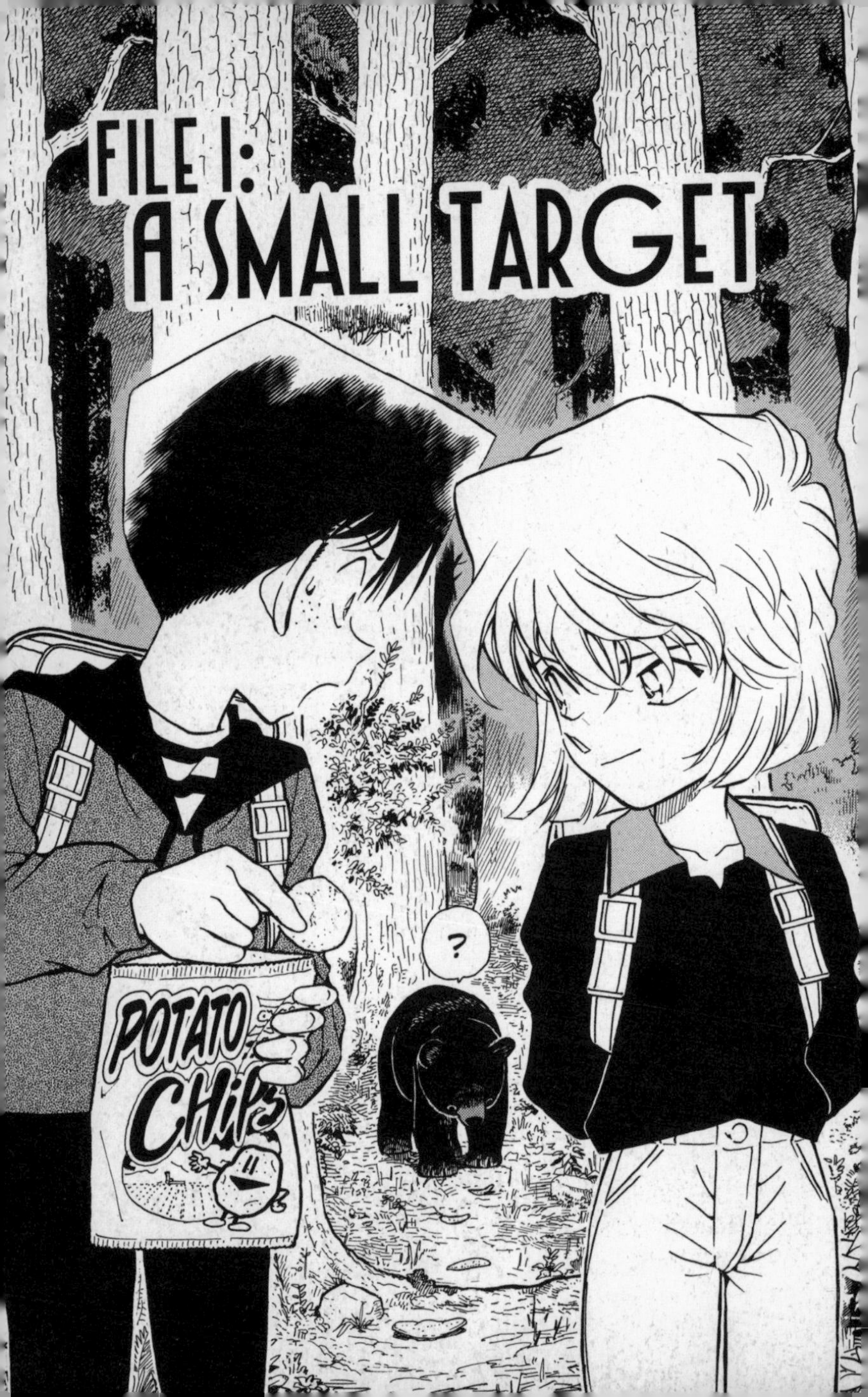

FILE 1: A SMALL TARGET
?
POTATO CHIPS

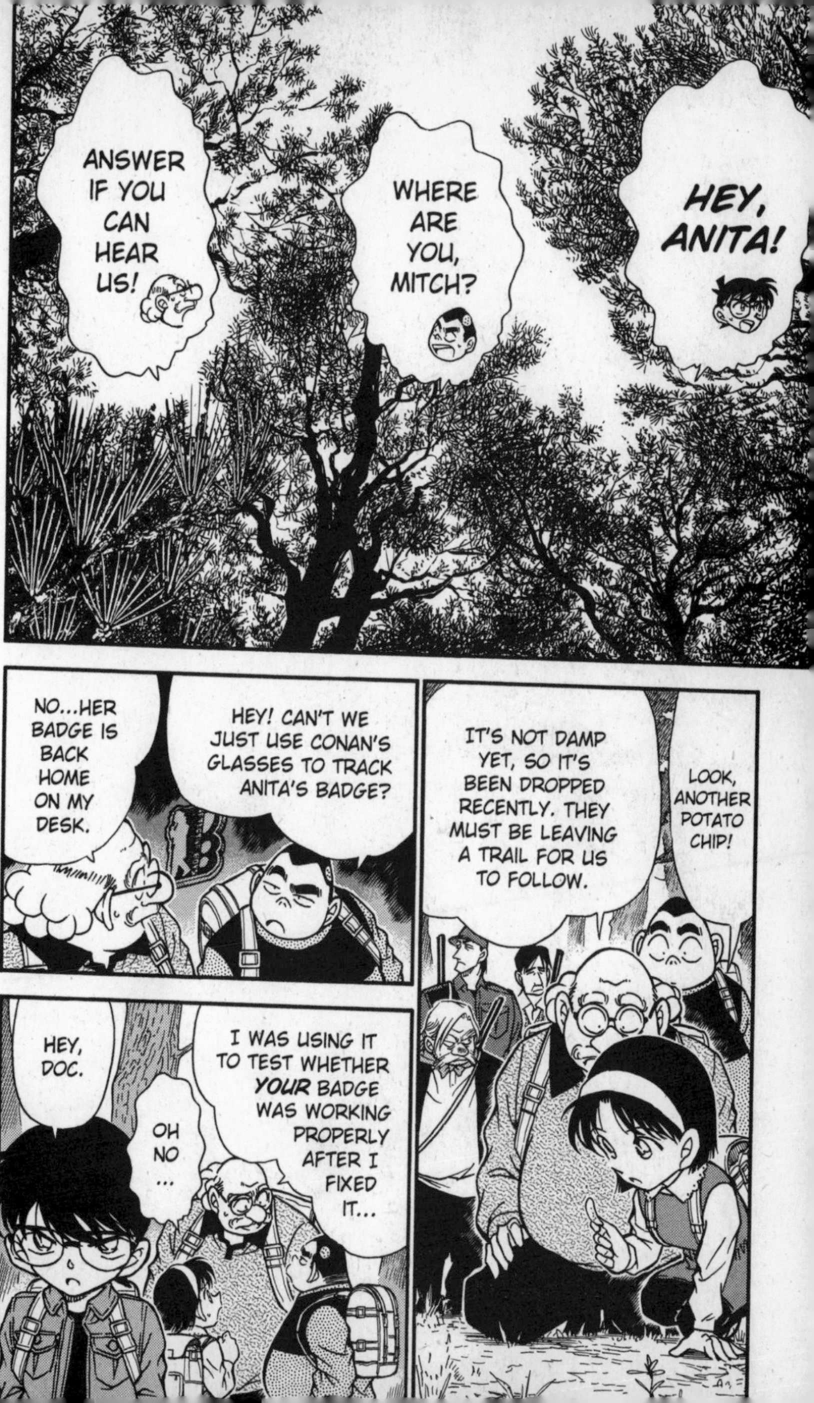
HEY, ANITA!
WHERE ARE YOU, MITCH?
ANSWER IF YOU CAN HEAR US!
LOOK, ANOTHER POTATO CHIP!
IT'S NOT DAMP YET, SO IT'S BEEN DROPPED RECENTLY. THEY MUST BE LEAVING A TRAIL FOR US TO FOLLOW.
HEY! CAN'T WE JUST USE CONAN'S GLASSES TO TRACK ANITA'S BADGE?
NO...HER BADGE IS BACK HOME ON MY DESK.
HEY, DOC.
I WAS USING IT TO TEST WHETHER *YOUR* BADGE WAS WORKING PROPERLY AFTER I FIXED IT...
OH NO ...

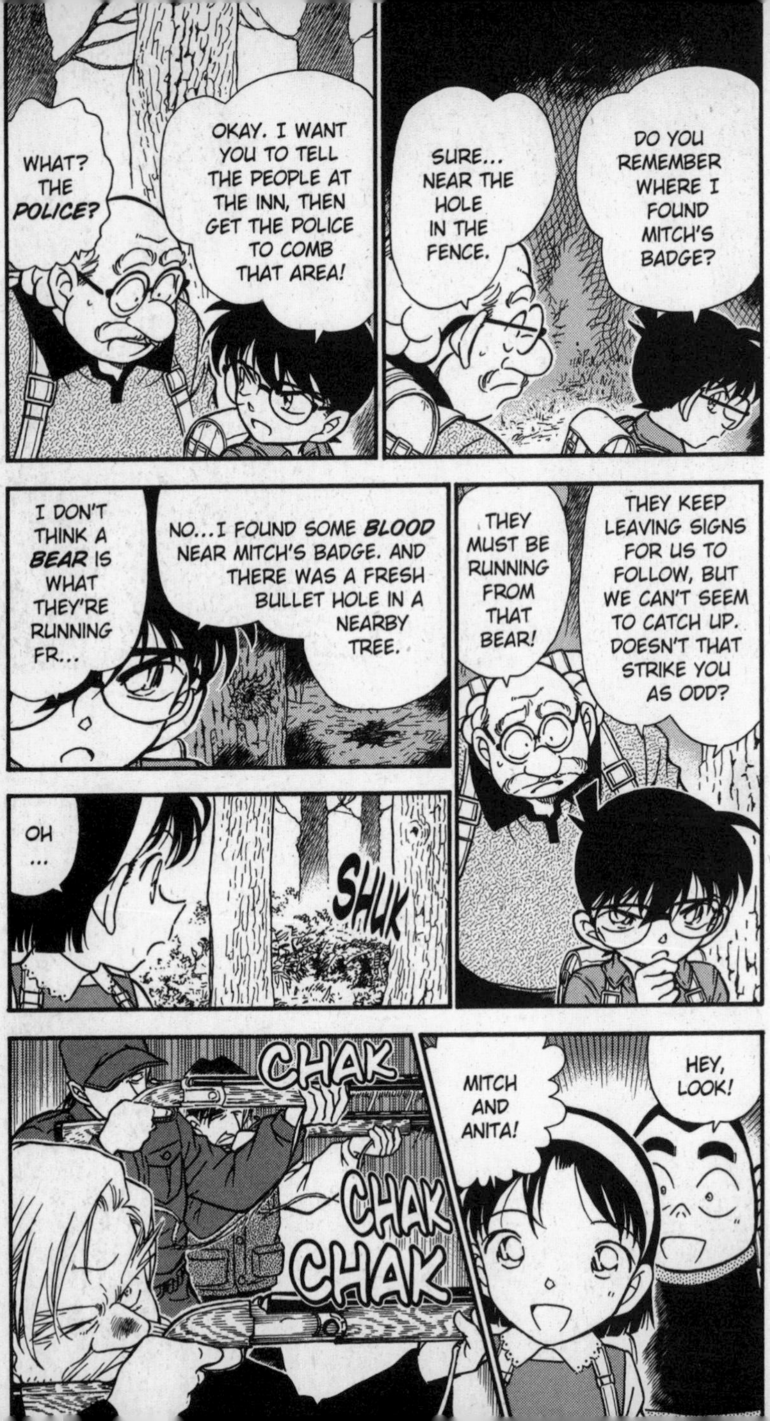
DO YOU REMEMBER WHERE I FOUND MITCH'S BADGE?
SURE... NEAR THE HOLE IN THE FENCE.
OKAY. I WANT YOU TO TELL THE PEOPLE AT THE INN, THEN GET THE POLICE TO COMB THAT AREA!
WHAT? THE *POLICE?*
THEY KEEP LEAVING SIGNS FOR US TO FOLLOW, BUT WE CAN'T SEEM TO CATCH UP. DOESN'T THAT STRIKE YOU AS ODD?
THEY MUST BE RUNNING FROM THAT BEAR!
NO...I FOUND SOME *BLOOD* NEAR MITCH'S BADGE. AND THERE WAS A FRESH BULLET HOLE IN A NEARBY TREE.
I DON'T THINK A *BEAR* IS WHAT THEY'RE RUNNING FR...
SHUK
OH ...
HEY, LOOK!
MITCH AND ANITA!
CHAK
CHAK
CHAK

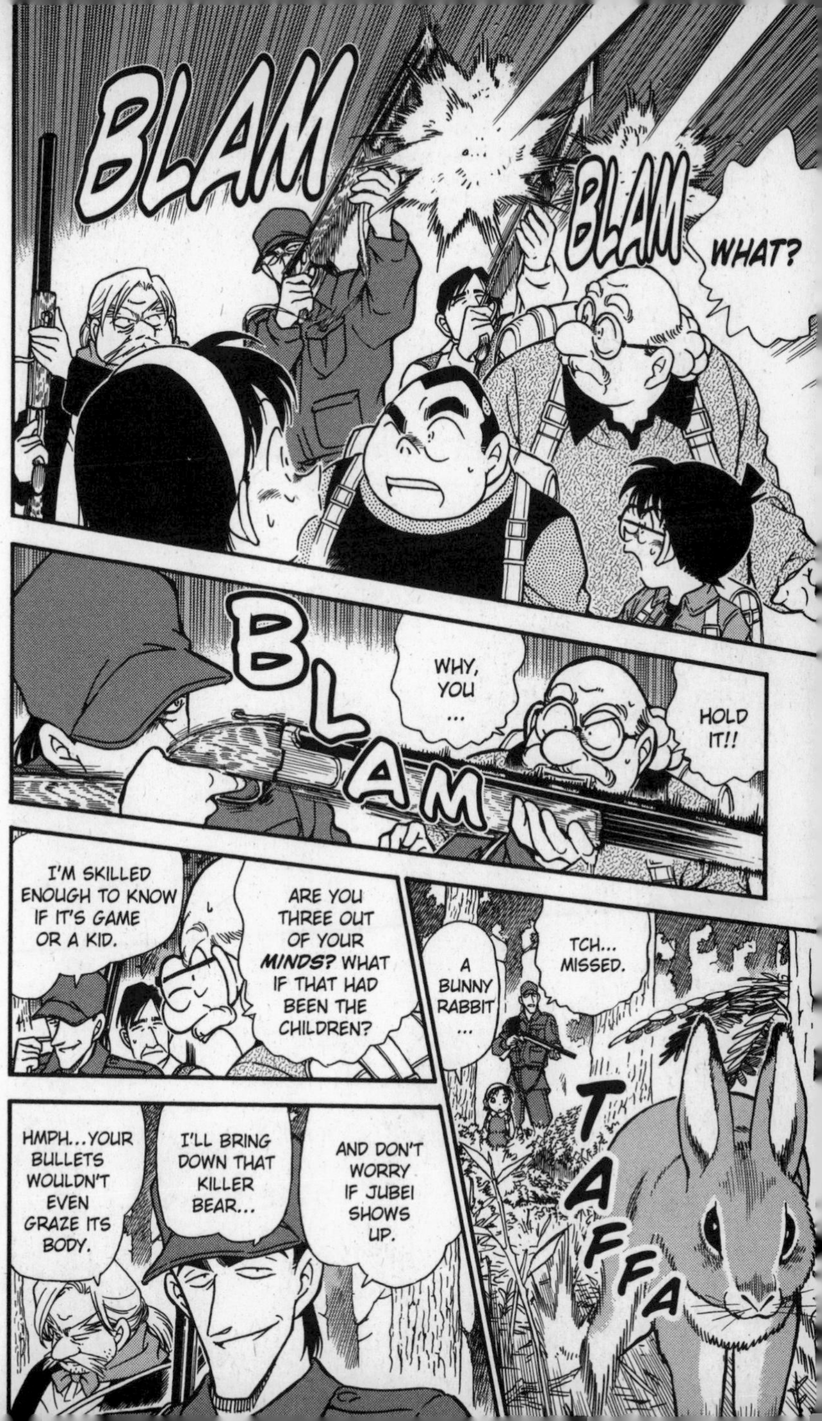
BLAM
WHAT?
BLAM
HOLD IT!!
WHY, YOU ...
BLAM
TCH... MISSED.
A BUNNY RABBIT ...
TAFFA
ARE YOU THREE OUT OF YOUR *MINDS?* WHAT IF THAT HAD BEEN THE CHILDREN?
I'M SKILLED ENOUGH TO KNOW IF IT'S GAME OR A KID.
AND DON'T WORRY IF JUBEI SHOWS UP.
I'LL BRING DOWN THAT KILLER BEAR...
HMPH...YOUR BULLETS WOULDN'T EVEN GRAZE ITS BODY.

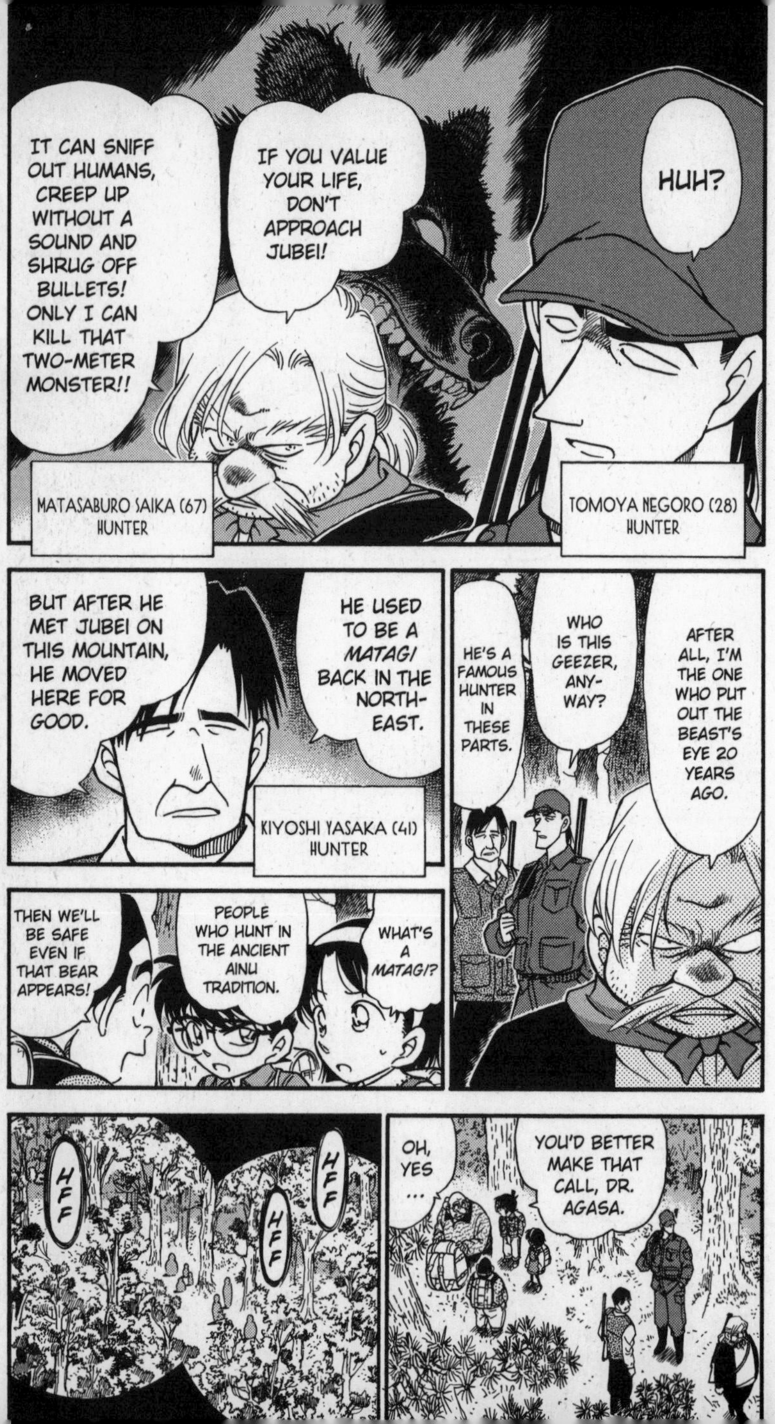
HUH?
IF YOU VALUE YOUR LIFE, DON'T APPROACH JUBEI!
IT CAN SNIFF OUT HUMANS, CREEP UP WITHOUT A SOUND AND SHRUG OFF BULLETS! ONLY I CAN KILL THAT TWO-METER MONSTER!!
TOMOYA NEGORO (28) HUNTER
MATASABURO SAIKA (67) HUNTER
AFTER ALL, I'M THE ONE WHO PUT OUT THE BEAST'S EYE 20 YEARS AGO.
WHO IS THIS GEEZER, ANYWAY?
HE'S A FAMOUS HUNTER IN THESE PARTS.
HE USED TO BE A *MATAGI* BACK IN THE NORTHEAST.
BUT AFTER HE MET JUBEI ON THIS MOUNTAIN, HE MOVED HERE FOR GOOD.
KIYOSHI YASAKA (41) HUNTER
WHAT'S A *MATAGI*?
PEOPLE WHO HUNT IN THE ANCIENT AINU TRADITION.
THEN WE'LL BE SAFE EVEN IF THAT BEAR APPEARS!
YOU'D BETTER MAKE THAT CALL, DR. AGASA.
OH, YES ...
HFF
HFF
HFF
HFF

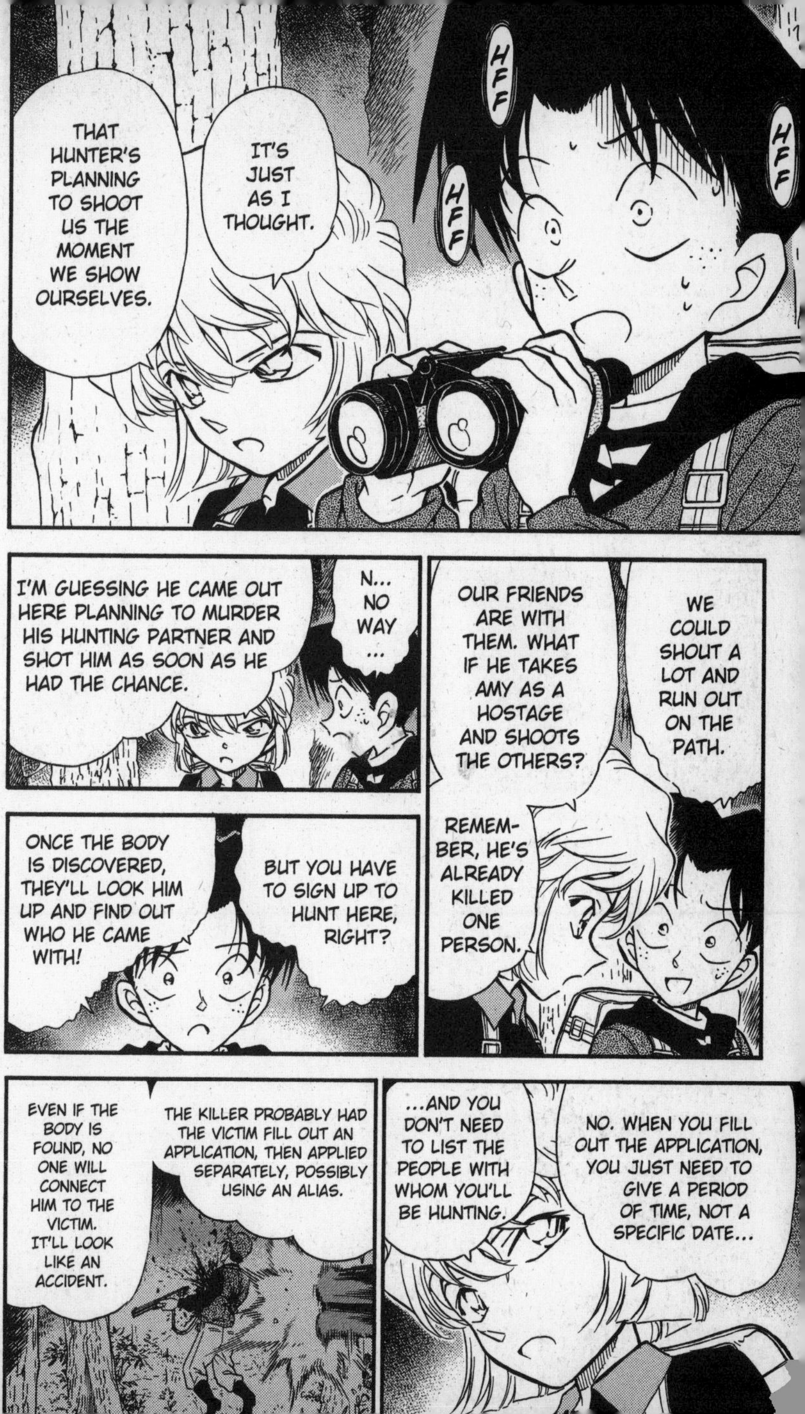
HFF
HFF
HFF
IT'S JUST AS I THOUGHT.
THAT HUNTER'S PLANNING TO SHOOT US THE MOMENT WE SHOW OURSELVES.
WE COULD SHOUT A LOT AND RUN OUT ON THE PATH.
OUR FRIENDS ARE WITH THEM. WHAT IF HE TAKES AMY AS A HOSTAGE AND SHOOTS THE OTHERS?
REMEMBER, HE'S ALREADY KILLED ONE PERSON.
N... NO WAY ...
I'M GUESSING HE CAME OUT HERE PLANNING TO MURDER HIS HUNTING PARTNER AND SHOT HIM AS SOON AS HE HAD THE CHANCE.
BUT YOU HAVE TO SIGN UP TO HUNT HERE, RIGHT?
ONCE THE BODY IS DISCOVERED, THEY'LL LOOK HIM UP AND FIND OUT WHO HE CAME WITH!
NO. WHEN YOU FILL OUT THE APPLICATION, YOU JUST NEED TO GIVE A PERIOD OF TIME, NOT A SPECIFIC DATE...
...AND YOU DON'T NEED TO LIST THE PEOPLE WITH WHOM YOU'LL BE HUNTING.
THE KILLER PROBABLY HAD THE VICTIM FILL OUT AN APPLICATION, THEN APPLIED SEPARATELY, POSSIBLY USING AN ALIAS.
EVEN IF THE BODY IS FOUND, NO ONE WILL CONNECT HIM TO THE VICTIM. IT'LL LOOK LIKE AN ACCIDENT.

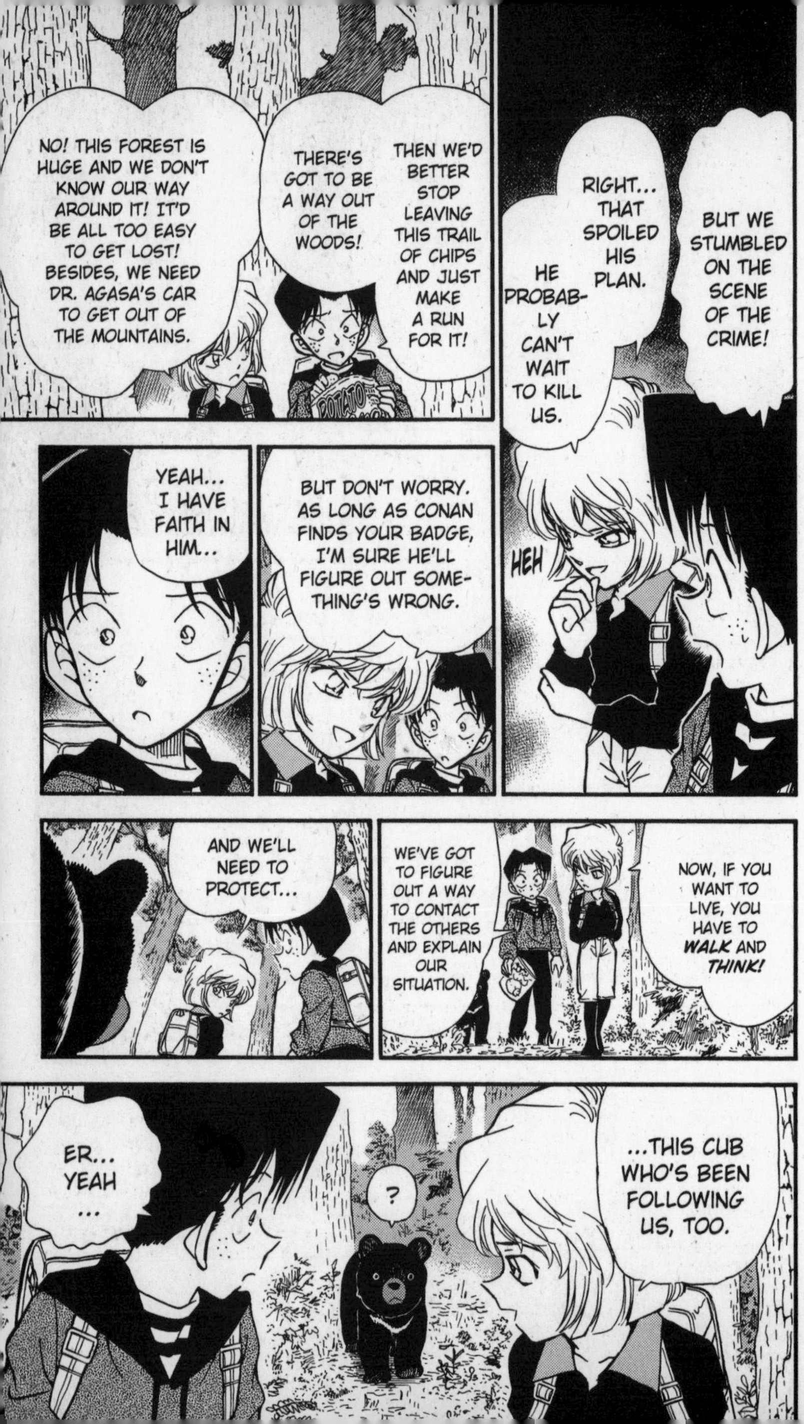
BUT WE STUMBLED ON THE SCENE OF THE CRIME!
RIGHT... THAT SPOILED HIS PLAN.
HE PROBAB-LY CAN'T WAIT TO KILL US.
HEH
THEN WE'D BETTER STOP LEAVING THIS TRAIL OF CHIPS AND JUST MAKE A RUN FOR IT!
THERE'S GOT TO BE A WAY OUT OF THE WOODS!
NO! THIS FOREST IS HUGE AND WE DON'T KNOW OUR WAY AROUND IT! IT'D BE ALL TOO EASY TO GET LOST! BESIDES, WE NEED DR. AGASA'S CAR TO GET OUT OF THE MOUNTAINS.
BUT DON'T WORRY. AS LONG AS CONAN FINDS YOUR BADGE, I'M SURE HE'LL FIGURE OUT SOME-THING'S WRONG.
YEAH... I HAVE FAITH IN HIM...
NOW, IF YOU WANT TO LIVE, YOU HAVE TO WALK AND THINK!
WE'VE GOT TO FIGURE OUT A WAY TO CONTACT THE OTHERS AND EXPLAIN OUR SITUATION.
AND WE'LL NEED TO PROTECT...
...THIS CUB WHO'S BEEN FOLLOWING US, TOO.
?
ER... YEAH ...

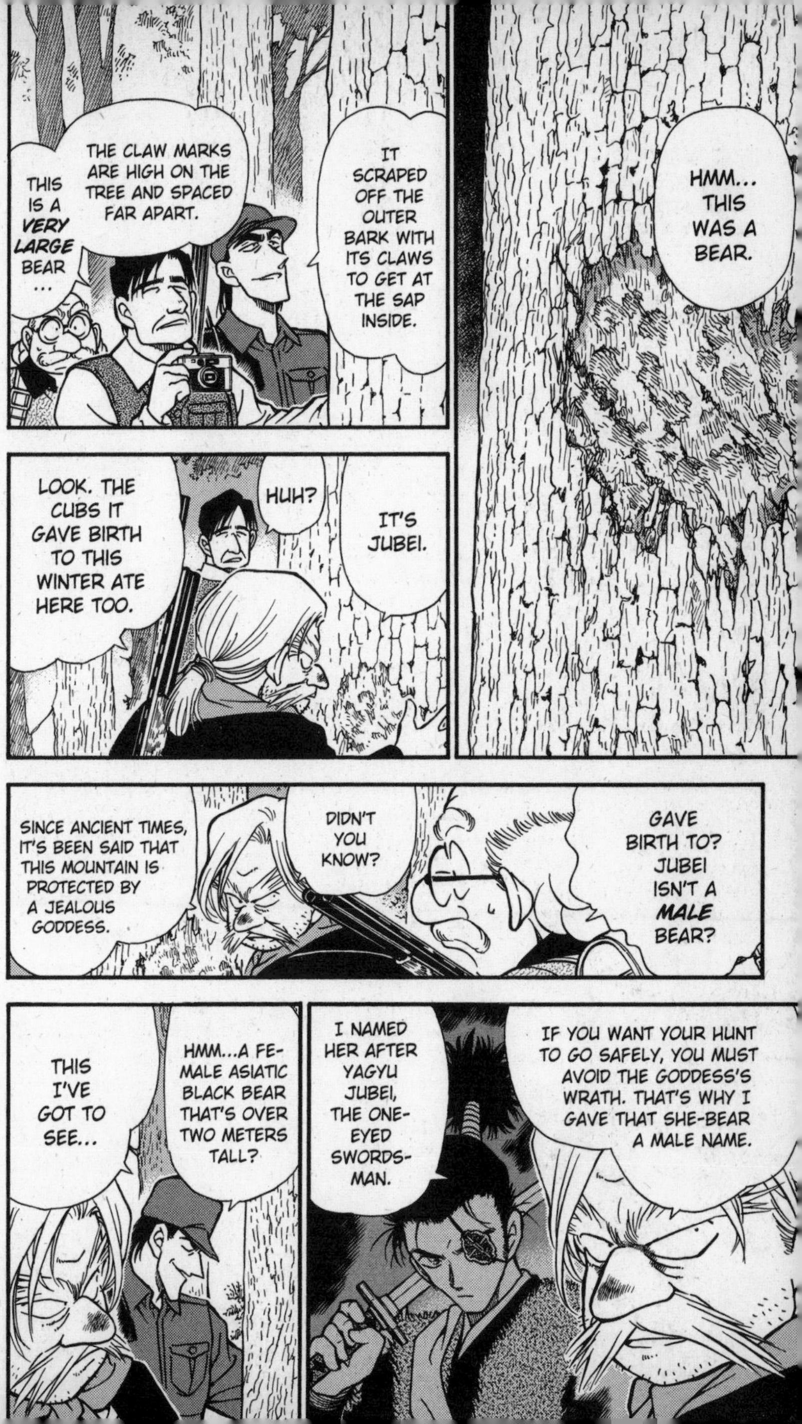
HMM... THIS WAS A BEAR.
IT SCRAPED OFF THE OUTER BARK WITH ITS CLAWS TO GET AT THE SAP INSIDE.
THE CLAW MARKS ARE HIGH ON THE TREE AND SPACED FAR APART.
THIS IS A ***VERY LARGE*** BEAR...
IT'S JUBEI.
HUH?
LOOK. THE CUBS IT GAVE BIRTH TO THIS WINTER ATE HERE TOO.
GAVE BIRTH TO? JUBEI ISN'T A ***MALE*** BEAR?
DIDN'T YOU KNOW?
SINCE ANCIENT TIMES, IT'S BEEN SAID THAT THIS MOUNTAIN IS PROTECTED BY A JEALOUS GODDESS.
IF YOU WANT YOUR HUNT TO GO SAFELY, YOU MUST AVOID THE GODDESS'S WRATH. THAT'S WHY I GAVE THAT SHE-BEAR A MALE NAME.
I NAMED HER AFTER YAGYU JUBEI, THE ONE-EYED SWORDSMAN.
HMM...A FEMALE ASIATIC BLACK BEAR THAT'S OVER TWO METERS TALL?
THIS I'VE GOT TO SEE...

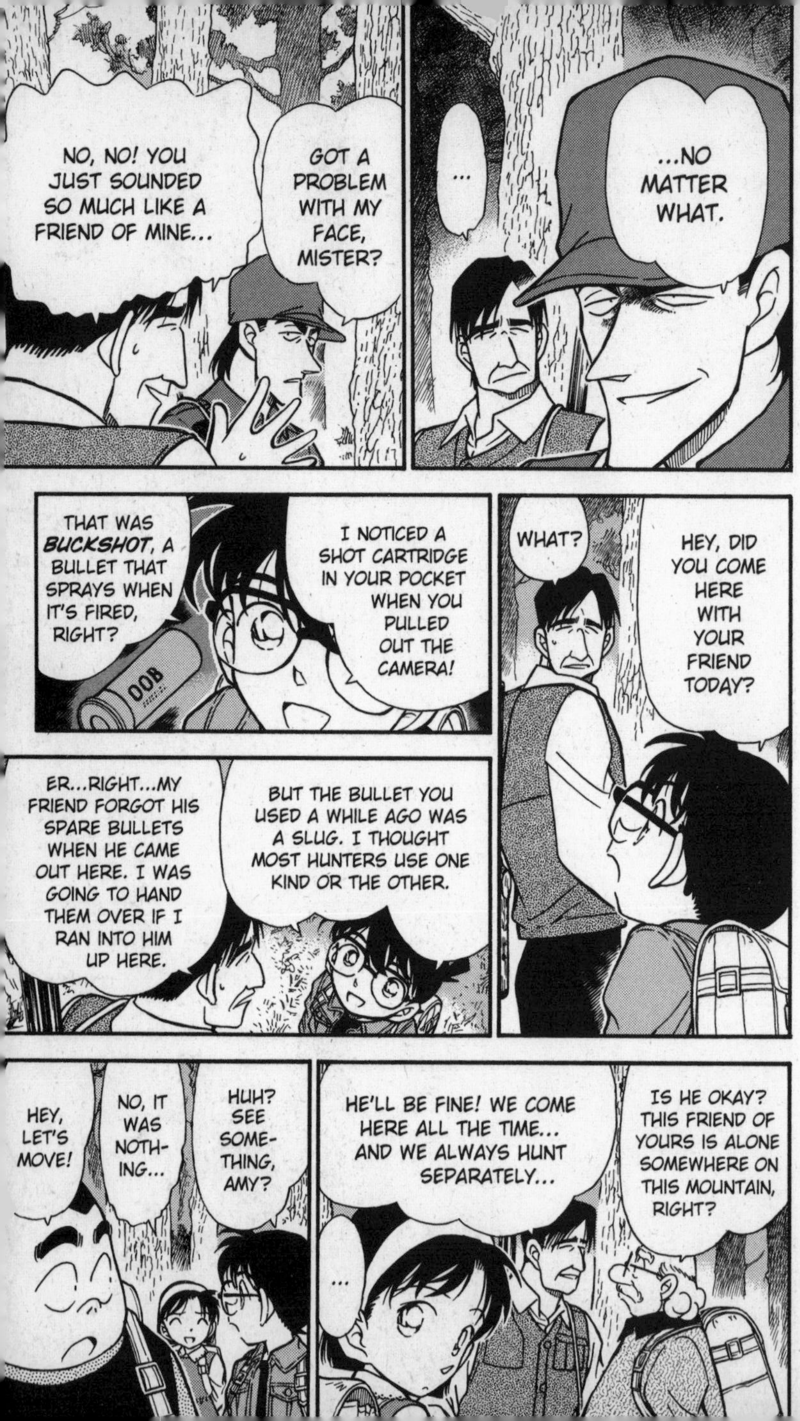
...NO MATTER WHAT.
...
GOT A PROBLEM WITH MY FACE, MISTER?
NO, NO! YOU JUST SOUNDED SO MUCH LIKE A FRIEND OF MINE...
HEY, DID YOU COME HERE WITH YOUR FRIEND TODAY?
WHAT?
I NOTICED A SHOT CARTRIDGE IN YOUR POCKET WHEN YOU PULLED OUT THE CAMERA!
THAT WAS BUCKSHOT, A BULLET THAT SPRAYS WHEN IT'S FIRED, RIGHT?
00B
BUT THE BULLET YOU USED A WHILE AGO WAS A SLUG. I THOUGHT MOST HUNTERS USE ONE KIND OR THE OTHER.
ER...RIGHT...MY FRIEND FORGOT HIS SPARE BULLETS WHEN HE CAME OUT HERE. I WAS GOING TO HAND THEM OVER IF I RAN INTO HIM UP HERE.
IS HE OKAY? THIS FRIEND OF YOURS IS ALONE SOMEWHERE ON THIS MOUNTAIN, RIGHT?
HE'LL BE FINE! WE COME HERE ALL THE TIME... AND WE ALWAYS HUNT SEPARATELY...
...
HUH? SEE SOMETHING, AMY?
NO, IT WAS NOTHING...
HEY, LET'S MOVE!

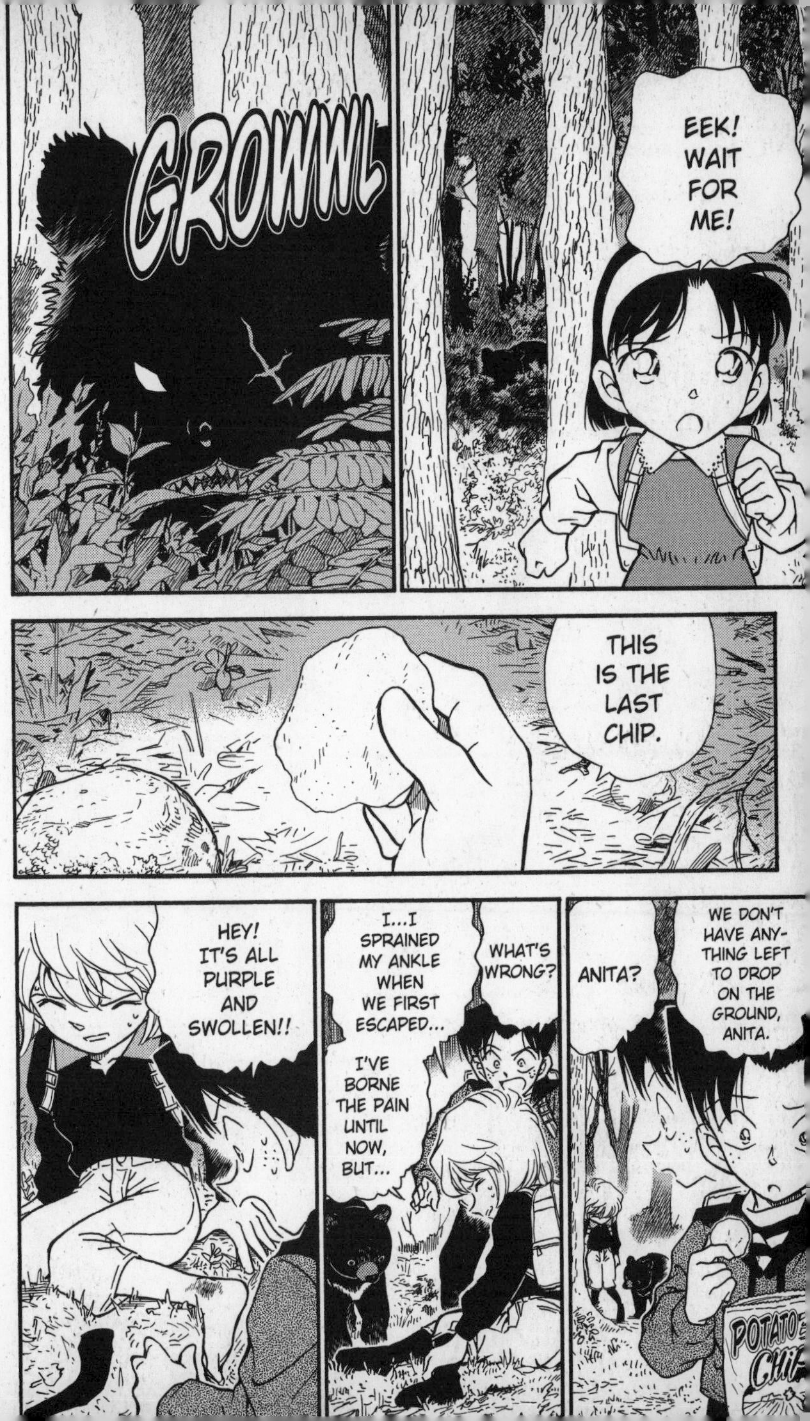
EEK! WAIT FOR ME!
GROWWL
THIS IS THE LAST CHIP.
WE DON'T HAVE ANY-THING LEFT TO DROP ON THE GROUND, ANITA.
ANITA?
WHAT'S WRONG?
I...I SPRAINED MY ANKLE WHEN WE FIRST ESCAPED...
I'VE BORNE THE PAIN UNTIL NOW, BUT...
HEY! IT'S ALL PURPLE AND SWOLLEN!!

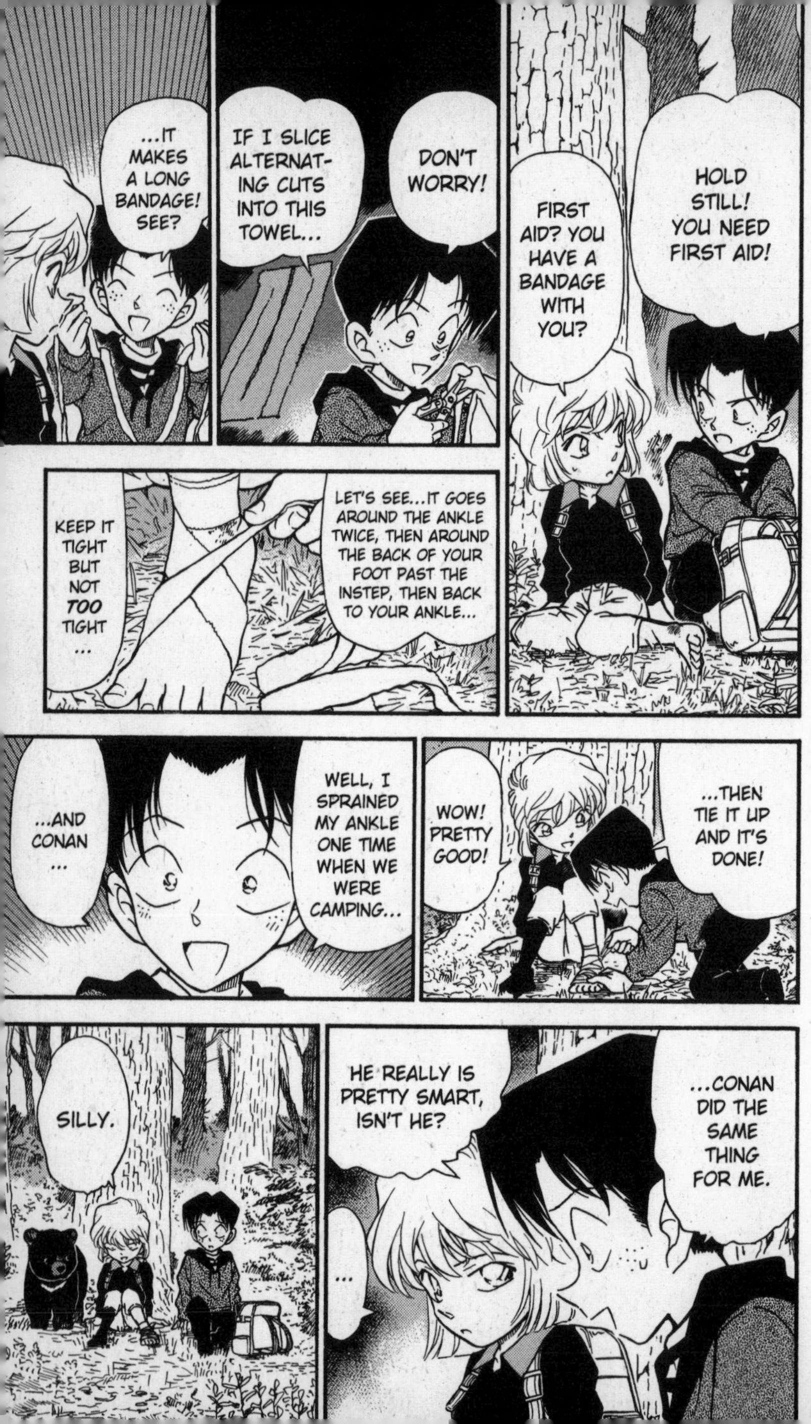
HOLD STILL! YOU NEED FIRST AID!
FIRST AID? YOU HAVE A BANDAGE WITH YOU?
DON'T WORRY!
IF I SLICE ALTERNATING CUTS INTO THIS TOWEL...
...IT MAKES A LONG BANDAGE! SEE?
LET'S SEE...IT GOES AROUND THE ANKLE TWICE, THEN AROUND THE BACK OF YOUR FOOT PAST THE INSTEP, THEN BACK TO YOUR ANKLE...
KEEP IT TIGHT BUT NOT *TOO* TIGHT ...
...THEN TIE IT UP AND IT'S DONE!
WOW! PRETTY GOOD!
WELL, I SPRAINED MY ANKLE ONE TIME WHEN WE WERE CAMPING...
...AND CONAN ...
...CONAN DID THE SAME THING FOR ME.
HE REALLY IS PRETTY SMART, ISN'T HE?
...
SILLY.

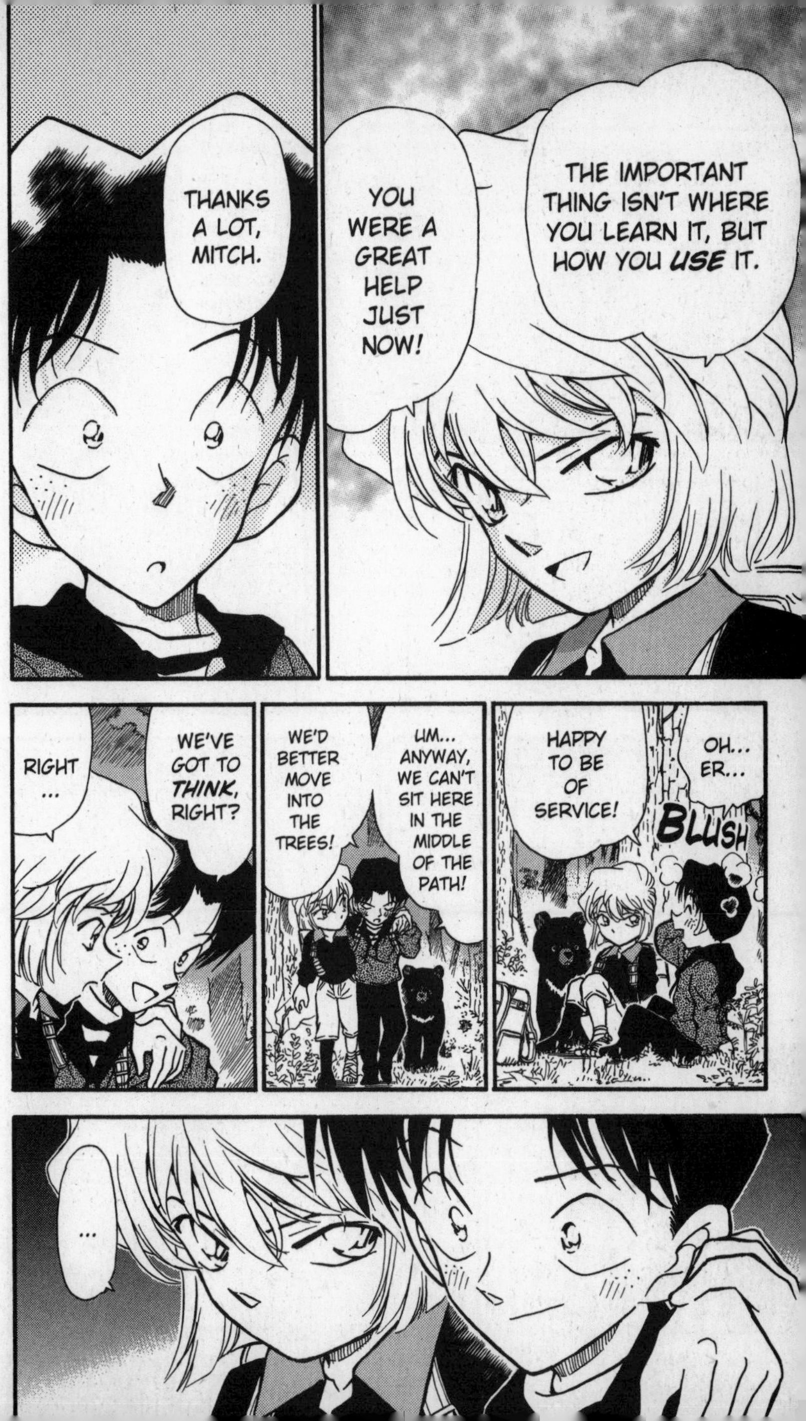
THE IMPORTANT THING ISN'T WHERE YOU LEARN IT, BUT HOW YOU USE IT.
YOU WERE A GREAT HELP JUST NOW!
THANKS A LOT, MITCH.
OH... ER...
BLUSH
HAPPY TO BE OF SERVICE!
UM... ANYWAY, WE CAN'T SIT HERE IN THE MIDDLE OF THE PATH!
WE'D BETTER MOVE INTO THE TREES!
WE'VE GOT TO THINK, RIGHT?
RIGHT ...
...

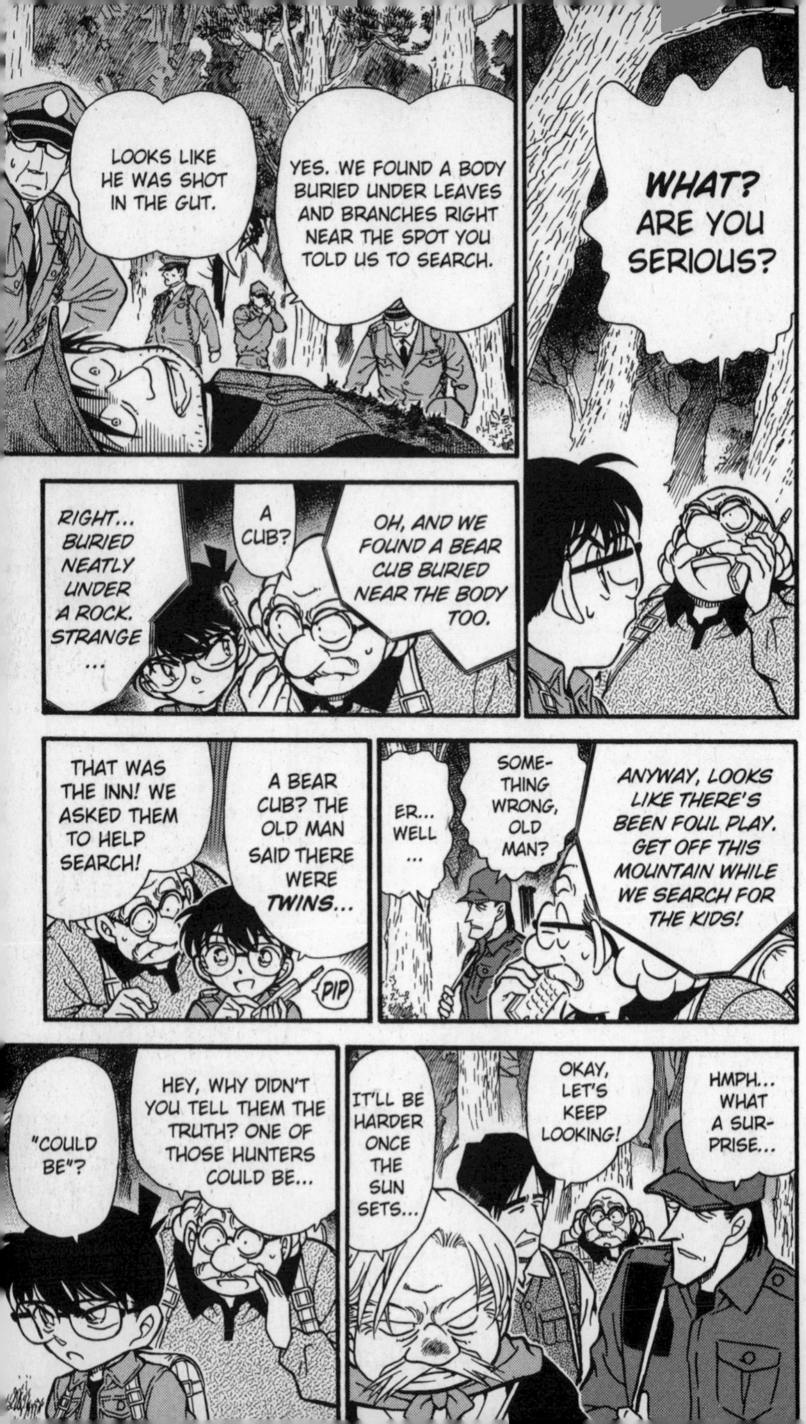
WHAT? ARE YOU SERIOUS?
YES. WE FOUND A BODY BURIED UNDER LEAVES AND BRANCHES RIGHT NEAR THE SPOT YOU TOLD US TO SEARCH.
LOOKS LIKE HE WAS SHOT IN THE GUT.
OH, AND WE FOUND A BEAR CUB BURIED NEAR THE BODY TOO.
A CUB?
RIGHT... BURIED NEATLY UNDER A ROCK. STRANGE...
ANYWAY, LOOKS LIKE THERE'S BEEN FOUL PLAY. GET OFF THIS MOUNTAIN WHILE WE SEARCH FOR THE KIDS!
SOME-THING WRONG, OLD MAN?
ER... WELL...
A BEAR CUB? THE OLD MAN SAID THERE WERE TWINS...
THAT WAS THE INN! WE ASKED THEM TO HELP SEARCH!
PIP
HMPH... WHAT A SUR-PRISE...
OKAY, LET'S KEEP LOOKING!
IT'LL BE HARDER ONCE THE SUN SETS...
HEY, WHY DIDN'T YOU TELL THEM THE TRUTH? ONE OF THOSE HUNTERS COULD BE...
"COULD BE"?

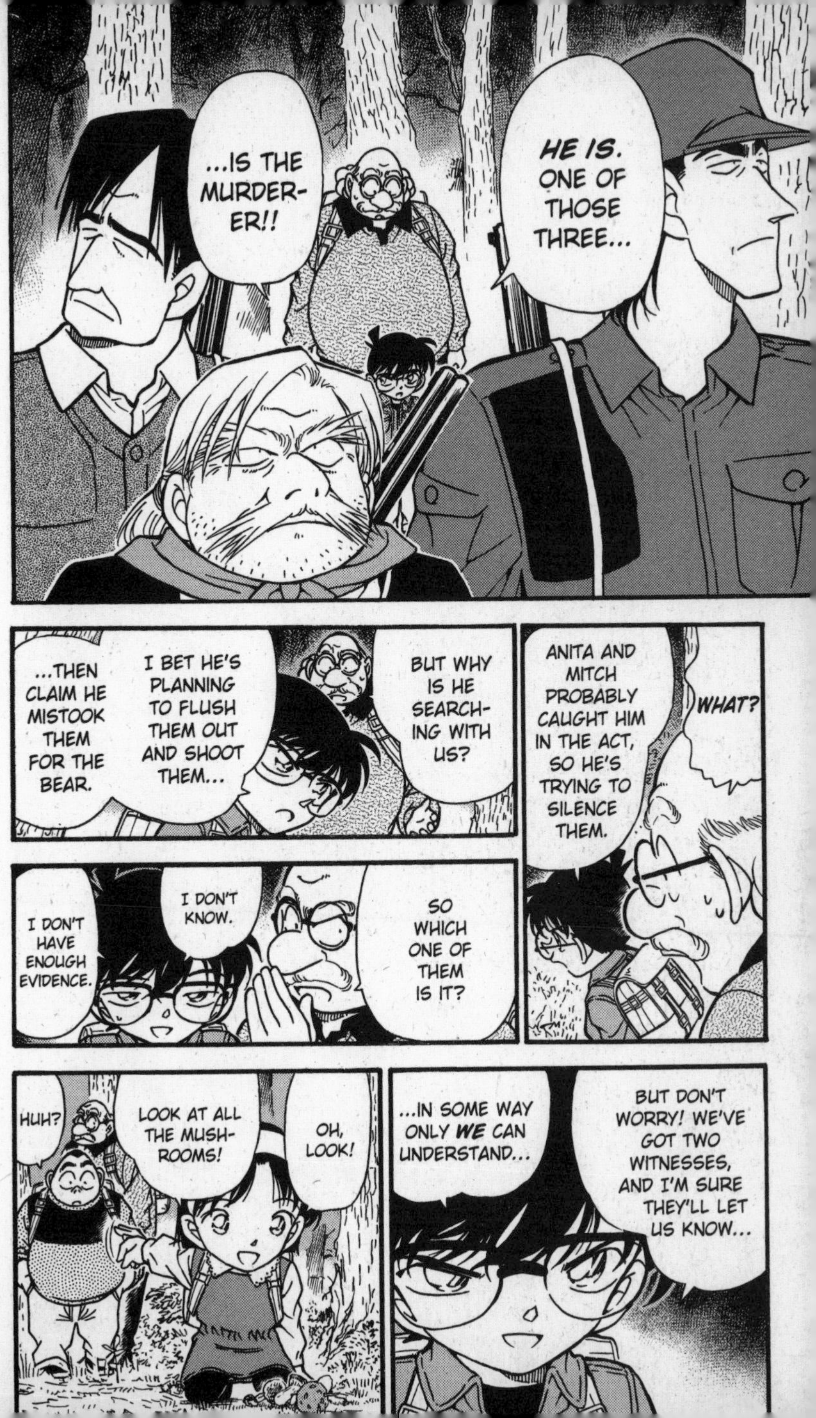
HE IS. ONE OF THOSE THREE...
...IS THE MURDERER!!
WHAT?
ANITA AND MITCH PROBABLY CAUGHT HIM IN THE ACT, SO HE'S TRYING TO SILENCE THEM.
BUT WHY IS HE SEARCHING WITH US?
I BET HE'S PLANNING TO FLUSH THEM OUT AND SHOOT THEM...
...THEN CLAIM HE MISTOOK THEM FOR THE BEAR.
SO WHICH ONE OF THEM IS IT?
I DON'T KNOW.
I DON'T HAVE ENOUGH EVIDENCE.
BUT DON'T WORRY! WE'VE GOT TWO WITNESSES, AND I'M SURE THEY'LL LET US KNOW...
...IN SOME WAY ONLY WE CAN UNDERSTAND...
OH, LOOK!
LOOK AT ALL THE MUSHROOMS!
HUH?

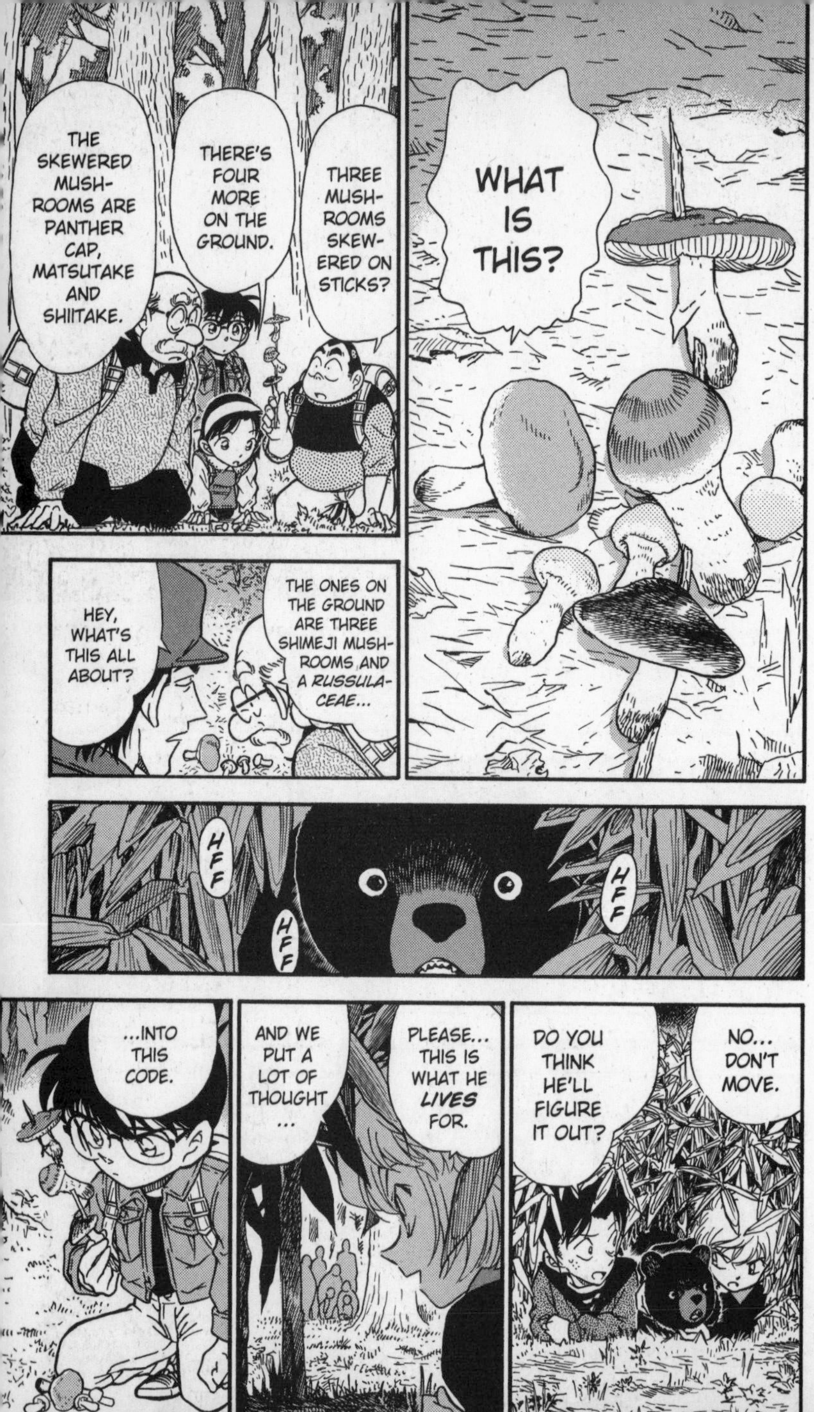
WHAT IS THIS?
THREE MUSH-ROOMS SKEW-ERED ON STICKS?
THERE'S FOUR MORE ON THE GROUND.
THE SKEWERED MUSH-ROOMS ARE PANTHER CAP, MATSUTAKE AND SHIITAKE.
THE ONES ON THE GROUND ARE THREE SHIMEJI MUSH-ROOMS AND A *RUSSULA-CEAE*...
HEY, WHAT'S THIS ALL ABOUT?
HFF
HFF
HFF
NO... DON'T MOVE.
DO YOU THINK HE'LL FIGURE IT OUT?
PLEASE... THIS IS WHAT HE *LIVES* FOR.
AND WE PUT A LOT OF THOUGHT ...
...INTO THIS CODE.

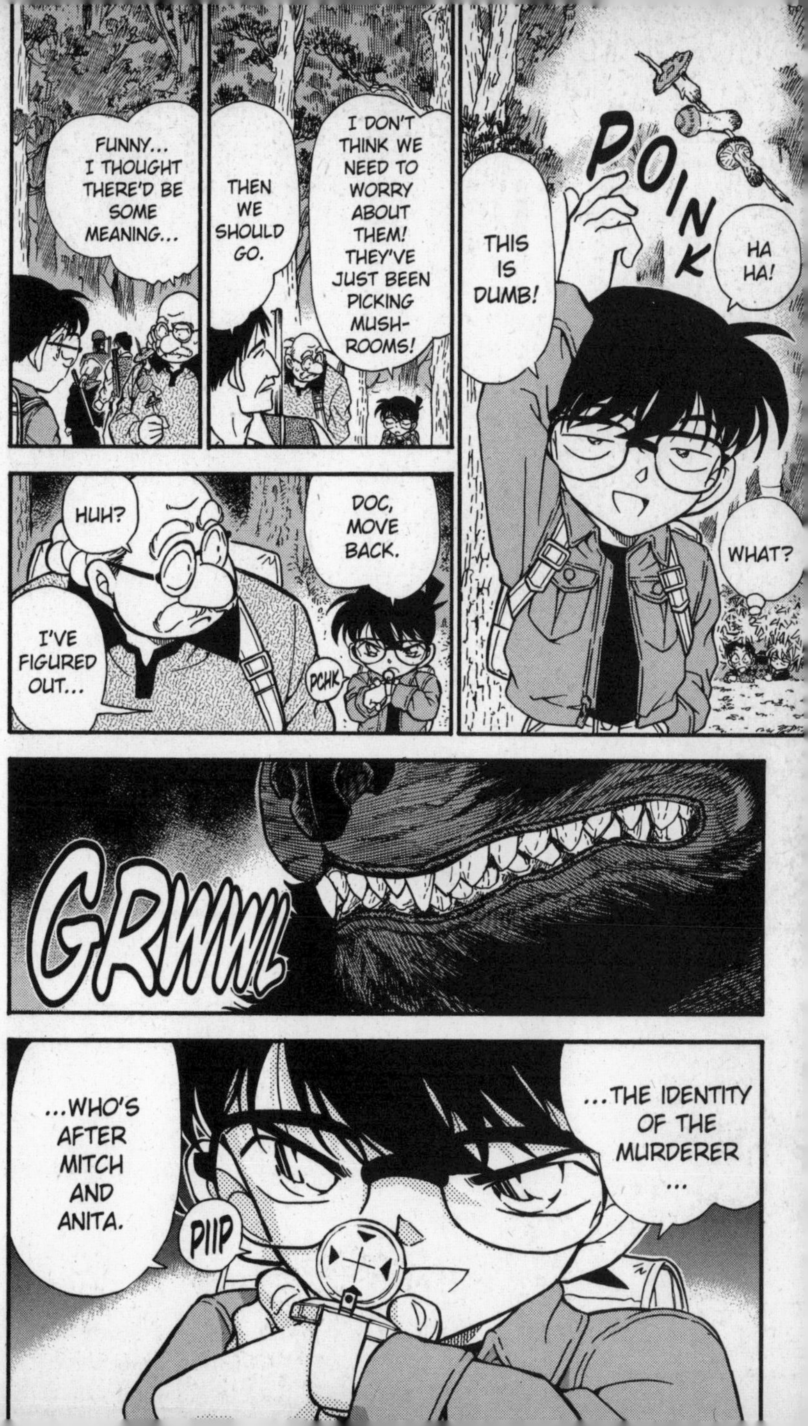
POINK
HA HA!
THIS IS DUMB!
WHAT?
I DON'T THINK WE NEED TO WORRY ABOUT THEM! THEY'VE JUST BEEN PICKING MUSH-ROOMS!
THEN WE SHOULD GO.
FUNNY... I THOUGHT THERE'D BE SOME MEANING...
DOC, MOVE BACK.
HUH?
PCHK
I'VE FIGURED OUT...
GRWWL
...THE IDENTITY OF THE MURDERER ...
PIIP
...WHO'S AFTER MITCH AND ANITA.

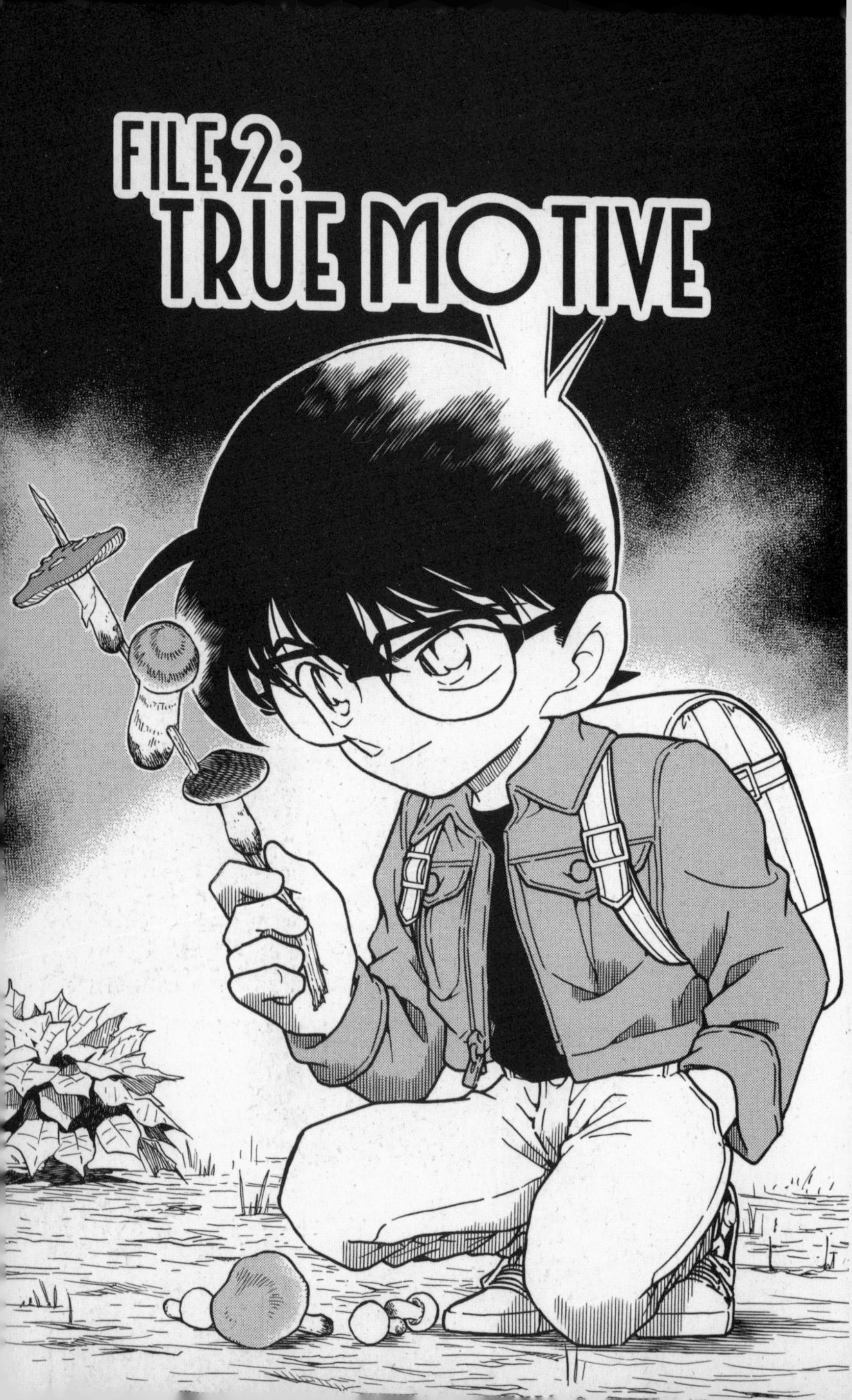
FILE 2:
TRUE MOTIVE

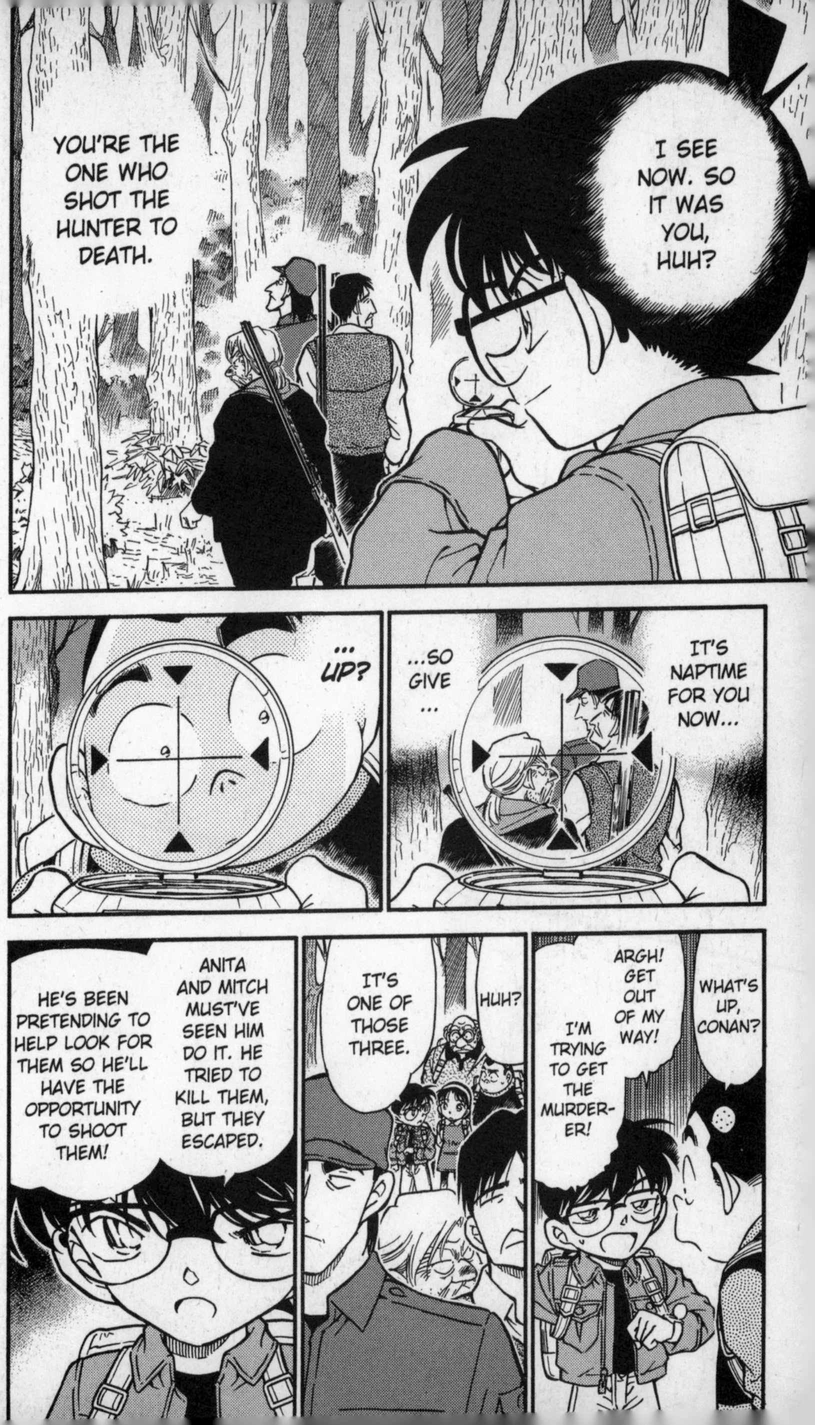
I SEE NOW. SO IT WAS YOU, HUH?
YOU'RE THE ONE WHO SHOT THE HUNTER TO DEATH.
IT'S NAPTIME FOR YOU NOW...
...SO GIVE ...
... UP?
WHAT'S UP, CONAN?
ARGH! GET OUT OF MY WAY!
I'M TRYING TO GET THE MURDER-ER!
HUH?
IT'S ONE OF THOSE THREE.
ANITA AND MITCH MUST'VE SEEN HIM DO IT. HE TRIED TO KILL THEM, BUT THEY ESCAPED.
HE'S BEEN PRETENDING TO HELP LOOK FOR THEM SO HE'LL HAVE THE OPPORTUNITY TO SHOOT THEM!

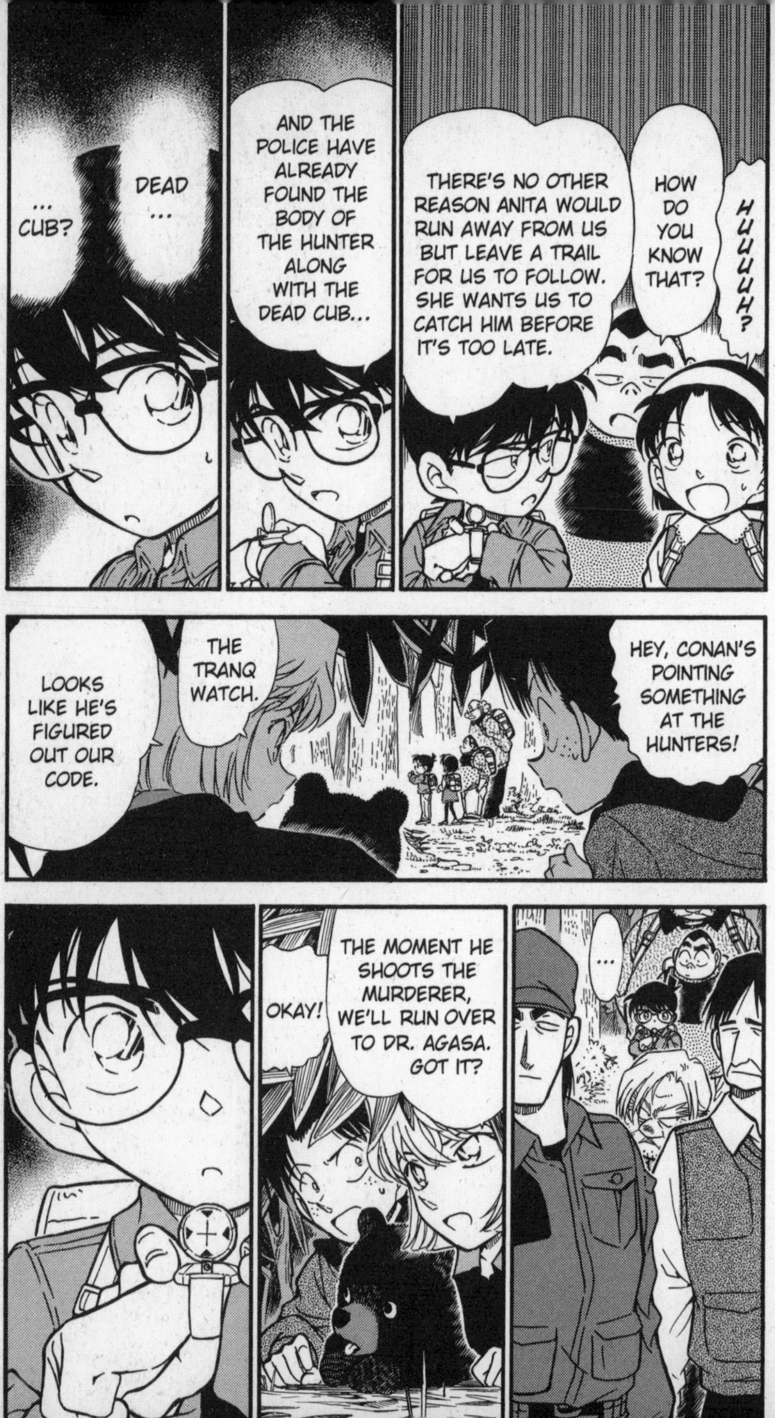
HUUUUH?
HOW DO YOU KNOW THAT?
THERE'S NO OTHER REASON ANITA WOULD RUN AWAY FROM US BUT LEAVE A TRAIL FOR US TO FOLLOW. SHE WANTS US TO CATCH HIM BEFORE IT'S TOO LATE.
AND THE POLICE HAVE ALREADY FOUND THE BODY OF THE HUNTER ALONG WITH THE DEAD CUB...
DEAD ...
... CUB?
HEY, CONAN'S POINTING SOMETHING AT THE HUNTERS!
THE TRANQ WATCH.
LOOKS LIKE HE'S FIGURED OUT OUR CODE.
...
THE MOMENT HE SHOOTS THE MURDERER, WE'LL RUN OVER TO DR. AGASA. GOT IT?
OKAY!

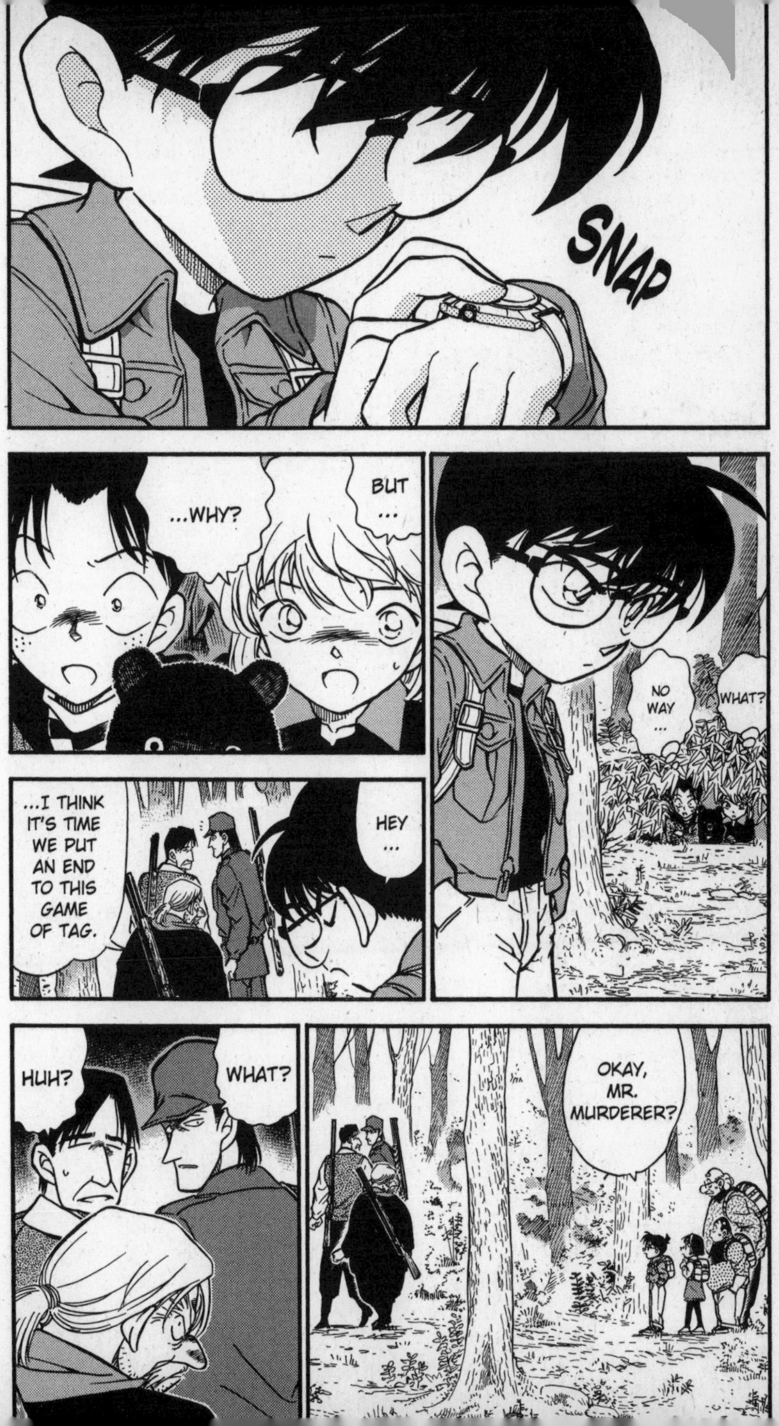
SNAP
WHAT?
NO WAY ...
BUT ...
...WHY?
HEY ...
...I THINK IT'S TIME WE PUT AN END TO THIS GAME OF TAG.
OKAY, MR. MURDERER?
WHAT?
HUH?

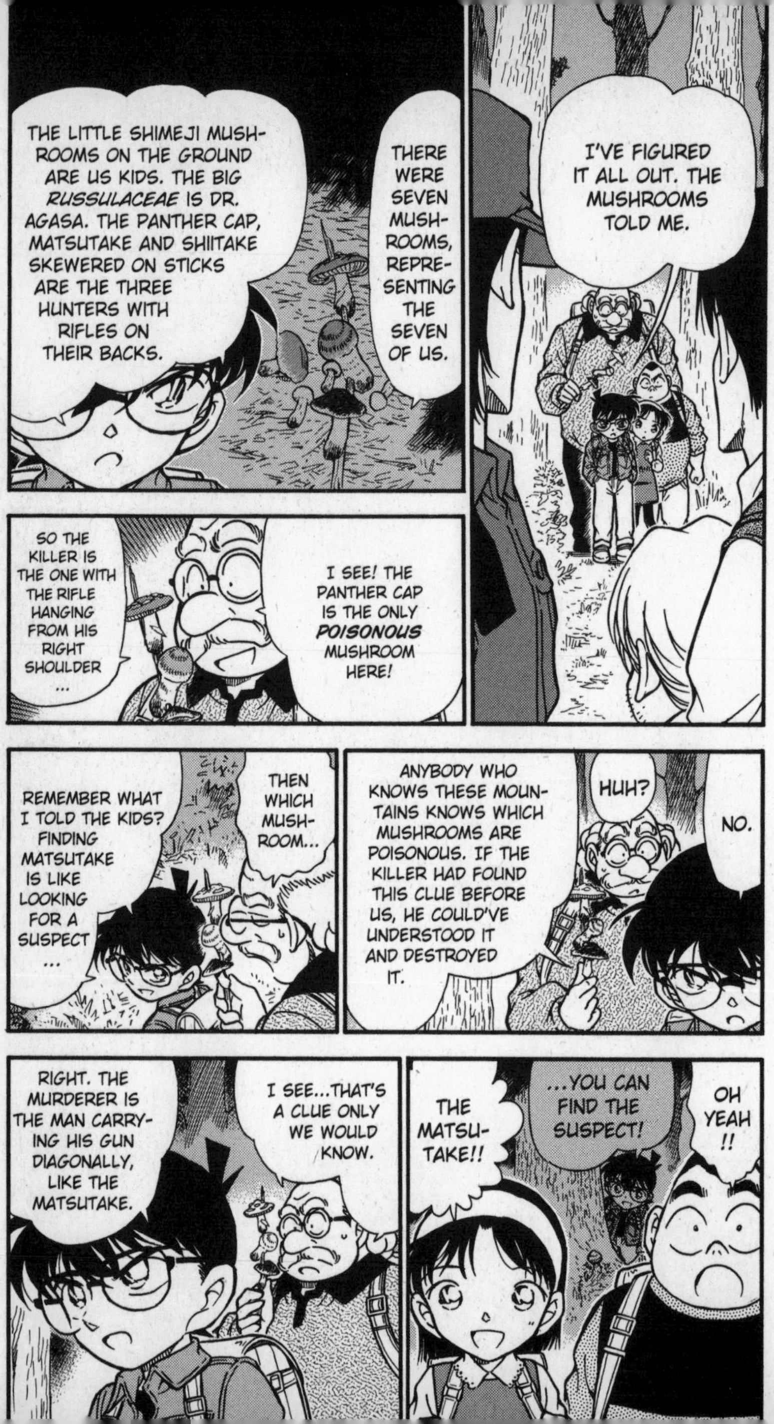
I'VE FIGURED IT ALL OUT. THE MUSHROOMS TOLD ME.
THERE WERE SEVEN MUSHROOMS, REPRESENTING THE SEVEN OF US.
THE LITTLE SHIMEJI MUSHROOMS ON THE GROUND ARE US KIDS. THE BIG *RUSSULACEAE* IS DR. AGASA. THE PANTHER CAP, MATSUTAKE AND SHIITAKE SKEWERED ON STICKS ARE THE THREE HUNTERS WITH RIFLES ON THEIR BACKS.
I SEE! THE PANTHER CAP IS THE ONLY ***POISONOUS*** MUSHROOM HERE!
SO THE KILLER IS THE ONE WITH THE RIFLE HANGING FROM HIS RIGHT SHOULDER ...
NO.
HUH?
ANYBODY WHO KNOWS THESE MOUNTAINS KNOWS WHICH MUSHROOMS ARE POISONOUS. IF THE KILLER HAD FOUND THIS CLUE BEFORE US, HE COULD'VE UNDERSTOOD IT AND DESTROYED IT.
THEN WHICH MUSHROOM...
REMEMBER WHAT I TOLD THE KIDS? FINDING MATSUTAKE IS LIKE LOOKING FOR A SUSPECT ...
OH YEAH !!
...YOU CAN FIND THE SUSPECT!
THE MATSUTAKE!!
I SEE...THAT'S A CLUE ONLY WE WOULD KNOW.
RIGHT. THE MURDERER IS THE MAN CARRYING HIS GUN DIAGONALLY, LIKE THE MATSUTAKE.

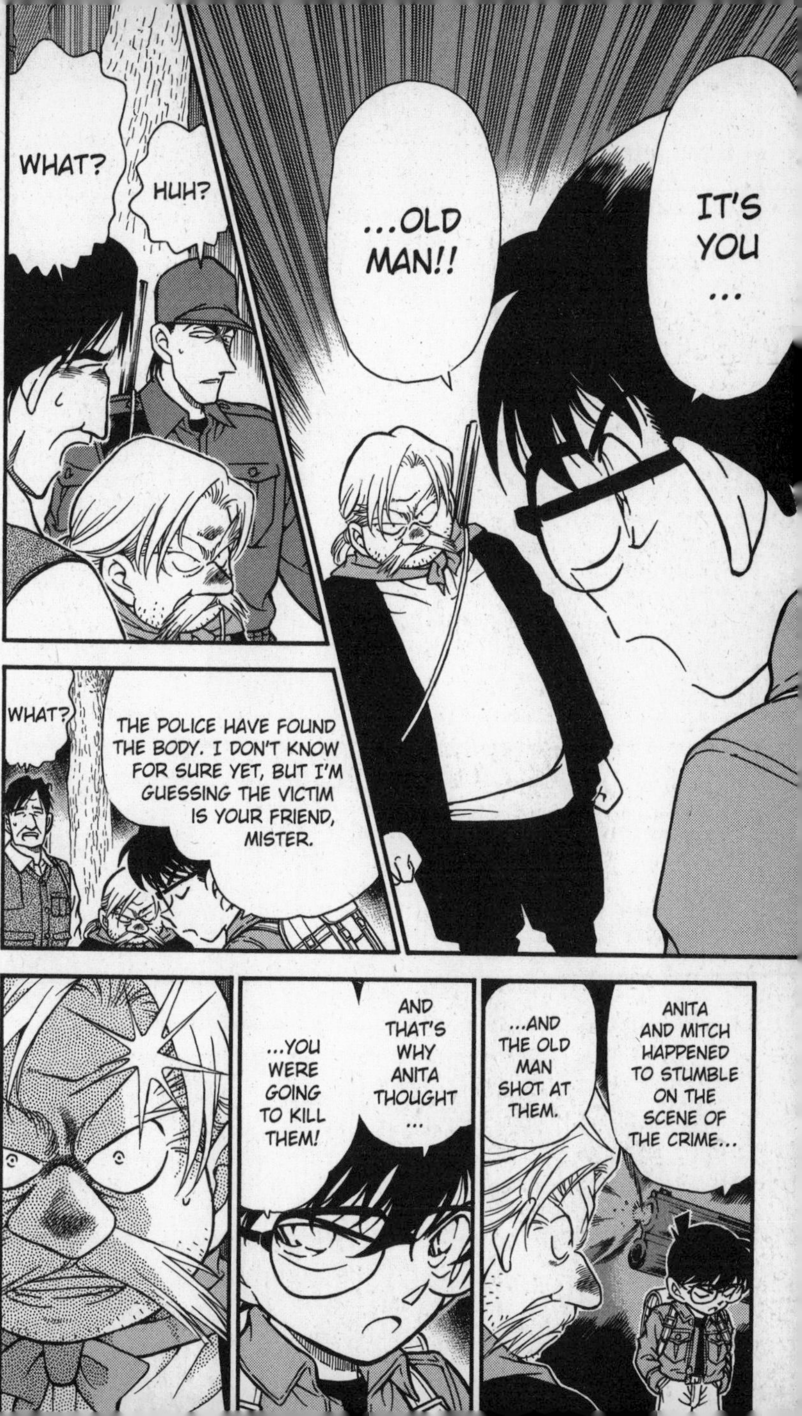
IT'S YOU ...
...OLD MAN!!
HUH?
WHAT?
THE POLICE HAVE FOUND THE BODY. I DON'T KNOW FOR SURE YET, BUT I'M GUESSING THE VICTIM IS YOUR FRIEND, MISTER.
WHAT?
ANITA AND MITCH HAPPENED TO STUMBLE ON THE SCENE OF THE CRIME...
...AND THE OLD MAN SHOT AT THEM.
AND THAT'S WHY ANITA THOUGHT ...
...YOU WERE GOING TO KILL THEM!

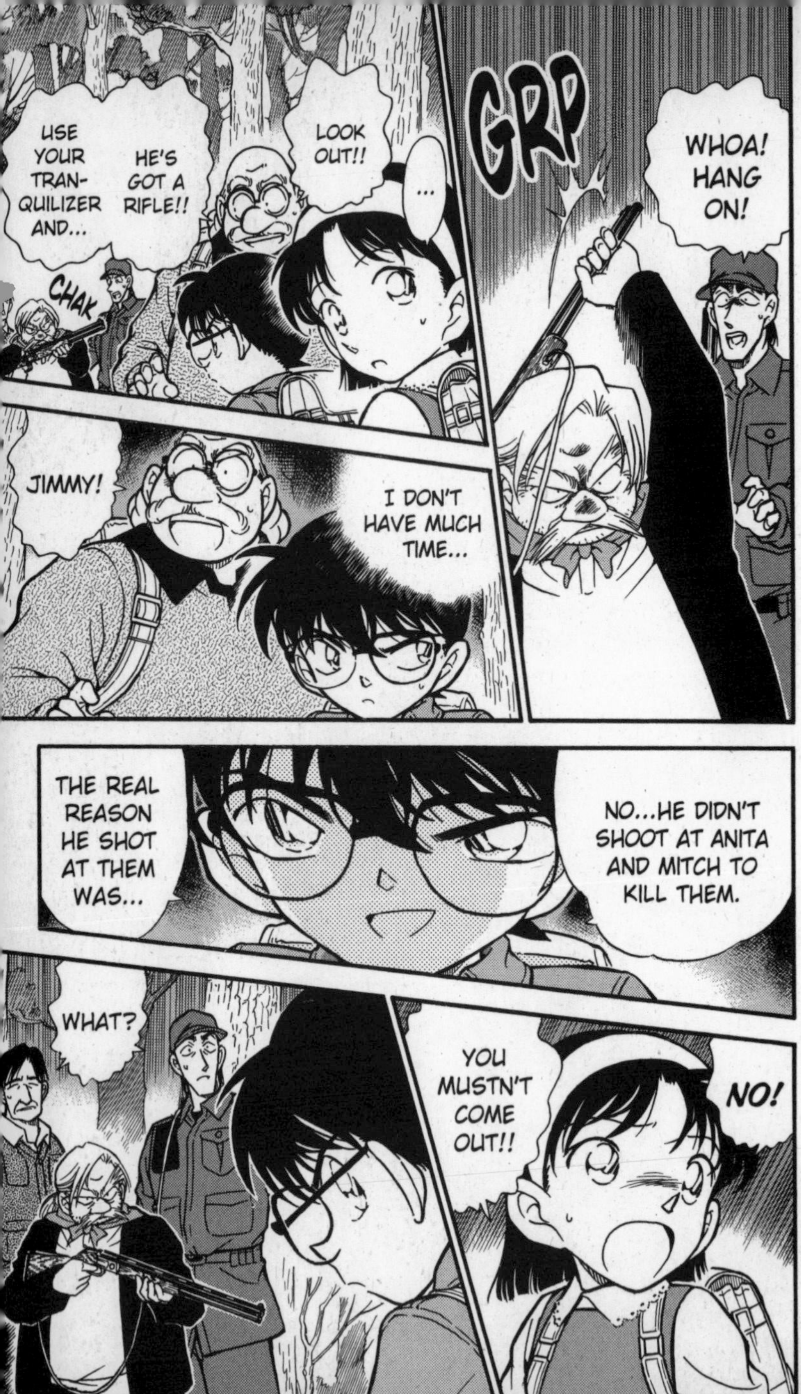
GRP
WHOA! HANG ON!
...
LOOK OUT!!
HE'S GOT A RIFLE!!
USE YOUR TRAN-QUILIZER AND...
CHAK
I DON'T HAVE MUCH TIME...
JIMMY!
NO...HE DIDN'T SHOOT AT ANITA AND MITCH TO KILL THEM.
THE REAL REASON HE SHOT AT THEM WAS...
NO!
YOU MUSTN'T COME OUT!!
WHAT?

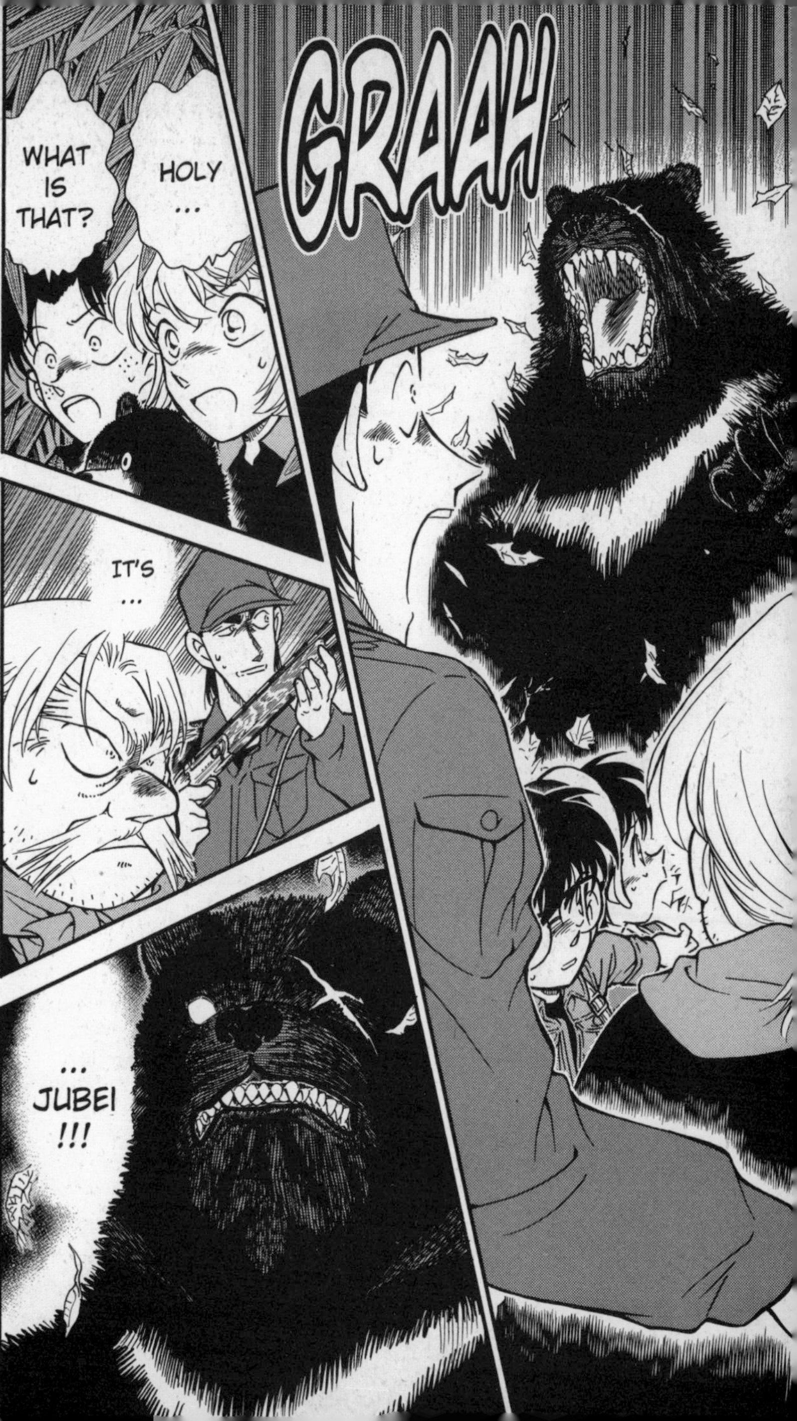
GRAAH
HOLY ...
WHAT IS THAT?
IT'S ...
... JUBEI !!!

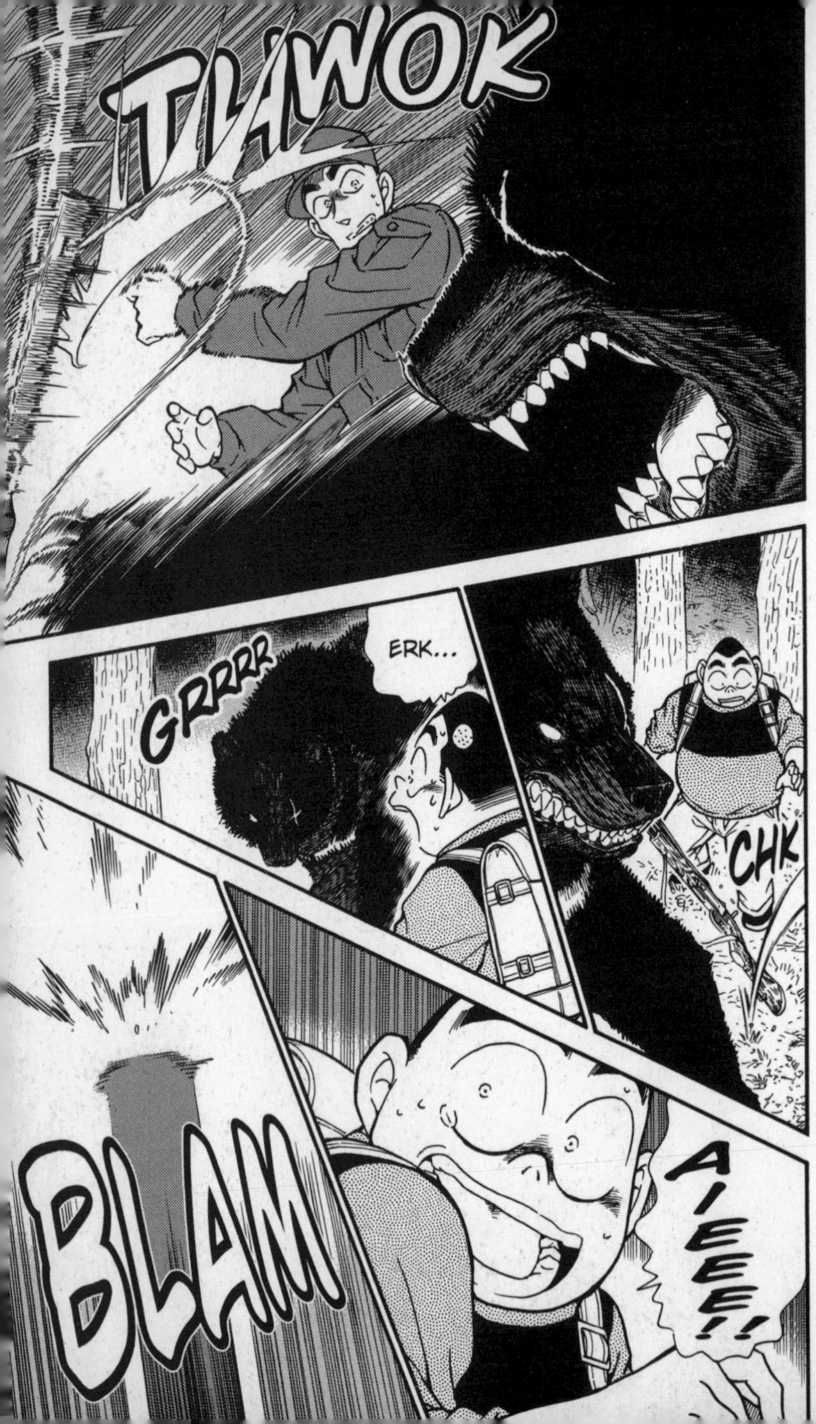
THWOK
CHK
ERK...
GRRRR
AIEEE!!
BLAM

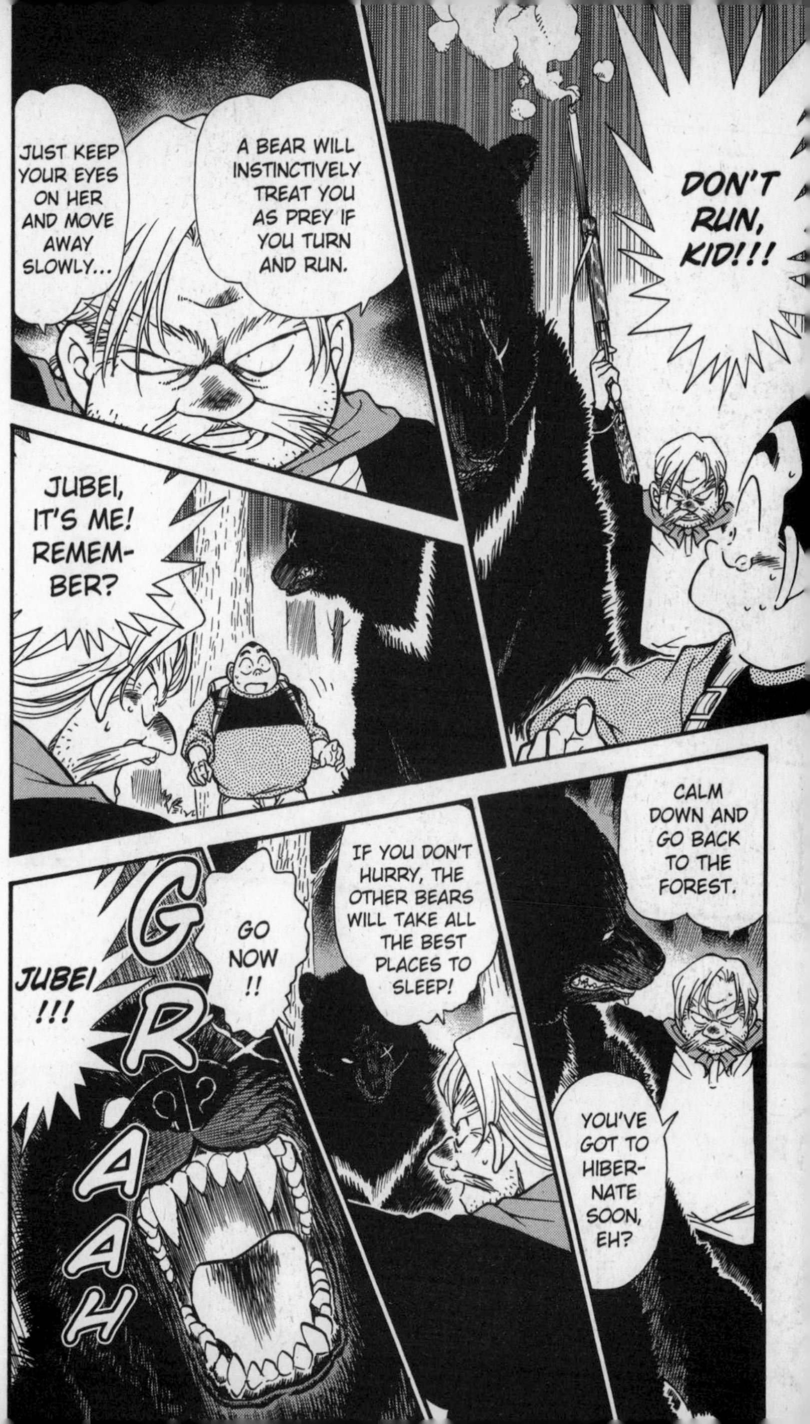
DON'T RUN, KID!!!
A BEAR WILL INSTINCTIVELY TREAT YOU AS PREY IF YOU TURN AND RUN.
JUST KEEP YOUR EYES ON HER AND MOVE AWAY SLOWLY...
JUBEI, IT'S ME! REMEMBER?
CALM DOWN AND GO BACK TO THE FOREST.
YOU'VE GOT TO HIBER-NATE SOON, EH?
IF YOU DON'T HURRY, THE OTHER BEARS WILL TAKE ALL THE BEST PLACES TO SLEEP!
GO NOW !!
JUBEI !!!
GRAAAH

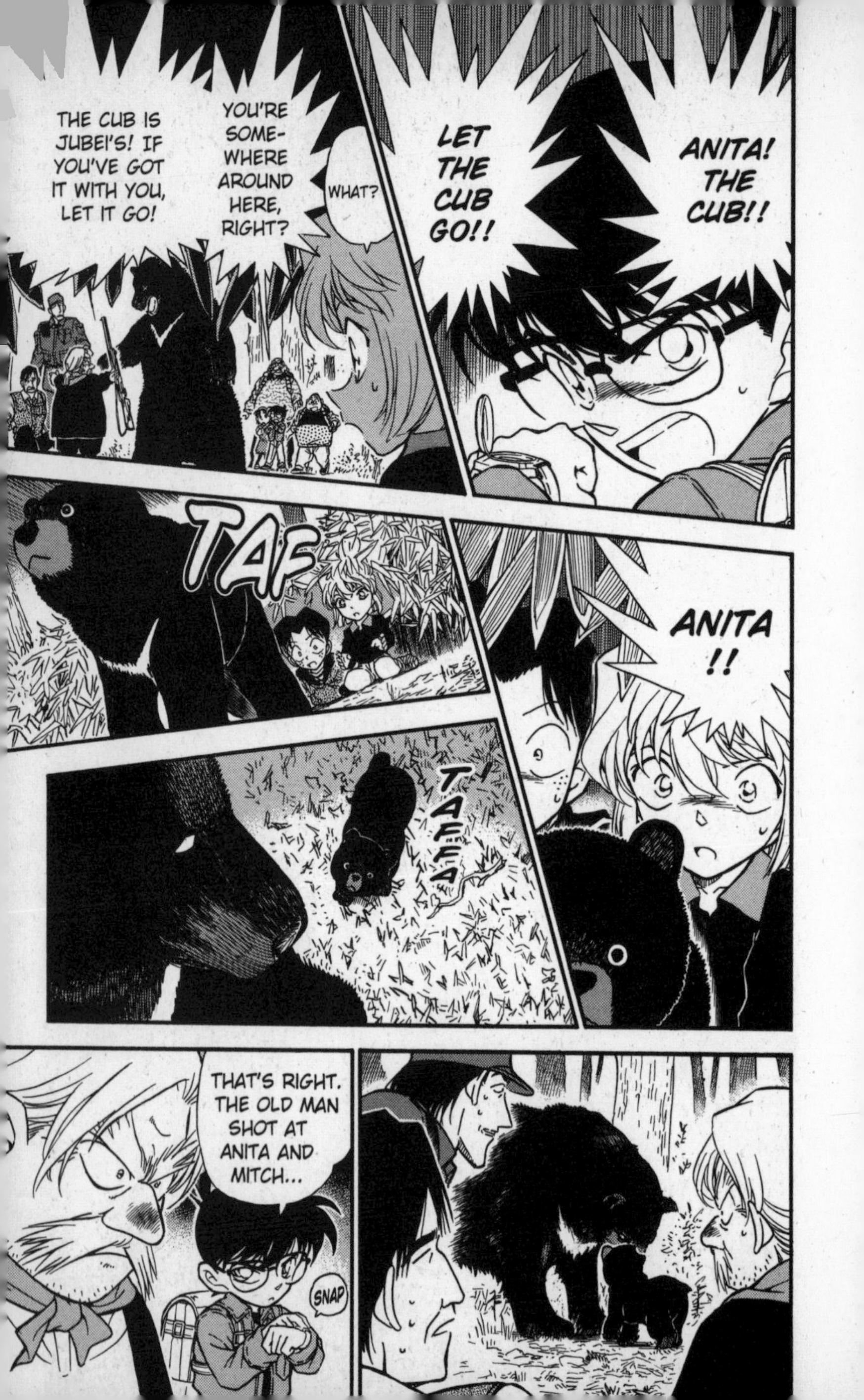
ANITA! THE CUB!!
LET THE CUB GO!!
WHAT?
YOU'RE SOME-WHERE AROUND HERE, RIGHT?
THE CUB IS JUBEI'S! IF YOU'VE GOT IT WITH YOU, LET IT GO!
ANITA !!
TAF
TAFFA
THAT'S RIGHT. THE OLD MAN SHOT AT ANITA AND MITCH...
SNAP

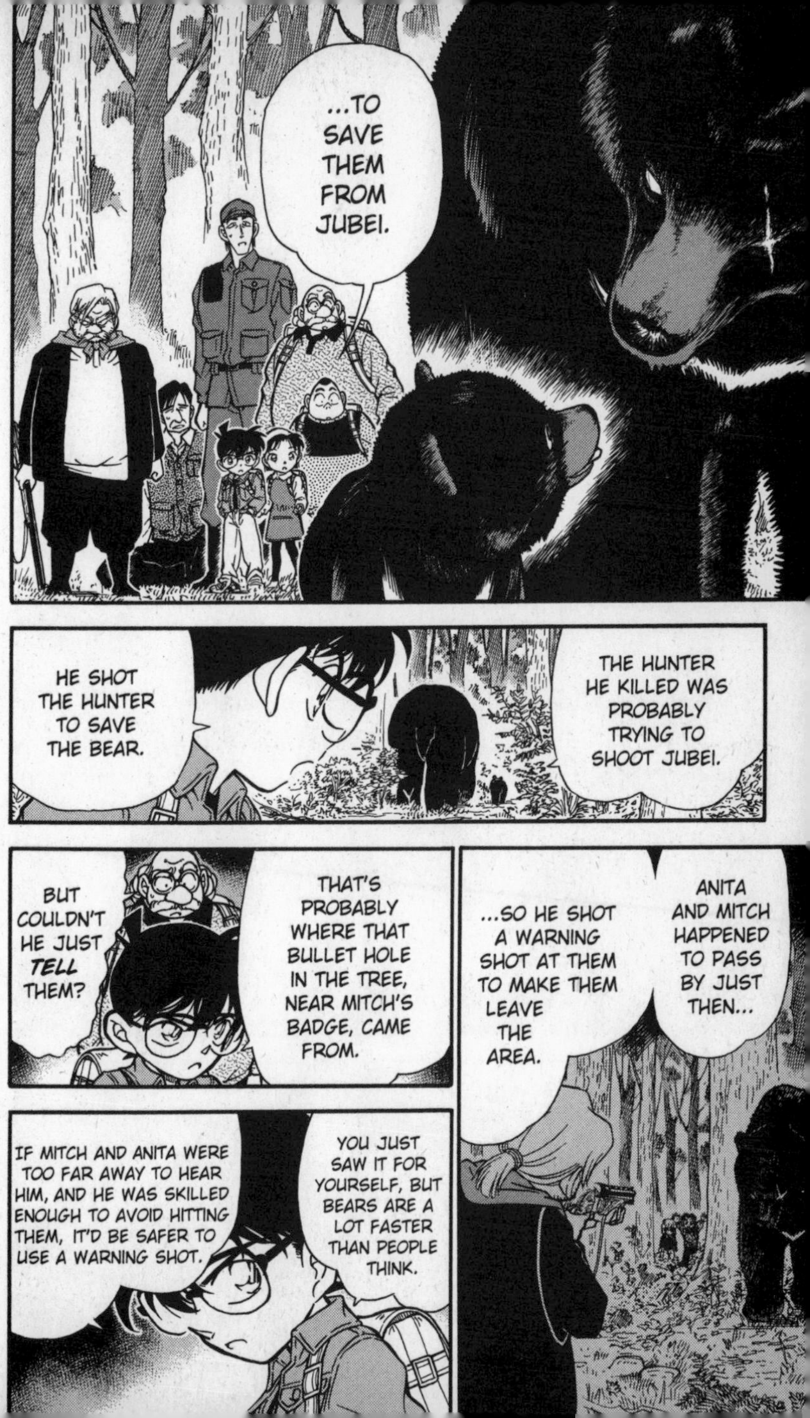
...TO SAVE THEM FROM JUBEI.
THE HUNTER HE KILLED WAS PROBABLY TRYING TO SHOOT JUBEI.
HE SHOT THE HUNTER TO SAVE THE BEAR.
ANITA AND MITCH HAPPENED TO PASS BY JUST THEN...
...SO HE SHOT A WARNING SHOT AT THEM TO MAKE THEM LEAVE THE AREA.
THAT'S PROBABLY WHERE THAT BULLET HOLE IN THE TREE, NEAR MITCH'S BADGE, CAME FROM.
BUT COULDN'T HE JUST *TELL* THEM?
YOU JUST SAW IT FOR YOURSELF, BUT BEARS ARE A LOT FASTER THAN PEOPLE THINK.
IF MITCH AND ANITA WERE TOO FAR AWAY TO HEAR HIM, AND HE WAS SKILLED ENOUGH TO AVOID HITTING THEM, IT'D BE SAFER TO USE A WARNING SHOT.

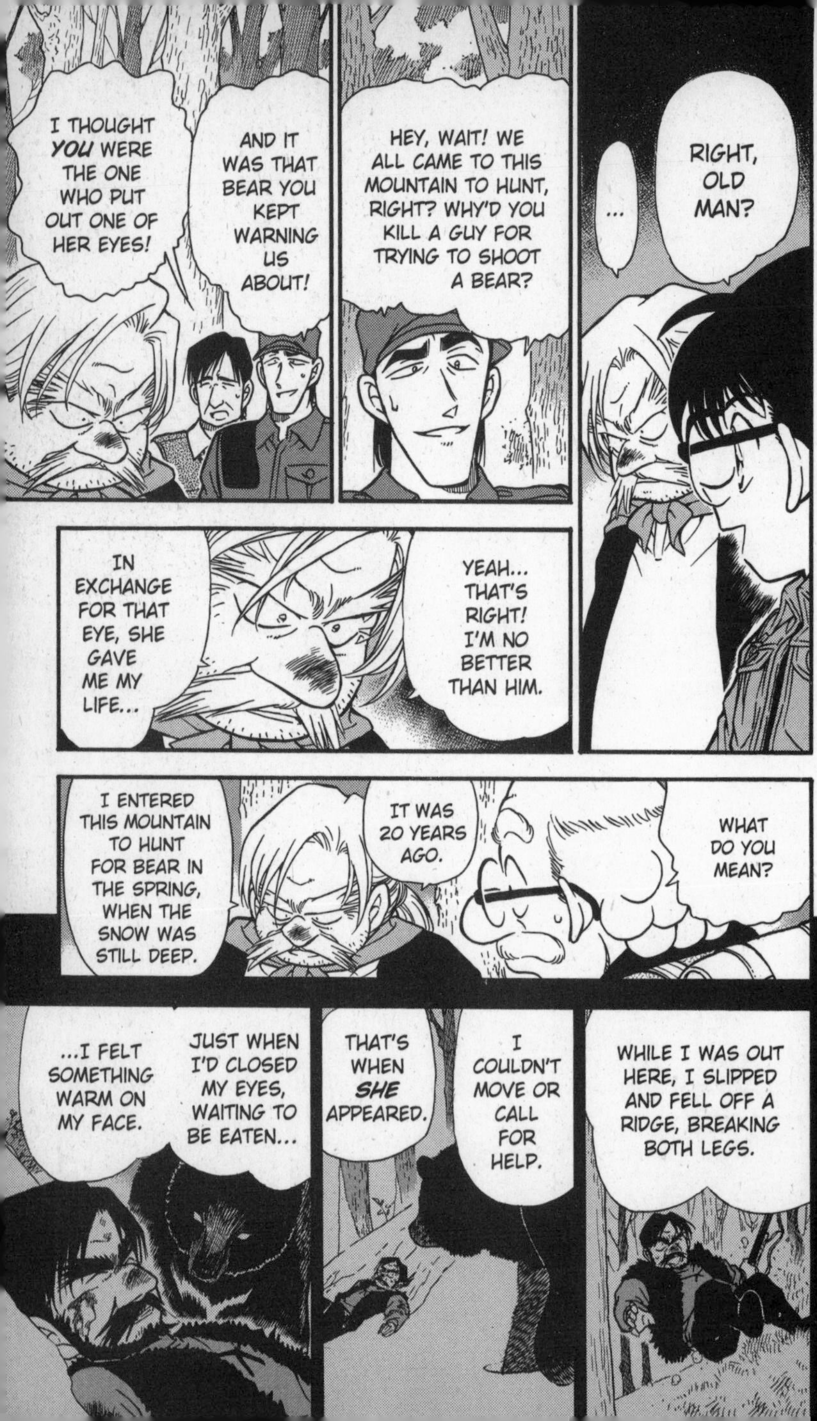

RIGHT, OLD MAN?
...
HEY, WAIT! WE ALL CAME TO THIS MOUNTAIN TO HUNT, RIGHT? WHY'D YOU KILL A GUY FOR TRYING TO SHOOT A BEAR?
AND IT WAS THAT BEAR YOU KEPT WARNING US ABOUT!
I THOUGHT *YOU* WERE THE ONE WHO PUT OUT ONE OF HER EYES!
YEAH... THAT'S RIGHT! I'M NO BETTER THAN HIM.
IN EXCHANGE FOR THAT EYE, SHE GAVE ME MY LIFE...
WHAT DO YOU MEAN?
IT WAS 20 YEARS AGO.
I ENTERED THIS MOUNTAIN TO HUNT FOR BEAR IN THE SPRING, WHEN THE SNOW WAS STILL DEEP.
WHILE I WAS OUT HERE, I SLIPPED AND FELL OFF A RIDGE, BREAKING BOTH LEGS.
I COULDN'T MOVE OR CALL FOR HELP.
THAT'S WHEN *SHE* APPEARED.
JUST WHEN I'D CLOSED MY EYES, WAITING TO BE EATEN...
...I FELT SOMETHING WARM ON MY FACE.

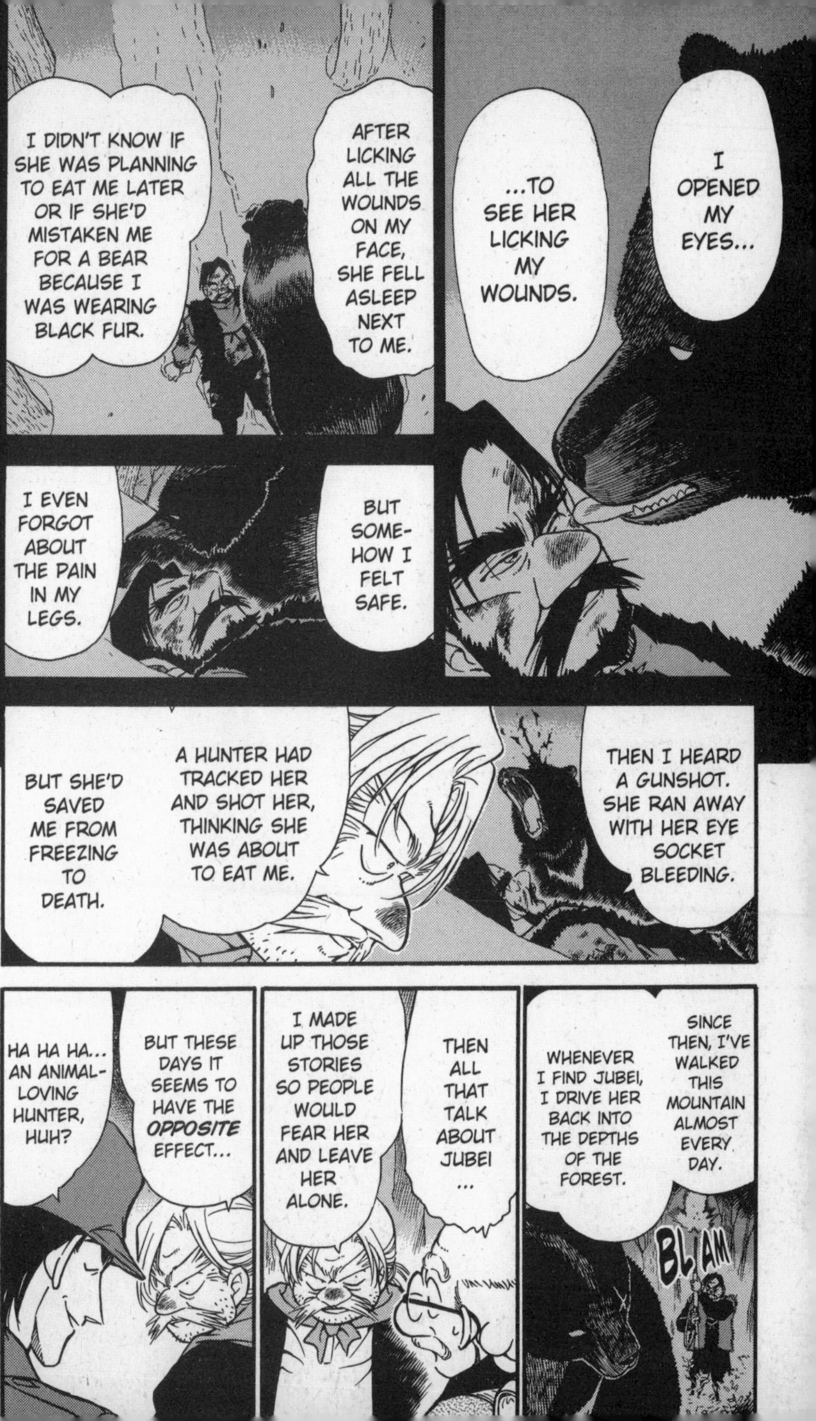
I OPENED MY EYES...
...TO SEE HER LICKING MY WOUNDS.
AFTER LICKING ALL THE WOUNDS ON MY FACE, SHE FELL ASLEEP NEXT TO ME.
I DIDN'T KNOW IF SHE WAS PLANNING TO EAT ME LATER OR IF SHE'D MISTAKEN ME FOR A BEAR BECAUSE I WAS WEARING BLACK FUR.
BUT SOME-HOW I FELT SAFE.
I EVEN FORGOT ABOUT THE PAIN IN MY LEGS.
THEN I HEARD A GUNSHOT. SHE RAN AWAY WITH HER EYE SOCKET BLEEDING.
A HUNTER HAD TRACKED HER AND SHOT HER, THINKING SHE WAS ABOUT TO EAT ME.
BUT SHE'D SAVED ME FROM FREEZING TO DEATH.
SINCE THEN, I'VE WALKED THIS MOUNTAIN ALMOST EVERY DAY.
WHENEVER I FIND JUBEI, I DRIVE HER BACK INTO THE DEPTHS OF THE FOREST.
BLAM
THEN ALL THAT TALK ABOUT JUBEI ...
I MADE UP THOSE STORIES SO PEOPLE WOULD FEAR HER AND LEAVE HER ALONE.
BUT THESE DAYS IT SEEMS TO HAVE THE *OPPOSITE* EFFECT...
HA HA HA... AN ANIMAL-LOVING HUNTER, HUH?

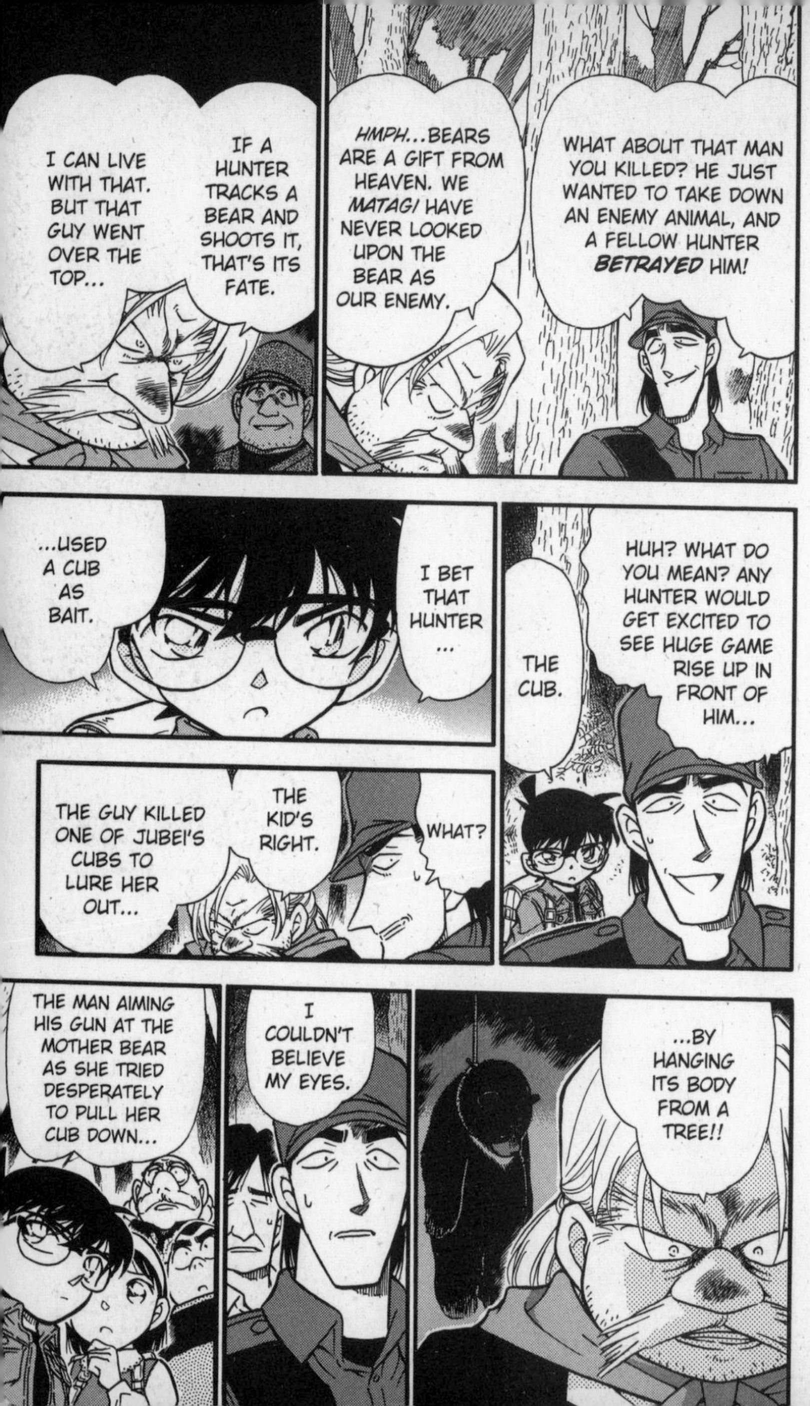
WHAT ABOUT THAT MAN YOU KILLED? HE JUST WANTED TO TAKE DOWN AN ENEMY ANIMAL, AND A FELLOW HUNTER *BETRAYED* HIM!
HMPH...BEARS ARE A GIFT FROM HEAVEN. WE *MATAGI* HAVE NEVER LOOKED UPON THE BEAR AS OUR ENEMY.
IF A HUNTER TRACKS A BEAR AND SHOOTS IT, THAT'S ITS FATE.
I CAN LIVE WITH THAT. BUT THAT GUY WENT OVER THE TOP...
HUH? WHAT DO YOU MEAN? ANY HUNTER WOULD GET EXCITED TO SEE HUGE GAME RISE UP IN FRONT OF HIM...
THE CUB.
I BET THAT HUNTER ...
...USED A CUB AS BAIT.
WHAT?
THE KID'S RIGHT.
THE GUY KILLED ONE OF JUBEI'S CUBS TO LURE HER OUT...
...BY HANGING ITS BODY FROM A TREE!!
I COULDN'T BELIEVE MY EYES.
THE MAN AIMING HIS GUN AT THE MOTHER BEAR AS SHE TRIED DESPERATELY TO PULL HER CUB DOWN...

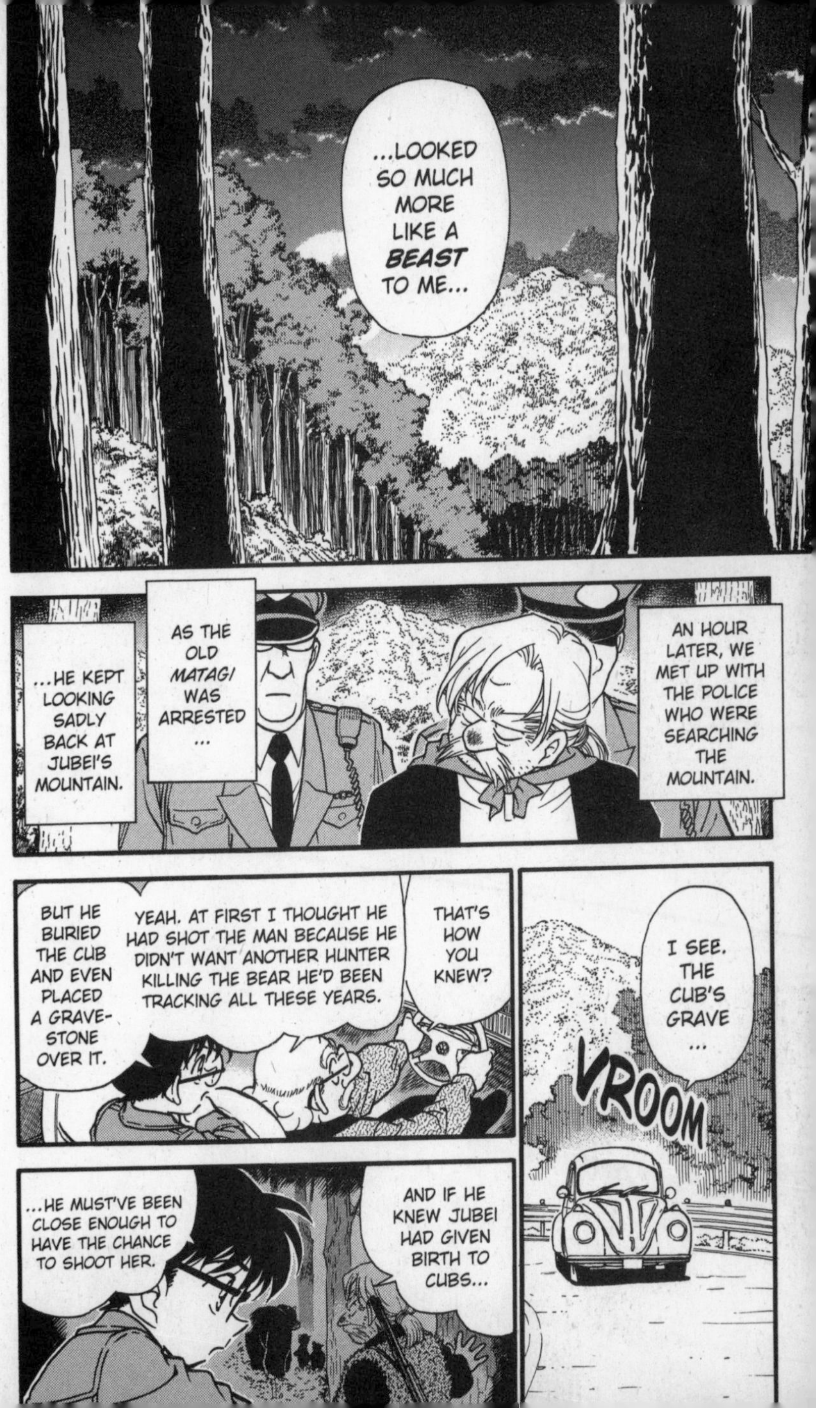
...LOOKED SO MUCH MORE LIKE A **BEAST** TO ME...
AN HOUR LATER, WE MET UP WITH THE POLICE WHO WERE SEARCHING THE MOUNTAIN.
AS THE OLD *MATAGI* WAS ARRESTED ...
...HE KEPT LOOKING SADLY BACK AT JUBEI'S MOUNTAIN.
I SEE. THE CUB'S GRAVE ...
VROOM
THAT'S HOW YOU KNEW?
YEAH. AT FIRST I THOUGHT HE HAD SHOT THE MAN BECAUSE HE DIDN'T WANT ANOTHER HUNTER KILLING THE BEAR HE'D BEEN TRACKING ALL THESE YEARS.
BUT HE BURIED THE CUB AND EVEN PLACED A GRAVE-STONE OVER IT.
AND IF HE KNEW JUBEI HAD GIVEN BIRTH TO CUBS...
...HE MUST'VE BEEN CLOSE ENOUGH TO HAVE THE CHANCE TO SHOOT HER.

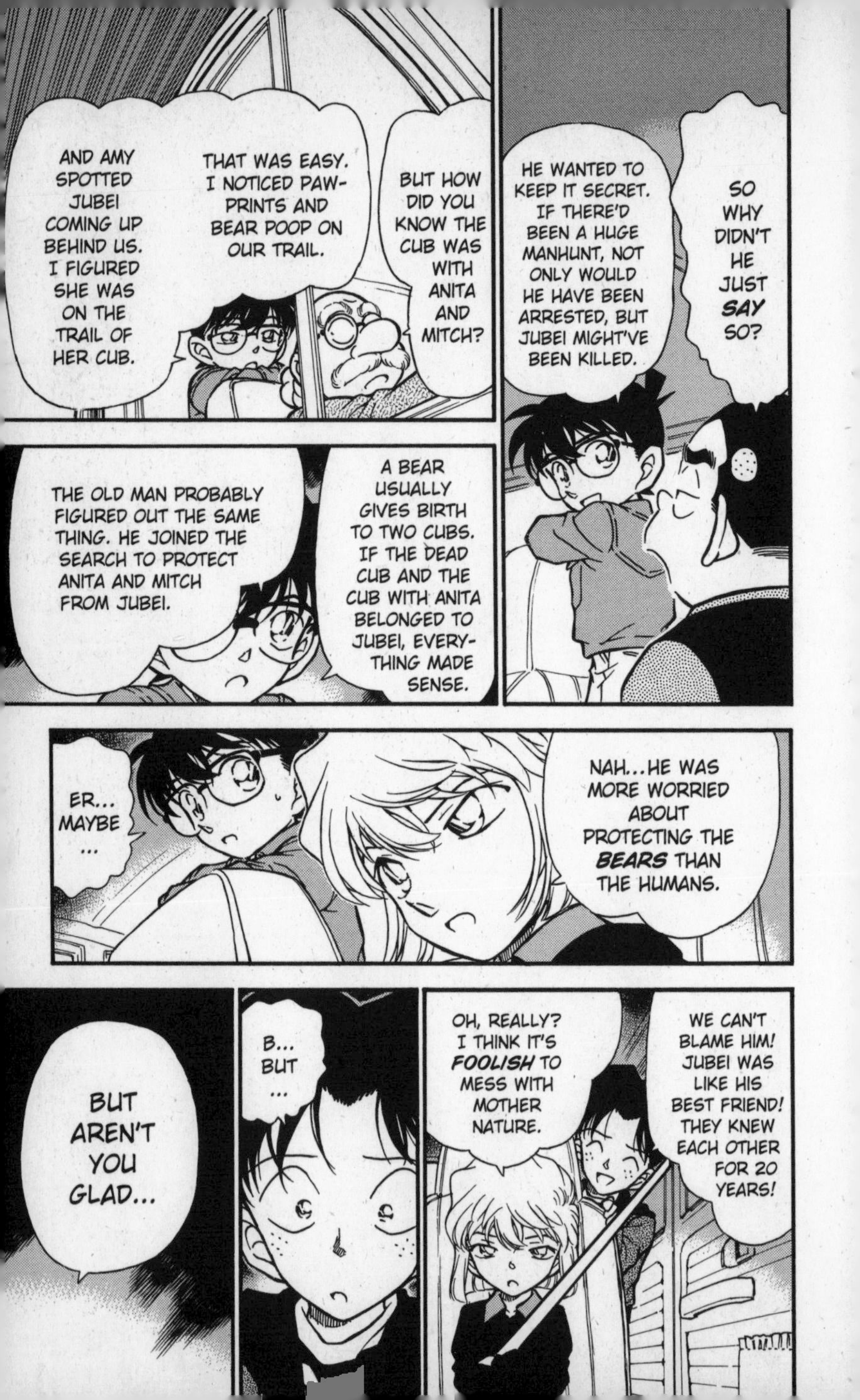
SO WHY DIDN'T HE JUST *SAY* SO?
HE WANTED TO KEEP IT SECRET. IF THERE'D BEEN A HUGE MANHUNT, NOT ONLY WOULD HE HAVE BEEN ARRESTED, BUT JUBEI MIGHT'VE BEEN KILLED.
BUT HOW DID YOU KNOW THE CUB WAS WITH ANITA AND MITCH?
THAT WAS EASY. I NOTICED PAW-PRINTS AND BEAR POOP ON OUR TRAIL.
AND AMY SPOTTED JUBEI COMING UP BEHIND US. I FIGURED SHE WAS ON THE TRAIL OF HER CUB.
A BEAR USUALLY GIVES BIRTH TO TWO CUBS. IF THE DEAD CUB AND THE CUB WITH ANITA BELONGED TO JUBEI, EVERY-THING MADE SENSE.
THE OLD MAN PROBABLY FIGURED OUT THE SAME THING. HE JOINED THE SEARCH TO PROTECT ANITA AND MITCH FROM JUBEI.
NAH...HE WAS MORE WORRIED ABOUT PROTECTING THE *BEARS* THAN THE HUMANS.
ER... MAYBE ...
WE CAN'T BLAME HIM! JUBEI WAS LIKE HIS BEST FRIEND! THEY KNEW EACH OTHER FOR 20 YEARS!
OH, REALLY? I THINK IT'S *FOOLISH* TO MESS WITH MOTHER NATURE.
B... BUT ...
BUT AREN'T YOU GLAD...

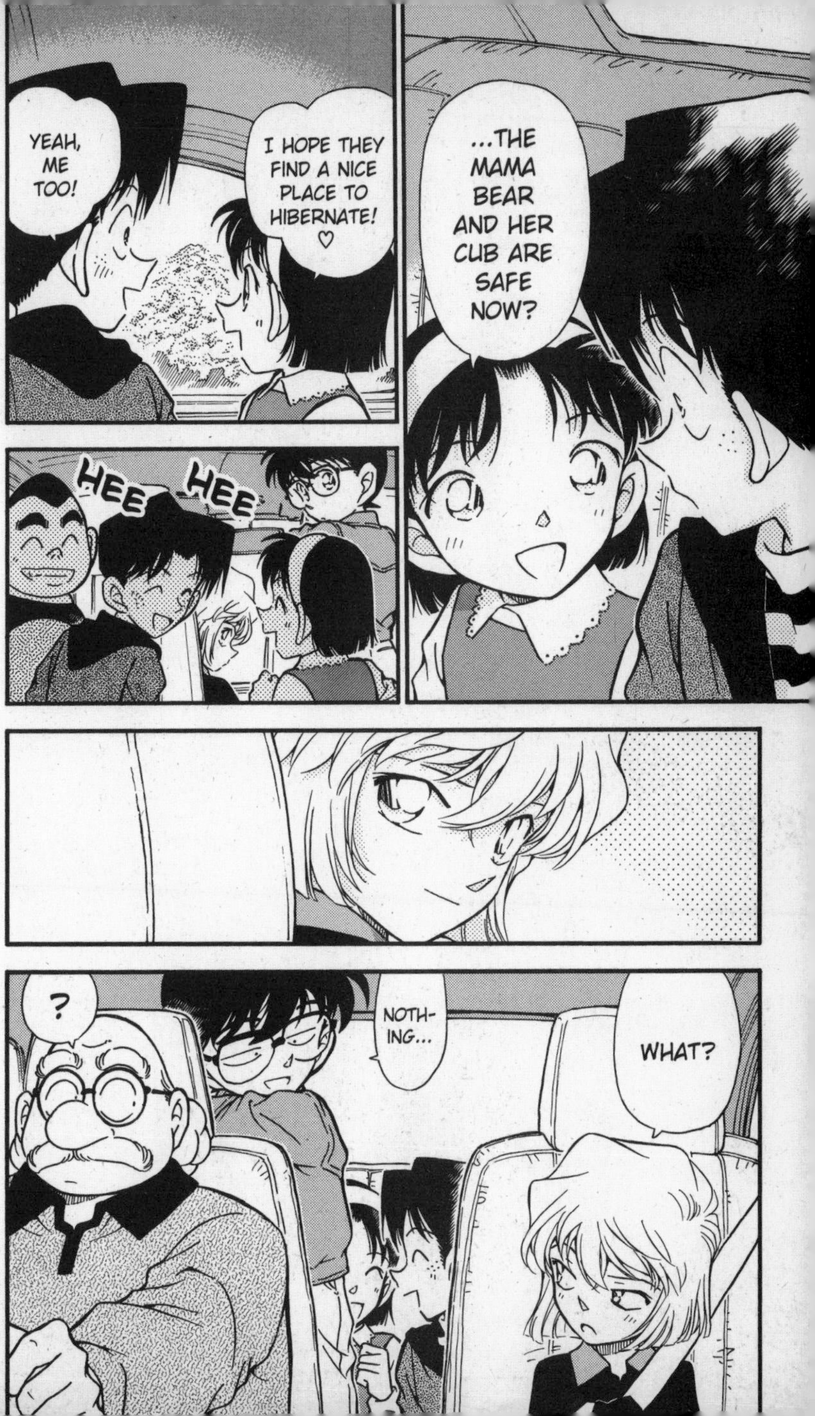
...THE MAMA BEAR AND HER CUB ARE SAFE NOW?
I HOPE THEY FIND A NICE PLACE TO HIBERNATE! ♡
YEAH, ME TOO!
HEE HEE
WHAT?
NOTH-ING...
?

FILE 3: A DECEITFUL WOMAN

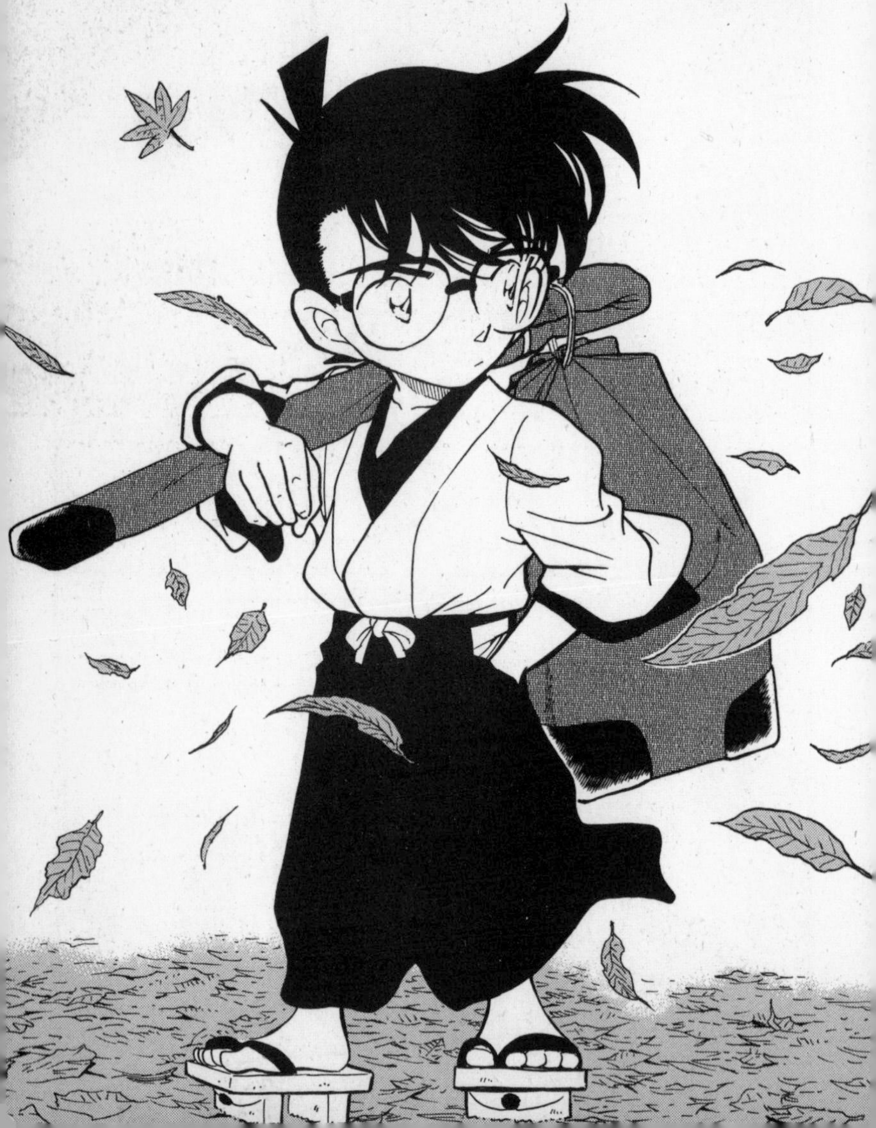

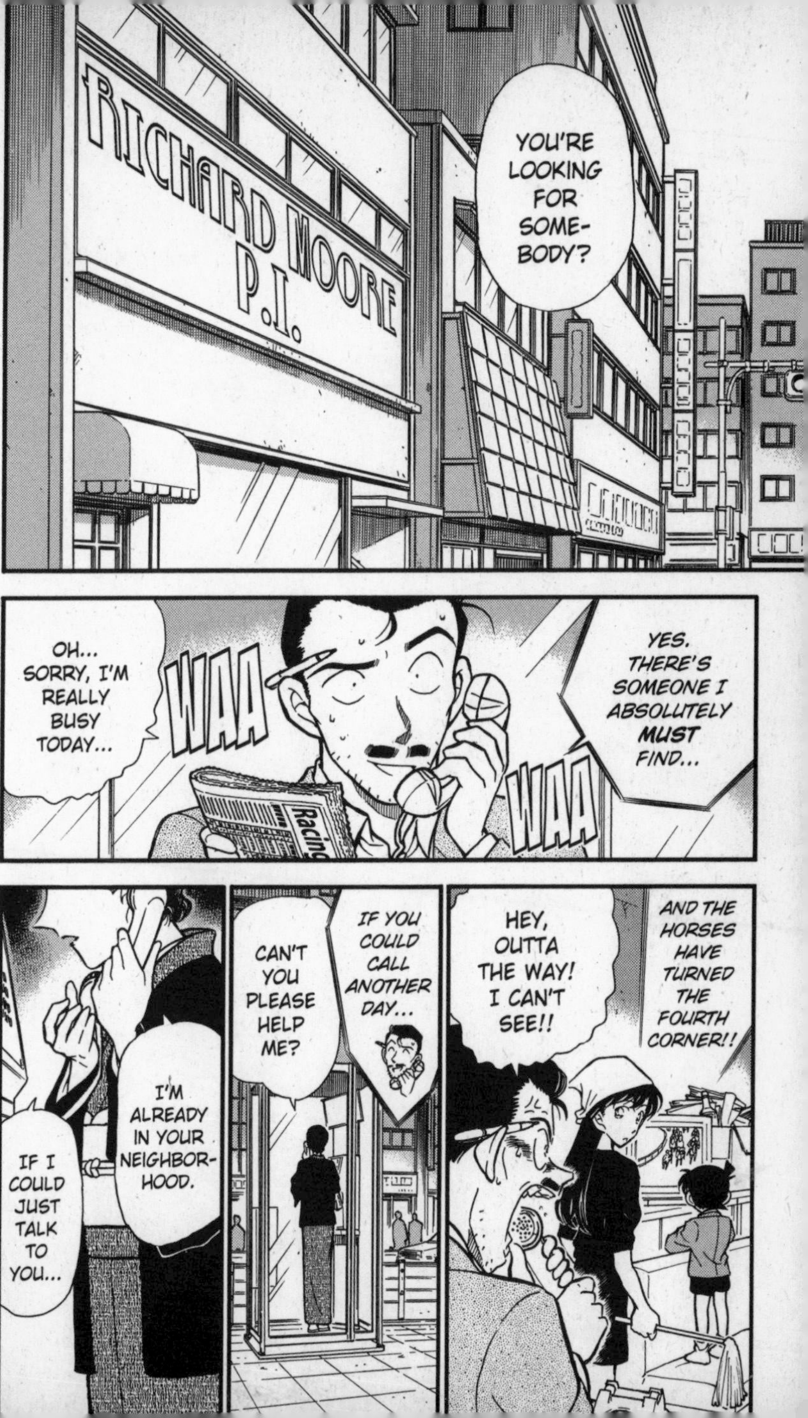
RICHARD MOORE P.I.
YOU'RE LOOKING FOR SOME-BODY?
YES. THERE'S SOMEONE I ABSOLUTELY **MUST** FIND...
WAA
WAA
OH... SORRY, I'M REALLY BUSY TODAY...
Racing
AND THE HORSES HAVE TURNED THE FOURTH CORNER!!
HEY, OUTTA THE WAY! I CAN'T SEE!!
IF YOU COULD CALL ANOTHER DAY...
CAN'T YOU PLEASE HELP ME?
I'M ALREADY IN YOUR NEIGHBOR-HOOD.
IF I COULD JUST TALK TO YOU...

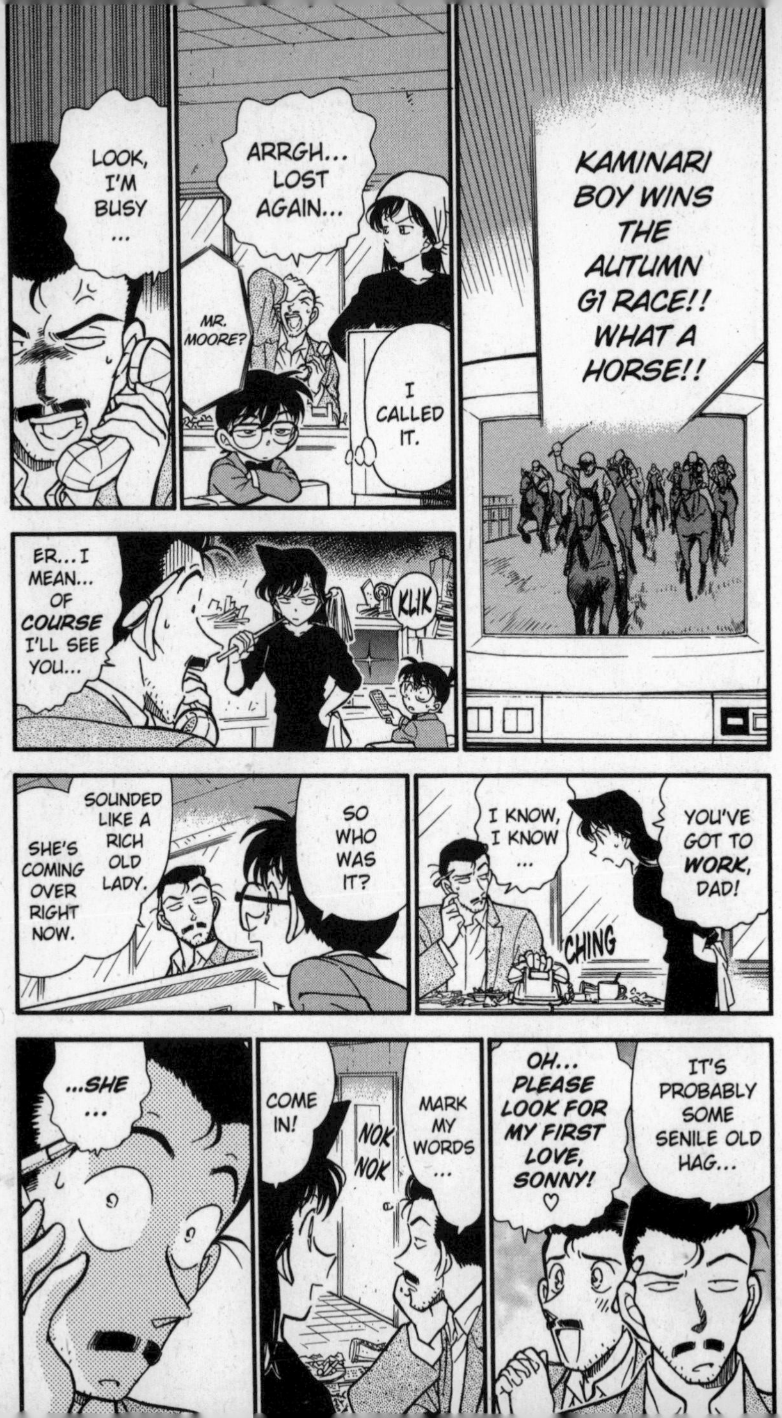
KAMINARI BOY WINS THE AUTUMN G1 RACE!! WHAT A HORSE!!
ARRGH... LOST AGAIN...
I CALLED IT.
MR. MOORE?
LOOK, I'M BUSY...
KLIK
ER... I MEAN... OF COURSE I'LL SEE YOU...
YOU'VE GOT TO WORK, DAD!
I KNOW, I KNOW...
CHING
SO WHO WAS IT?
SOUNDED LIKE A RICH OLD LADY.
SHE'S COMING OVER RIGHT NOW.
IT'S PROBABLY SOME SENILE OLD HAG...
OH... PLEASE LOOK FOR MY FIRST LOVE, SONNY! ♡
MARK MY WORDS...
NOK NOK
COME IN!
...SHE...

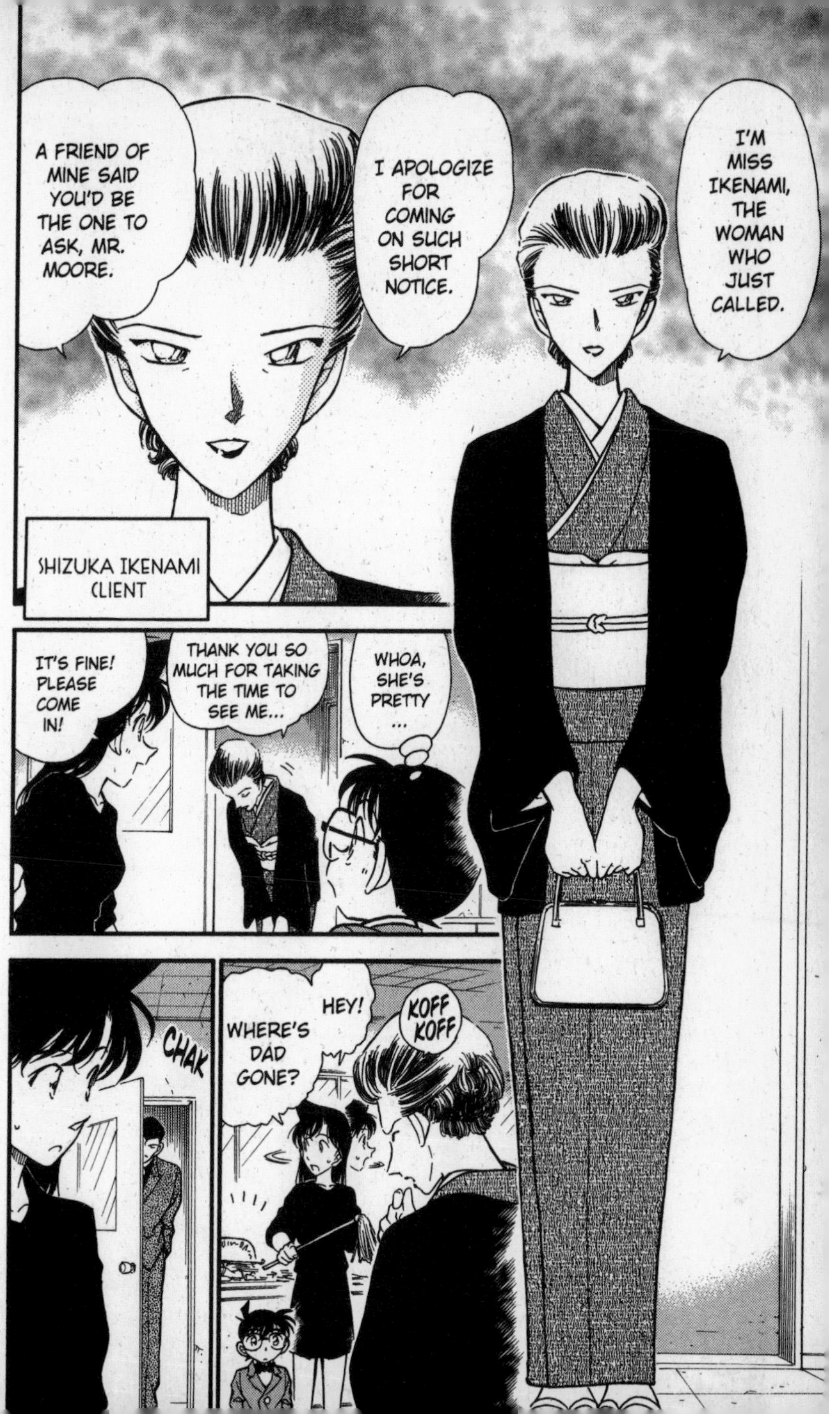

I'M MISS IKENAMI, THE WOMAN WHO JUST CALLED.
I APOLOGIZE FOR COMING ON SUCH SHORT NOTICE.
A FRIEND OF MINE SAID YOU'D BE THE ONE TO ASK, MR. MOORE.
SHIZUKA IKENAMI
CLIENT
WHOA, SHE'S PRETTY ...
THANK YOU SO MUCH FOR TAKING THE TIME TO SEE ME...
IT'S FINE! PLEASE COME IN!
KOFF KOFF
HEY!
WHERE'S DAD GONE?
CHAK

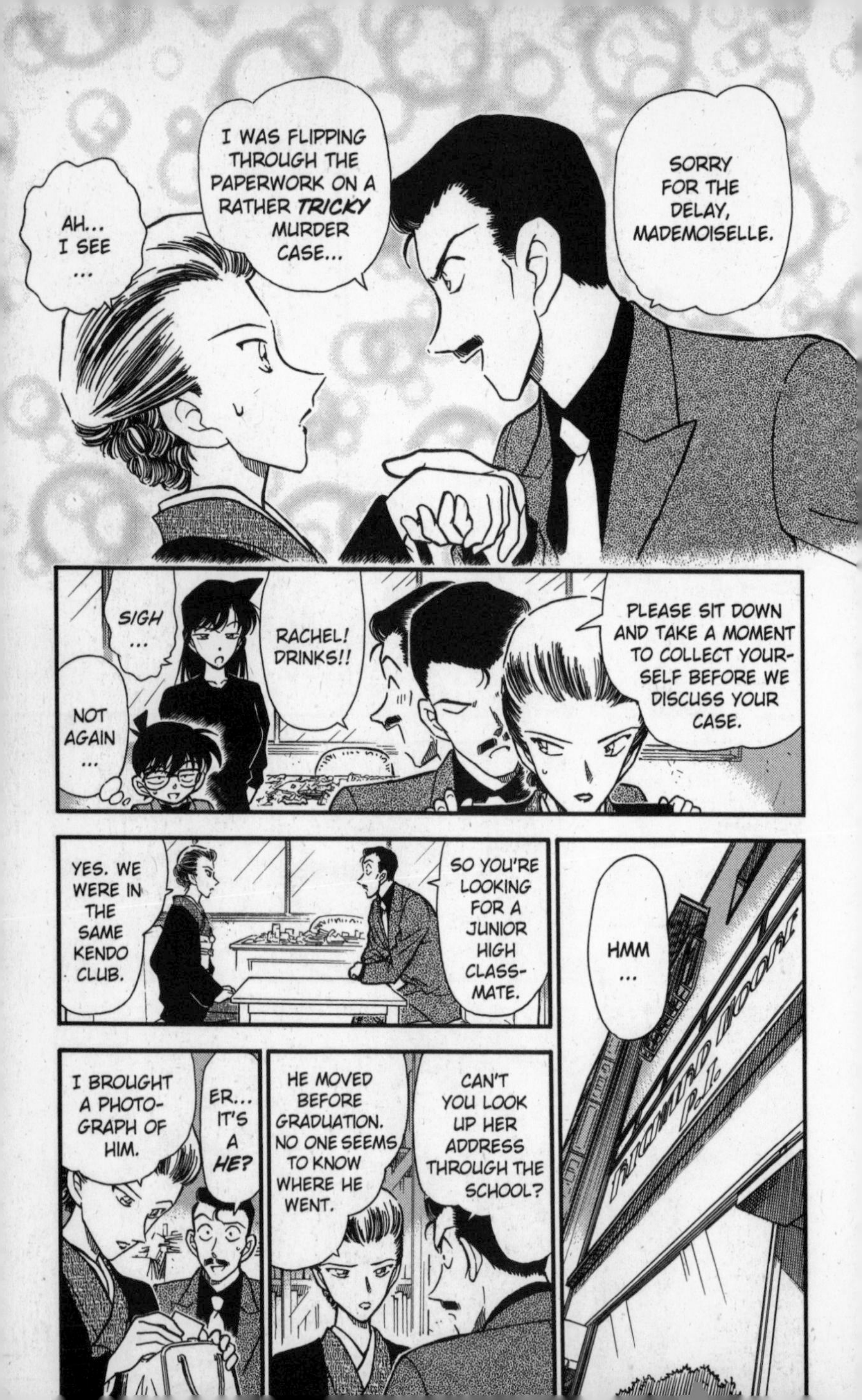
SORRY FOR THE DELAY, MADEMOISELLE.
I WAS FLIPPING THROUGH THE PAPERWORK ON A RATHER *TRICKY* MURDER CASE...
AH... I SEE ...
PLEASE SIT DOWN AND TAKE A MOMENT TO COLLECT YOURSELF BEFORE WE DISCUSS YOUR CASE.
RACHEL! DRINKS!!
SIGH ...
NOT AGAIN ...
HMM ...
SO YOU'RE LOOKING FOR A JUNIOR HIGH CLASSMATE.
YES. WE WERE IN THE SAME KENDO CLUB.
CAN'T YOU LOOK UP HER ADDRESS THROUGH THE SCHOOL?
HE MOVED BEFORE GRADUATION. NO ONE SEEMS TO KNOW WHERE HE WENT.
ER... IT'S A *HE*?
I BROUGHT A PHOTOGRAPH OF HIM.

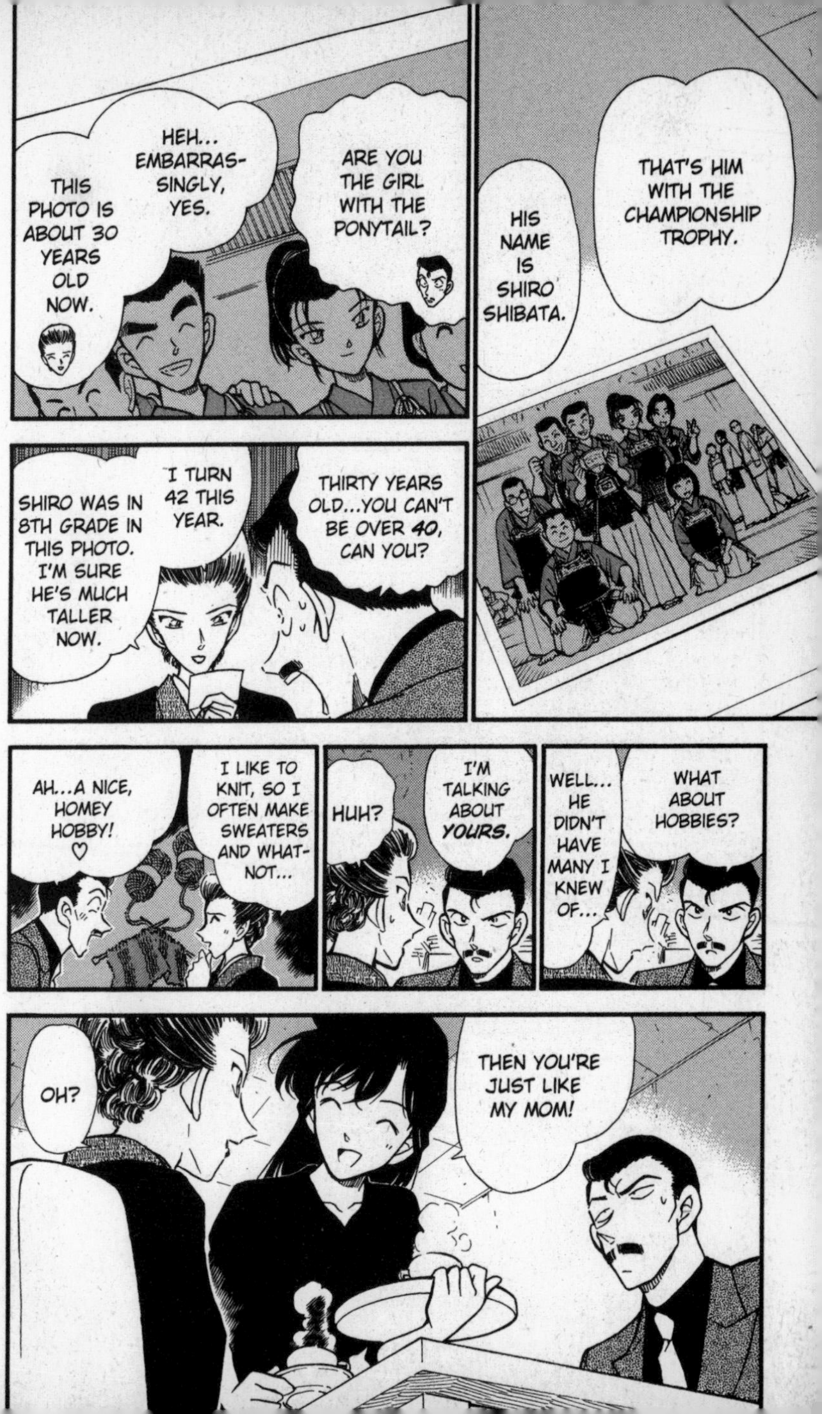
THAT'S HIM WITH THE CHAMPIONSHIP TROPHY.
HIS NAME IS SHIRO SHIBATA.
ARE YOU THE GIRL WITH THE PONYTAIL?
HEH... EMBARRASSINGLY, YES.
THIS PHOTO IS ABOUT 30 YEARS OLD NOW.
THIRTY YEARS OLD...YOU CAN'T BE OVER 40, CAN YOU?
I TURN 42 THIS YEAR.
SHIRO WAS IN 8TH GRADE IN THIS PHOTO. I'M SURE HE'S MUCH TALLER NOW.
WHAT ABOUT HOBBIES?
WELL... HE DIDN'T HAVE MANY I KNEW OF...
I'M TALKING ABOUT ***YOURS.***
HUH?
I LIKE TO KNIT, SO I OFTEN MAKE SWEATERS AND WHATNOT...
AH...A NICE, HOMEY HOBBY! ♡
THEN YOU'RE JUST LIKE MY MOM!
OH?

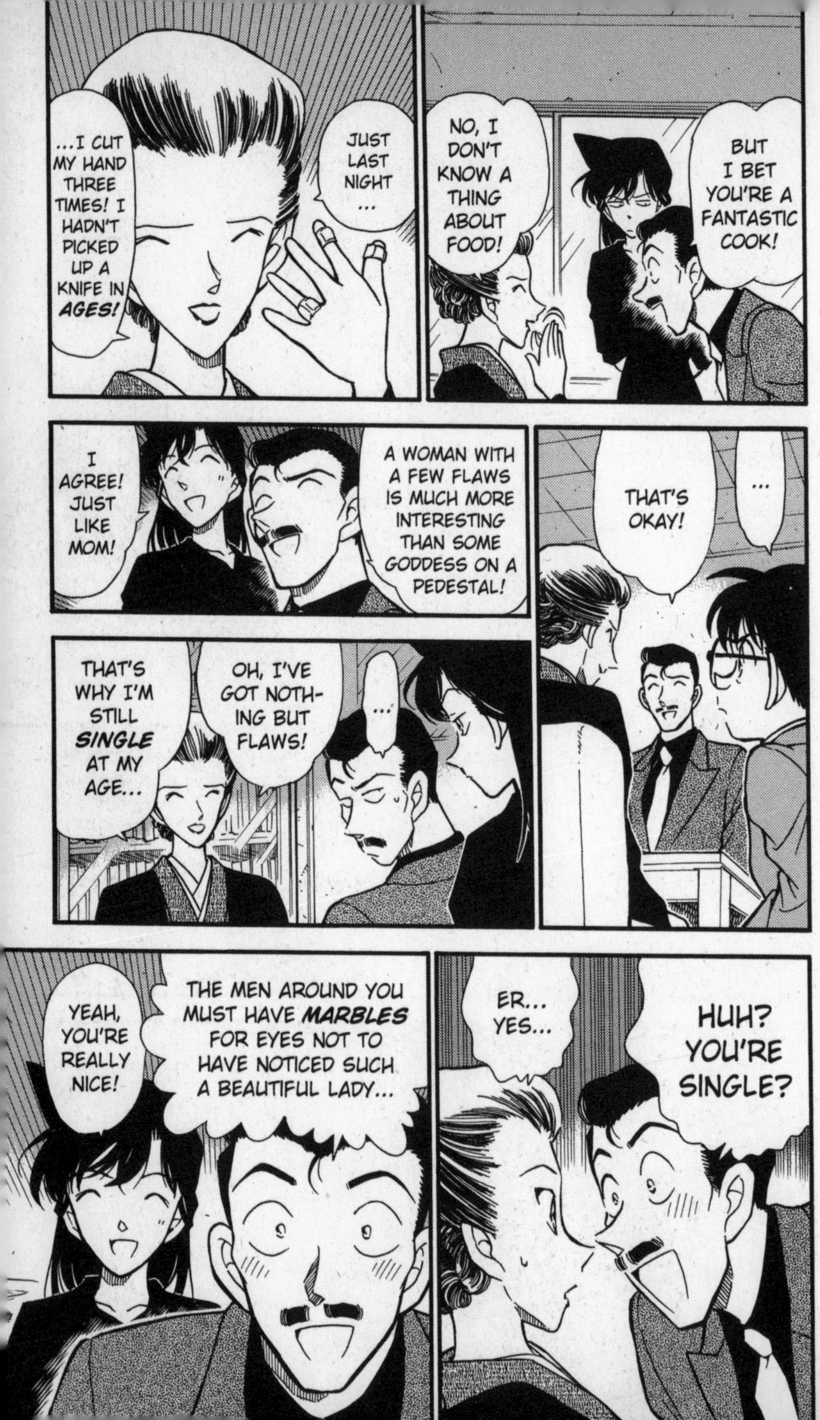
BUT I BET YOU'RE A FANTASTIC COOK!
NO, I DON'T KNOW A THING ABOUT FOOD!
JUST LAST NIGHT...
...I CUT MY HAND THREE TIMES! I HADN'T PICKED UP A KNIFE IN *AGES!*
...
THAT'S OKAY!
A WOMAN WITH A FEW FLAWS IS MUCH MORE INTERESTING THAN SOME GODDESS ON A PEDESTAL!
I AGREE! JUST LIKE MOM!
...
OH, I'VE GOT NOTHING BUT FLAWS!
THAT'S WHY I'M STILL *SINGLE* AT MY AGE...
HUH? YOU'RE SINGLE?
ER... YES...
THE MEN AROUND YOU MUST HAVE *MARBLES* FOR EYES NOT TO HAVE NOTICED SUCH A BEAUTIFUL LADY...
YEAH, YOU'RE REALLY NICE!

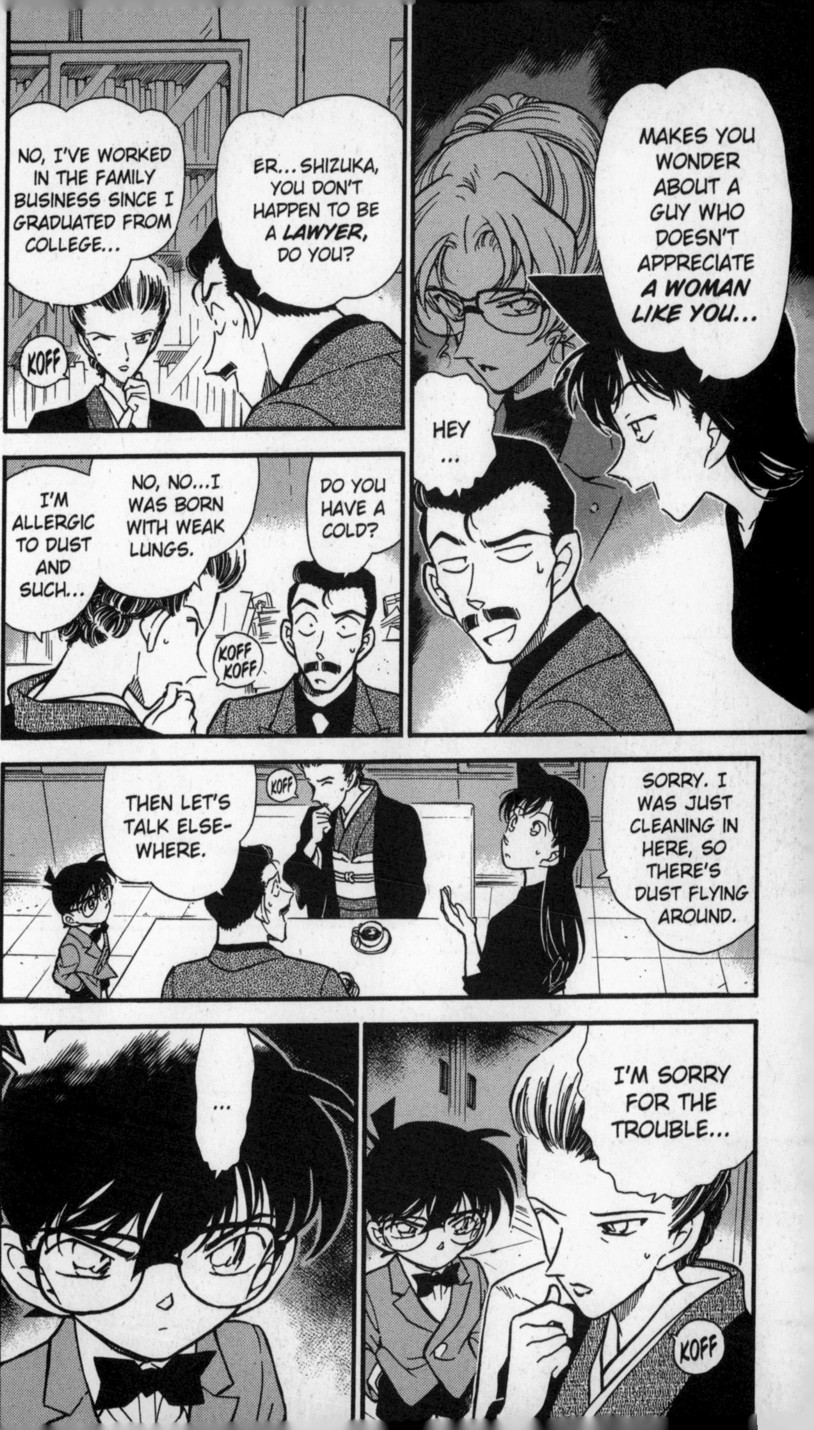
MAKES YOU WONDER ABOUT A GUY WHO DOESN'T APPRECIATE **A WOMAN LIKE YOU...**
HEY ...
ER... SHIZUKA, YOU DON'T HAPPEN TO BE A ***LAWYER,*** DO YOU?
NO, I'VE WORKED IN THE FAMILY BUSINESS SINCE I GRADUATED FROM COLLEGE...
KOFF
DO YOU HAVE A COLD?
KOFF KOFF
NO, NO...I WAS BORN WITH WEAK LUNGS.
I'M ALLERGIC TO DUST AND SUCH...
SORRY. I WAS JUST CLEANING IN HERE, SO THERE'S DUST FLYING AROUND.
KOFF
THEN LET'S TALK ELSE-WHERE.
I'M SORRY FOR THE TROUBLE...
KOFF
...

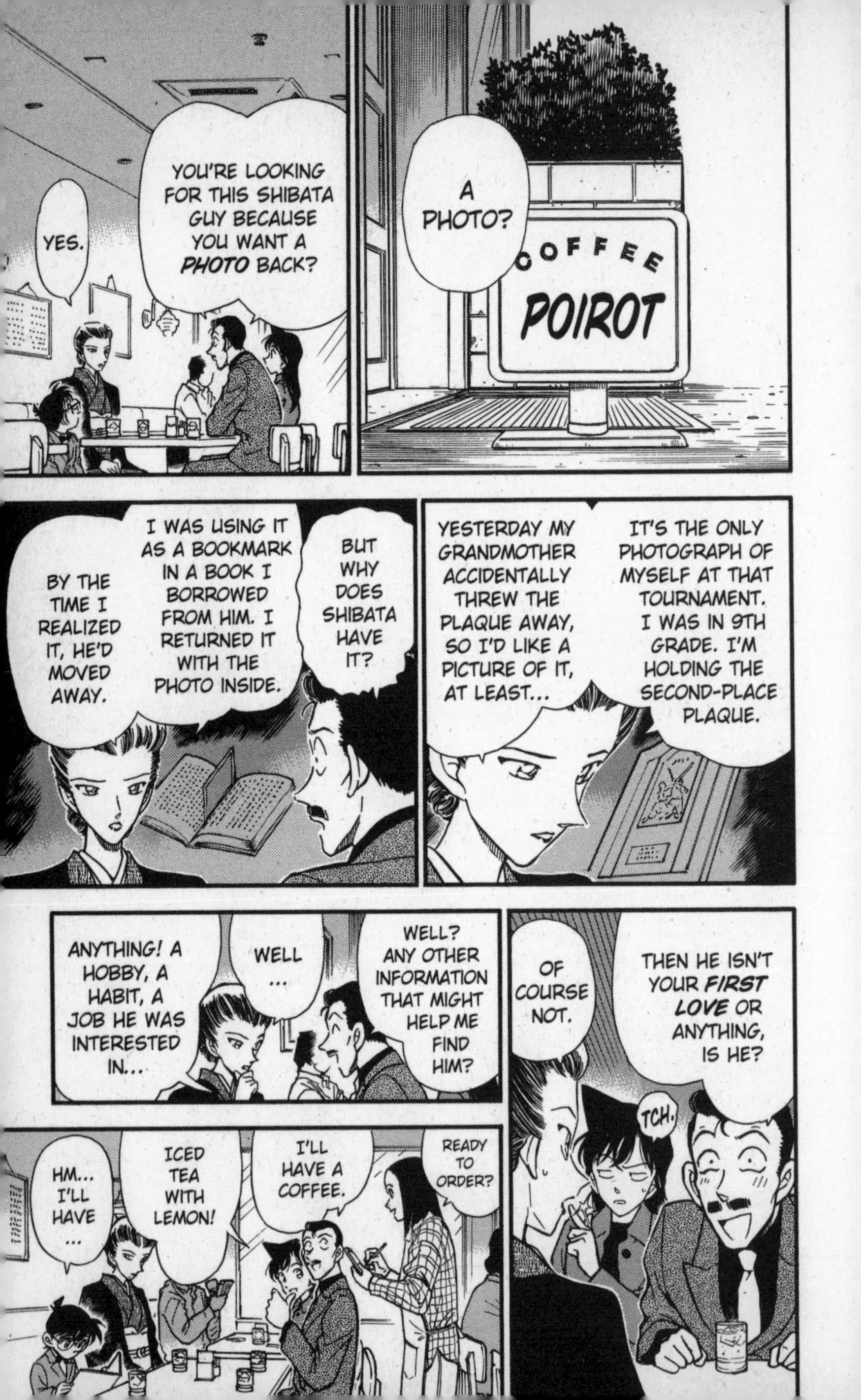
A PHOTO?
COFFEE
POIROT
YOU'RE LOOKING FOR THIS SHIBATA GUY BECAUSE YOU WANT A PHOTO BACK?
YES.
IT'S THE ONLY PHOTOGRAPH OF MYSELF AT THAT TOURNAMENT. I WAS IN 9TH GRADE. I'M HOLDING THE SECOND-PLACE PLAQUE.
YESTERDAY MY GRANDMOTHER ACCIDENTALLY THREW THE PLAQUE AWAY, SO I'D LIKE A PICTURE OF IT, AT LEAST...
BUT WHY DOES SHIBATA HAVE IT?
I WAS USING IT AS A BOOKMARK IN A BOOK I BORROWED FROM HIM. I RETURNED IT WITH THE PHOTO INSIDE.
BY THE TIME I REALIZED IT, HE'D MOVED AWAY.
THEN HE ISN'T YOUR FIRST LOVE OR ANYTHING, IS HE?
OF COURSE NOT.
TCH.
WELL? ANY OTHER INFORMATION THAT MIGHT HELP ME FIND HIM?
WELL ...
ANYTHING! A HOBBY, A HABIT, A JOB HE WAS INTERESTED IN...
READY TO ORDER?
I'LL HAVE A COFFEE.
ICED TEA WITH LEMON!
HM... I'LL HAVE ...

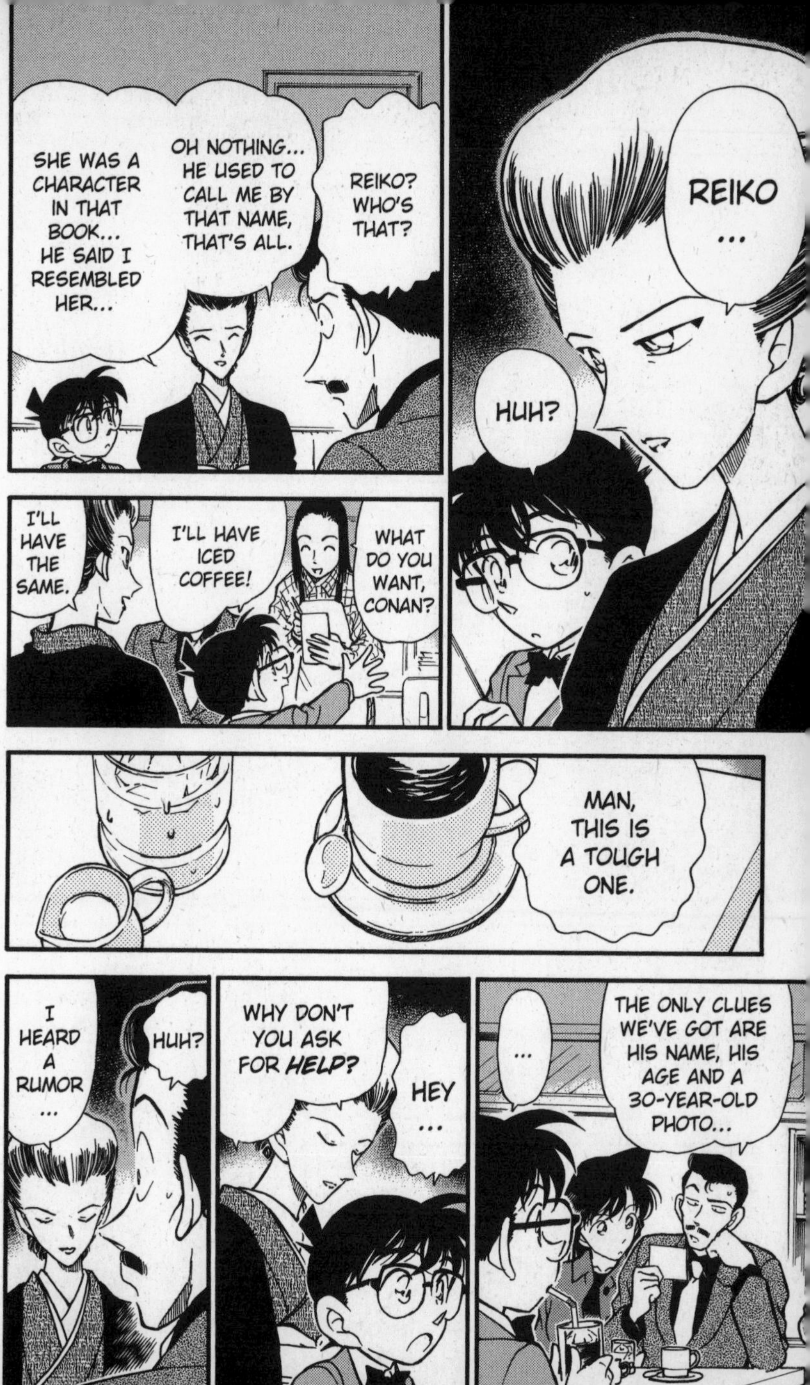
REIKO ...
HUH?
REIKO? WHO'S THAT?
OH NOTHING... HE USED TO CALL ME BY THAT NAME, THAT'S ALL.
SHE WAS A CHARACTER IN THAT BOOK... HE SAID I RESEMBLED HER...
WHAT DO YOU WANT, CONAN?
I'LL HAVE ICED COFFEE!
I'LL HAVE THE SAME.
MAN, THIS IS A TOUGH ONE.
THE ONLY CLUES WE'VE GOT ARE HIS NAME, HIS AGE AND A 30-YEAR-OLD PHOTO...
...
HEY ...
WHY DON'T YOU ASK FOR ***HELP***?
HUH?
I HEARD A RUMOR ...

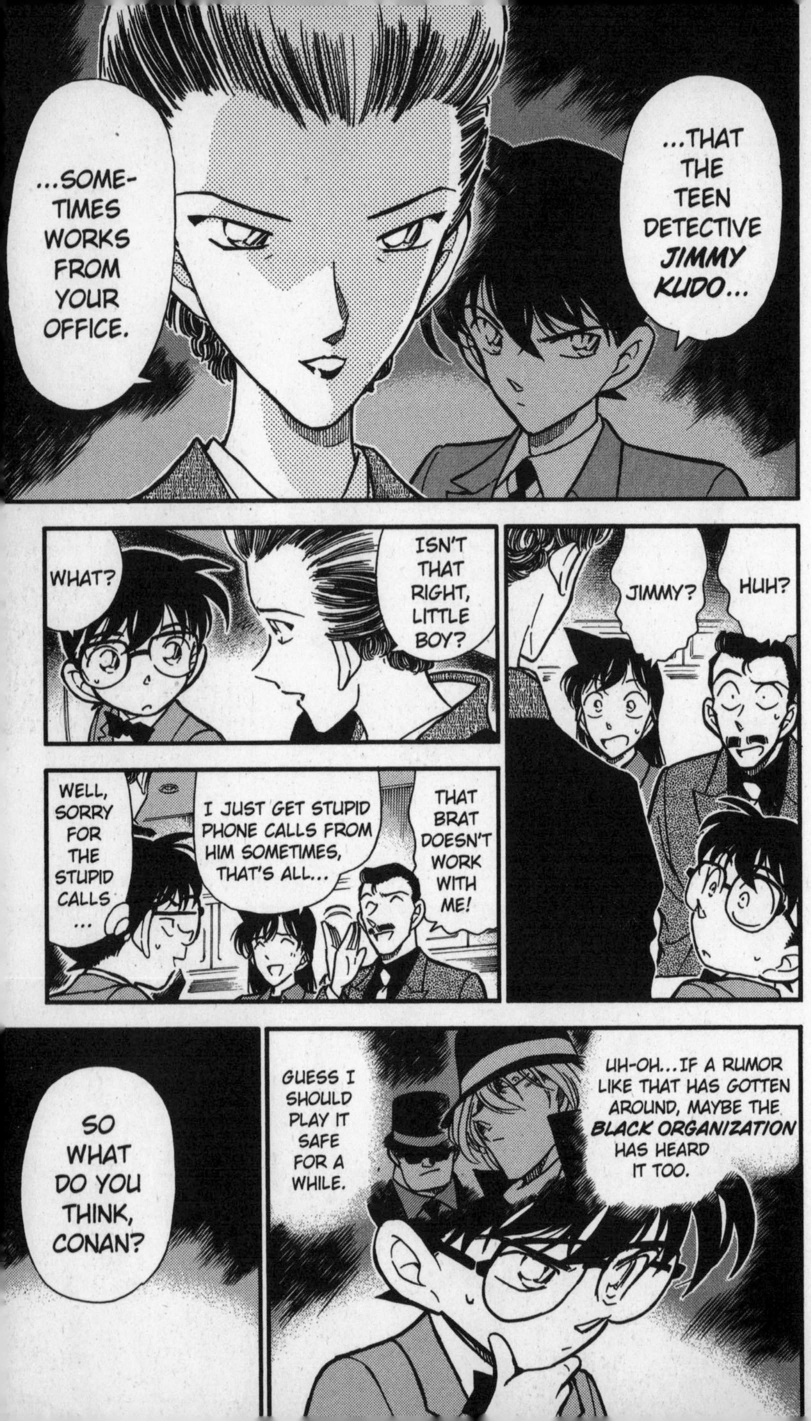
...THAT THE TEEN DETECTIVE *JIMMY KUDO*...
...SOMETIMES WORKS FROM YOUR OFFICE.
HUH?
JIMMY?
ISN'T THAT RIGHT, LITTLE BOY?
WHAT?
THAT BRAT DOESN'T WORK WITH ME!
I JUST GET STUPID PHONE CALLS FROM HIM SOMETIMES, THAT'S ALL...
WELL, SORRY FOR THE STUPID CALLS...
UH-OH...IF A RUMOR LIKE THAT HAS GOTTEN AROUND, MAYBE THE *BLACK ORGANIZATION* HAS HEARD IT TOO.
GUESS I SHOULD PLAY IT SAFE FOR A WHILE.
SO WHAT DO YOU THINK, CONAN?

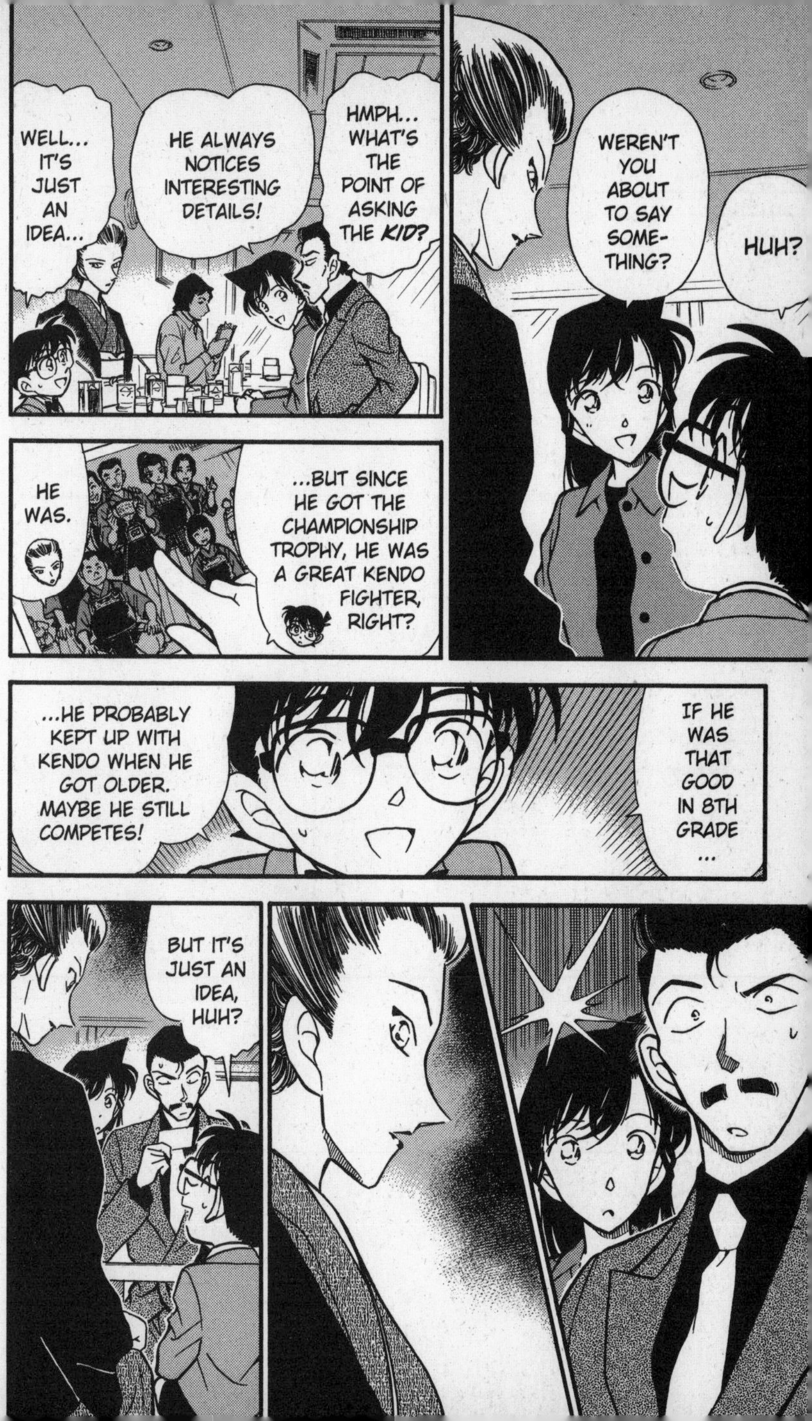
WEREN'T YOU ABOUT TO SAY SOME-THING?
HUH?
HMPH... WHAT'S THE POINT OF ASKING THE *KID*?
HE ALWAYS NOTICES INTERESTING DETAILS!
WELL... IT'S JUST AN IDEA...
...BUT SINCE HE GOT THE CHAMPIONSHIP TROPHY, HE WAS A GREAT KENDO FIGHTER, RIGHT?
HE WAS.
IF HE WAS THAT GOOD IN 8TH GRADE ...
...HE PROBABLY KEPT UP WITH KENDO WHEN HE GOT OLDER. MAYBE HE STILL COMPETES!
BUT IT'S JUST AN IDEA, HUH?

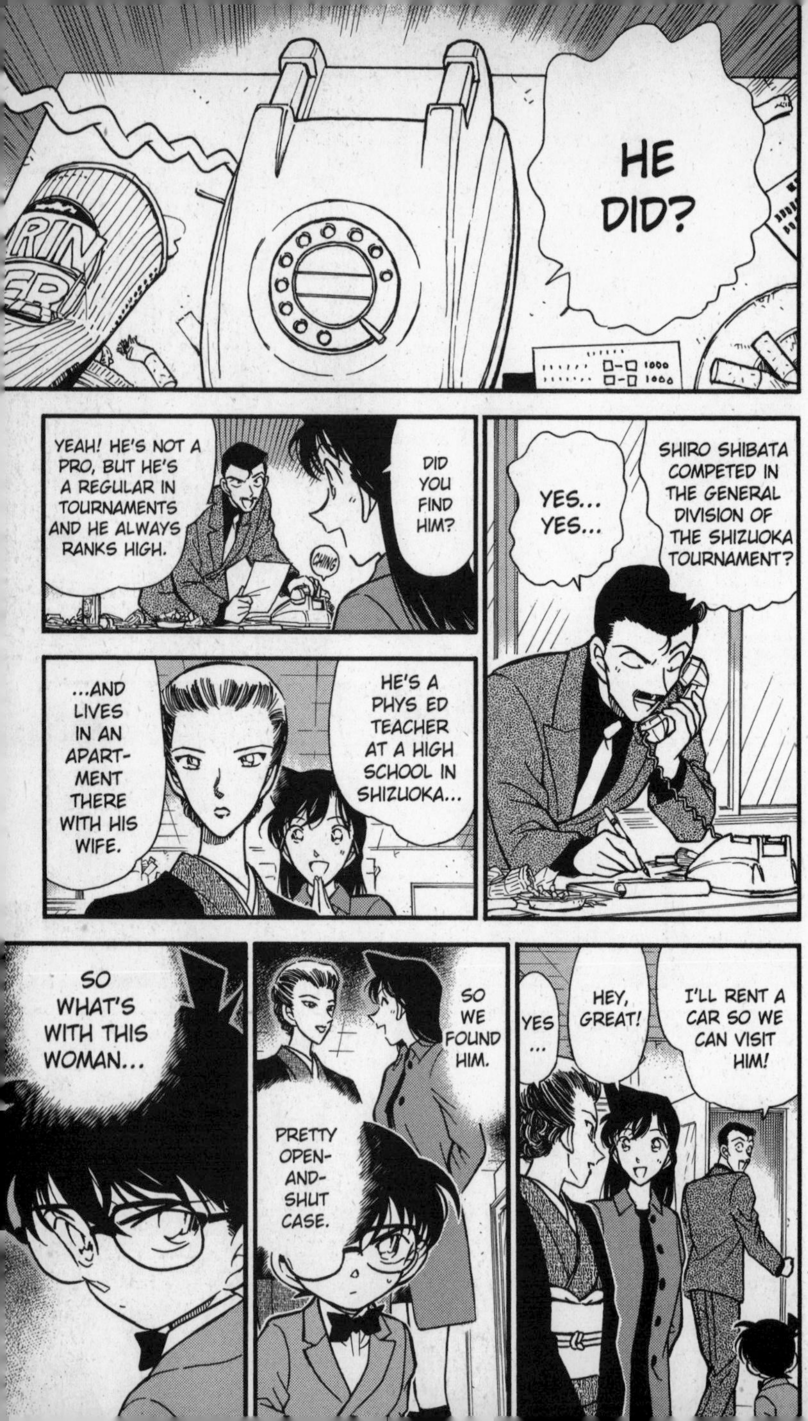
HE DID?
SHIRO SHIBATA COMPETED IN THE GENERAL DIVISION OF THE SHIZUOKA TOURNAMENT?
YES... YES...
DID YOU FIND HIM?
CHING
YEAH! HE'S NOT A PRO, BUT HE'S A REGULAR IN TOURNAMENTS AND HE ALWAYS RANKS HIGH.
HE'S A PHYS ED TEACHER AT A HIGH SCHOOL IN SHIZUOKA...
...AND LIVES IN AN APARTMENT THERE WITH HIS WIFE.
I'LL RENT A CAR SO WE CAN VISIT HIM!
HEY, GREAT!
YES...
SO WE FOUND HIM.
PRETTY OPEN-AND-SHUT CASE.
SO WHAT'S WITH THIS WOMAN...

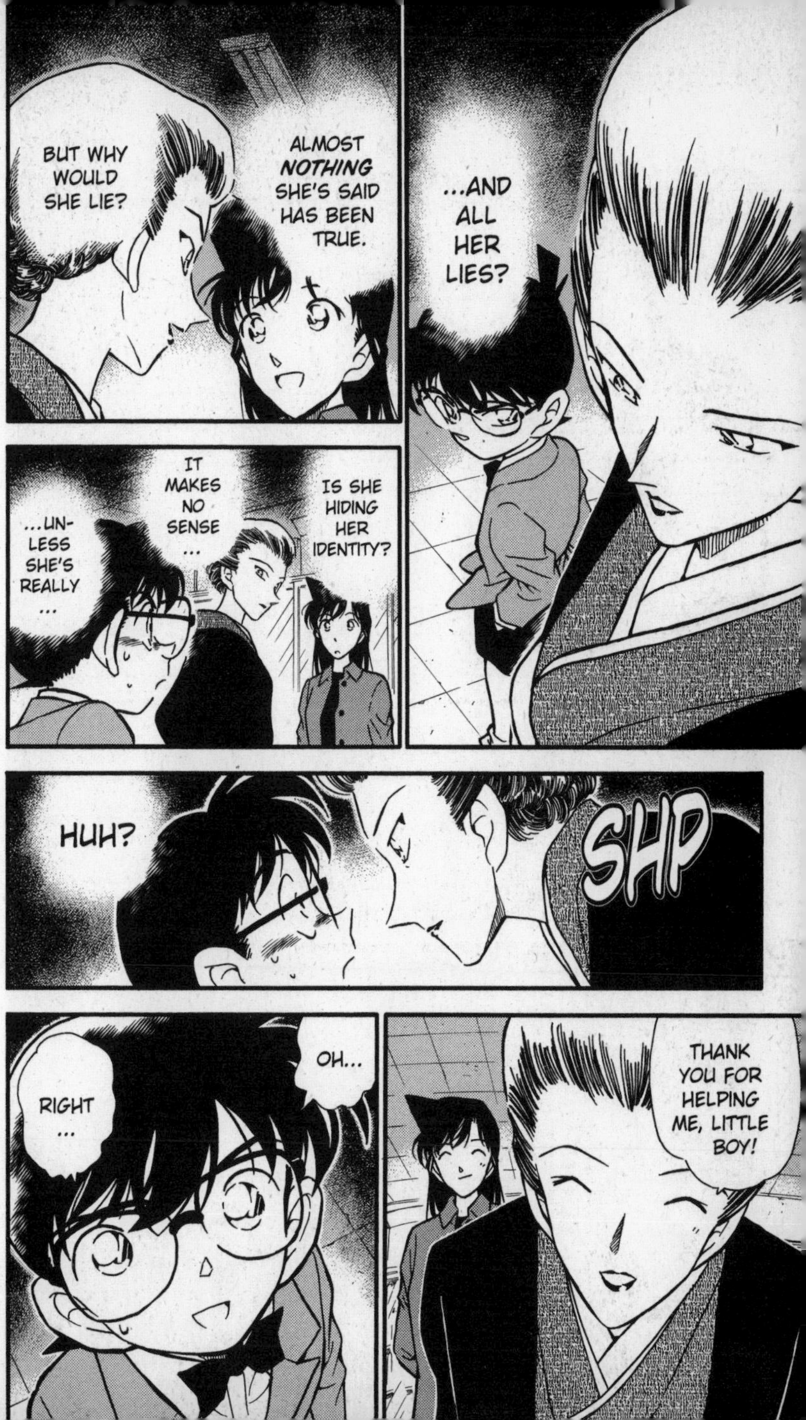
...AND ALL HER LIES?
ALMOST NOTHING SHE'S SAID HAS BEEN TRUE.
BUT WHY WOULD SHE LIE?
IS SHE HIDING HER IDENTITY?
IT MAKES NO SENSE...
...UNLESS SHE'S REALLY...
SHP
HUH?
THANK YOU FOR HELPING ME, LITTLE BOY!
OH...
RIGHT...

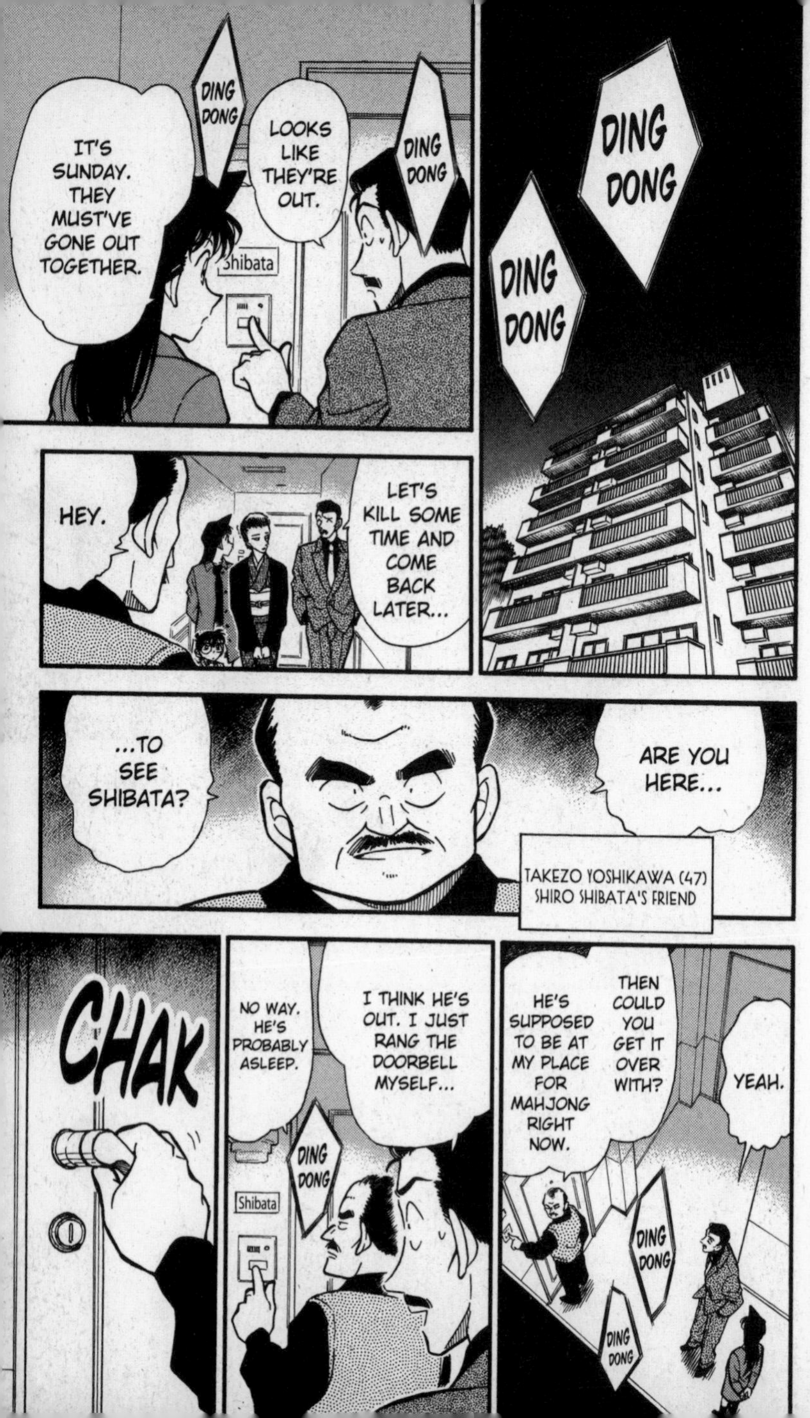
DING DONG
DING DONG
DING DONG
LOOKS LIKE THEY'RE OUT.
DING DONG
IT'S SUNDAY. THEY MUST'VE GONE OUT TOGETHER.
Shibata
LET'S KILL SOME TIME AND COME BACK LATER...
HEY.
ARE YOU HERE...
TAKEZO YOSHIKAWA (47) SHIRO SHIBATA'S FRIEND
...TO SEE SHIBATA?
YEAH.
THEN COULD YOU GET IT OVER WITH?
HE'S SUPPOSED TO BE AT MY PLACE FOR MAHJONG RIGHT NOW.
DING DONG
DING DONG
I THINK HE'S OUT. I JUST RANG THE DOORBELL MYSELF...
NO WAY. HE'S PROBABLY ASLEEP.
DING DONG
Shibata
CHAK

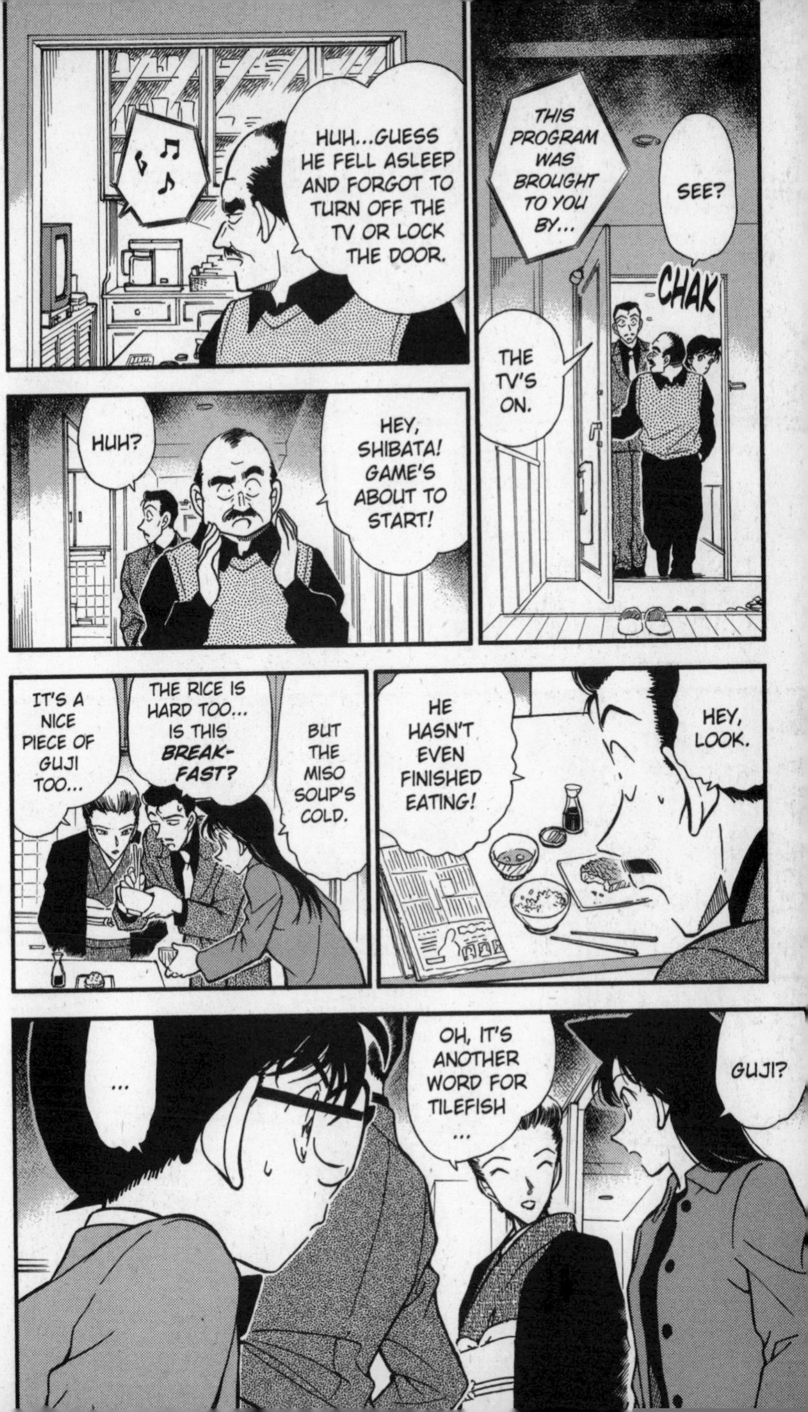
SEE?
THIS PROGRAM WAS BROUGHT TO YOU BY...
CHAK
THE TV'S ON.
♪ ♪ ♪
HUH...GUESS HE FELL ASLEEP AND FORGOT TO TURN OFF THE TV OR LOCK THE DOOR.
HEY, SHIBATA! GAME'S ABOUT TO START!
HUH?
HEY, LOOK.
HE HASN'T EVEN FINISHED EATING!
BUT THE MISO SOUP'S COLD.
THE RICE IS HARD TOO... IS THIS *BREAK-FAST?*
IT'S A NICE PIECE OF GUJI TOO...
GUJI?
OH, IT'S ANOTHER WORD FOR TILEFISH...
...

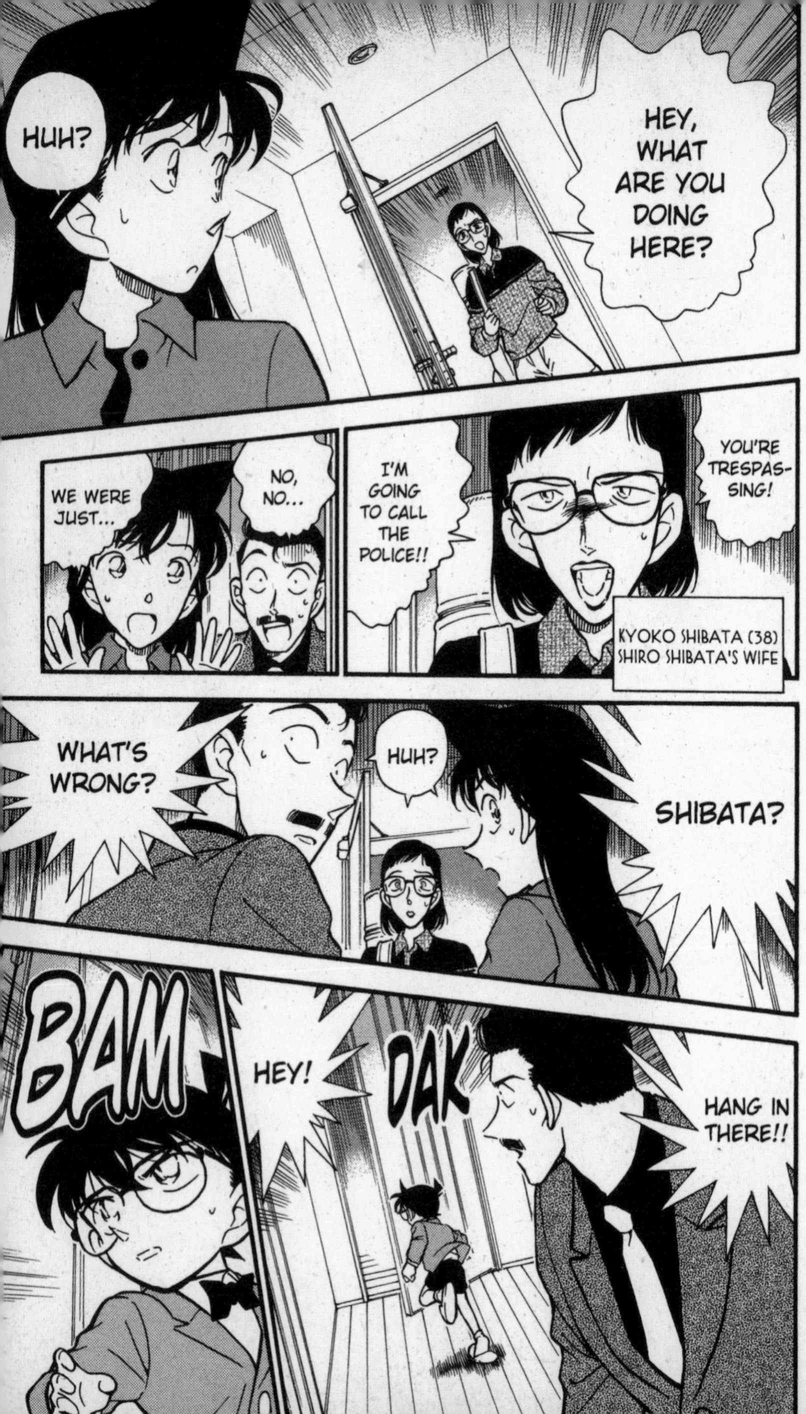
HEY, WHAT ARE YOU DOING HERE?
HUH?
YOU'RE TRESPAS-SING!
I'M GOING TO CALL THE POLICE!!
KYOKO SHIBATA (38) SHIRO SHIBATA'S WIFE
NO, NO...
WE WERE JUST...
SHIBATA?
HUH?
WHAT'S WRONG?
HANG IN THERE!!
DAK
HEY!
BAM

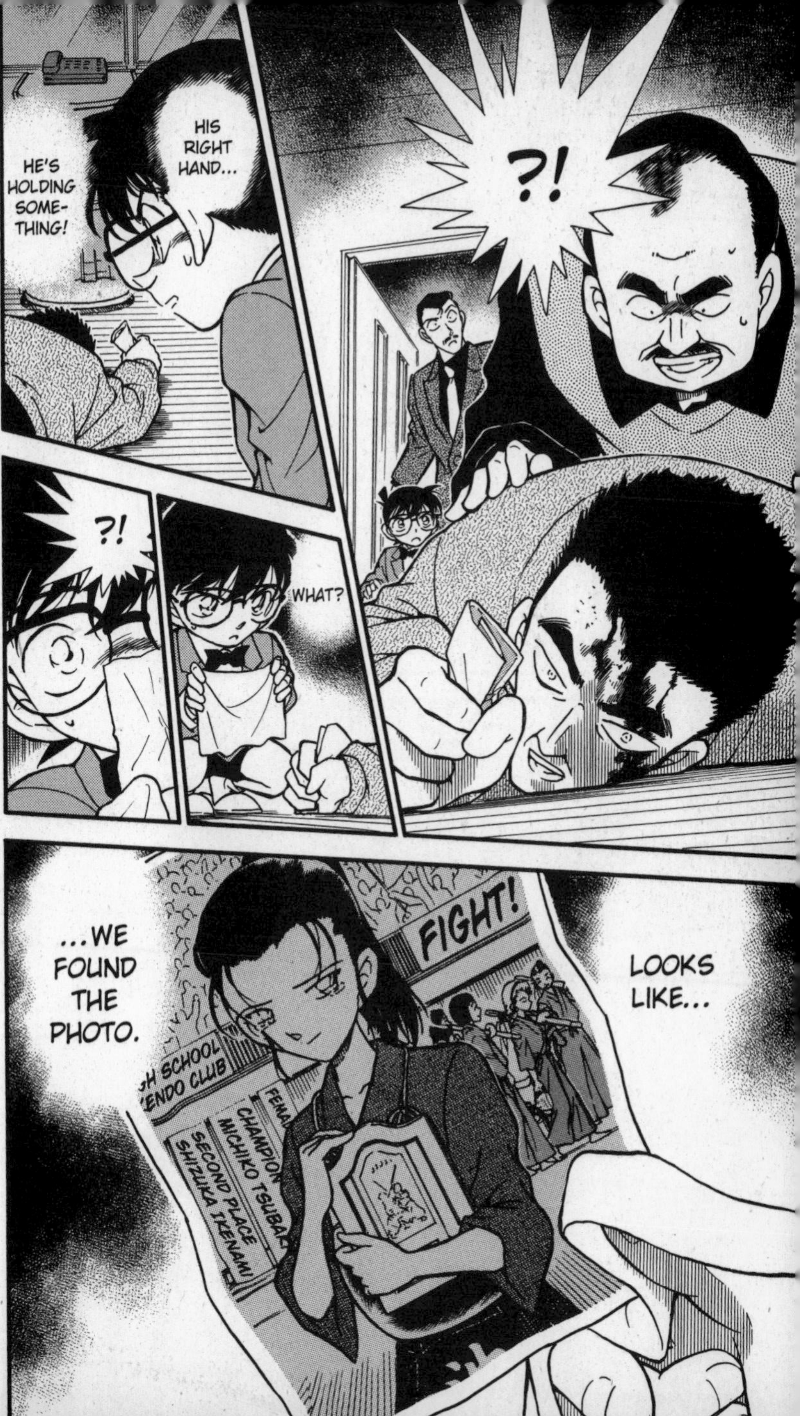
?!
HIS RIGHT HAND...
HE'S HOLDING SOME-THING!
WHAT?
?!
LOOKS LIKE...
...WE FOUND THE PHOTO.
FIGHT!
GH SCHOOL
ENDO CLUB
FEMA
CHAMPION
MICHIKO TSUBA
SECOND PLACE
SHIZUKA IKENAMI

FILE 4: A HANDFUL OF PROOF

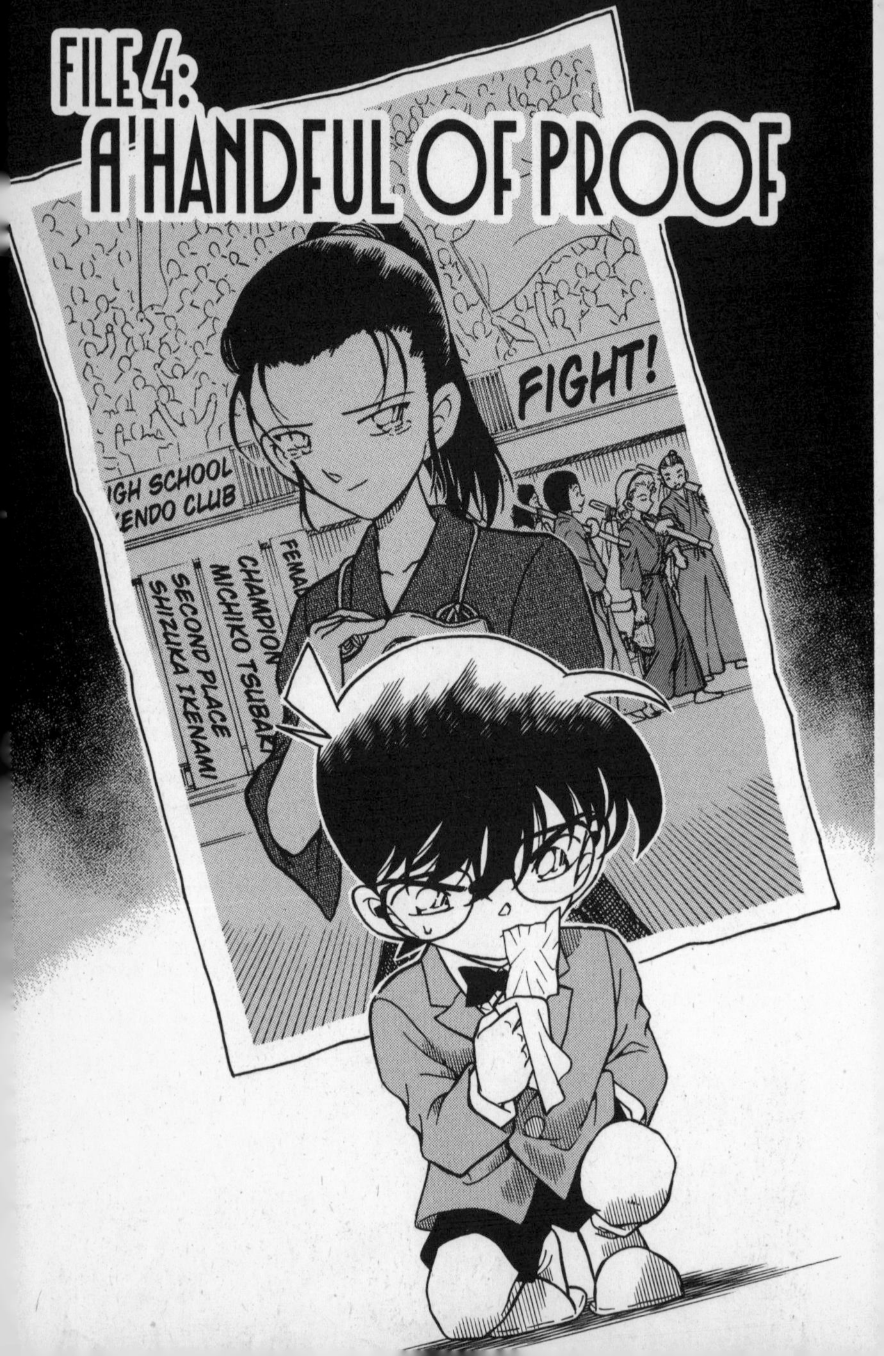
FIGHT!
IGH SCHOOL
ENDO CLUB
CHAMPION
MICHIKO TSUBAKI
SECOND PLACE
SHIZUKA IKENAMI

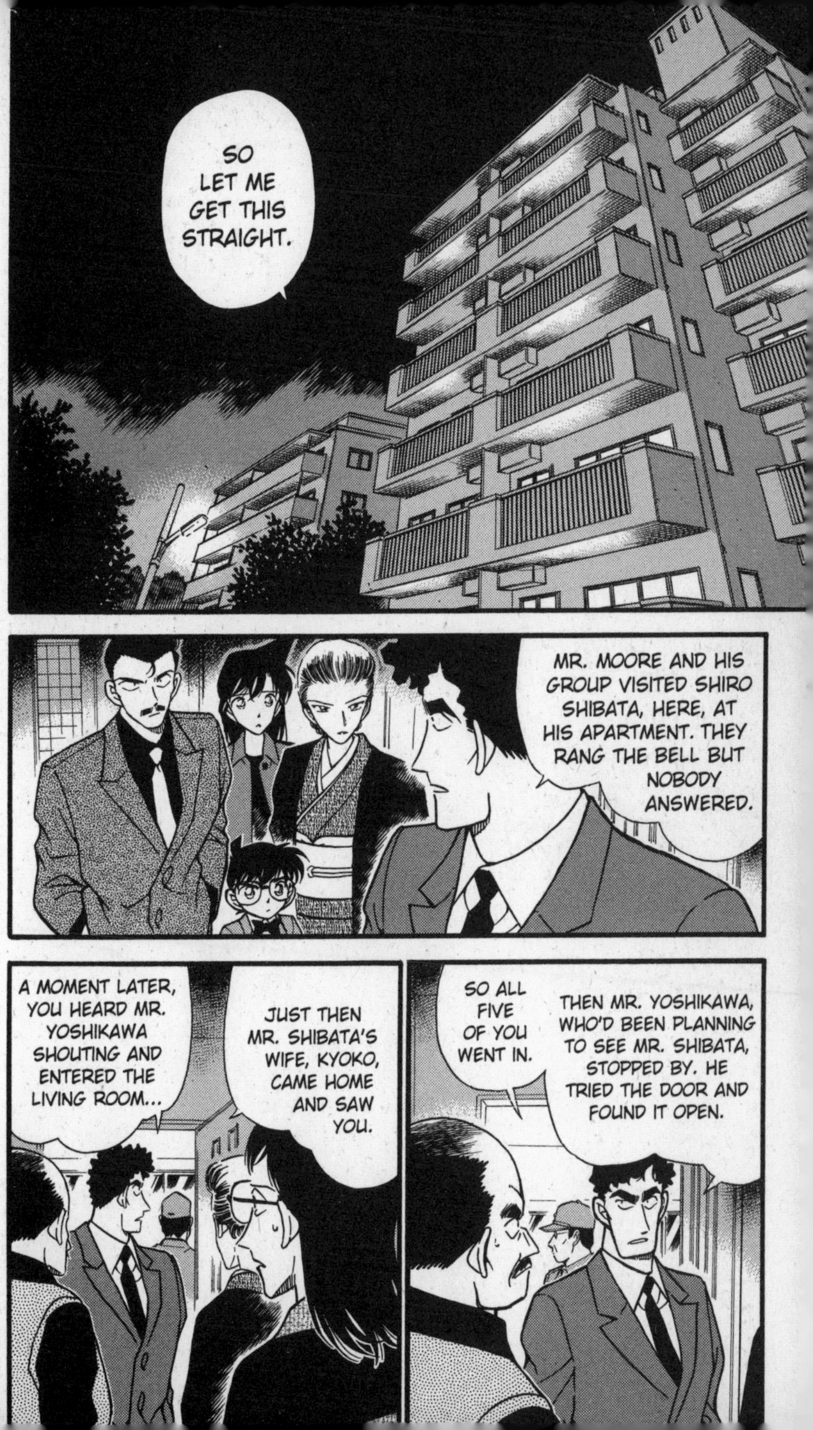
SO LET ME GET THIS STRAIGHT.
MR. MOORE AND HIS GROUP VISITED SHIRO SHIBATA, HERE, AT HIS APARTMENT. THEY RANG THE BELL BUT NOBODY ANSWERED.
THEN MR. YOSHIKAWA, WHO'D BEEN PLANNING TO SEE MR. SHIBATA, STOPPED BY. HE TRIED THE DOOR AND FOUND IT OPEN.
SO ALL FIVE OF YOU WENT IN.
JUST THEN MR. SHIBATA'S WIFE, KYOKO, CAME HOME AND SAW YOU.
A MOMENT LATER, YOU HEARD MR. YOSHIKAWA SHOUTING AND ENTERED THE LIVING ROOM...

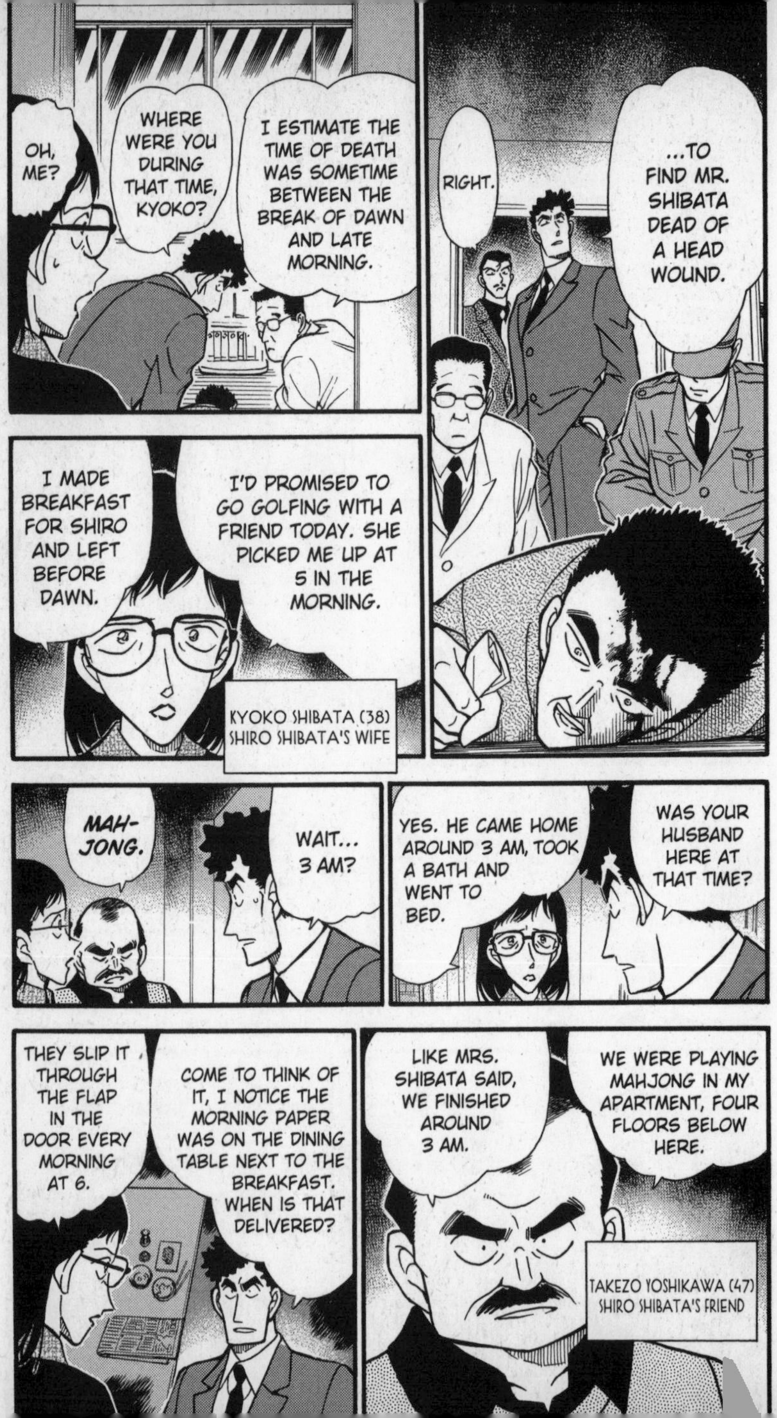
...TO FIND MR. SHIBATA DEAD OF A HEAD WOUND.
RIGHT.
I ESTIMATE THE TIME OF DEATH WAS SOMETIME BETWEEN THE BREAK OF DAWN AND LATE MORNING.
WHERE WERE YOU DURING THAT TIME, KYOKO?
OH, ME?
I'D PROMISED TO GO GOLFING WITH A FRIEND TODAY. SHE PICKED ME UP AT 5 IN THE MORNING.
I MADE BREAKFAST FOR SHIRO AND LEFT BEFORE DAWN.
KYOKO SHIBATA (38) SHIRO SHIBATA'S WIFE
WAS YOUR HUSBAND HERE AT THAT TIME?
YES. HE CAME HOME AROUND 3 AM, TOOK A BATH AND WENT TO BED.
WAIT... 3 AM?
MAH-JONG.
WE WERE PLAYING MAHJONG IN MY APARTMENT, FOUR FLOORS BELOW HERE.
LIKE MRS. SHIBATA SAID, WE FINISHED AROUND 3 AM.
TAKEZO YOSHIKAWA (47) SHIRO SHIBATA'S FRIEND
COME TO THINK OF IT, I NOTICE THE MORNING PAPER WAS ON THE DINING TABLE NEXT TO THE BREAKFAST. WHEN IS THAT DELIVERED?
THEY SLIP IT THROUGH THE FLAP IN THE DOOR EVERY MORNING AT 6.

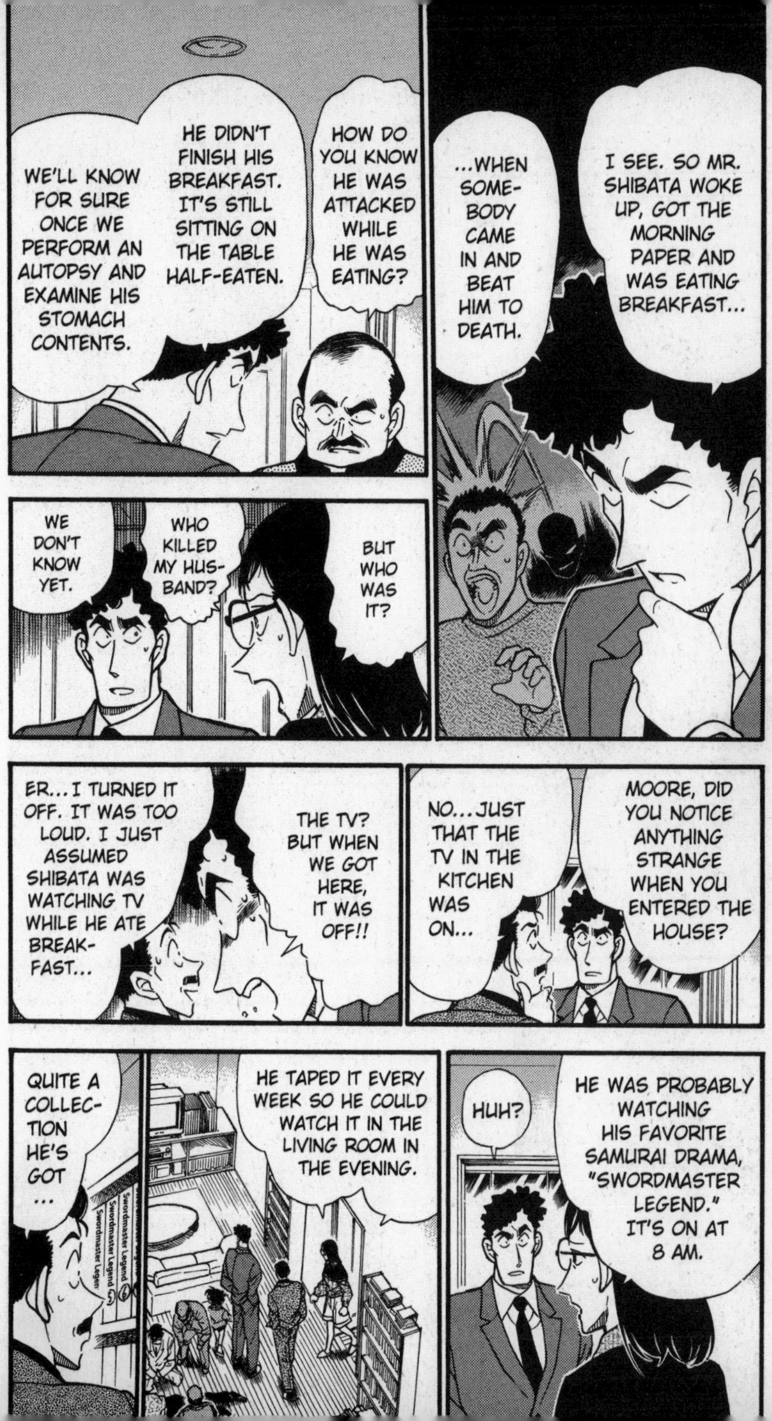
I SEE. SO MR. SHIBATA WOKE UP, GOT THE MORNING PAPER AND WAS EATING BREAKFAST...
...WHEN SOME-BODY CAME IN AND BEAT HIM TO DEATH.
HOW DO YOU KNOW HE WAS ATTACKED WHILE HE WAS EATING?
HE DIDN'T FINISH HIS BREAKFAST. IT'S STILL SITTING ON THE TABLE HALF-EATEN.
WE'LL KNOW FOR SURE ONCE WE PERFORM AN AUTOPSY AND EXAMINE HIS STOMACH CONTENTS.
BUT WHO WAS IT?
WHO KILLED MY HUS-BAND?
WE DON'T KNOW YET.
MOORE, DID YOU NOTICE ANYTHING STRANGE WHEN YOU ENTERED THE HOUSE?
NO...JUST THAT THE TV IN THE KITCHEN WAS ON...
THE TV? BUT WHEN WE GOT HERE, IT WAS OFF!!
ER...I TURNED IT OFF. IT WAS TOO LOUD. I JUST ASSUMED SHIBATA WAS WATCHING TV WHILE HE ATE BREAK-FAST...
HE WAS PROBABLY WATCHING HIS FAVORITE SAMURAI DRAMA, "SWORDMASTER LEGEND." IT'S ON AT 8 AM.
HUH?
HE TAPED IT EVERY WEEK SO HE COULD WATCH IT IN THE LIVING ROOM IN THE EVENING.
QUITE A COLLEC-TION HE'S GOT ...
Swordmaster Legend
Swordmaster Legend
Swordmaster Legend

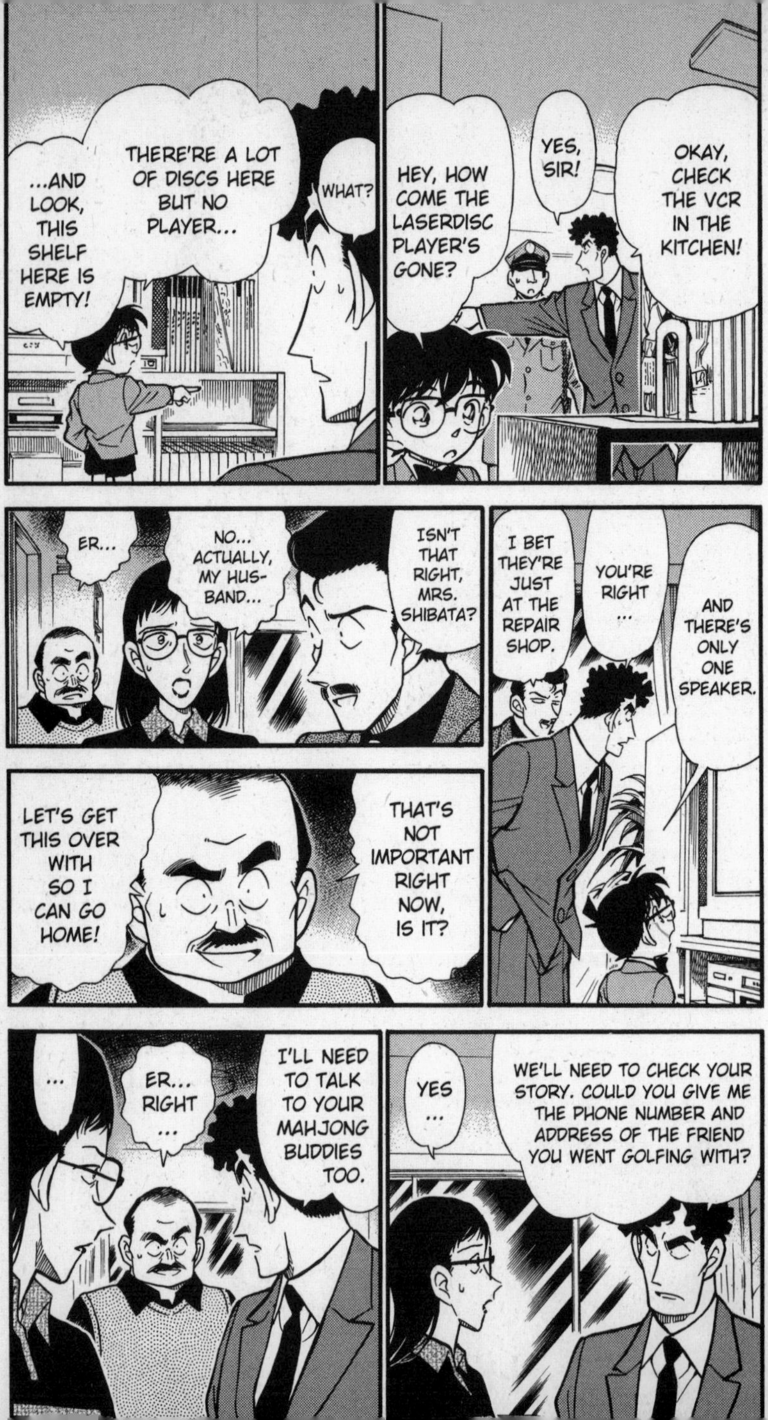
OKAY, CHECK THE VCR IN THE KITCHEN!
YES, SIR!
HEY, HOW COME THE LASERDISC PLAYER'S GONE?
WHAT?
THERE'RE A LOT OF DISCS HERE BUT NO PLAYER...
...AND LOOK, THIS SHELF HERE IS EMPTY!
AND THERE'S ONLY ONE SPEAKER.
YOU'RE RIGHT ...
I BET THEY'RE JUST AT THE REPAIR SHOP.
ISN'T THAT RIGHT, MRS. SHIBATA?
NO... ACTUALLY, MY HUS-BAND...
ER...
THAT'S NOT IMPORTANT RIGHT NOW, IS IT?
LET'S GET THIS OVER WITH SO I CAN GO HOME!
WE'LL NEED TO CHECK YOUR STORY. COULD YOU GIVE ME THE PHONE NUMBER AND ADDRESS OF THE FRIEND YOU WENT GOLFING WITH?
YES ...
I'LL NEED TO TALK TO YOUR MAHJONG BUDDIES TOO.
ER... RIGHT ...
...

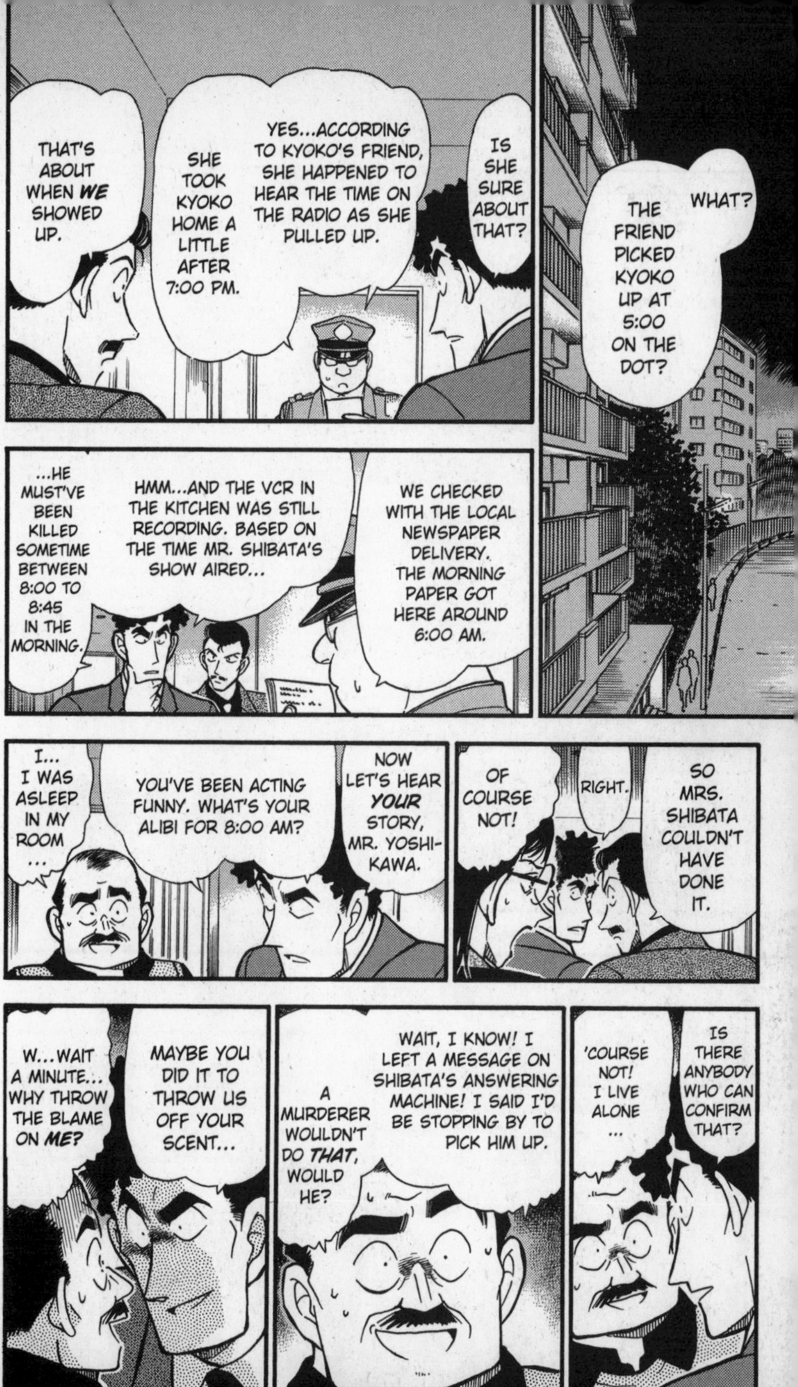
WHAT?
THE FRIEND PICKED KYOKO UP AT 5:00 ON THE DOT?
IS SHE SURE ABOUT THAT?
YES...ACCORDING TO KYOKO'S FRIEND, SHE HAPPENED TO HEAR THE TIME ON THE RADIO AS SHE PULLED UP.
SHE TOOK KYOKO HOME A LITTLE AFTER 7:00 PM.
THAT'S ABOUT WHEN WE SHOWED UP.
WE CHECKED WITH THE LOCAL NEWSPAPER DELIVERY. THE MORNING PAPER GOT HERE AROUND 6:00 AM.
HMM...AND THE VCR IN THE KITCHEN WAS STILL RECORDING. BASED ON THE TIME MR. SHIBATA'S SHOW AIRED...
...HE MUST'VE BEEN KILLED SOMETIME BETWEEN 8:00 TO 8:45 IN THE MORNING.
SO MRS. SHIBATA COULDN'T HAVE DONE IT.
RIGHT.
OF COURSE NOT!
NOW LET'S HEAR YOUR STORY, MR. YOSHI-KAWA.
YOU'VE BEEN ACTING FUNNY. WHAT'S YOUR ALIBI FOR 8:00 AM?
I... I WAS ASLEEP IN MY ROOM ...
IS THERE ANYBODY WHO CAN CONFIRM THAT?
'COURSE NOT! I LIVE ALONE ...
WAIT, I KNOW! I LEFT A MESSAGE ON SHIBATA'S ANSWERING MACHINE! I SAID I'D BE STOPPING BY TO PICK HIM UP.
A MURDERER WOULDN'T DO THAT, WOULD HE?
MAYBE YOU DID IT TO THROW US OFF YOUR SCENT...
W...WAIT A MINUTE... WHY THROW THE BLAME ON ME?

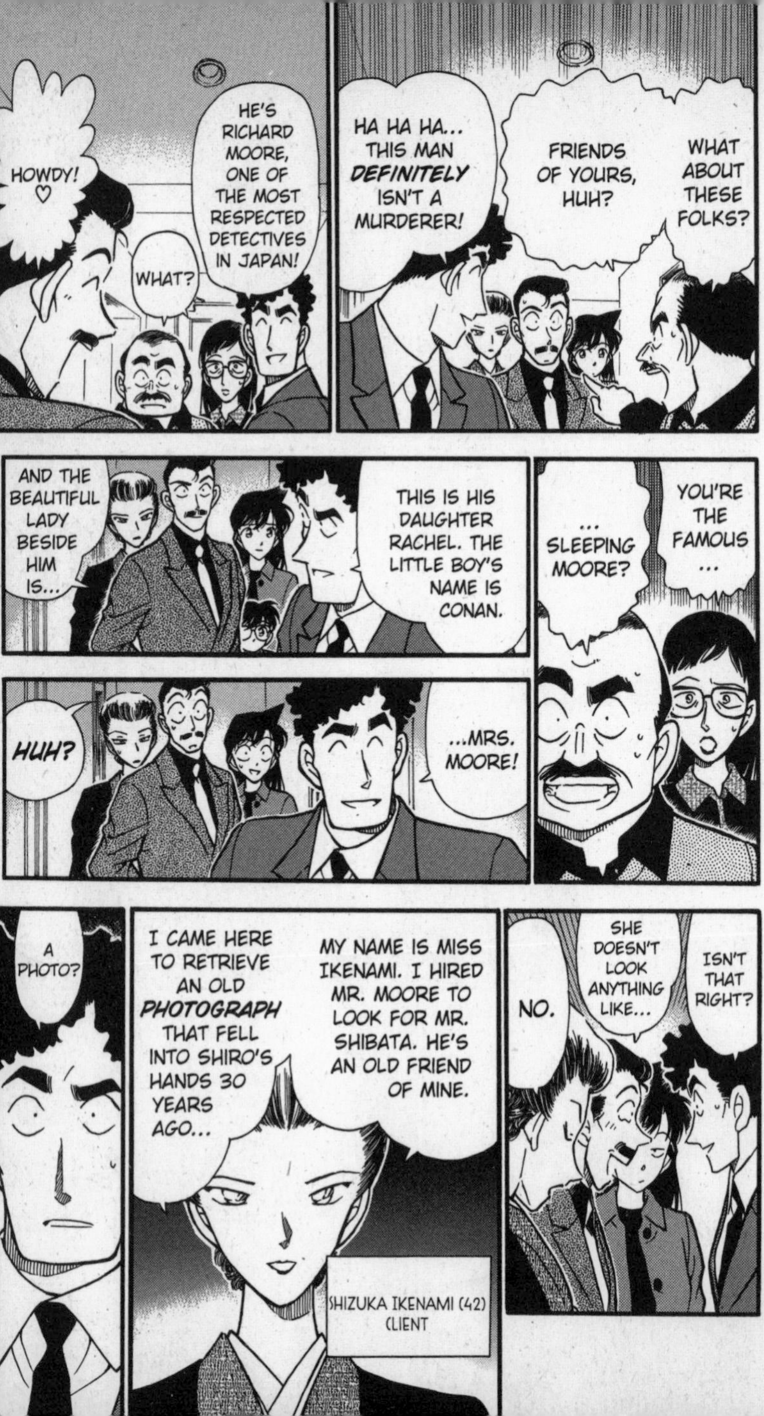
WHAT ABOUT THESE FOLKS?
FRIENDS OF YOURS, HUH?
HA HA HA... THIS MAN *DEFINITELY* ISN'T A MURDERER!
HE'S RICHARD MOORE, ONE OF THE MOST RESPECTED DETECTIVES IN JAPAN!
HOWDY! ♡
WHAT?
YOU'RE THE FAMOUS ...
... SLEEPING MOORE?
THIS IS HIS DAUGHTER RACHEL. THE LITTLE BOY'S NAME IS CONAN.
AND THE BEAUTIFUL LADY BESIDE HIM IS...
...MRS. MOORE!
HUH?
ISN'T THAT RIGHT?
SHE DOESN'T LOOK ANYTHING LIKE...
NO.
MY NAME IS MISS IKENAMI. I HIRED MR. MOORE TO LOOK FOR MR. SHIBATA. HE'S AN OLD FRIEND OF MINE.
I CAME HERE TO RETRIEVE AN OLD *PHOTOGRAPH* THAT FELL INTO SHIRO'S HANDS 30 YEARS AGO...
SHIZUKA IKENAMI (42) CLIENT
A PHOTO?

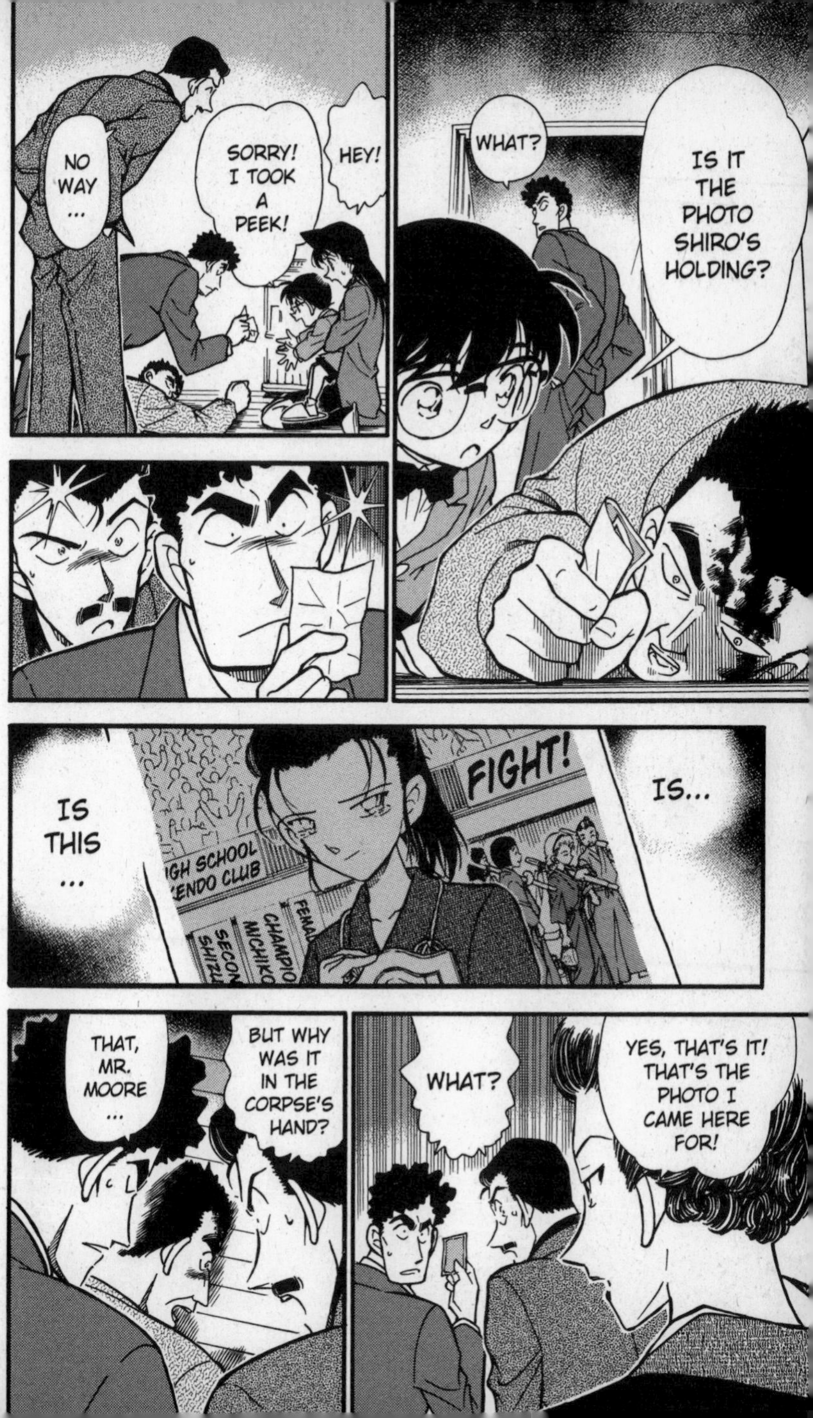
IS IT THE PHOTO SHIRO'S HOLDING?
WHAT?
HEY!
SORRY! I TOOK A PEEK!
NO WAY ...
IS...
FIGHT!
IGH SCHOOL
ENDO CLUB
IS THIS ...
YES, THAT'S IT! THAT'S THE PHOTO I CAME HERE FOR!
WHAT?
BUT WHY WAS IT IN THE CORPSE'S HAND?
THAT, MR. MOORE ...

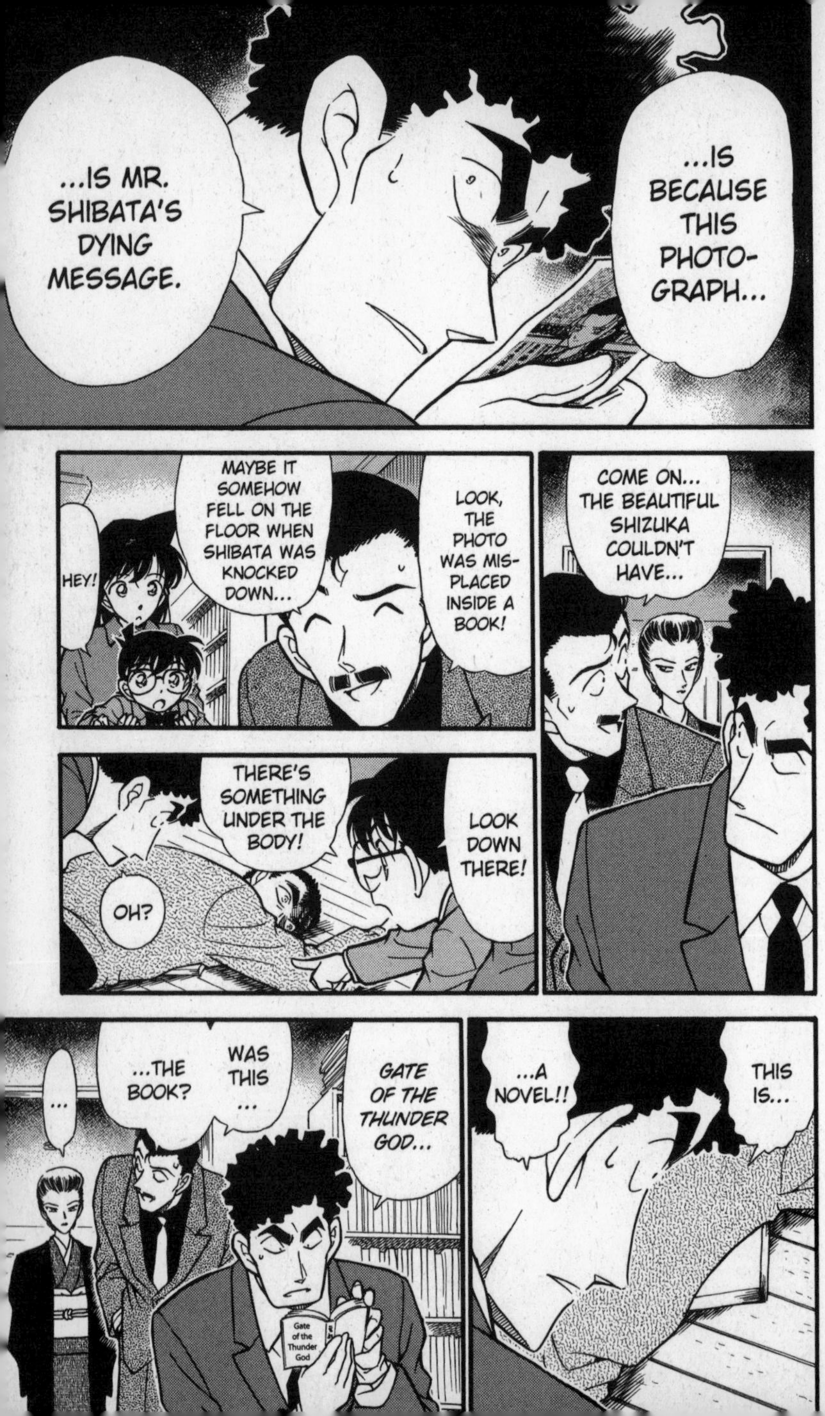
...IS BECAUSE THIS PHOTO-GRAPH...
...IS MR. SHIBATA'S DYING MESSAGE.
COME ON... THE BEAUTIFUL SHIZUKA COULDN'T HAVE...
LOOK, THE PHOTO WAS MIS-PLACED INSIDE A BOOK!
MAYBE IT SOMEHOW FELL ON THE FLOOR WHEN SHIBATA WAS KNOCKED DOWN...
HEY!
LOOK DOWN THERE!
THERE'S SOMETHING UNDER THE BODY!
OH?
THIS IS...
...A NOVEL!!
GATE OF THE THUNDER GOD...
WAS THIS ...
...THE BOOK?
...
Gate of the Thunder God

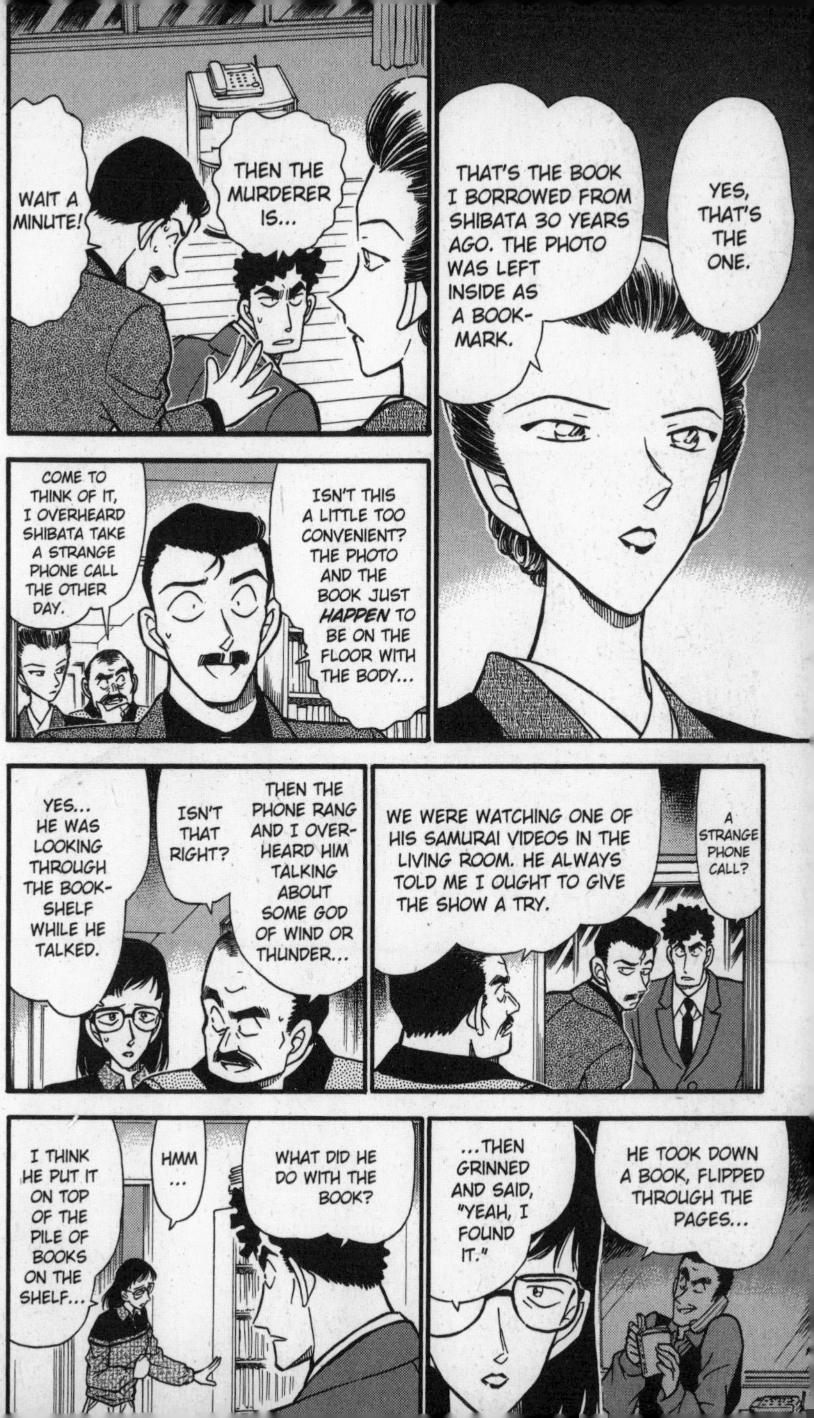
YES, THAT'S THE ONE.
THAT'S THE BOOK I BORROWED FROM SHIBATA 30 YEARS AGO. THE PHOTO WAS LEFT INSIDE AS A BOOK-MARK.
THEN THE MURDERER IS...
WAIT A MINUTE!
ISN'T THIS A LITTLE TOO CONVENIENT? THE PHOTO AND THE BOOK JUST *HAPPEN* TO BE ON THE FLOOR WITH THE BODY...
COME TO THINK OF IT, I OVERHEARD SHIBATA TAKE A STRANGE PHONE CALL THE OTHER DAY.
A STRANGE PHONE CALL?
WE WERE WATCHING ONE OF HIS SAMURAI VIDEOS IN THE LIVING ROOM. HE ALWAYS TOLD ME I OUGHT TO GIVE THE SHOW A TRY.
THEN THE PHONE RANG AND I OVER-HEARD HIM TALKING ABOUT SOME GOD OF WIND OR THUNDER...
ISN'T THAT RIGHT?
YES... HE WAS LOOKING THROUGH THE BOOK-SHELF WHILE HE TALKED.
HE TOOK DOWN A BOOK, FLIPPED THROUGH THE PAGES...
...THEN GRINNED AND SAID, "YEAH, I FOUND IT."
WHAT DID HE DO WITH THE BOOK?
HMM...
I THINK HE PUT IT ON TOP OF THE PILE OF BOOKS ON THE SHELF...

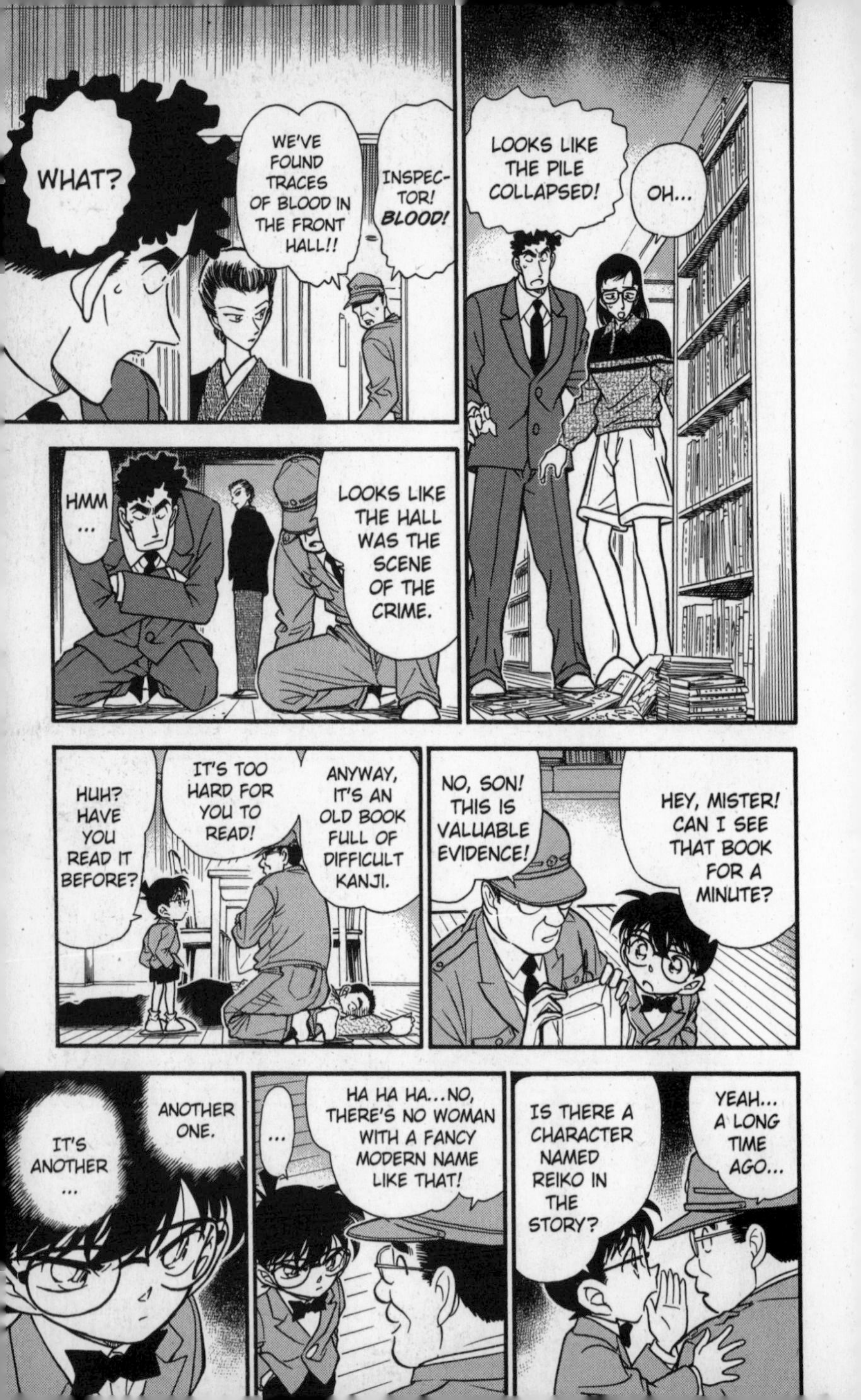
OH...
LOOKS LIKE THE PILE COLLAPSED!
INSPECTOR! BLOOD!
WE'VE FOUND TRACES OF BLOOD IN THE FRONT HALL!!
WHAT?
LOOKS LIKE THE HALL WAS THE SCENE OF THE CRIME.
HMM ...
HEY, MISTER! CAN I SEE THAT BOOK FOR A MINUTE?
NO, SON! THIS IS VALUABLE EVIDENCE!
ANYWAY, IT'S AN OLD BOOK FULL OF DIFFICULT KANJI.
IT'S TOO HARD FOR YOU TO READ!
HUH? HAVE YOU READ IT BEFORE?
YEAH... A LONG TIME AGO...
IS THERE A CHARACTER NAMED REIKO IN THE STORY?
HA HA HA...NO, THERE'S NO WOMAN WITH A FANCY MODERN NAME LIKE THAT!
...
ANOTHER ONE.
IT'S ANOTHER ...

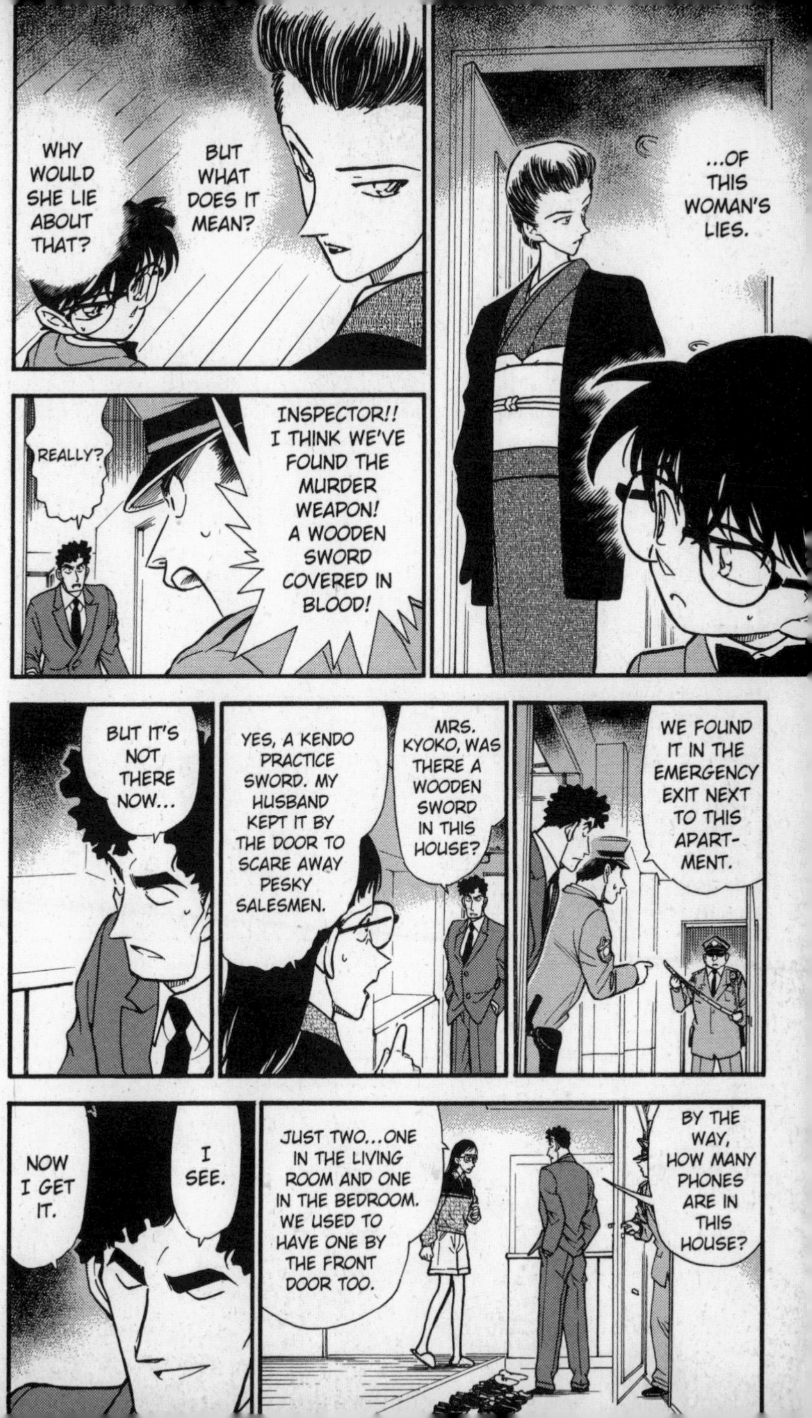
...OF THIS WOMAN'S LIES.
BUT WHAT DOES IT MEAN?
WHY WOULD SHE LIE ABOUT THAT?
INSPECTOR!! I THINK WE'VE FOUND THE MURDER WEAPON! A WOODEN SWORD COVERED IN BLOOD!
REALLY?
WE FOUND IT IN THE EMERGENCY EXIT NEXT TO THIS APARTMENT.
MRS. KYOKO, WAS THERE A WOODEN SWORD IN THIS HOUSE?
YES, A KENDO PRACTICE SWORD. MY HUSBAND KEPT IT BY THE DOOR TO SCARE AWAY PESKY SALESMEN.
BUT IT'S NOT THERE NOW...
BY THE WAY, HOW MANY PHONES ARE IN THIS HOUSE?
JUST TWO...ONE IN THE LIVING ROOM AND ONE IN THE BEDROOM. WE USED TO HAVE ONE BY THE FRONT DOOR TOO.
I SEE.
NOW I GET IT.

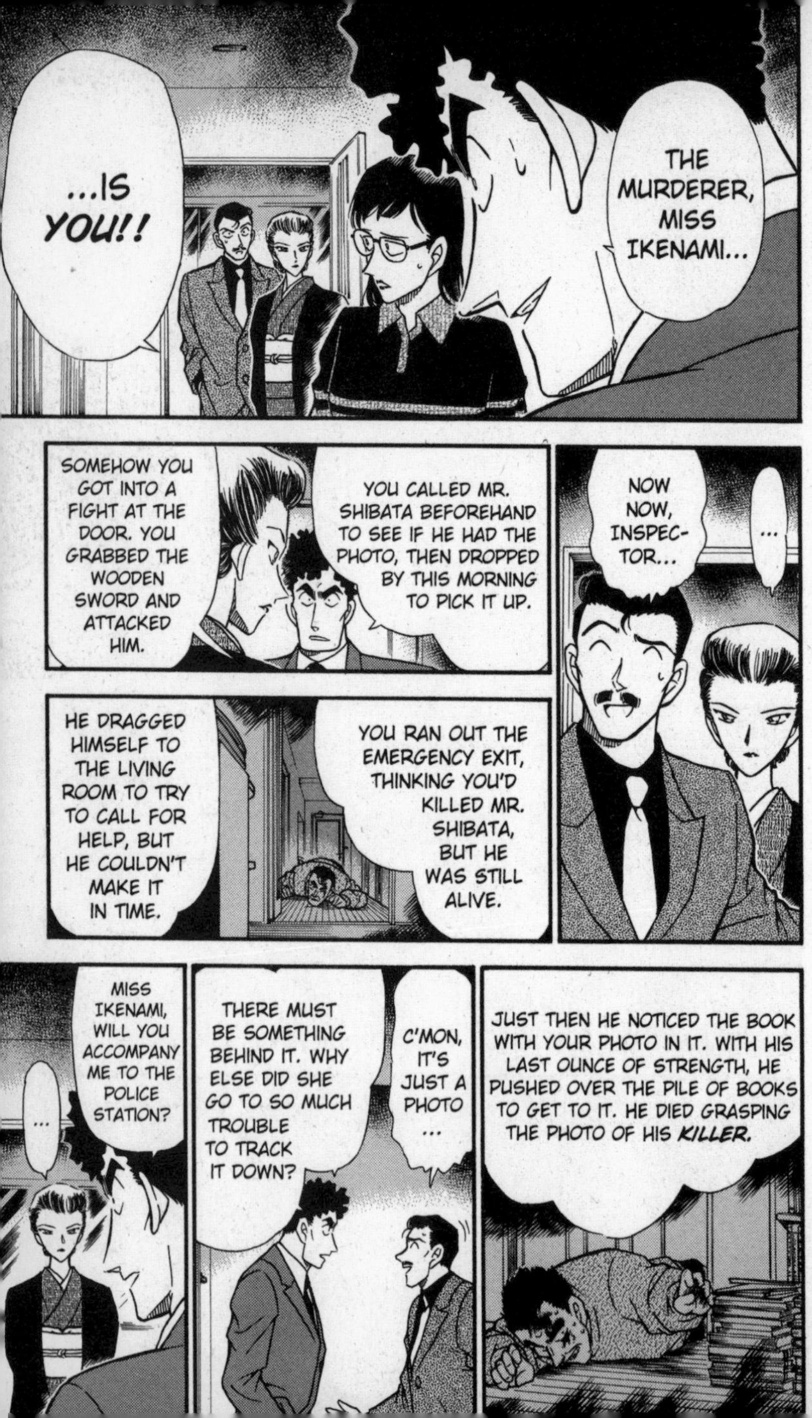
THE MURDERER, MISS IKENAMI...
...IS *YOU!!*
NOW NOW, INSPECTOR...
...
YOU CALLED MR. SHIBATA BEFOREHAND TO SEE IF HE HAD THE PHOTO, THEN DROPPED BY THIS MORNING TO PICK IT UP.
SOMEHOW YOU GOT INTO A FIGHT AT THE DOOR. YOU GRABBED THE WOODEN SWORD AND ATTACKED HIM.
YOU RAN OUT THE EMERGENCY EXIT, THINKING YOU'D KILLED MR. SHIBATA, BUT HE WAS STILL ALIVE.
HE DRAGGED HIMSELF TO THE LIVING ROOM TO TRY TO CALL FOR HELP, BUT HE COULDN'T MAKE IT IN TIME.
JUST THEN HE NOTICED THE BOOK WITH YOUR PHOTO IN IT. WITH HIS LAST OUNCE OF STRENGTH, HE PUSHED OVER THE PILE OF BOOKS TO GET TO IT. HE DIED GRASPING THE PHOTO OF HIS *KILLER.*
C'MON, IT'S JUST A PHOTO ...
THERE MUST BE SOMETHING BEHIND IT. WHY ELSE DID SHE GO TO SO MUCH TROUBLE TO TRACK IT DOWN?
MISS IKENAMI, WILL YOU ACCOMPANY ME TO THE POLICE STATION?
...

IF YOU WANT TO TAKE ME IN FOR QUESTIONING, YOU'LL HAVE TO WAIT UNTIL *AFTER* YOU'VE ACQUIRED A WARRANT FOR MY ARREST.

WHAT?

I'M SORRY, BUT I MUST DECLINE.

...I FIND IT HARD TO BELIEVE YOU COULD OBTAIN A WARRANT AT THIS TIME.

AND SINCE YOU LACK THE HARD EVIDENCE YOU'D NEED TO PERSUADE A JUDGE...

HEH

OF COURSE, IF THE WIFE THERE WANTS US TAKEN IN FOR TRESPASSING, THAT'S ANOTHER STORY...

WHAT THE...?

HUH?

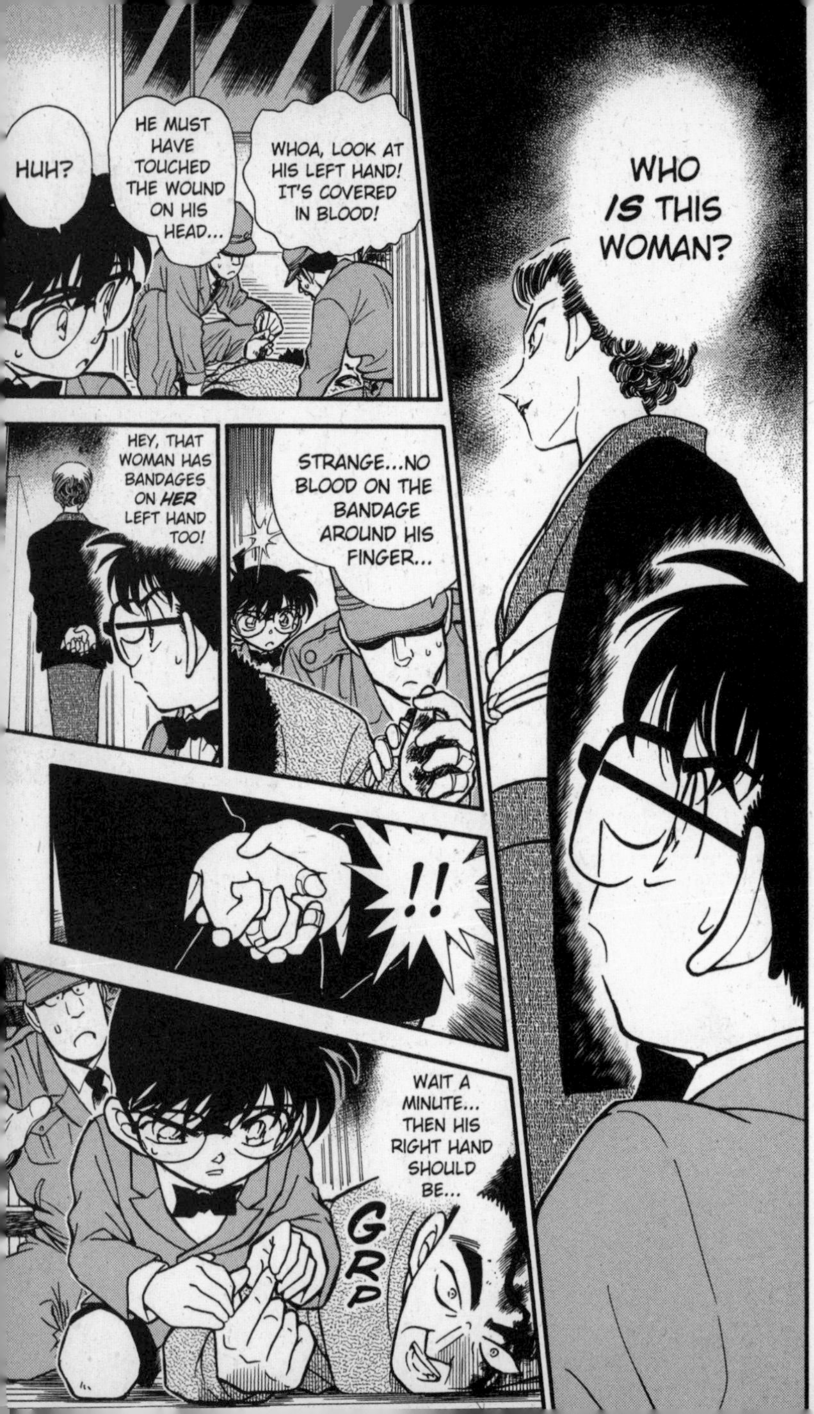
WHO *IS* THIS WOMAN?
WHOA, LOOK AT HIS LEFT HAND! IT'S COVERED IN BLOOD!
HE MUST HAVE TOUCHED THE WOUND ON HIS HEAD...
HUH?
STRANGE...NO BLOOD ON THE BANDAGE AROUND HIS FINGER...
HEY, THAT WOMAN HAS BANDAGES ON *HER* LEFT HAND TOO!
!!
WAIT A MINUTE... THEN HIS RIGHT HAND SHOULD BE...
GRP

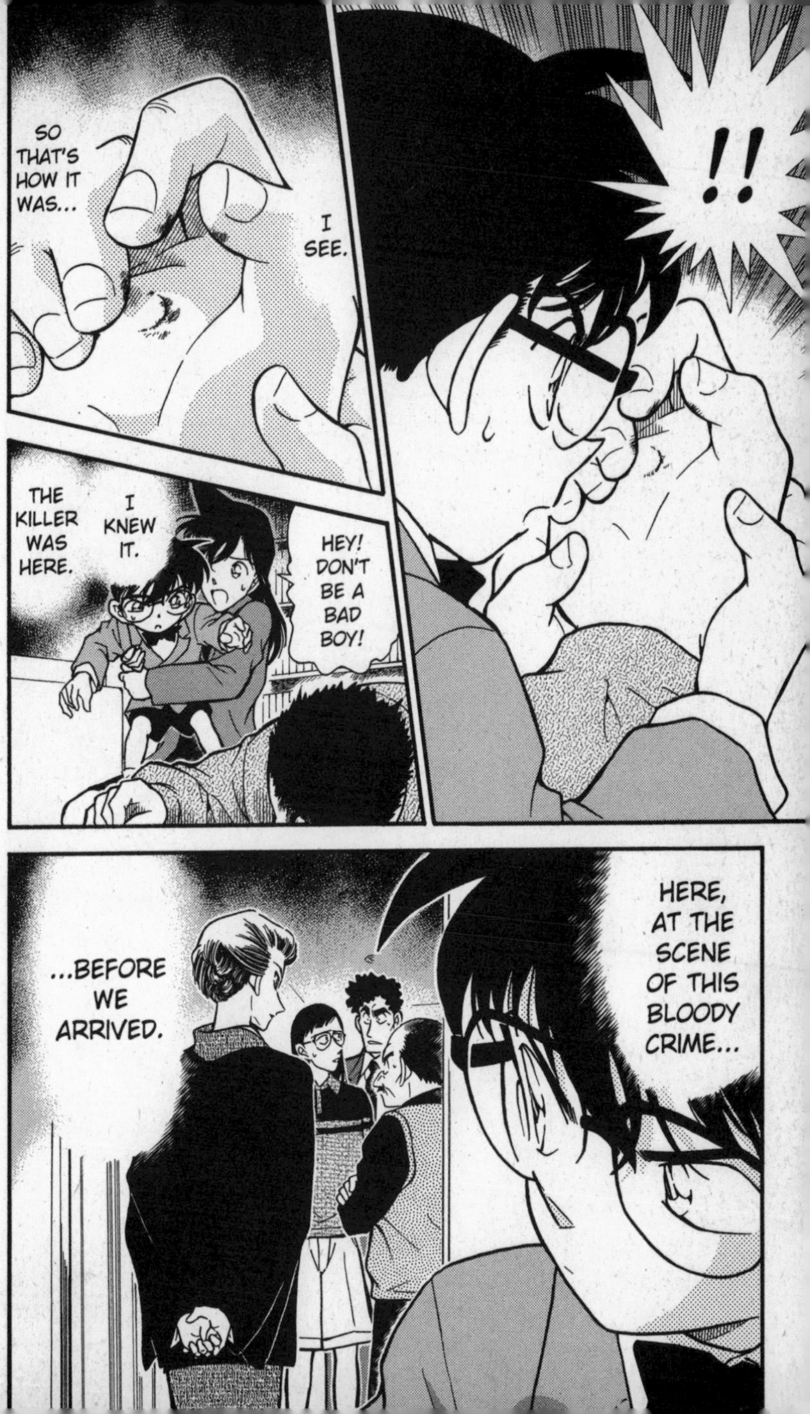
!!
I SEE.
SO THAT'S HOW IT WAS...
HEY! DON'T BE A BAD BOY!
I KNEW IT.
THE KILLER WAS HERE.
HERE, AT THE SCENE OF THIS BLOODY CRIME...
...BEFORE WE ARRIVED.

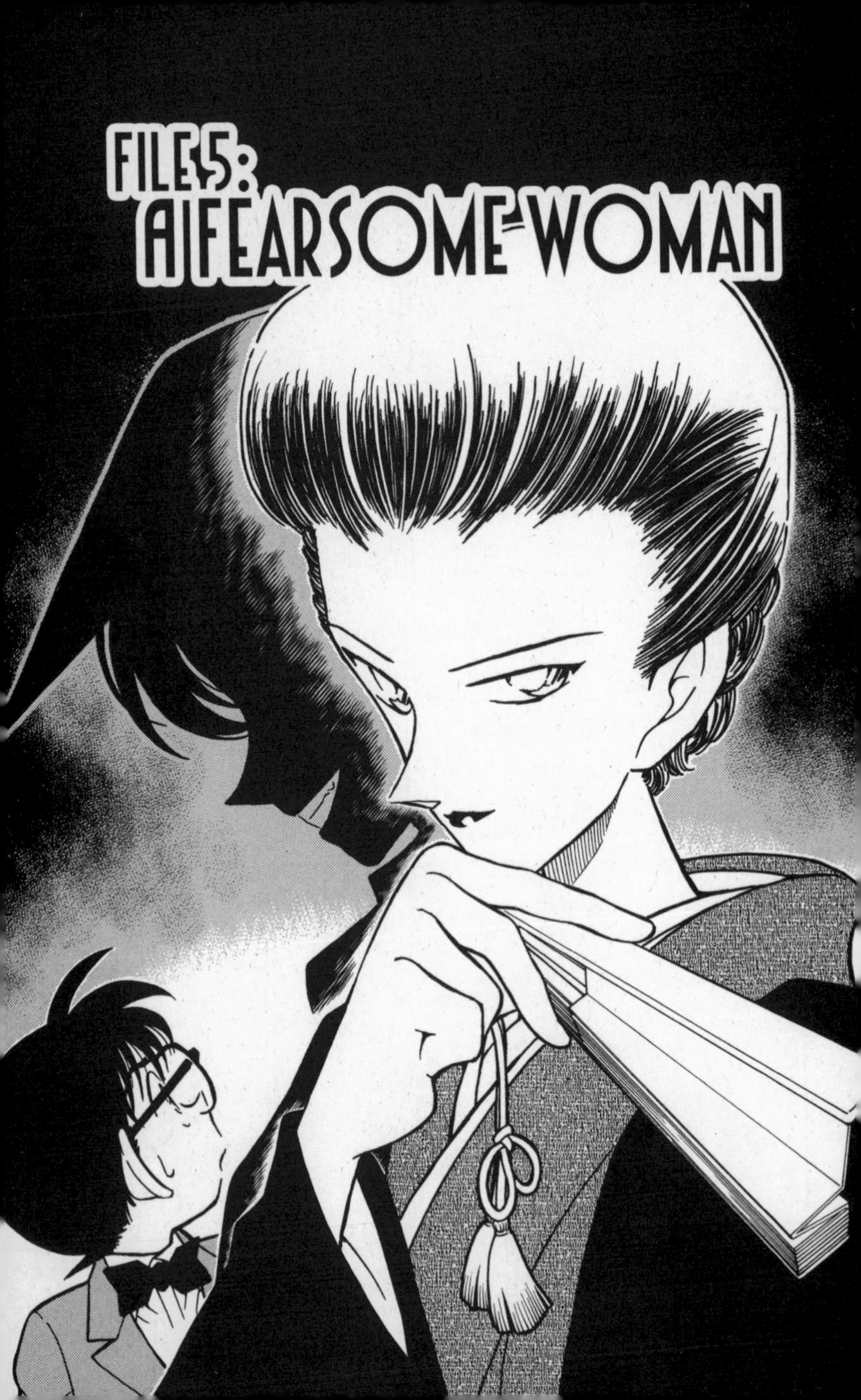
FILE 5:
A FEARSOME WOMAN

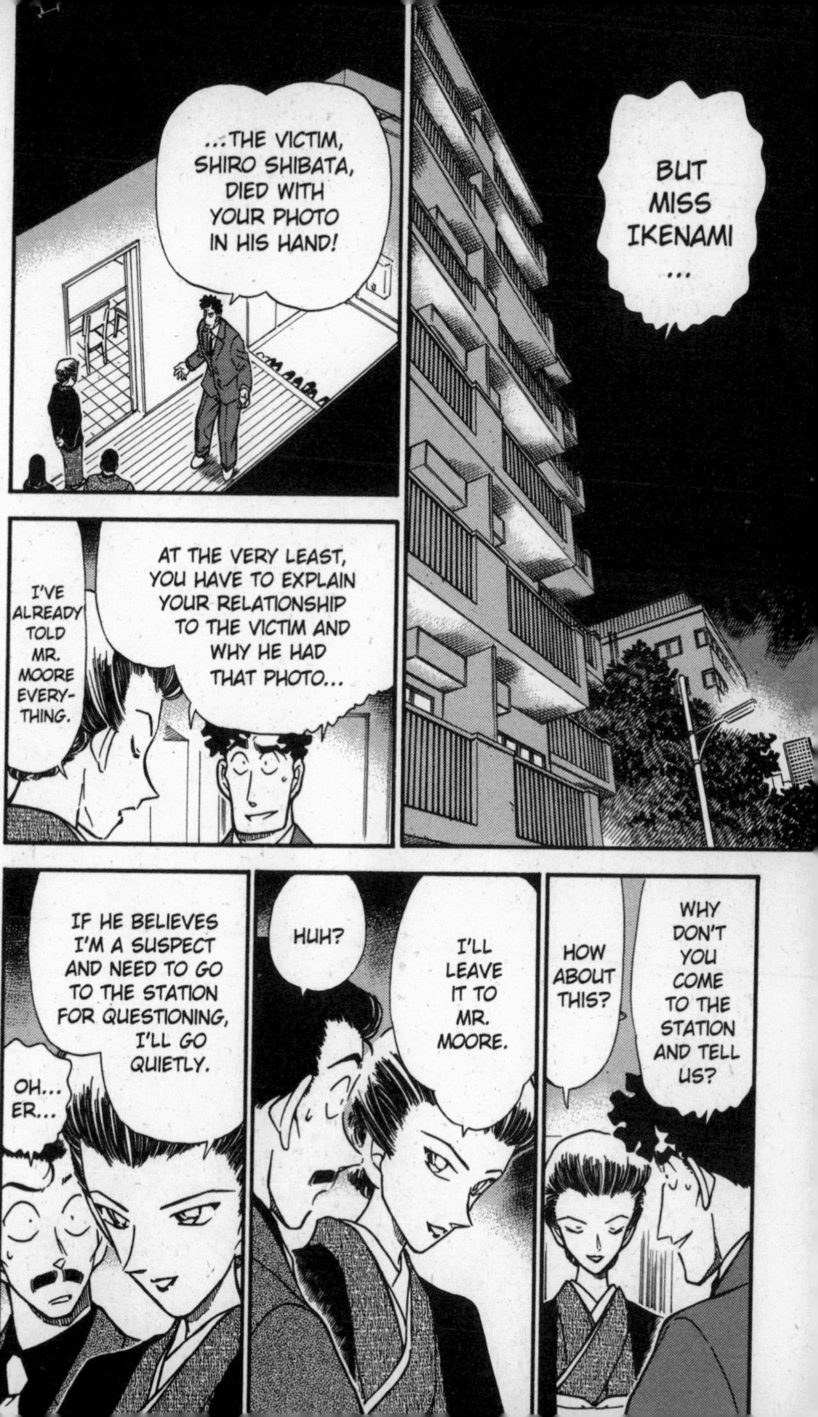
BUT MISS IKENAMI ...
...THE VICTIM, SHIRO SHIBATA, DIED WITH YOUR PHOTO IN HIS HAND!
AT THE VERY LEAST, YOU HAVE TO EXPLAIN YOUR RELATIONSHIP TO THE VICTIM AND WHY HE HAD THAT PHOTO...
I'VE ALREADY TOLD MR. MOORE EVERYTHING.
WHY DON'T YOU COME TO THE STATION AND TELL US?
HOW ABOUT THIS?
I'LL LEAVE IT TO MR. MOORE.
HUH?
IF HE BELIEVES I'M A SUSPECT AND NEED TO GO TO THE STATION FOR QUESTIONING, I'LL GO QUIETLY.
OH... ER...

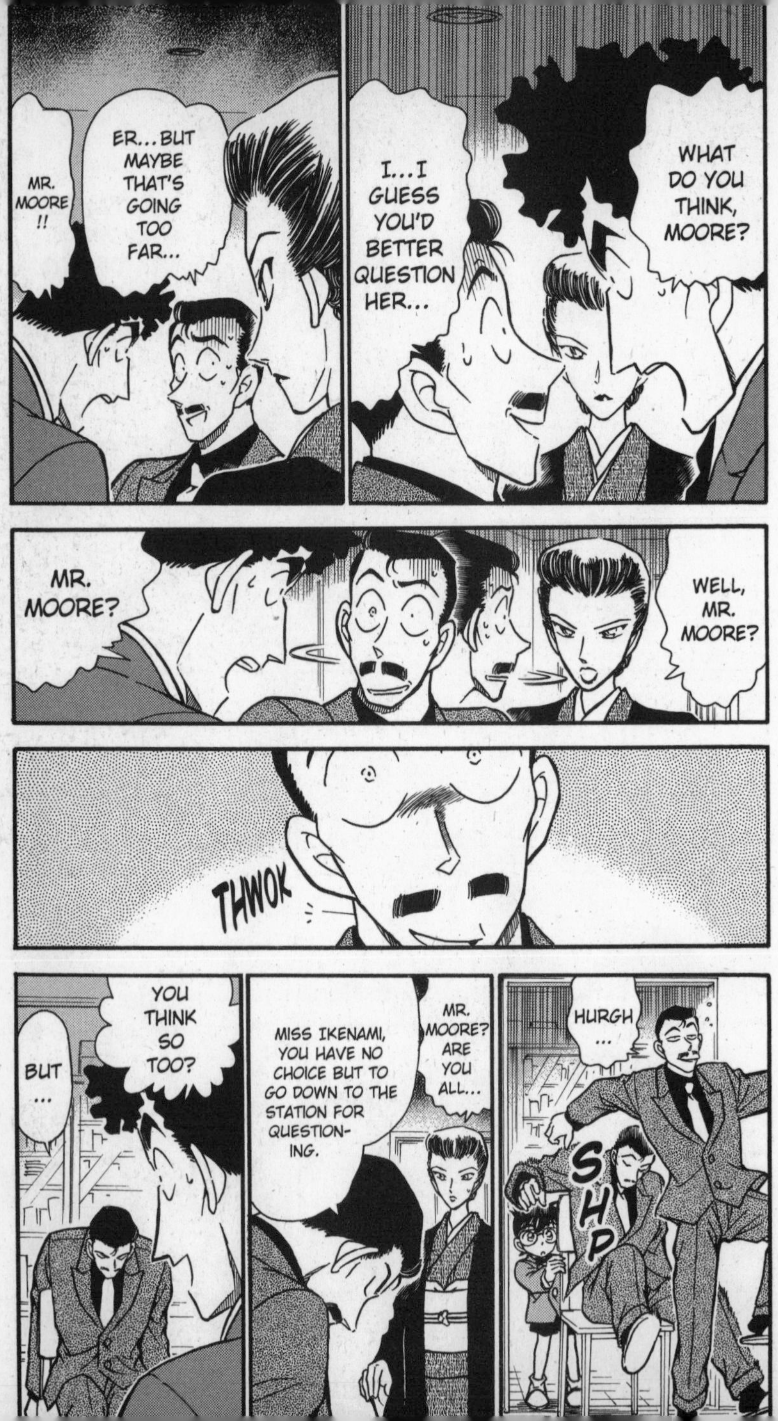
WHAT DO YOU THINK, MOORE?
I...I GUESS YOU'D BETTER QUESTION HER...
ER...BUT MAYBE THAT'S GOING TOO FAR...
MR. MOORE !!
WELL, MR. MOORE?
MR. MOORE?
THWOK
HURGH ...
SHP
MR. MOORE? ARE YOU ALL...
MISS IKENAMI, YOU HAVE NO CHOICE BUT TO GO DOWN TO THE STATION FOR QUESTION-ING.
YOU THINK SO TOO?
BUT ...

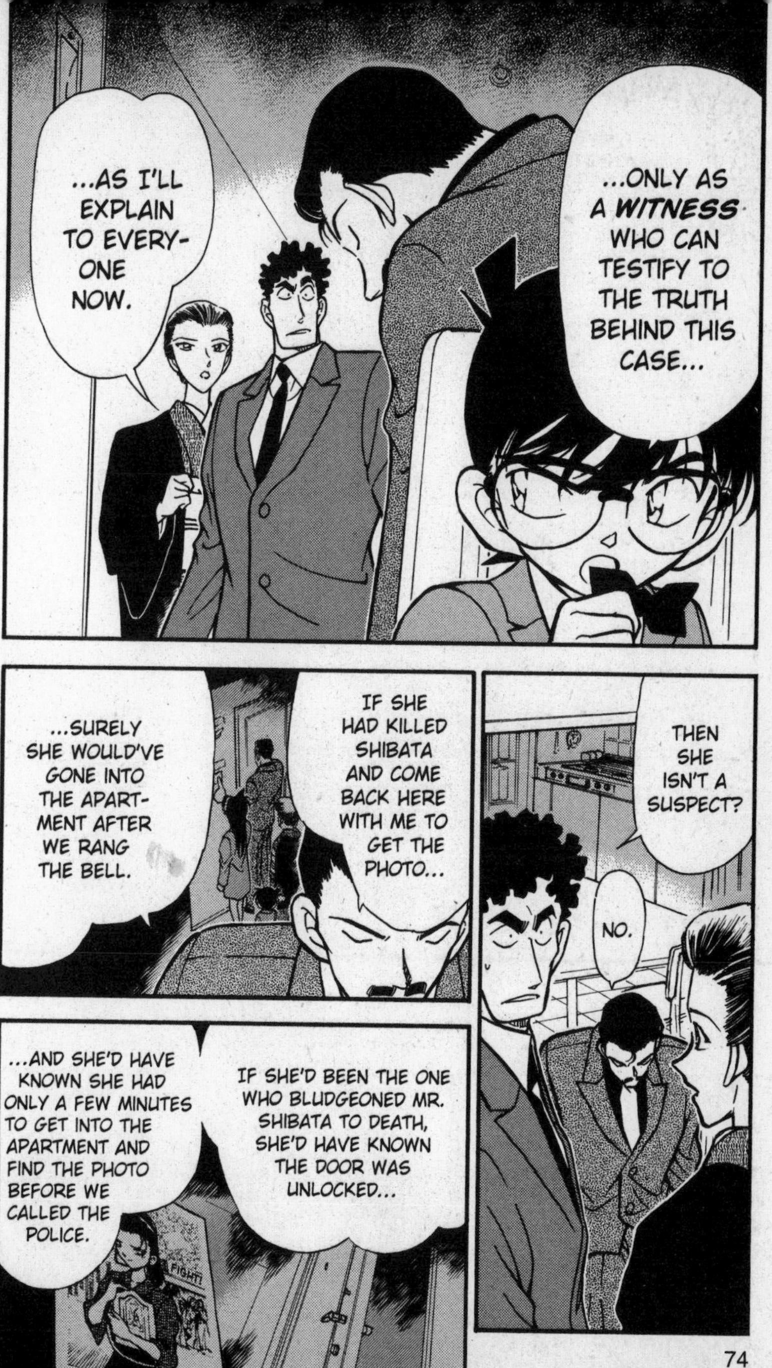
...ONLY AS A *WITNESS* WHO CAN TESTIFY TO THE TRUTH BEHIND THIS CASE...
...AS I'LL EXPLAIN TO EVERY-ONE NOW.
THEN SHE ISN'T A SUSPECT?
NO.
IF SHE HAD KILLED SHIBATA AND COME BACK HERE WITH ME TO GET THE PHOTO...
...SURELY SHE WOULD'VE GONE INTO THE APART-MENT AFTER WE RANG THE BELL.
IF SHE'D BEEN THE ONE WHO BLUDGEONED MR. SHIBATA TO DEATH, SHE'D HAVE KNOWN THE DOOR WAS UNLOCKED...
...AND SHE'D HAVE KNOWN SHE HAD ONLY A FEW MINUTES TO GET INTO THE APARTMENT AND FIND THE PHOTO BEFORE WE CALLED THE POLICE.
FIGHT!

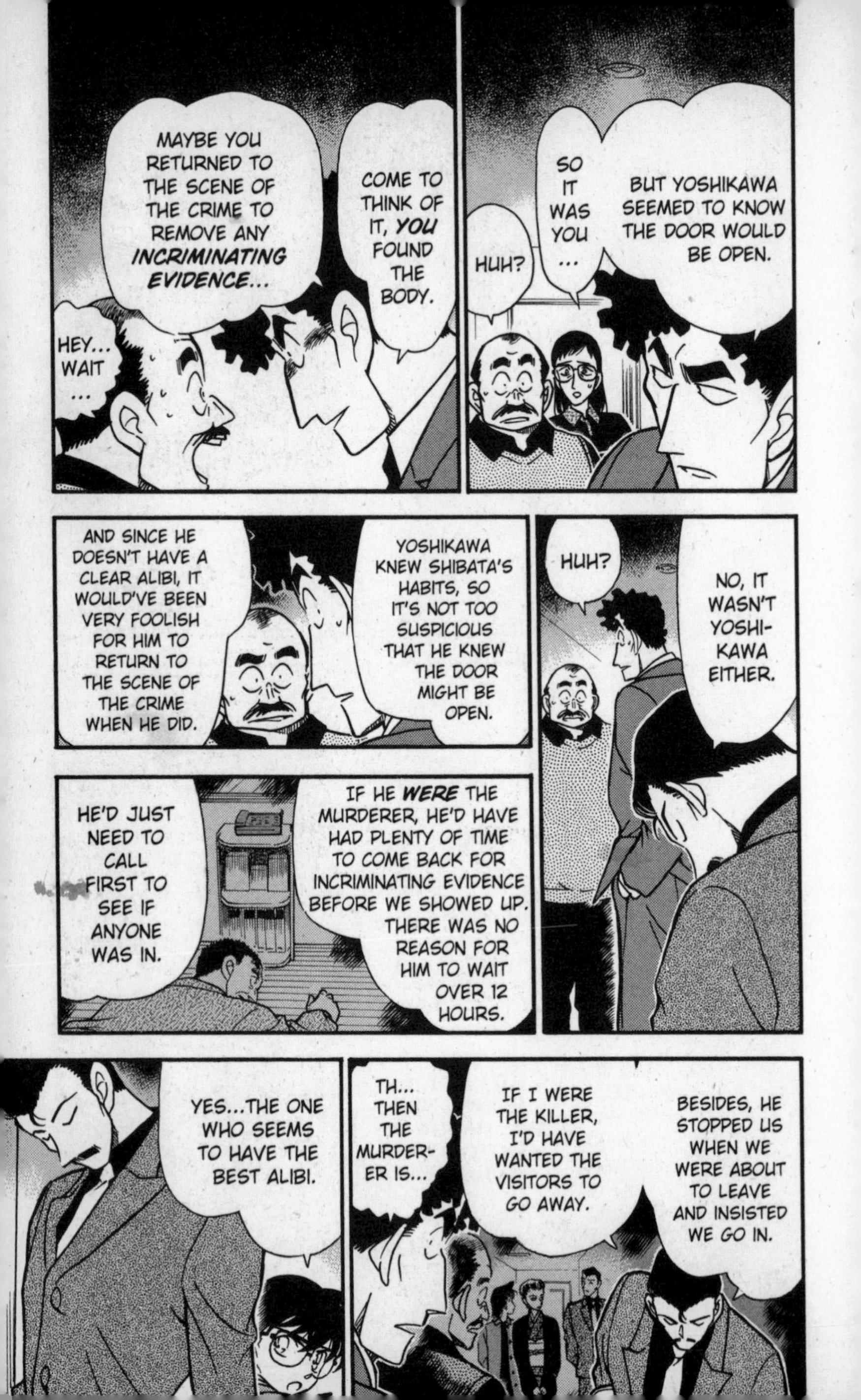
BUT YOSHIKAWA SEEMED TO KNOW THE DOOR WOULD BE OPEN.
SO IT WAS YOU ...
HUH?
COME TO THINK OF IT, *YOU* FOUND THE BODY.
MAYBE YOU RETURNED TO THE SCENE OF THE CRIME TO REMOVE ANY *INCRIMINATING EVIDENCE...*
HEY... WAIT ...
NO, IT WASN'T YOSHI-KAWA EITHER.
HUH?
YOSHIKAWA KNEW SHIBATA'S HABITS, SO IT'S NOT TOO SUSPICIOUS THAT HE KNEW THE DOOR MIGHT BE OPEN.
AND SINCE HE DOESN'T HAVE A CLEAR ALIBI, IT WOULD'VE BEEN VERY FOOLISH FOR HIM TO RETURN TO THE SCENE OF THE CRIME WHEN HE DID.
IF HE *WERE* THE MURDERER, HE'D HAVE HAD PLENTY OF TIME TO COME BACK FOR INCRIMINATING EVIDENCE BEFORE WE SHOWED UP. THERE WAS NO REASON FOR HIM TO WAIT OVER 12 HOURS.
HE'D JUST NEED TO CALL FIRST TO SEE IF ANYONE WAS IN.
BESIDES, HE STOPPED US WHEN WE WERE ABOUT TO LEAVE AND INSISTED WE GO IN.
IF I WERE THE KILLER, I'D HAVE WANTED THE VISITORS TO GO AWAY.
TH... THEN THE MURDER-ER IS...
YES...THE ONE WHO SEEMS TO HAVE THE BEST ALIBI.

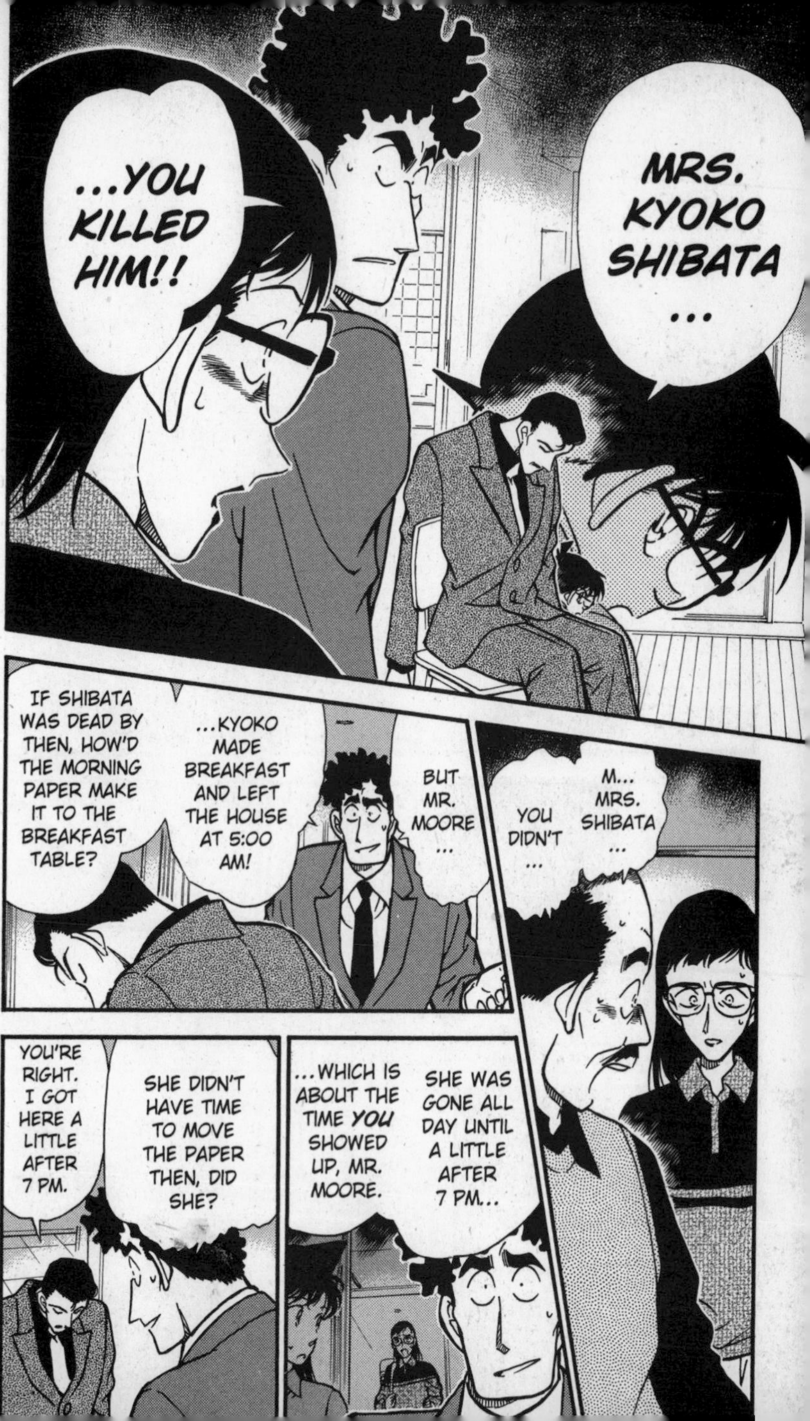
MRS. KYOKO SHIBATA ...
...YOU KILLED HIM!!
M... MRS. SHIBATA ...
YOU DIDN'T ...
BUT MR. MOORE ...
...KYOKO MADE BREAKFAST AND LEFT THE HOUSE AT 5:00 AM!
IF SHIBATA WAS DEAD BY THEN, HOW'D THE MORNING PAPER MAKE IT TO THE BREAKFAST TABLE?
SHE WAS GONE ALL DAY UNTIL A LITTLE AFTER 7 PM...
...WHICH IS ABOUT THE TIME YOU SHOWED UP, MR. MOORE.
SHE DIDN'T HAVE TIME TO MOVE THE PAPER THEN, DID SHE?
YOU'RE RIGHT. I GOT HERE A LITTLE AFTER 7 PM.

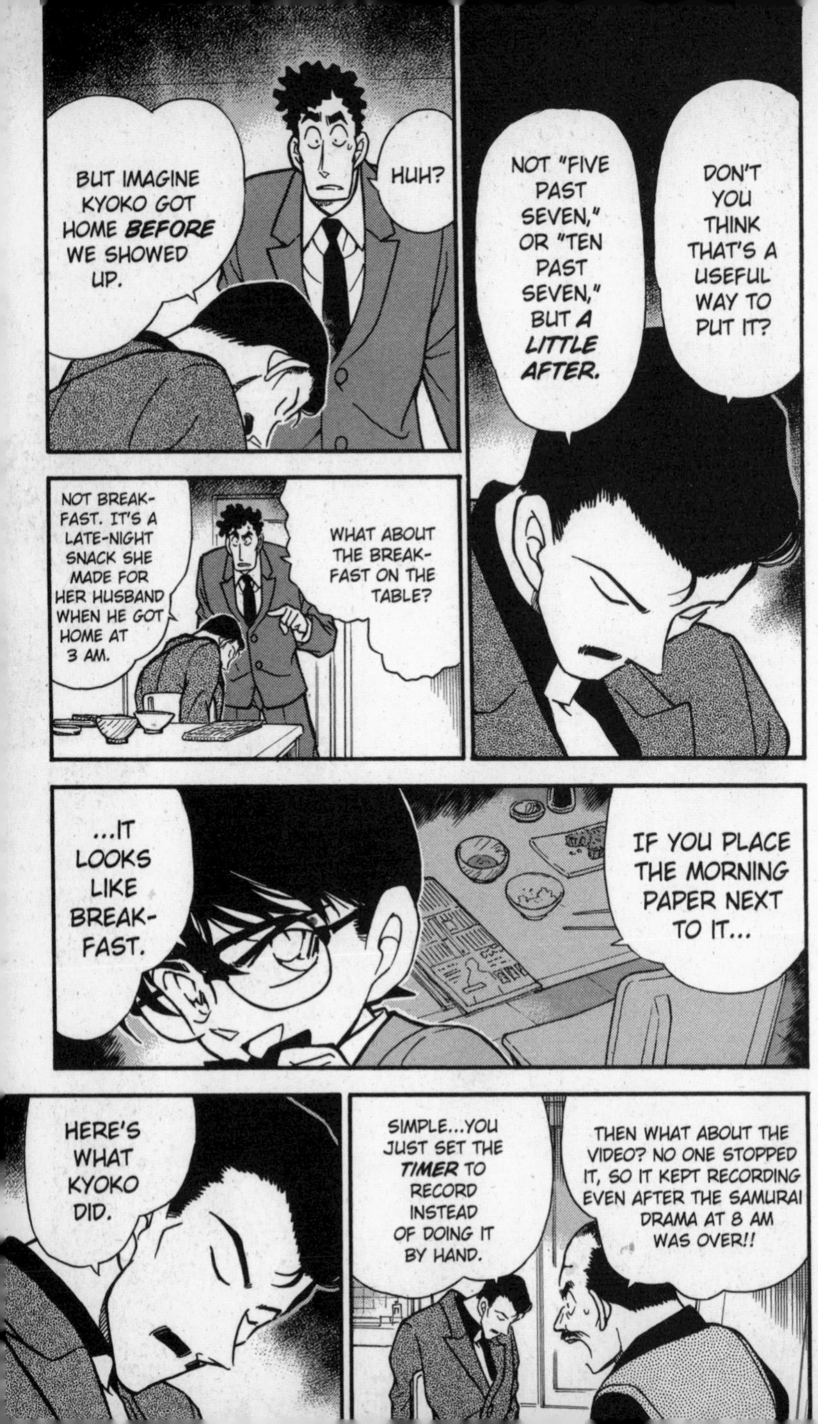
DON'T YOU THINK THAT'S A USEFUL WAY TO PUT IT?
NOT "FIVE PAST SEVEN," OR "TEN PAST SEVEN," BUT *A LITTLE AFTER.*
HUH?
BUT IMAGINE KYOKO GOT HOME *BEFORE* WE SHOWED UP.
WHAT ABOUT THE BREAKFAST ON THE TABLE?
NOT BREAKFAST. IT'S A LATE-NIGHT SNACK SHE MADE FOR HER HUSBAND WHEN HE GOT HOME AT 3 AM.
IF YOU PLACE THE MORNING PAPER NEXT TO IT...
...IT LOOKS LIKE BREAKFAST.
THEN WHAT ABOUT THE VIDEO? NO ONE STOPPED IT, SO IT KEPT RECORDING EVEN AFTER THE SAMURAI DRAMA AT 8 AM WAS OVER!!
SIMPLE...YOU JUST SET THE *TIMER* TO RECORD INSTEAD OF DOING IT BY HAND.
HERE'S WHAT KYOKO DID.

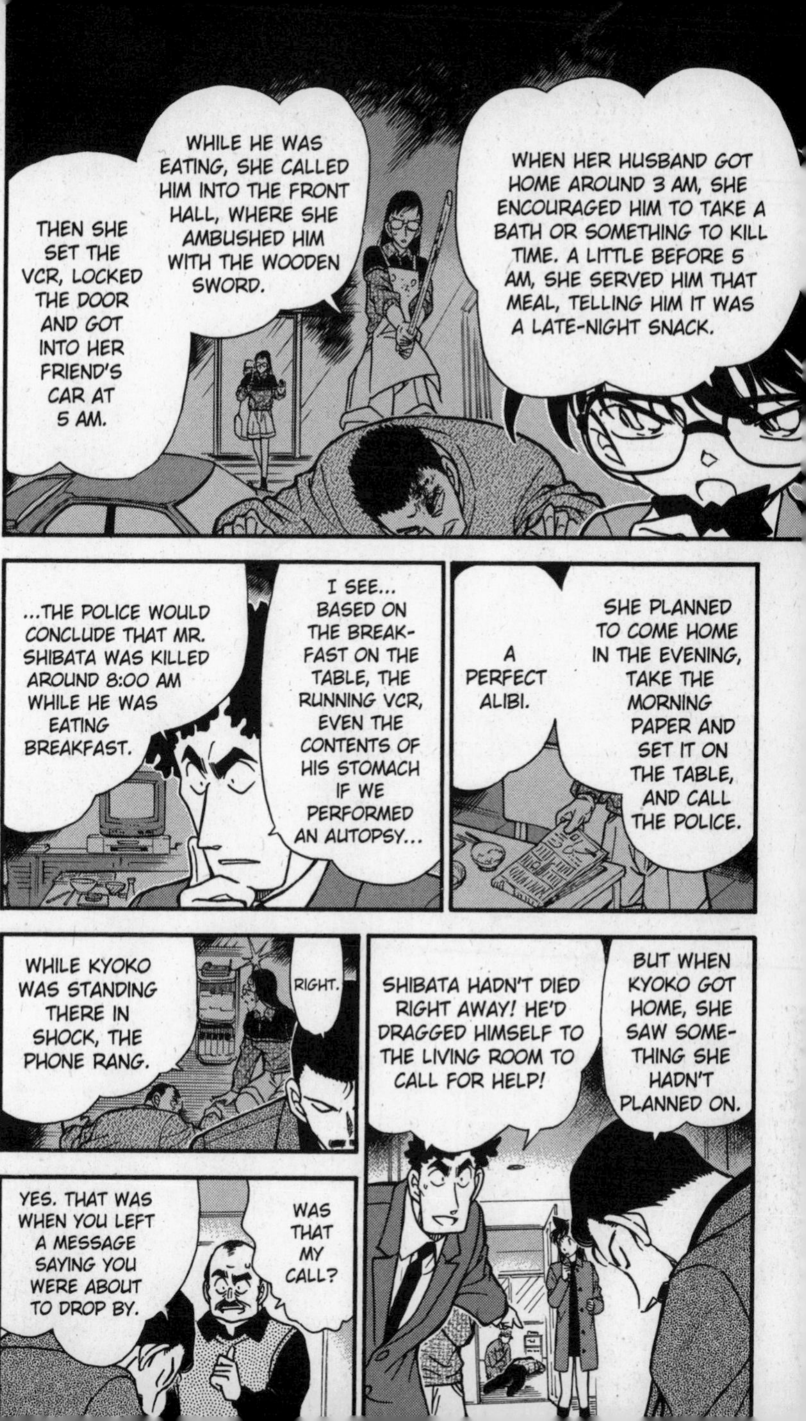
WHEN HER HUSBAND GOT HOME AROUND 3 AM, SHE ENCOURAGED HIM TO TAKE A BATH OR SOMETHING TO KILL TIME. A LITTLE BEFORE 5 AM, SHE SERVED HIM THAT MEAL, TELLING HIM IT WAS A LATE-NIGHT SNACK.
WHILE HE WAS EATING, SHE CALLED HIM INTO THE FRONT HALL, WHERE SHE AMBUSHED HIM WITH THE WOODEN SWORD.
THEN SHE SET THE VCR, LOCKED THE DOOR AND GOT INTO HER FRIEND'S CAR AT 5 AM.
SHE PLANNED TO COME HOME IN THE EVENING, TAKE THE MORNING PAPER AND SET IT ON THE TABLE, AND CALL THE POLICE.
A PERFECT ALIBI.
I SEE... BASED ON THE BREAK-FAST ON THE TABLE, THE RUNNING VCR, EVEN THE CONTENTS OF HIS STOMACH IF WE PERFORMED AN AUTOPSY...
...THE POLICE WOULD CONCLUDE THAT MR. SHIBATA WAS KILLED AROUND 8:00 AM WHILE HE WAS EATING BREAKFAST.
BUT WHEN KYOKO GOT HOME, SHE SAW SOME-THING SHE HADN'T PLANNED ON.
SHIBATA HADN'T DIED RIGHT AWAY! HE'D DRAGGED HIMSELF TO THE LIVING ROOM TO CALL FOR HELP!
RIGHT.
WHILE KYOKO WAS STANDING THERE IN SHOCK, THE PHONE RANG.
WAS THAT MY CALL?
YES. THAT WAS WHEN YOU LEFT A MESSAGE SAYING YOU WERE ABOUT TO DROP BY.

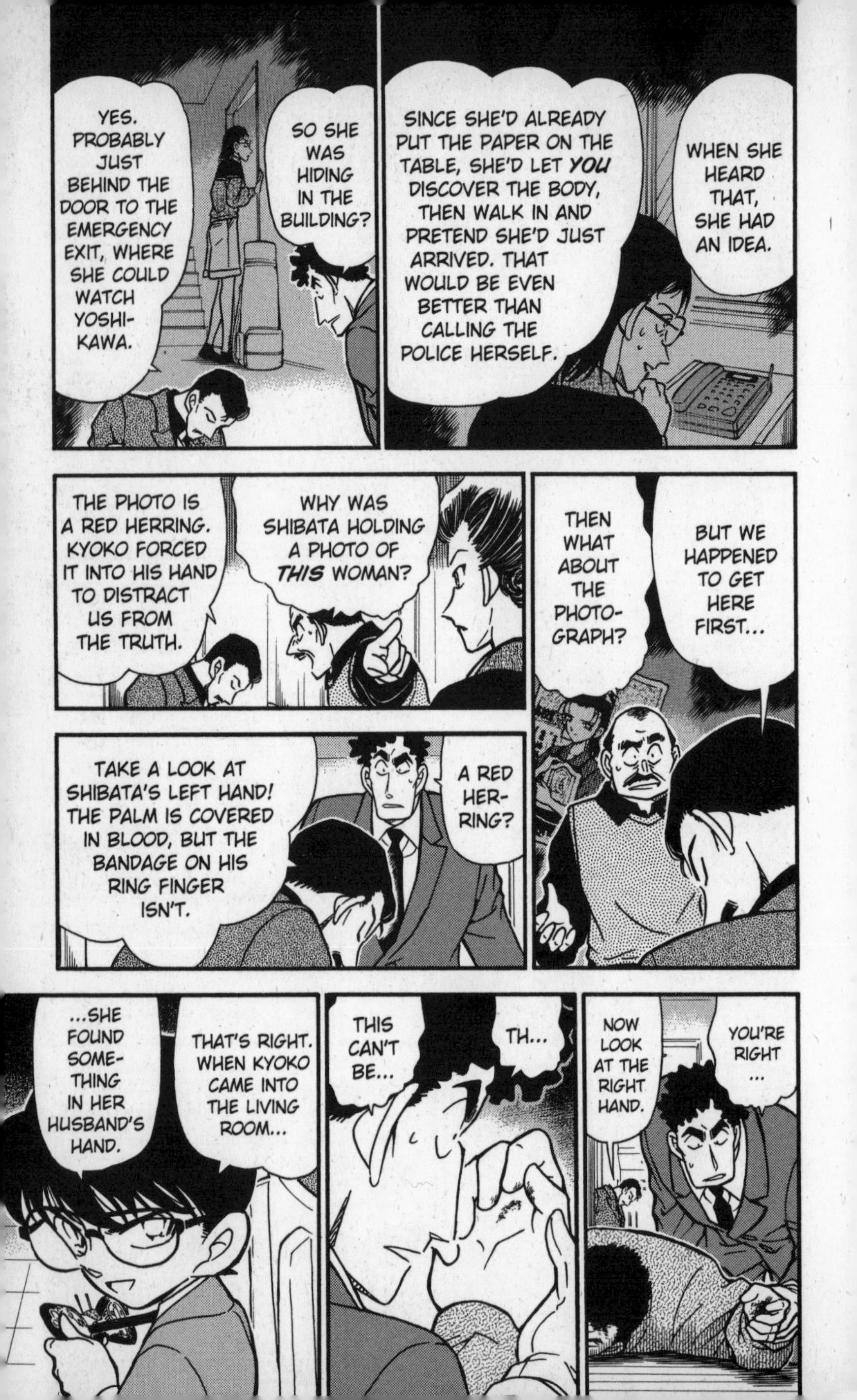
WHEN SHE HEARD THAT, SHE HAD AN IDEA.
SINCE SHE'D ALREADY PUT THE PAPER ON THE TABLE, SHE'D LET *YOU* DISCOVER THE BODY, THEN WALK IN AND PRETEND SHE'D JUST ARRIVED. THAT WOULD BE EVEN BETTER THAN CALLING THE POLICE HERSELF.
SO SHE WAS HIDING IN THE BUILDING?
YES. PROBABLY JUST BEHIND THE DOOR TO THE EMERGENCY EXIT, WHERE SHE COULD WATCH YOSHIKAWA.
BUT WE HAPPENED TO GET HERE FIRST...
THEN WHAT ABOUT THE PHOTOGRAPH?
WHY WAS SHIBATA HOLDING A PHOTO OF *THIS* WOMAN?
THE PHOTO IS A RED HERRING. KYOKO FORCED IT INTO HIS HAND TO DISTRACT US FROM THE TRUTH.
A RED HERRING?
TAKE A LOOK AT SHIBATA'S LEFT HAND! THE PALM IS COVERED IN BLOOD, BUT THE BANDAGE ON HIS RING FINGER ISN'T.
YOU'RE RIGHT...
NOW LOOK AT THE RIGHT HAND.
TH...
THIS CAN'T BE...
THAT'S RIGHT. WHEN KYOKO CAME INTO THE LIVING ROOM...
...SHE FOUND SOMETHING IN HER HUSBAND'S HAND.

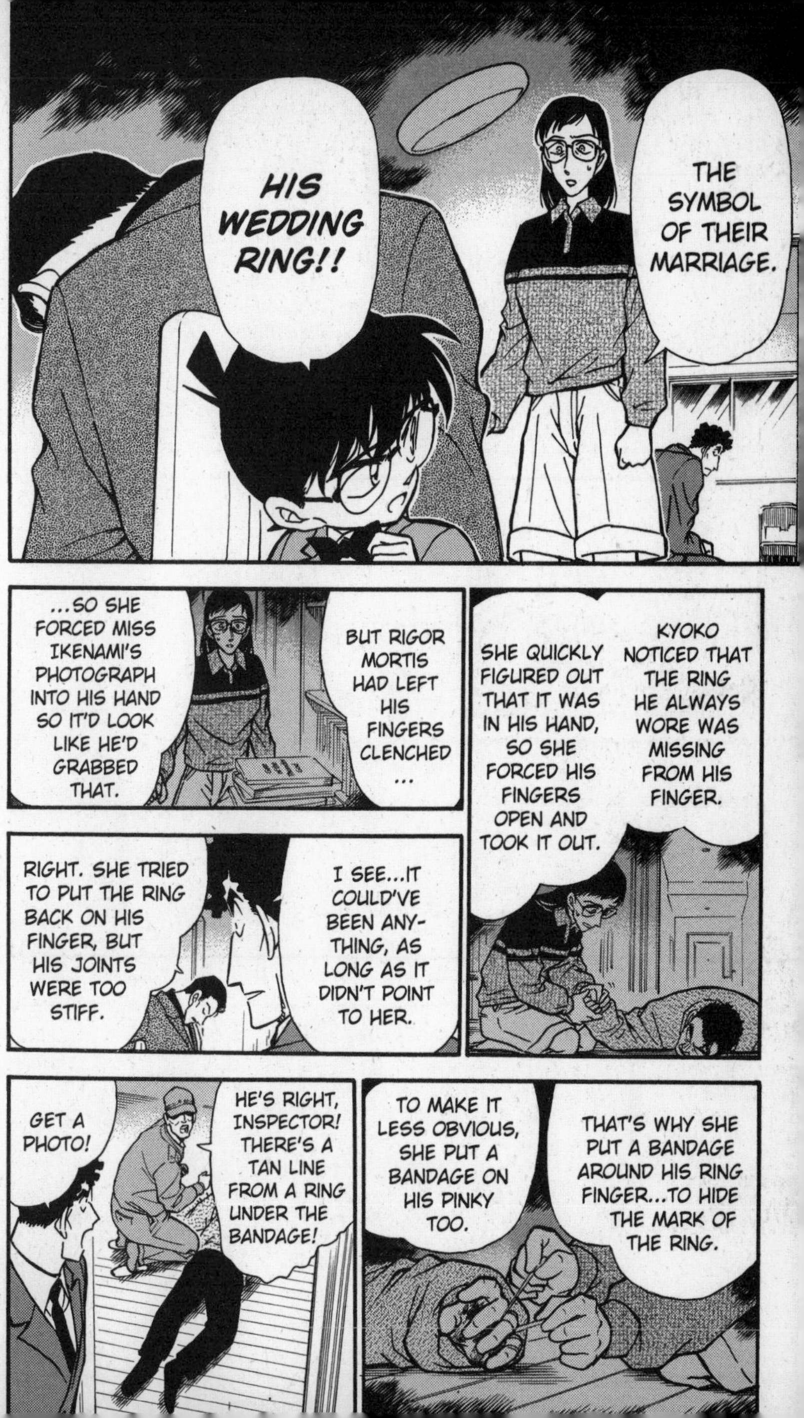
THE SYMBOL OF THEIR MARRIAGE.
HIS WEDDING RING!!
KYOKO NOTICED THAT THE RING HE ALWAYS WORE WAS MISSING FROM HIS FINGER.
SHE QUICKLY FIGURED OUT THAT IT WAS IN HIS HAND, SO SHE FORCED HIS FINGERS OPEN AND TOOK IT OUT.
BUT RIGOR MORTIS HAD LEFT HIS FINGERS CLENCHED ...
...SO SHE FORCED MISS IKENAMI'S PHOTOGRAPH INTO HIS HAND SO IT'D LOOK LIKE HE'D GRABBED THAT.
I SEE...IT COULD'VE BEEN ANY-THING, AS LONG AS IT DIDN'T POINT TO HER.
RIGHT. SHE TRIED TO PUT THE RING BACK ON HIS FINGER, BUT HIS JOINTS WERE TOO STIFF.
THAT'S WHY SHE PUT A BANDAGE AROUND HIS RING FINGER...TO HIDE THE MARK OF THE RING.
TO MAKE IT LESS OBVIOUS, SHE PUT A BANDAGE ON HIS PINKY TOO.
HE'S RIGHT, INSPECTOR! THERE'S A TAN LINE FROM A RING UNDER THE BANDAGE!
GET A PHOTO!

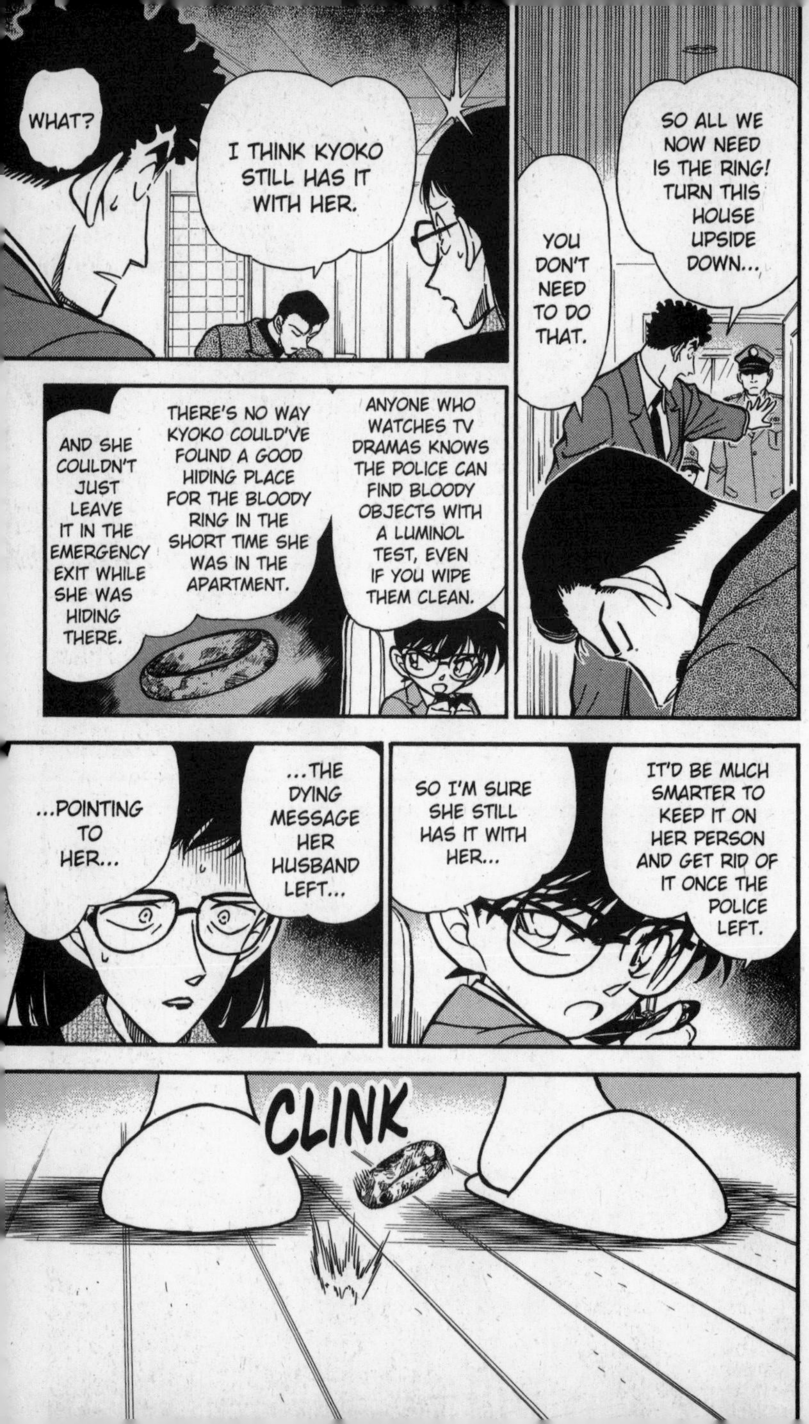
SO ALL WE NOW NEED IS THE RING! TURN THIS HOUSE UPSIDE DOWN...,
YOU DON'T NEED TO DO THAT.
I THINK KYOKO STILL HAS IT WITH HER.
WHAT?
ANYONE WHO WATCHES TV DRAMAS KNOWS THE POLICE CAN FIND BLOODY OBJECTS WITH A LUMINOL TEST, EVEN IF YOU WIPE THEM CLEAN.
THERE'S NO WAY KYOKO COULD'VE FOUND A GOOD HIDING PLACE FOR THE BLOODY RING IN THE SHORT TIME SHE WAS IN THE APARTMENT.
AND SHE COULDN'T JUST LEAVE IT IN THE EMERGENCY EXIT WHILE SHE WAS HIDING THERE.
IT'D BE MUCH SMARTER TO KEEP IT ON HER PERSON AND GET RID OF IT ONCE THE POLICE LEFT.
SO I'M SURE SHE STILL HAS IT WITH HER...
...THE DYING MESSAGE HER HUSBAND LEFT...
...POINTING TO HER...
CLINK

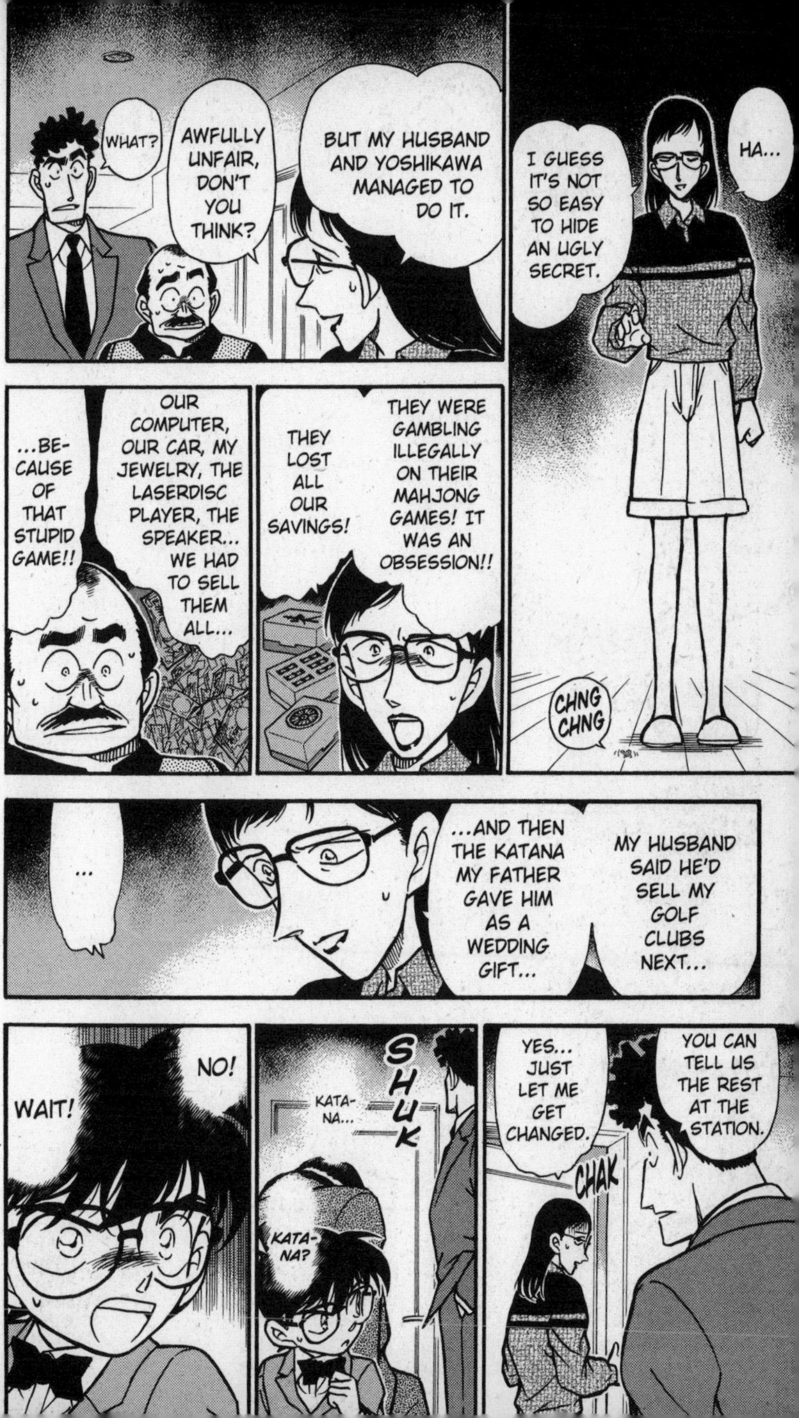
HA...
I GUESS IT'S NOT SO EASY TO HIDE AN UGLY SECRET.
CHNG CHNG
BUT MY HUSBAND AND YOSHIKAWA MANAGED TO DO IT.
AWFULLY UNFAIR, DON'T YOU THINK?
WHAT?
THEY WERE GAMBLING ILLEGALLY ON THEIR MAHJONG GAMES! IT WAS AN OBSESSION!!
THEY LOST ALL OUR SAVINGS!
OUR COMPUTER, OUR CAR, MY JEWELRY, THE LASERDISC PLAYER, THE SPEAKER... WE HAD TO SELL THEM ALL...
...BE-CAUSE OF THAT STUPID GAME!!
MY HUSBAND SAID HE'D SELL MY GOLF CLUBS NEXT...
...AND THEN THE KATANA MY FATHER GAVE HIM AS A WEDDING GIFT...
...
YOU CAN TELL US THE REST AT THE STATION.
YES... JUST LET ME GET CHANGED.
CHAK
SHUK
KATA-NA...
KATA-NA?
NO!
WAIT!

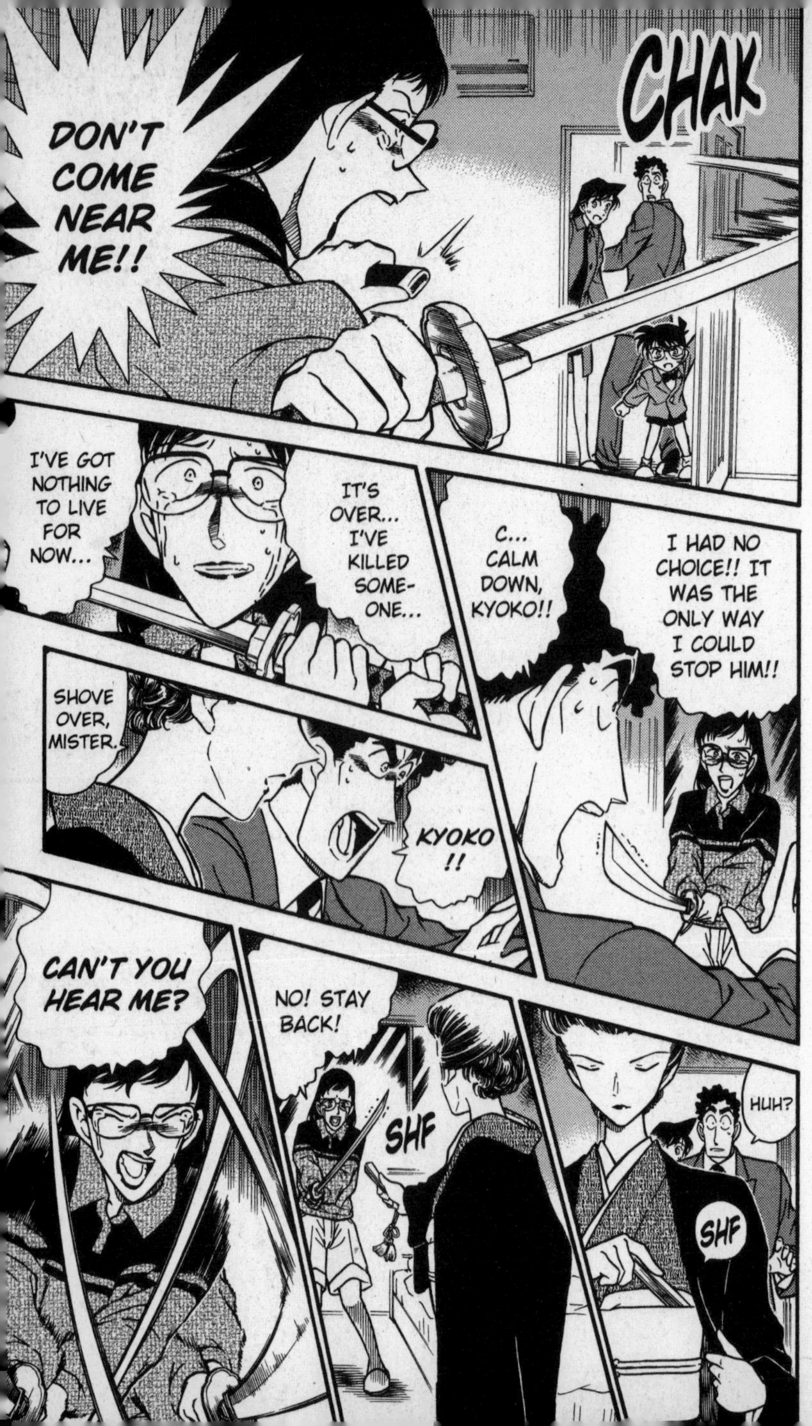
CHAK
DON'T COME NEAR ME!!
C... CALM DOWN, KYOKO!!
I HAD NO CHOICE!! IT WAS THE ONLY WAY I COULD STOP HIM!!
IT'S OVER... I'VE KILLED SOME-ONE...
I'VE GOT NOTHING TO LIVE FOR NOW...
KYOKO !!
SHOVE OVER, MISTER.
HUH?
SHF
SHF
NO! STAY BACK!
CAN'T YOU HEAR ME?

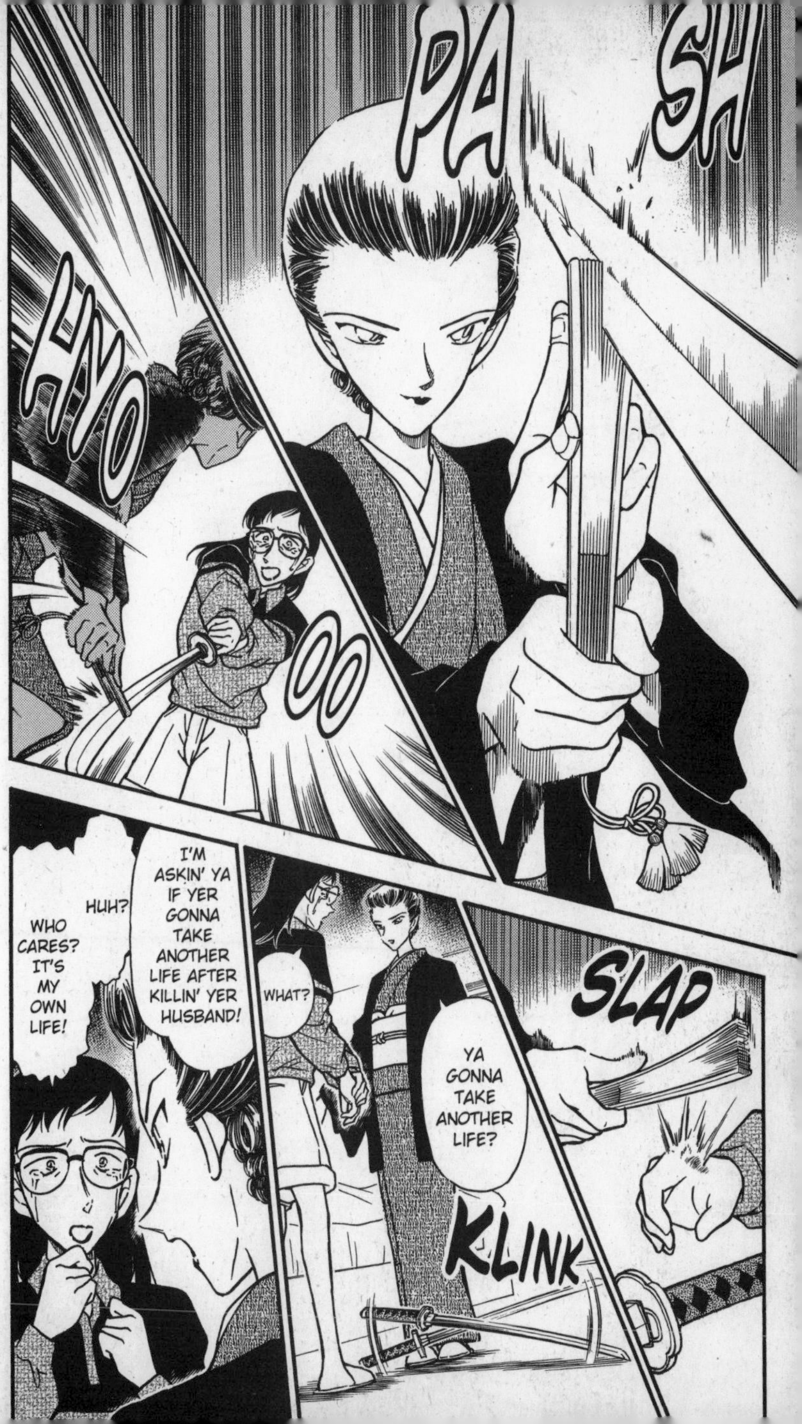
PASH
HYO
OO
SLAP
YA GONNA TAKE ANOTHER LIFE?
KLINK
WHAT?
I'M ASKIN' YA IF YER GONNA TAKE ANOTHER LIFE AFTER KILLIN' YER HUSBAND!
HUH?
WHO CARES? IT'S MY OWN LIFE!

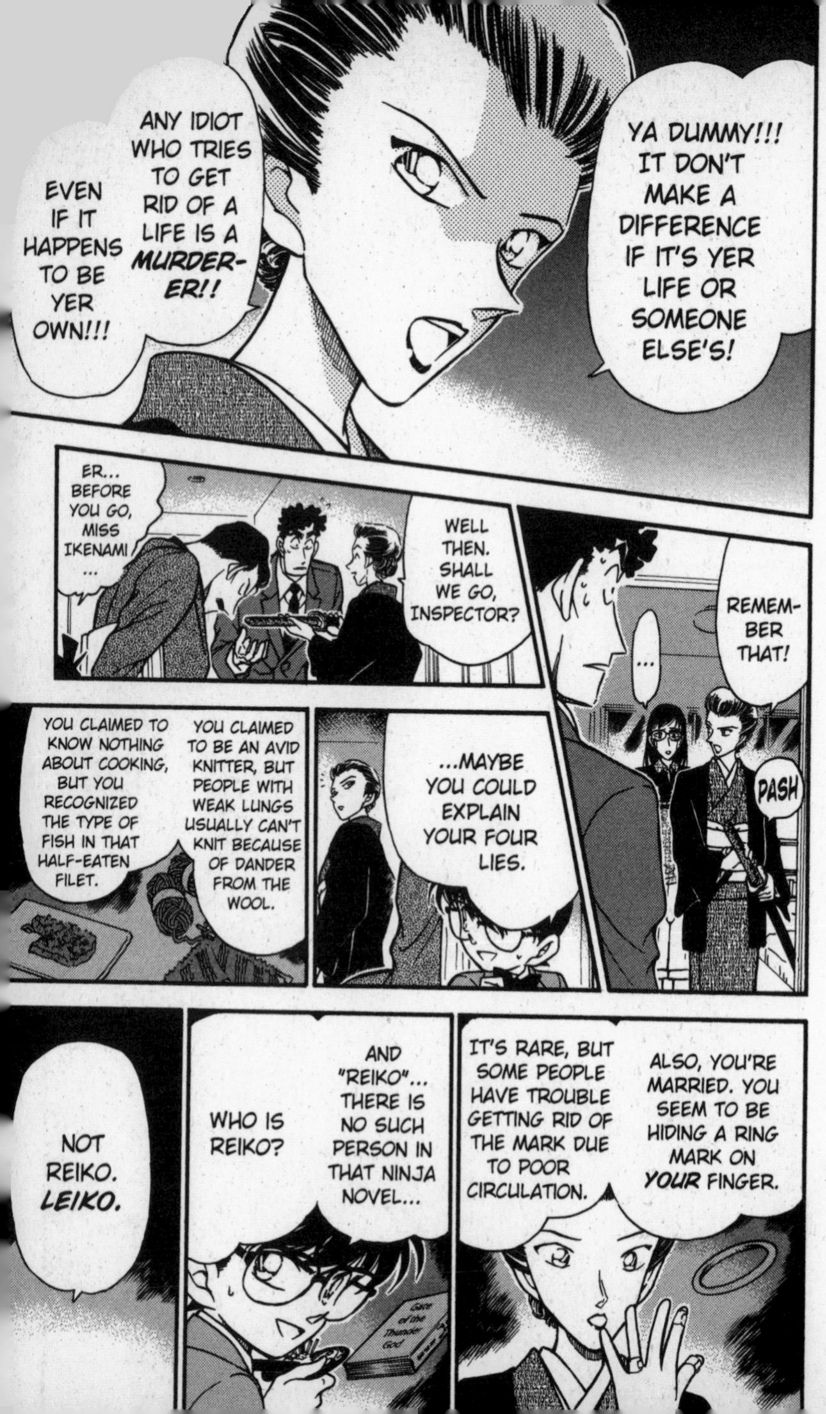

YA DUMMY!!! IT DON'T MAKE A DIFFERENCE IF IT'S YER LIFE OR SOMEONE ELSE'S!
ANY IDIOT WHO TRIES TO GET RID OF A LIFE IS A MURDER-ER!!
EVEN IF IT HAPPENS TO BE YER OWN!!!
REMEMBER THAT!
...
PASH
WELL THEN. SHALL WE GO, INSPECTOR?
ER... BEFORE YOU GO, MISS IKENAMI...
...MAYBE YOU COULD EXPLAIN YOUR FOUR LIES.
YOU CLAIMED TO BE AN AVID KNITTER, BUT PEOPLE WITH WEAK LUNGS USUALLY CAN'T KNIT BECAUSE OF DANDER FROM THE WOOL.
YOU CLAIMED TO KNOW NOTHING ABOUT COOKING, BUT YOU RECOGNIZED THE TYPE OF FISH IN THAT HALF-EATEN FILET.
ALSO, YOU'RE MARRIED. YOU SEEM TO BE HIDING A RING MARK ON YOUR FINGER.
IT'S RARE, BUT SOME PEOPLE HAVE TROUBLE GETTING RID OF THE MARK DUE TO POOR CIRCULATION.
AND "REIKO"... THERE IS NO SUCH PERSON IN THAT NINJA NOVEL...
WHO IS REIKO?
Gate of the Thunder God
NOT REIKO. LEIKO.

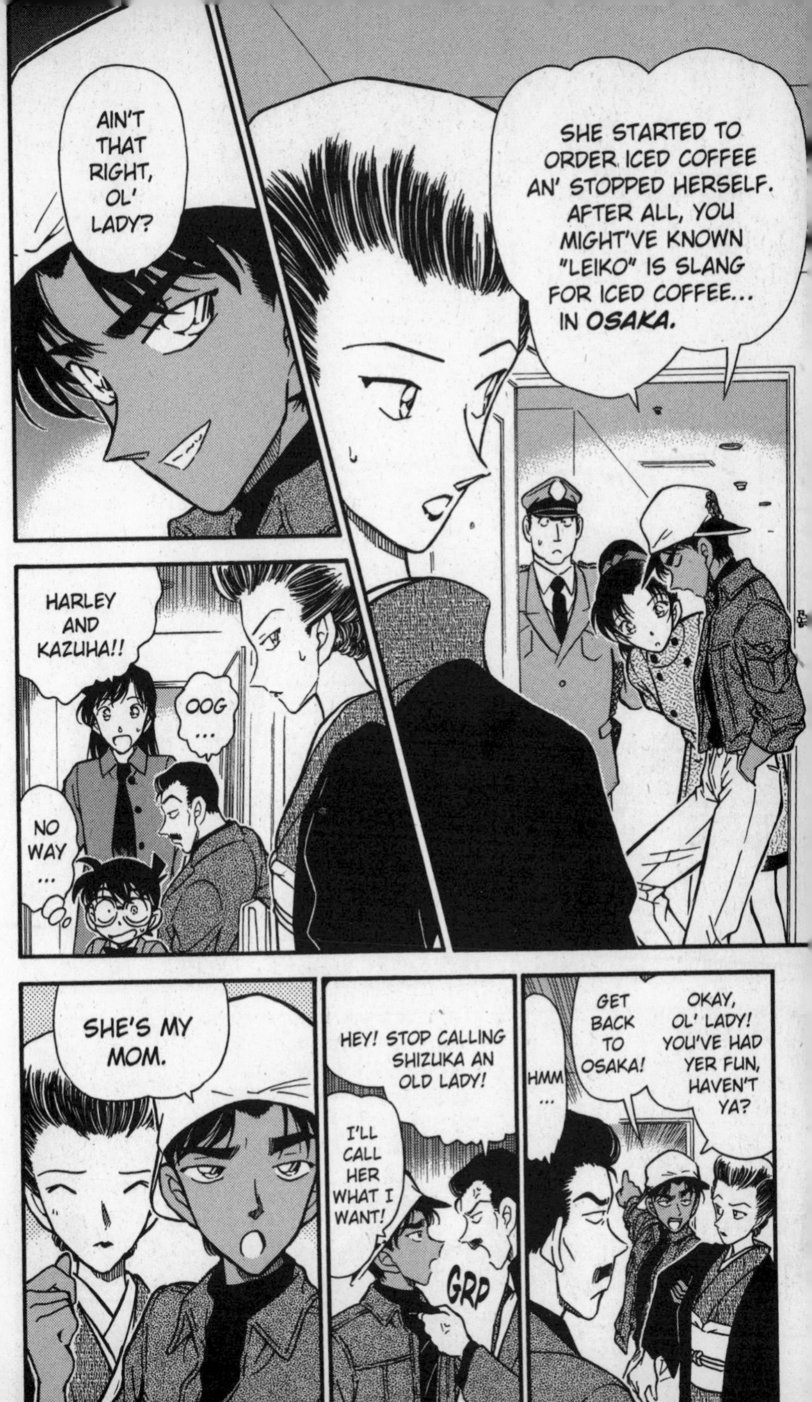
SHE STARTED TO ORDER ICED COFFEE AN' STOPPED HERSELF. AFTER ALL, YOU MIGHT'VE KNOWN "LEIKO" IS SLANG FOR ICED COFFEE... IN OSAKA.
AIN'T THAT RIGHT, OL' LADY?
HARLEY AND KAZUHA!!
OOG...
NO WAY...
OKAY, OL' LADY! YOU'VE HAD YER FUN, HAVEN'T YA?
GET BACK TO OSAKA!
HMM...
HEY! STOP CALLING SHIZUKA AN OLD LADY!
I'LL CALL HER WHAT I WANT!
GRP
SHE'S MY MOM.

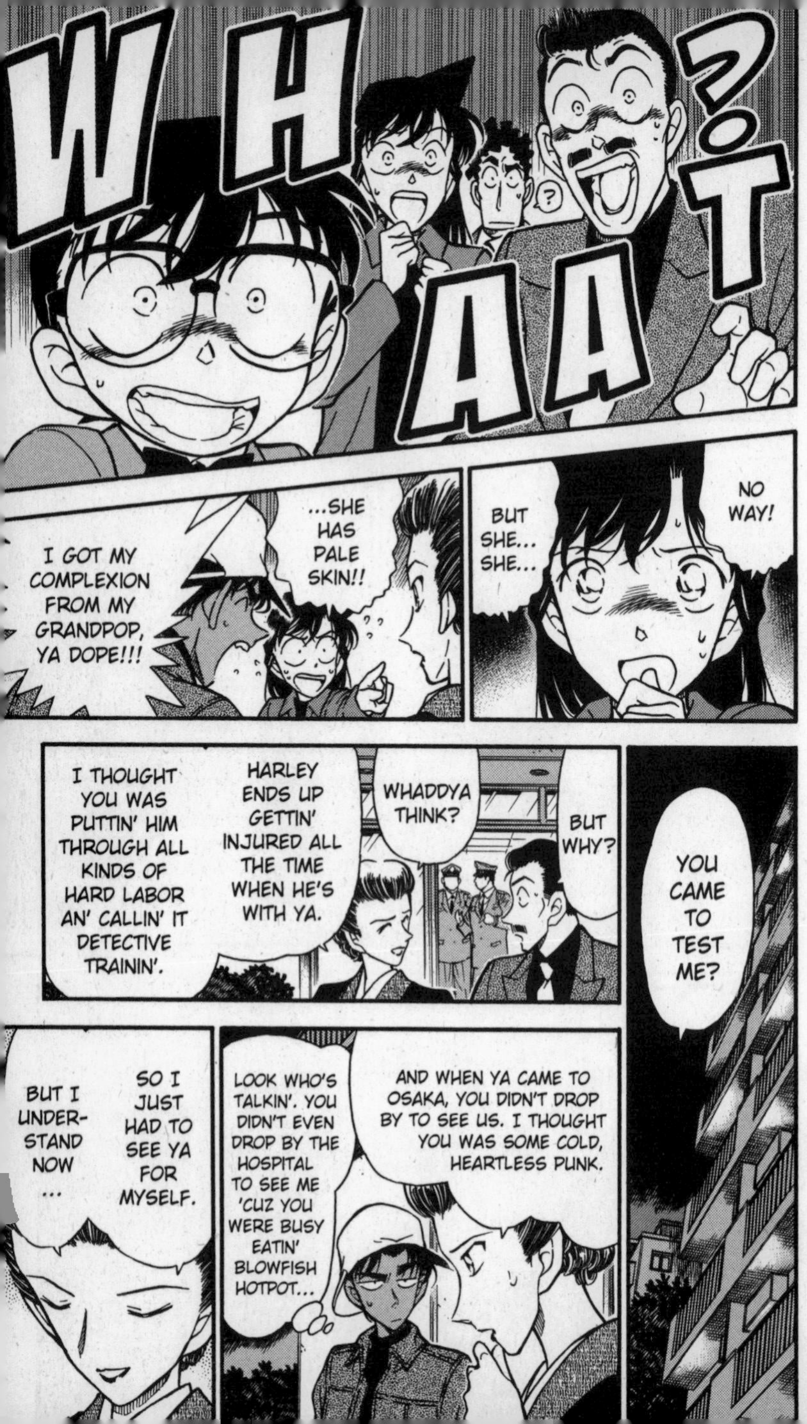
WHAAT?
?
NO WAY!
BUT SHE... SHE...
...SHE HAS PALE SKIN!!
I GOT MY COMPLEXION FROM MY GRANDPOP, YA DOPE!!!
YOU CAME TO TEST ME?
BUT WHY?
WHADDYA THINK?
HARLEY ENDS UP GETTIN' INJURED ALL THE TIME WHEN HE'S WITH YA.
I THOUGHT YOU WAS PUTTIN' HIM THROUGH ALL KINDS OF HARD LABOR AN' CALLIN' IT DETECTIVE TRAININ'.
AND WHEN YA CAME TO OSAKA, YOU DIDN'T DROP BY TO SEE US. I THOUGHT YOU WAS SOME COLD, HEARTLESS PUNK.
LOOK WHO'S TALKIN'. YOU DIDN'T EVEN DROP BY THE HOSPITAL TO SEE ME 'CUZ YOU WERE BUSY EATIN' BLOWFISH HOTPOT...
SO I JUST HAD TO SEE YA FOR MYSELF.
BUT I UNDER-STAND NOW ...

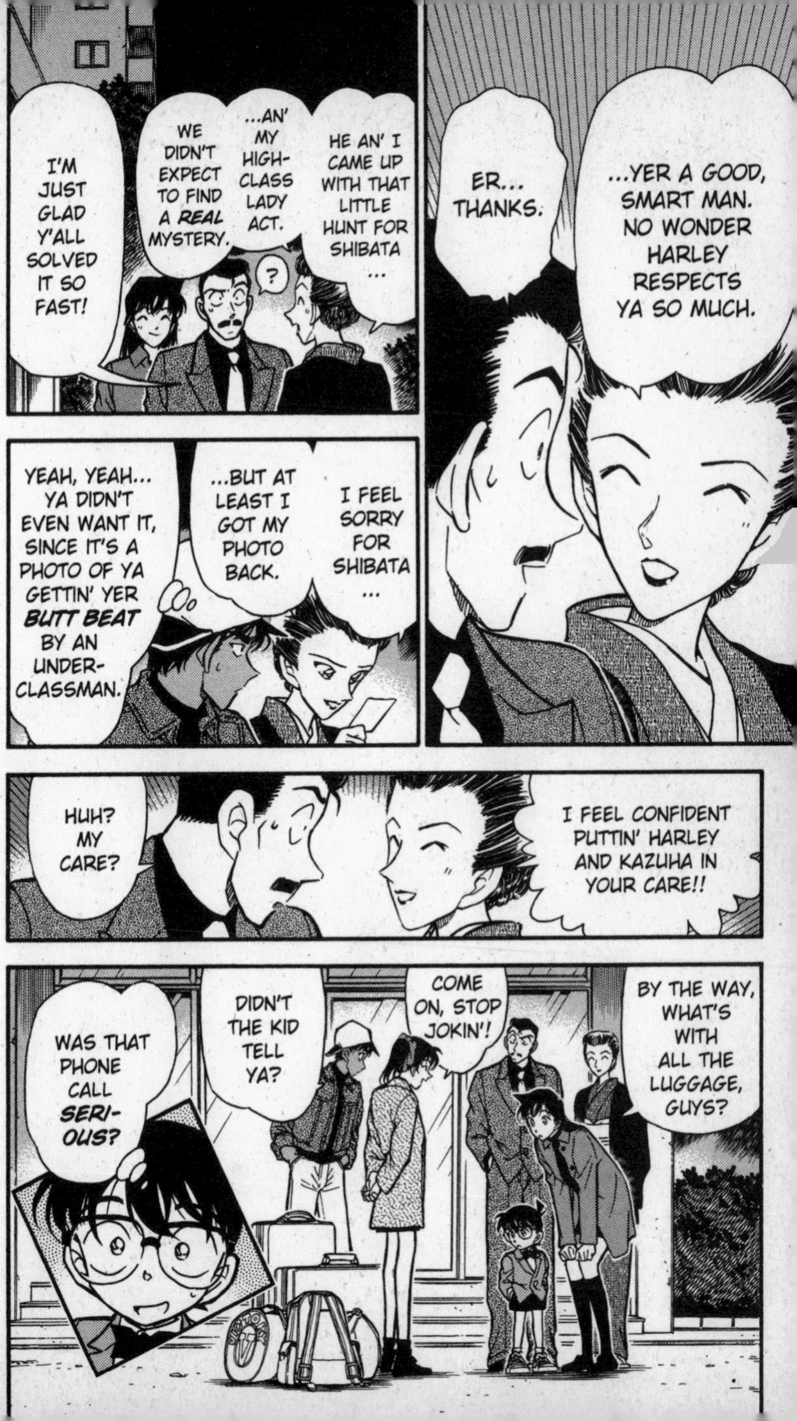
...YER A GOOD, SMART MAN. NO WONDER HARLEY RESPECTS YA SO MUCH.
ER... THANKS.
HE AN' I CAME UP WITH THAT LITTLE HUNT FOR SHIBATA ...
...AN' MY HIGH-CLASS LADY ACT.
WE DIDN'T EXPECT TO FIND A *REAL* MYSTERY.
?
I'M JUST GLAD Y'ALL SOLVED IT SO FAST!
I FEEL SORRY FOR SHIBATA ...
...BUT AT LEAST I GOT MY PHOTO BACK.
YEAH, YEAH... YA DIDN'T EVEN WANT IT, SINCE IT'S A PHOTO OF YA GETTIN' YER ***BUTT BEAT*** BY AN UNDER-CLASSMAN.
I FEEL CONFIDENT PUTTIN' HARLEY AND KAZUHA IN YOUR CARE!!
HUH? MY CARE?
BY THE WAY, WHAT'S WITH ALL THE LUGGAGE, GUYS?
COME ON, STOP JOKIN'!
DIDN'T THE KID TELL YA?
WAS THAT PHONE CALL *SERI-OUS?*

FILE 6: THE MERMAID'S CURSE?

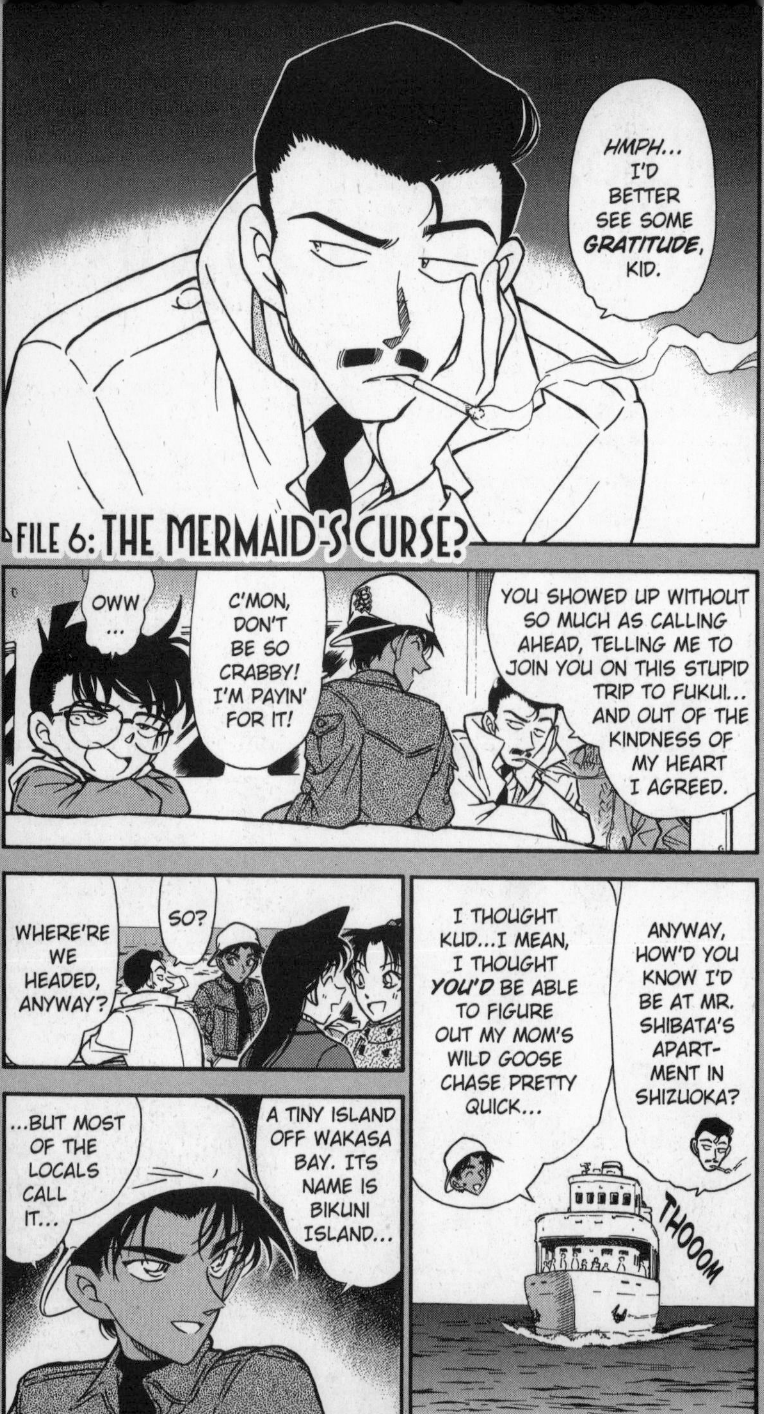
HMPH... I'D BETTER SEE SOME *GRATITUDE,* KID.
YOU SHOWED UP WITHOUT SO MUCH AS CALLING AHEAD, TELLING ME TO JOIN YOU ON THIS STUPID TRIP TO FUKUI... AND OUT OF THE KINDNESS OF MY HEART I AGREED.
C'MON, DON'T BE SO CRABBY! I'M PAYIN' FOR IT!
OWW ...
ANYWAY, HOW'D YOU KNOW I'D BE AT MR. SHIBATA'S APARTMENT IN SHIZUOKA?
I THOUGHT KUD...I MEAN, I THOUGHT *YOU'D* BE ABLE TO FIGURE OUT MY MOM'S WILD GOOSE CHASE PRETTY QUICK...
THOOOM
SO?
WHERE'RE WE HEADED, ANYWAY?
A TINY ISLAND OFF WAKASA BAY. ITS NAME IS BIKUNI ISLAND...
...BUT MOST OF THE LOCALS CALL IT...

FILE 6: THE MERMAID'S CURSE?

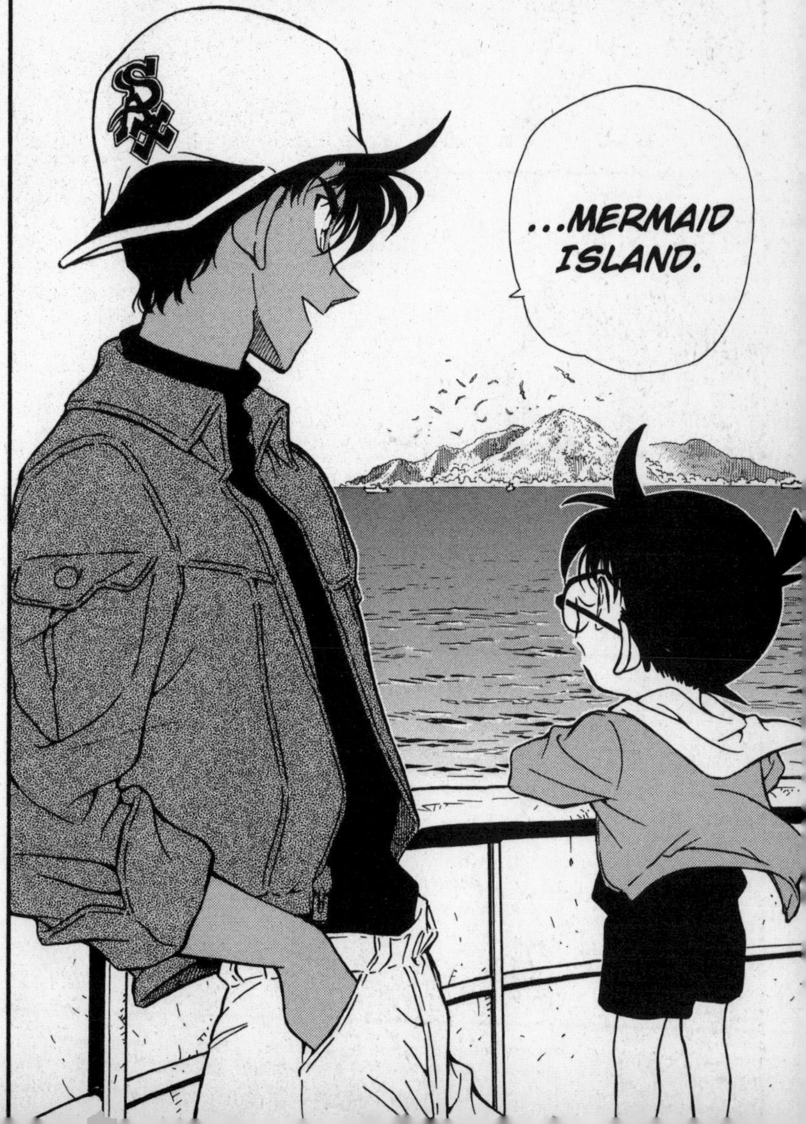
...MERMAID ISLAND.

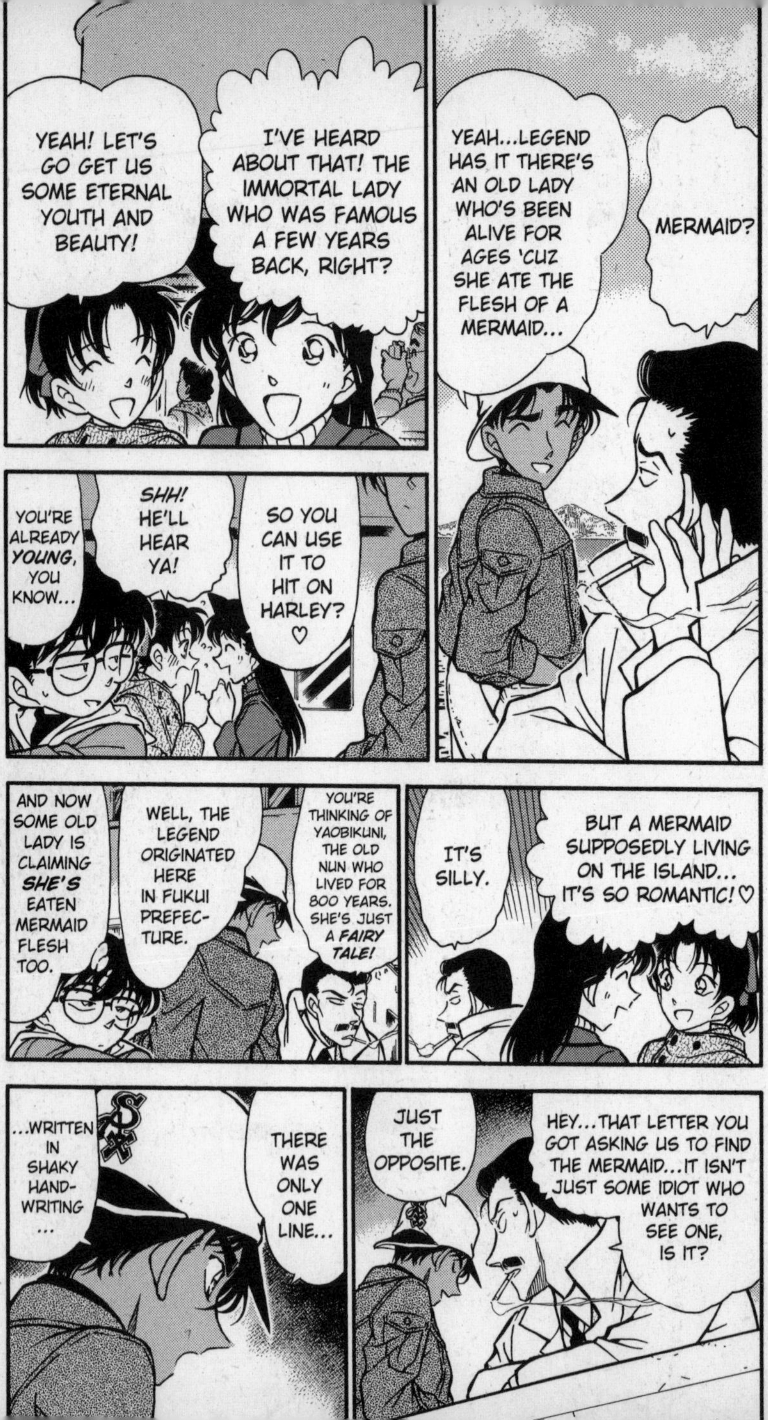
MERMAID?
YEAH...LEGEND HAS IT THERE'S AN OLD LADY WHO'S BEEN ALIVE FOR AGES 'CUZ SHE ATE THE FLESH OF A MERMAID...
I'VE HEARD ABOUT THAT! THE IMMORTAL LADY WHO WAS FAMOUS A FEW YEARS BACK, RIGHT?
YEAH! LET'S GO GET US SOME ETERNAL YOUTH AND BEAUTY!
SO YOU CAN USE IT TO HIT ON HARLEY? ♡
SHH! HE'LL HEAR YA!
YOU'RE ALREADY YOUNG, YOU KNOW...
BUT A MERMAID SUPPOSEDLY LIVING ON THE ISLAND... IT'S SO ROMANTIC! ♡
IT'S SILLY.
YOU'RE THINKING OF YAOBIKUNI, THE OLD NUN WHO LIVED FOR 800 YEARS. SHE'S JUST A FAIRY TALE!
WELL, THE LEGEND ORIGINATED HERE IN FUKUI PREFECTURE.
AND NOW SOME OLD LADY IS CLAIMING SHE'S EATEN MERMAID FLESH TOO.
HEY...THAT LETTER YOU GOT ASKING US TO FIND THE MERMAID...IT ISN'T JUST SOME IDIOT WHO WANTS TO SEE ONE, IS IT?
JUST THE OPPOSITE.
THERE WAS ONLY ONE LINE...
...WRITTEN IN SHAKY HANDWRITING...

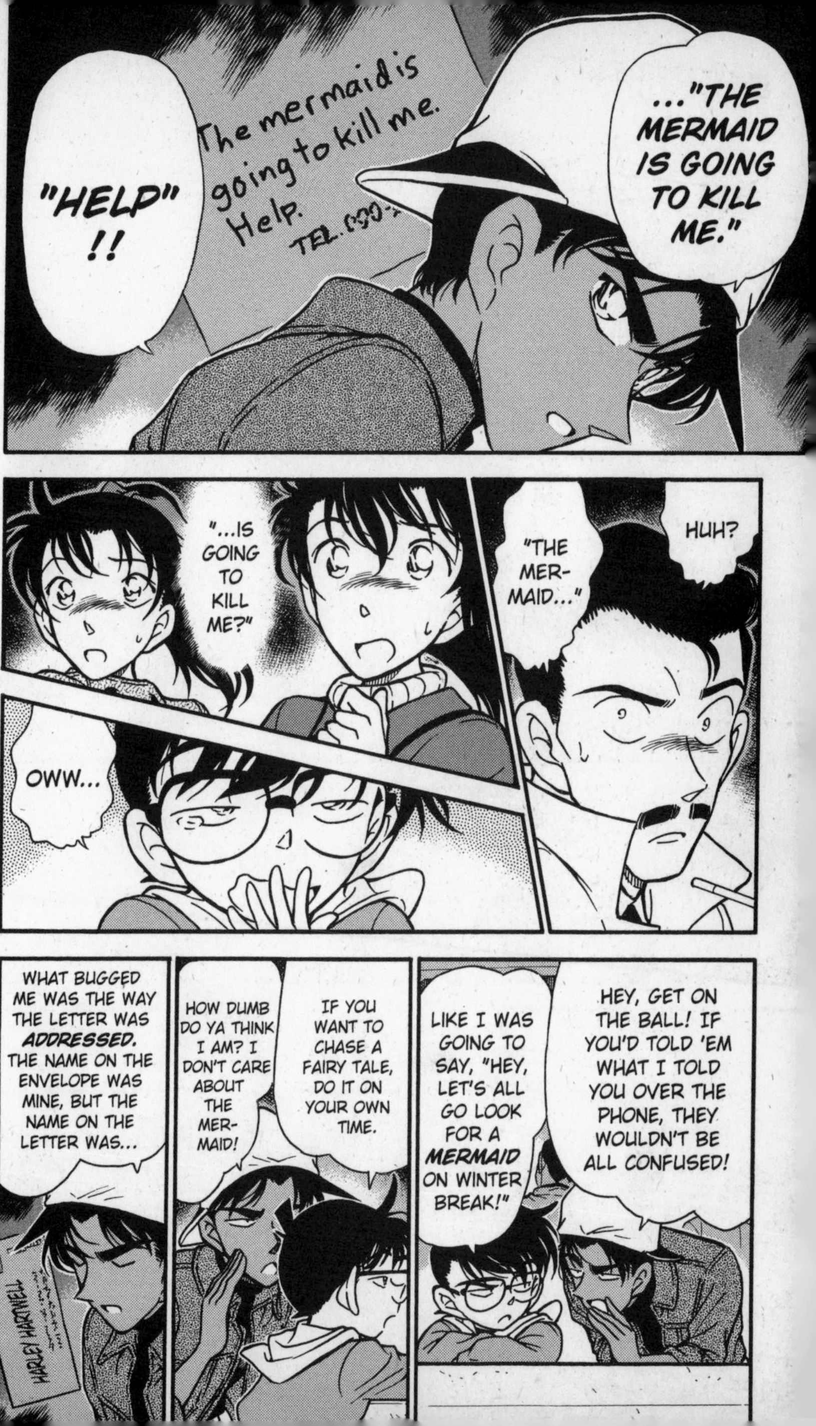
..."THE MERMAID IS GOING TO KILL ME."
The mermaid is going to kill me. Help. TEL.
"HELP" !!
HUH?
"THE MER-MAID..."
"...IS GOING TO KILL ME?"
OWW...
HEY, GET ON THE BALL! IF YOU'D TOLD 'EM WHAT I TOLD YOU OVER THE PHONE, THEY WOULDN'T BE ALL CONFUSED!
LIKE I WAS GOING TO SAY, "HEY, LET'S ALL GO LOOK FOR A ***MERMAID*** ON WINTER BREAK!"
IF YOU WANT TO CHASE A FAIRY TALE, DO IT ON YOUR OWN TIME.
HOW DUMB DO YA THINK I AM? I DON'T CARE ABOUT THE MER-MAID!
WHAT BUGGED ME WAS THE WAY THE LETTER WAS ***ADDRESSED.*** THE NAME ON THE ENVELOPE WAS MINE, BUT THE NAME ON THE LETTER WAS...
HARLEY HARTWELL

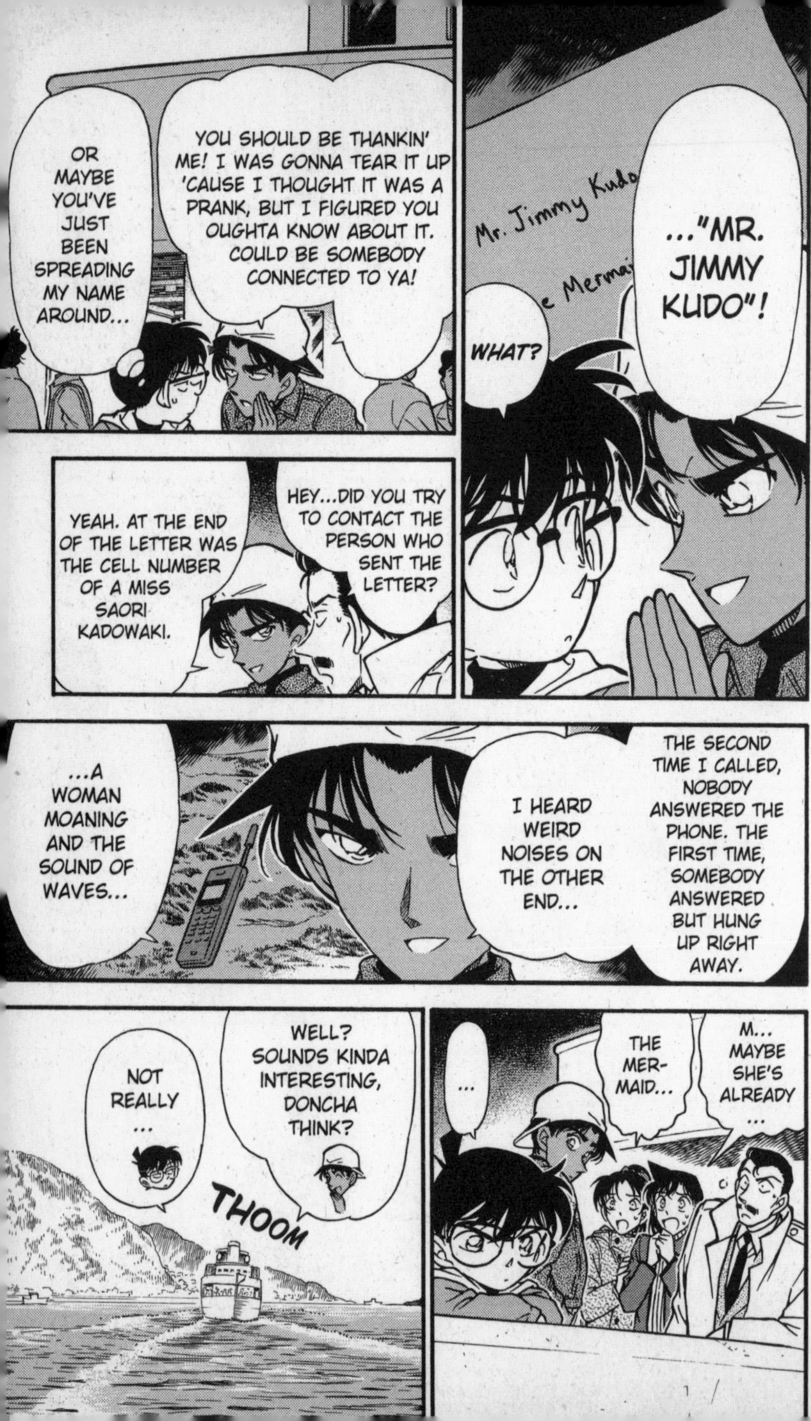
..."MR. JIMMY KUDO"!
WHAT?
YOU SHOULD BE THANKIN' ME! I WAS GONNA TEAR IT UP 'CAUSE I THOUGHT IT WAS A PRANK, BUT I FIGURED YOU OUGHTA KNOW ABOUT IT. COULD BE SOMEBODY CONNECTED TO YA!
OR MAYBE YOU'VE JUST BEEN SPREADING MY NAME AROUND...
HEY...DID YOU TRY TO CONTACT THE PERSON WHO SENT THE LETTER?
YEAH. AT THE END OF THE LETTER WAS THE CELL NUMBER OF A MISS SAORI KADOWAKI.
THE SECOND TIME I CALLED, NOBODY ANSWERED THE PHONE. THE FIRST TIME, SOMEBODY ANSWERED BUT HUNG UP RIGHT AWAY.
I HEARD WEIRD NOISES ON THE OTHER END...
...A WOMAN MOANING AND THE SOUND OF WAVES...
M... MAYBE SHE'S ALREADY ...
THE MER-MAID...
...
WELL? SOUNDS KINDA INTERESTING, DONCHA THINK?
NOT REALLY ...
THOOM

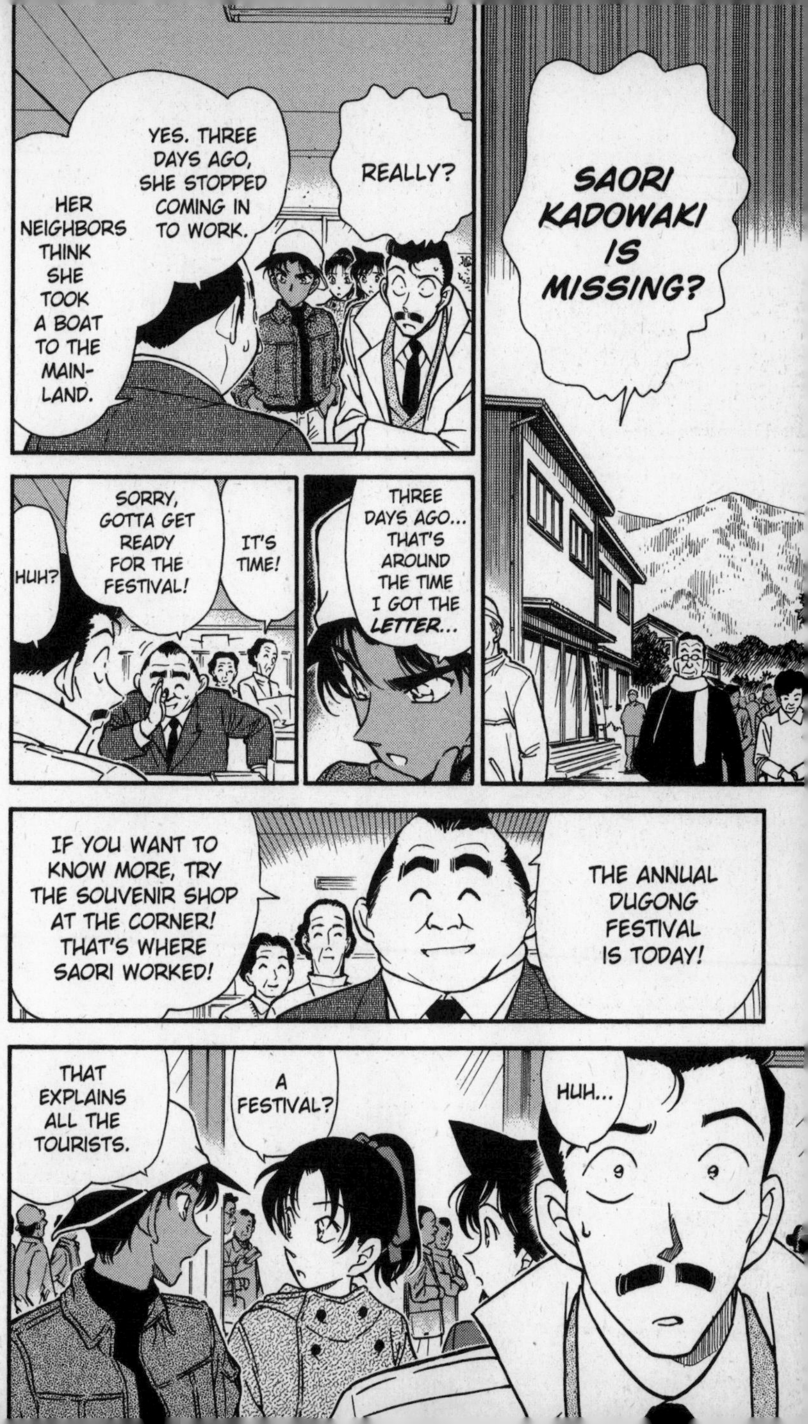
SAORI KADOWAKI IS MISSING?
REALLY?
YES. THREE DAYS AGO, SHE STOPPED COMING IN TO WORK.
HER NEIGHBORS THINK SHE TOOK A BOAT TO THE MAIN-LAND.
THREE DAYS AGO... THAT'S AROUND THE TIME I GOT THE *LETTER*...
IT'S TIME!
SORRY, GOTTA GET READY FOR THE FESTIVAL!
HUH?
THE ANNUAL DUGONG FESTIVAL IS TODAY!
IF YOU WANT TO KNOW MORE, TRY THE SOUVENIR SHOP AT THE CORNER! THAT'S WHERE SAORI WORKED!
HUH...
A FESTIVAL?
THAT EXPLAINS ALL THE TOURISTS.

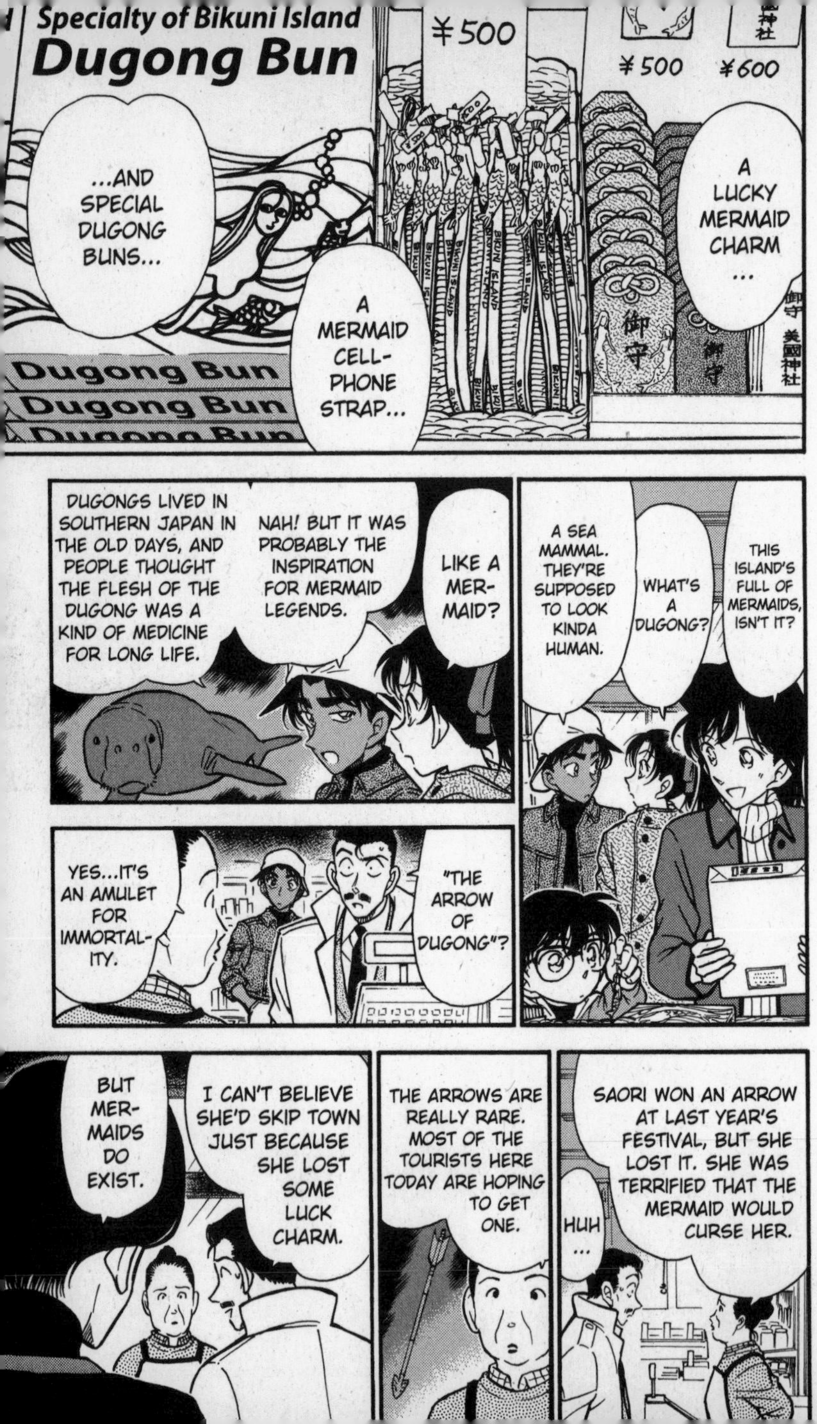
Specialty of Bikuni Island
Dugong Bun
¥500
¥500 ¥600
A LUCKY MERMAID CHARM...
A MERMAID CELL-PHONE STRAP...
...AND SPECIAL DUGONG BUNS...
Dugong Bun
Dugong Bun
THIS ISLAND'S FULL OF MERMAIDS, ISN'T IT?
WHAT'S A DUGONG?
A SEA MAMMAL. THEY'RE SUPPOSED TO LOOK KINDA HUMAN.
LIKE A MERMAID?
NAH! BUT IT WAS PROBABLY THE INSPIRATION FOR MERMAID LEGENDS.
DUGONGS LIVED IN SOUTHERN JAPAN IN THE OLD DAYS, AND PEOPLE THOUGHT THE FLESH OF THE DUGONG WAS A KIND OF MEDICINE FOR LONG LIFE.
"THE ARROW OF DUGONG"?
YES...IT'S AN AMULET FOR IMMORTALITY.
SAORI WON AN ARROW AT LAST YEAR'S FESTIVAL, BUT SHE LOST IT. SHE WAS TERRIFIED THAT THE MERMAID WOULD CURSE HER.
HUH...
THE ARROWS ARE REALLY RARE. MOST OF THE TOURISTS HERE TODAY ARE HOPING TO GET ONE.
I CAN'T BELIEVE SHE'D SKIP TOWN JUST BECAUSE SHE LOST SOME LUCK CHARM.
BUT MERMAIDS DO EXIST.

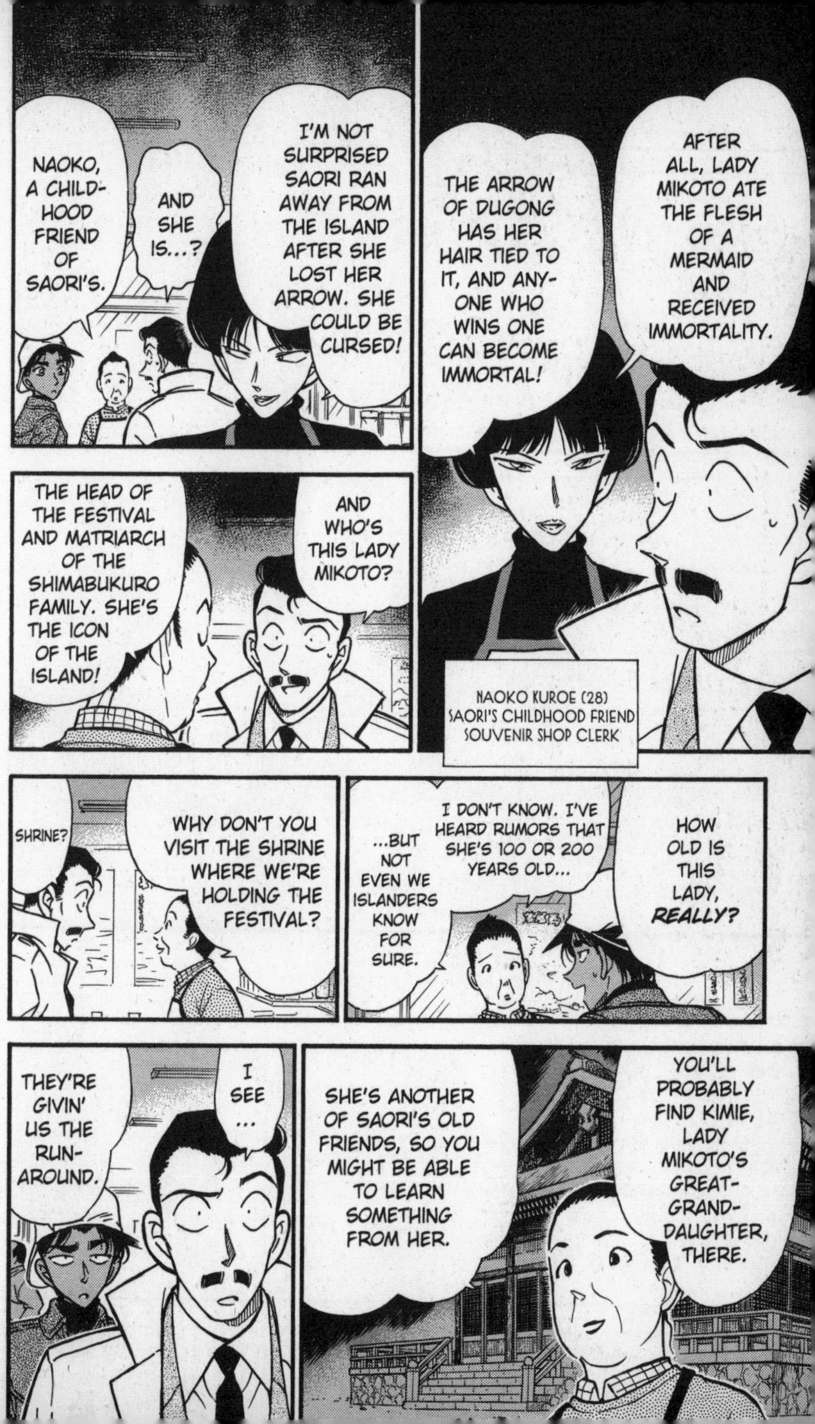
NAOKO, A CHILDHOOD FRIEND OF SAORI'S.
AND SHE IS...?
I'M NOT SURPRISED SAORI RAN AWAY FROM THE ISLAND AFTER SHE LOST HER ARROW. SHE COULD BE CURSED!
THE ARROW OF DUGONG HAS HER HAIR TIED TO IT, AND ANYONE WHO WINS ONE CAN BECOME IMMORTAL!
AFTER ALL, LADY MIKOTO ATE THE FLESH OF A MERMAID AND RECEIVED IMMORTALITY.
NAOKO KUROE (28) SAORI'S CHILDHOOD FRIEND SOUVENIR SHOP CLERK
AND WHO'S THIS LADY MIKOTO?
THE HEAD OF THE FESTIVAL AND MATRIARCH OF THE SHIMABUKURO FAMILY. SHE'S THE ICON OF THE ISLAND!
HOW OLD IS THIS LADY, ***REALLY?***
I DON'T KNOW. I'VE HEARD RUMORS THAT SHE'S 100 OR 200 YEARS OLD...
...BUT NOT EVEN WE ISLANDERS KNOW FOR SURE.
WHY DON'T YOU VISIT THE SHRINE WHERE WE'RE HOLDING THE FESTIVAL?
SHRINE?
YOU'LL PROBABLY FIND KIMIE, LADY MIKOTO'S GREAT-GRANDDAUGHTER, THERE.
SHE'S ANOTHER OF SAORI'S OLD FRIENDS, SO YOU MIGHT BE ABLE TO LEARN SOMETHING FROM HER.
I SEE...
THEY'RE GIVIN' US THE RUN-AROUND.

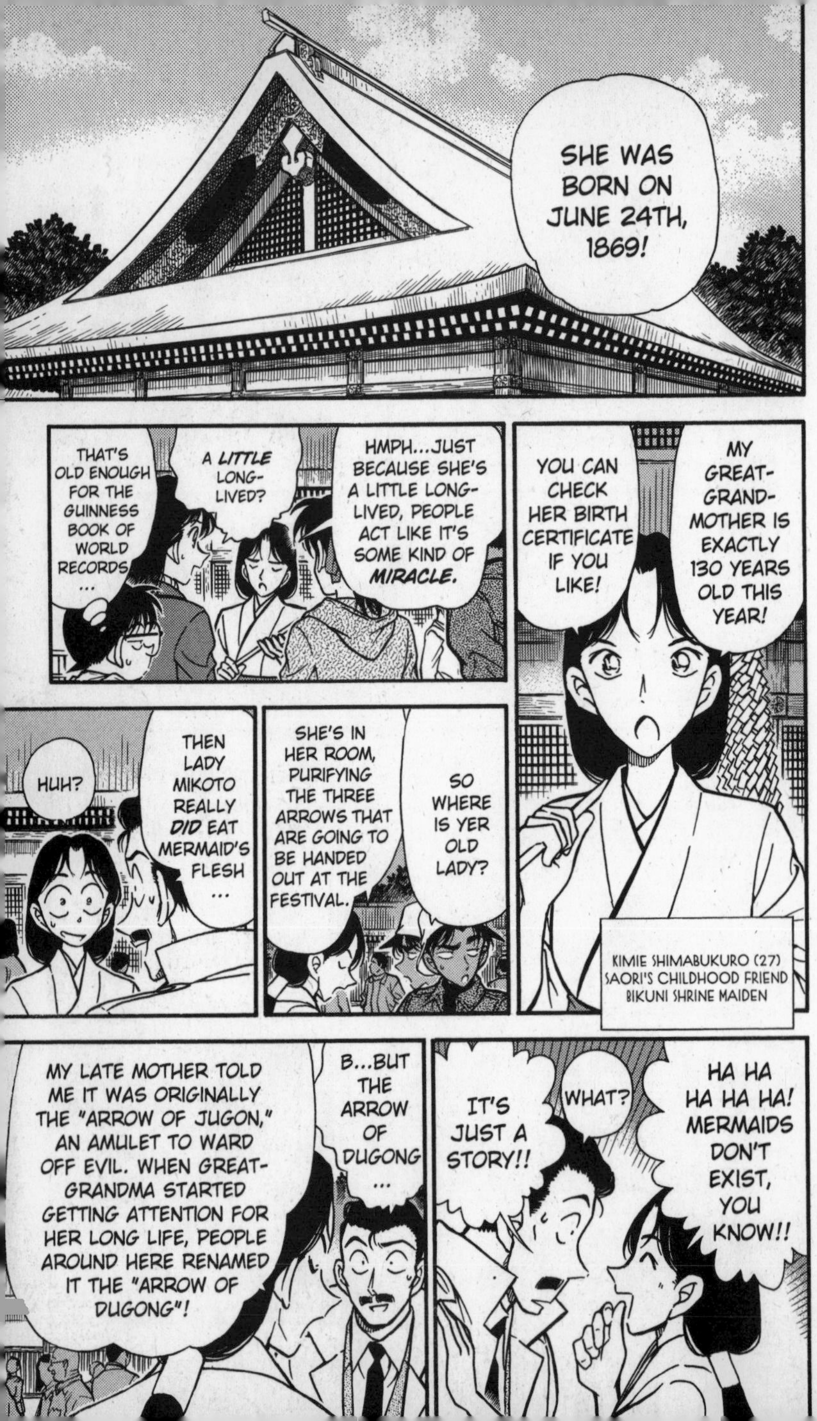
SHE WAS BORN ON JUNE 24TH, 1869!
MY GREAT-GRANDMOTHER IS EXACTLY 130 YEARS OLD THIS YEAR!
YOU CAN CHECK HER BIRTH CERTIFICATE IF YOU LIKE!
KIMIE SHIMABUKURO (27) SAORI'S CHILDHOOD FRIEND BIKUNI SHRINE MAIDEN
HMPH...JUST BECAUSE SHE'S A LITTLE LONG-LIVED, PEOPLE ACT LIKE IT'S SOME KIND OF *MIRACLE.*
A *LITTLE* LONG-LIVED?
THAT'S OLD ENOUGH FOR THE GUINNESS BOOK OF WORLD RECORDS...
SO WHERE IS YER OLD LADY?
SHE'S IN HER ROOM, PURIFYING THE THREE ARROWS THAT ARE GOING TO BE HANDED OUT AT THE FESTIVAL.
THEN LADY MIKOTO REALLY *DID* EAT MERMAID'S FLESH...
HUH?
HA HA HA HA HA! MERMAIDS DON'T EXIST, YOU KNOW!!
WHAT?
IT'S JUST A STORY!!
B...BUT THE ARROW OF DUGONG...
MY LATE MOTHER TOLD ME IT WAS ORIGINALLY THE "ARROW OF JUGON," AN AMULET TO WARD OFF EVIL. WHEN GREAT-GRANDMA STARTED GETTING ATTENTION FOR HER LONG LIFE, PEOPLE AROUND HERE RENAMED IT THE "ARROW OF DUGONG"!

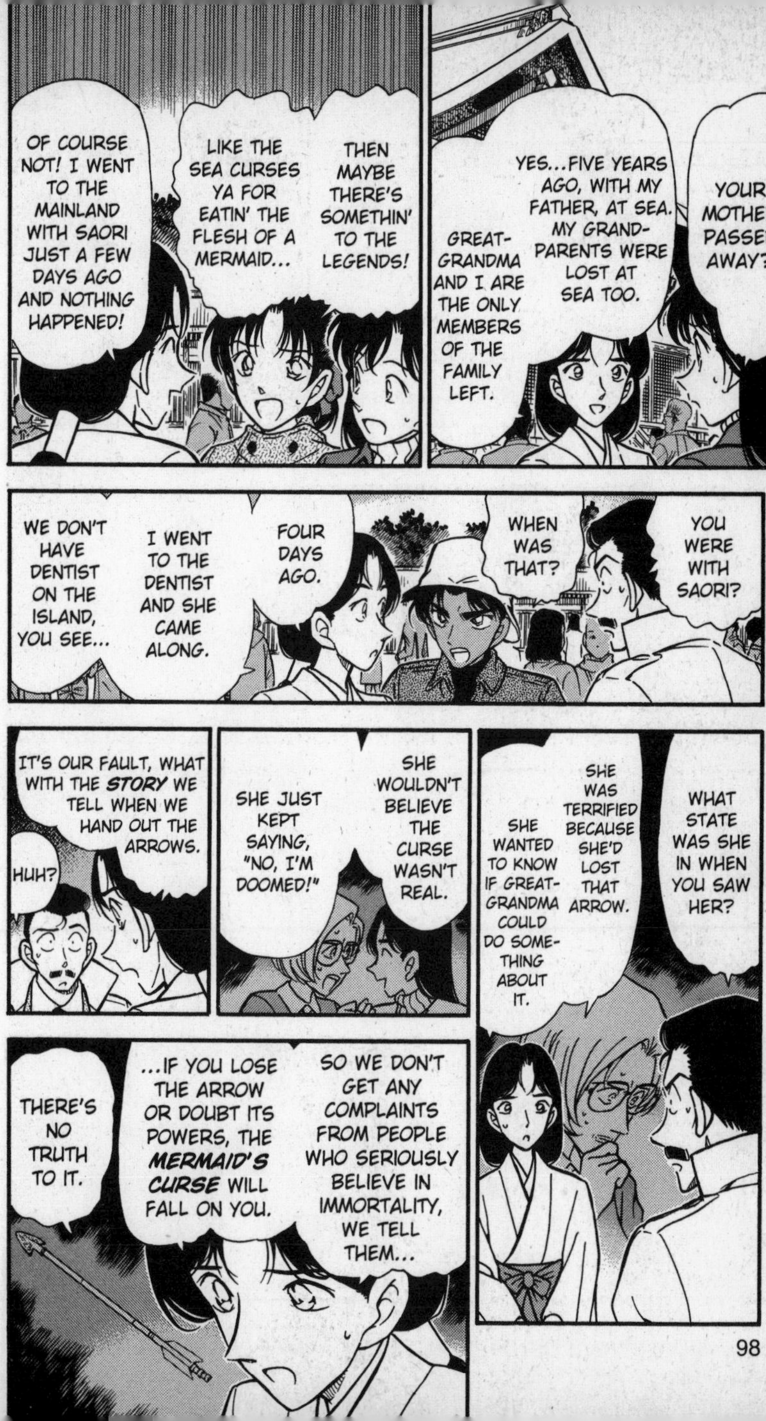
YOUR MOTHER PASSED AWAY?
YES...FIVE YEARS AGO, WITH MY FATHER, AT SEA. MY GRAND-PARENTS WERE LOST AT SEA TOO.
GREAT-GRANDMA AND I ARE THE ONLY MEMBERS OF THE FAMILY LEFT.
THEN MAYBE THERE'S SOMETHIN' TO THE LEGENDS!
LIKE THE SEA CURSES YA FOR EATIN' THE FLESH OF A MERMAID...
OF COURSE NOT! I WENT TO THE MAINLAND WITH SAORI JUST A FEW DAYS AGO AND NOTHING HAPPENED!
YOU WERE WITH SAORI?
WHEN WAS THAT?
FOUR DAYS AGO.
I WENT TO THE DENTIST AND SHE CAME ALONG.
WE DON'T HAVE DENTIST ON THE ISLAND, YOU SEE...
WHAT STATE WAS SHE IN WHEN YOU SAW HER?
SHE WAS TERRIFIED BECAUSE SHE'D LOST THAT ARROW.
SHE WANTED TO KNOW IF GREAT-GRANDMA COULD DO SOME-THING ABOUT IT.
SHE WOULDN'T BELIEVE THE CURSE WASN'T REAL.
SHE JUST KEPT SAYING, "NO, I'M DOOMED!"
IT'S OUR FAULT, WHAT WITH THE **STORY** WE TELL WHEN WE HAND OUT THE ARROWS.
HUH?
SO WE DON'T GET ANY COMPLAINTS FROM PEOPLE WHO SERIOUSLY BELIEVE IN IMMORTALITY, WE TELL THEM...
...IF YOU LOSE THE ARROW OR DOUBT ITS POWERS, THE **MERMAID'S CURSE** WILL FALL ON YOU.
THERE'S NO TRUTH TO IT.

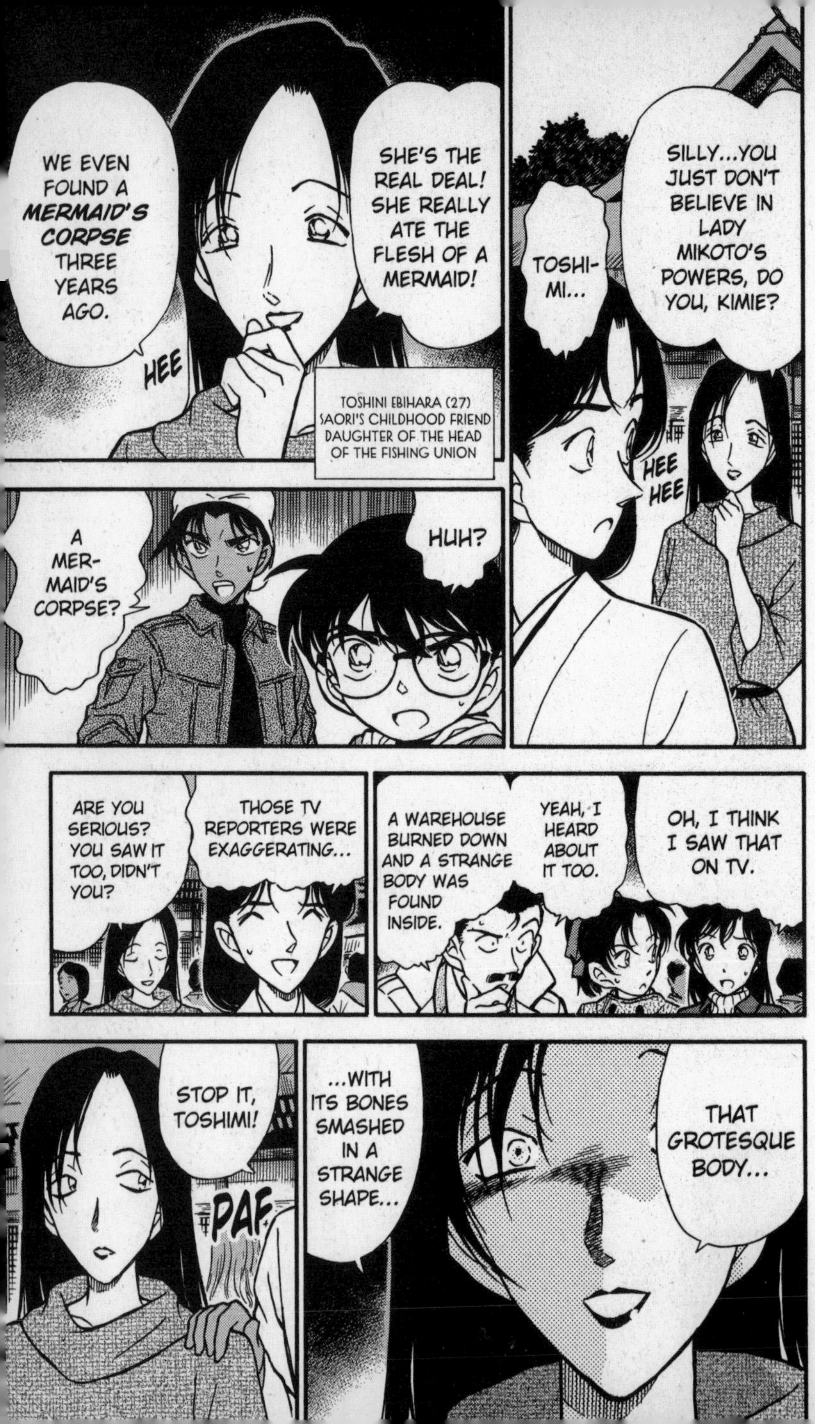
SILLY...YOU JUST DON'T BELIEVE IN LADY MIKOTO'S POWERS, DO YOU, KIMIE?
TOSHI-MI...
HEE HEE
SHE'S THE REAL DEAL! SHE REALLY ATE THE FLESH OF A MERMAID!
WE EVEN FOUND A MERMAID'S CORPSE THREE YEARS AGO.
HEE
TOSHINI EBIHARA (27)
SAORI'S CHILDHOOD FRIEND
DAUGHTER OF THE HEAD OF THE FISHING UNION
HUH?
A MER-MAID'S CORPSE?
OH, I THINK I SAW THAT ON TV.
YEAH, I HEARD ABOUT IT TOO.
A WAREHOUSE BURNED DOWN AND A STRANGE BODY WAS FOUND INSIDE.
THOSE TV REPORTERS WERE EXAGGERATING...
ARE YOU SERIOUS? YOU SAW IT TOO, DIDN'T YOU?
THAT GROTESQUE BODY...
...WITH ITS BONES SMASHED IN A STRANGE SHAPE...
STOP IT, TOSHIMI!
PAF

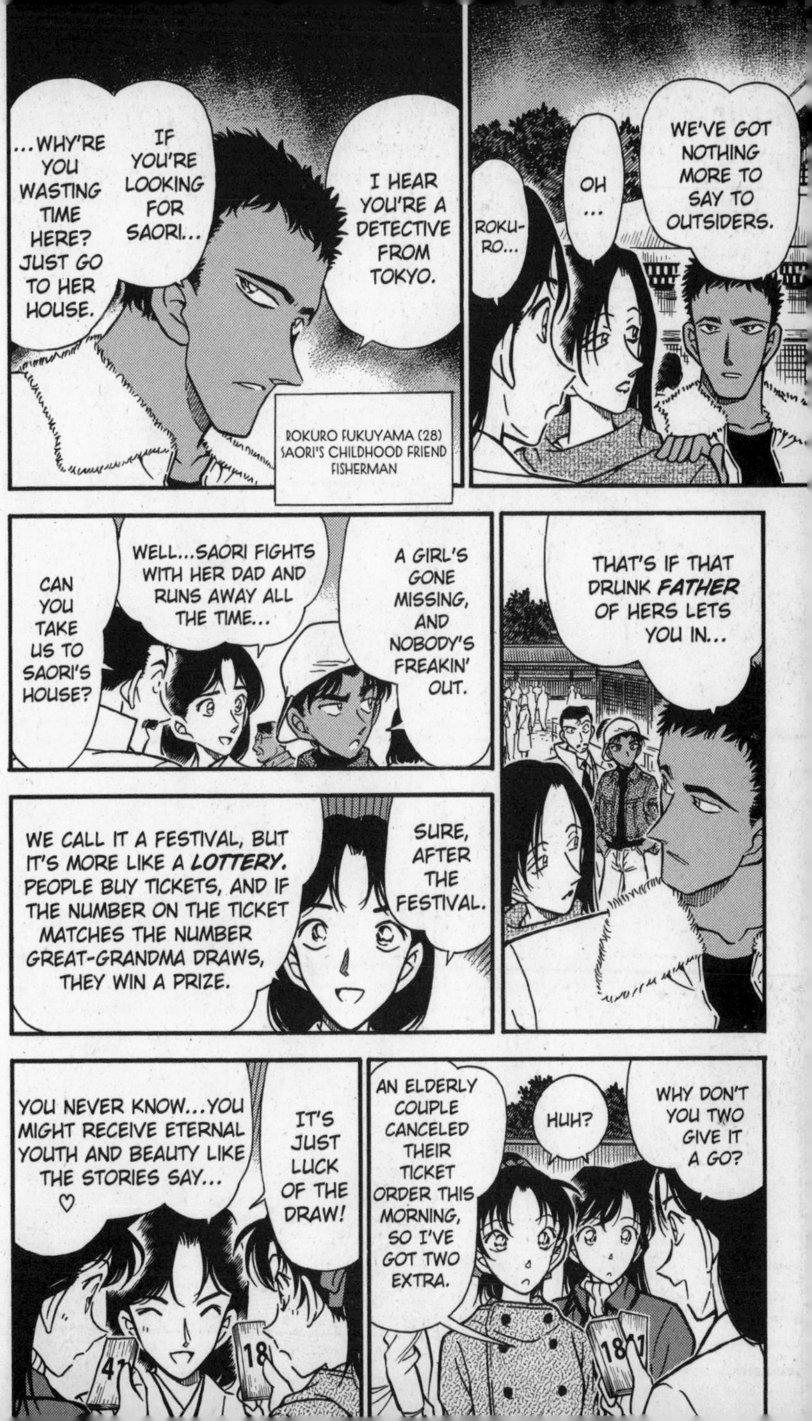
WE'VE GOT NOTHING MORE TO SAY TO OUTSIDERS.
OH...
ROKURO...
I HEAR YOU'RE A DETECTIVE FROM TOKYO.
IF YOU'RE LOOKING FOR SAORI...
...WHY'RE YOU WASTING TIME HERE? JUST GO TO HER HOUSE.
ROKURO FUKUYAMA (28)
SAORI'S CHILDHOOD FRIEND
FISHERMAN
THAT'S IF THAT DRUNK FATHER OF HERS LETS YOU IN...
A GIRL'S GONE MISSING, AND NOBODY'S FREAKIN' OUT.
WELL...SAORI FIGHTS WITH HER DAD AND RUNS AWAY ALL THE TIME...
CAN YOU TAKE US TO SAORI'S HOUSE?
SURE, AFTER THE FESTIVAL.
WE CALL IT A FESTIVAL, BUT IT'S MORE LIKE A LOTTERY. PEOPLE BUY TICKETS, AND IF THE NUMBER ON THE TICKET MATCHES THE NUMBER GREAT-GRANDMA DRAWS, THEY WIN A PRIZE.
WHY DON'T YOU TWO GIVE IT A GO?
HUH?
AN ELDERLY COUPLE CANCELED THEIR TICKET ORDER THIS MORNING, SO I'VE GOT TWO EXTRA.
IT'S JUST LUCK OF THE DRAW!
YOU NEVER KNOW...YOU MIGHT RECEIVE ETERNAL YOUTH AND BEAUTY LIKE THE STORIES SAY... ♡

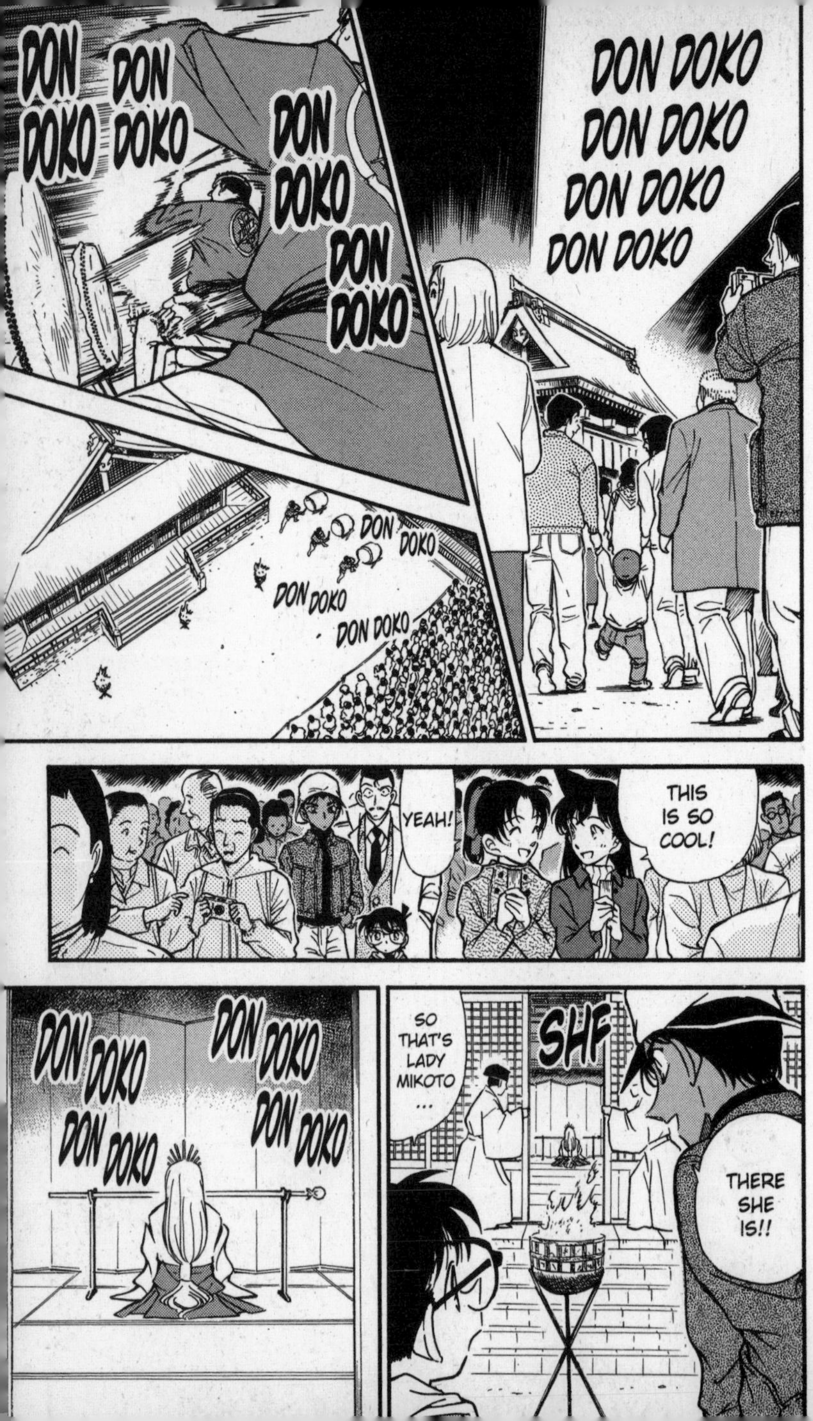
DON DOKO DON DOKO DON DOKO DON DOKO
DON DOKO
DON DOKO
DON DOKO
DON DOKO
DON DOKO
DON DOKO
DON DOKO
THIS IS SO COOL!
YEAH!
SHF
THERE SHE IS!!
SO THAT'S LADY MIKOTO ...
DON DOKO
DON DOKO
DON DOKO
DON DOKO

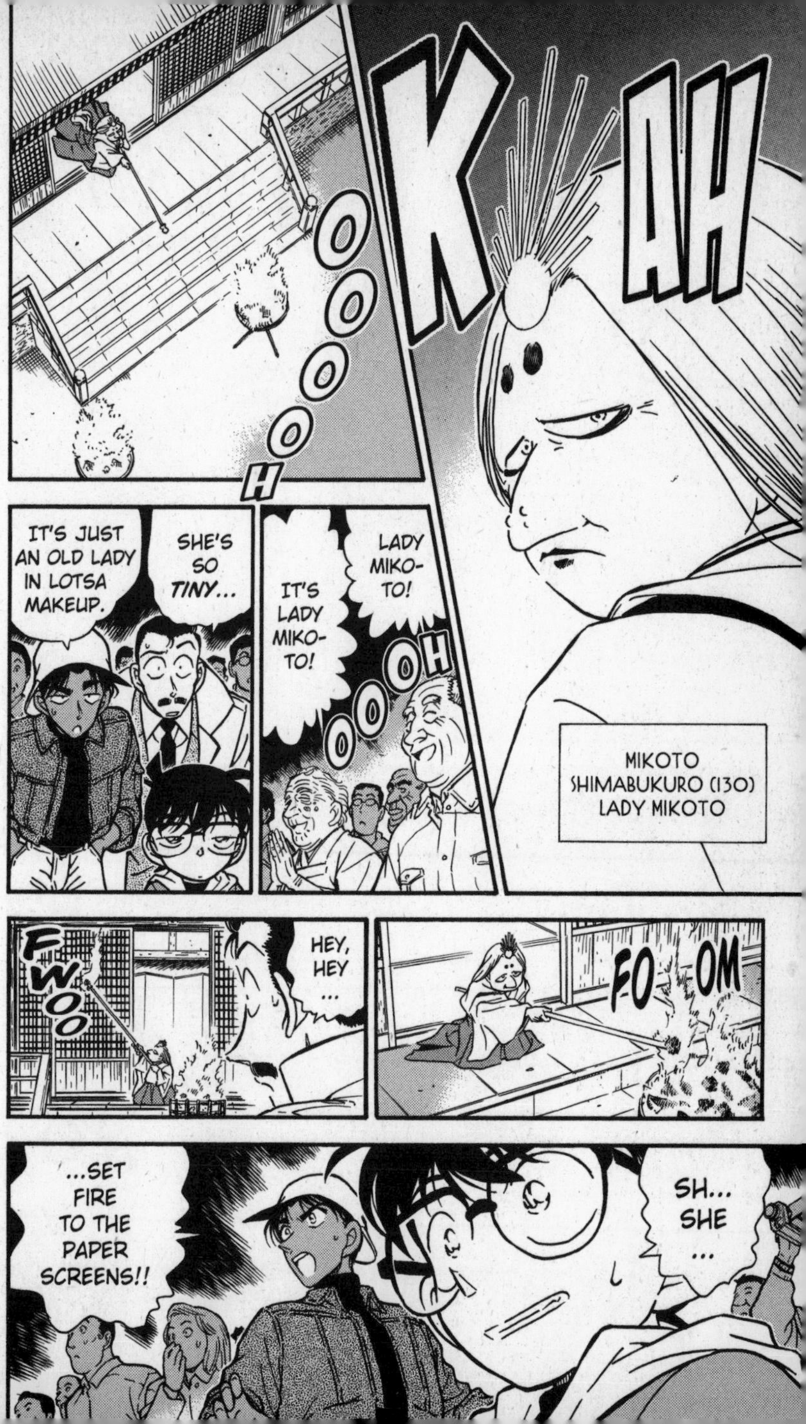
KAH
MIKOTO SHIMABUKURO (130) LADY MIKOTO
OOOOOOH
LADY MIKO-TO!
IT'S LADY MIKO-TO!
OOOOH
SHE'S SO *TINY*...
IT'S JUST AN OLD LADY IN LOTSA MAKEUP.
FO OM
HEY, HEY ...
FWOO
SH... SHE ...
...SET FIRE TO THE PAPER SCREENS!!

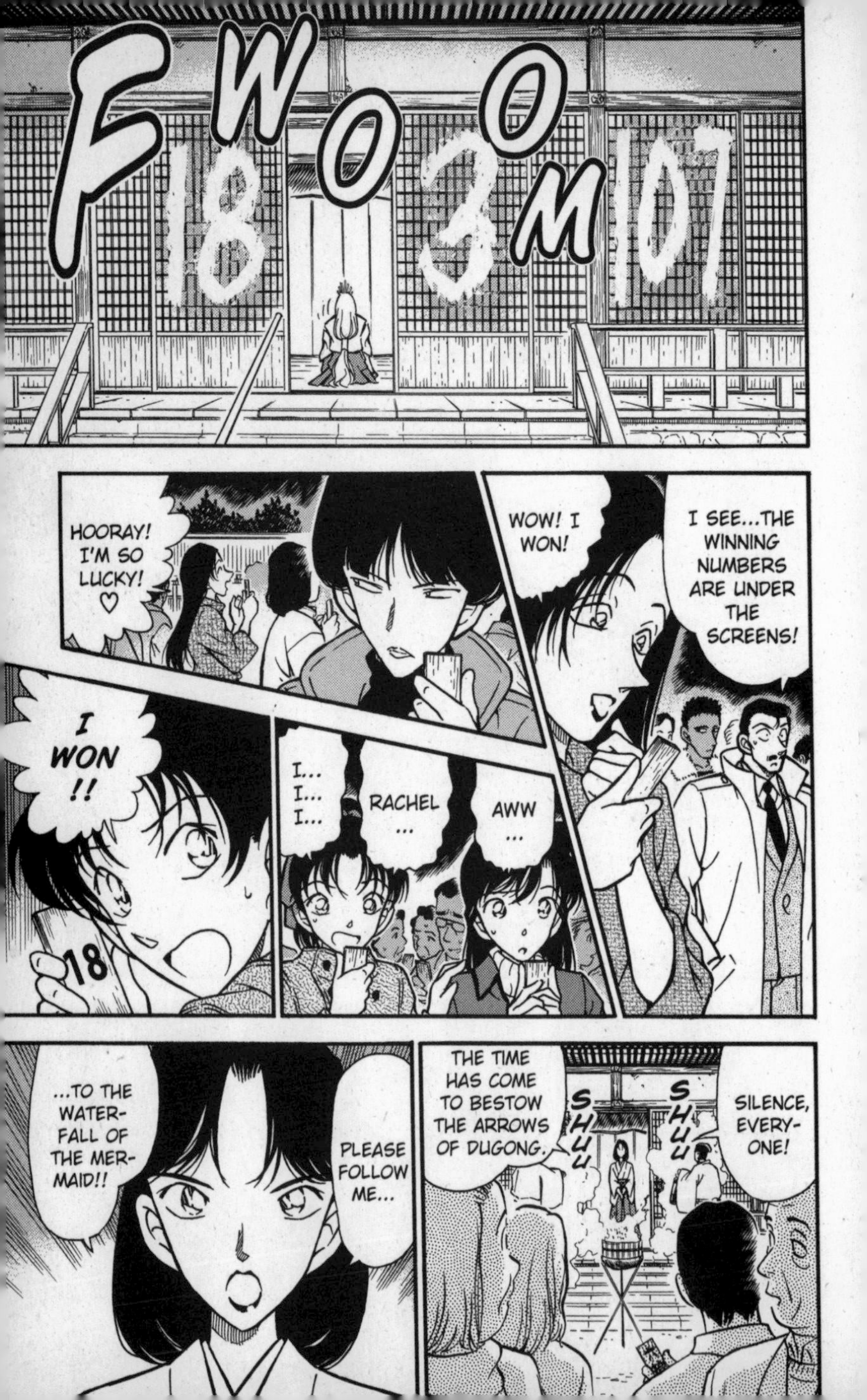
FWOOOM
18
3
107
I SEE...THE WINNING NUMBERS ARE UNDER THE SCREENS!
WOW! I WON!
HOORAY! I'M SO LUCKY! ♡
AWW ...
RACHEL ...
I... I... I...
I WON!!
18
SILENCE, EVERYONE!
SHUU
SHUU
THE TIME HAS COME TO BESTOW THE ARROWS OF DUGONG.
PLEASE FOLLOW ME...
...TO THE WATER-FALL OF THE MER-MAID!!

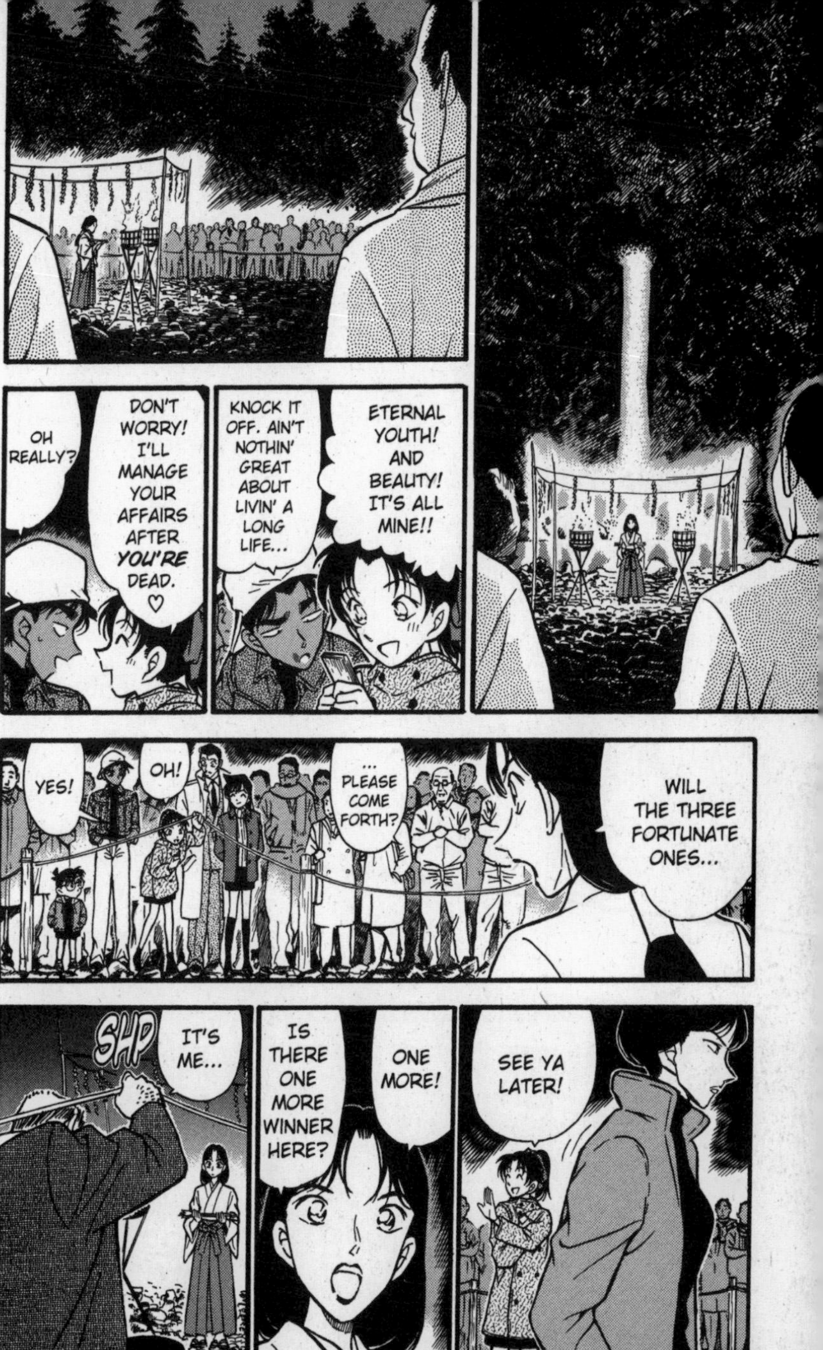
ETERNAL YOUTH! AND BEAUTY! IT'S ALL MINE!!
KNOCK IT OFF. AIN'T NOTHIN' GREAT ABOUT LIVIN' A LONG LIFE...
DON'T WORRY! I'LL MANAGE YOUR AFFAIRS AFTER *YOU'RE* DEAD. ♡
OH REALLY?
WILL THE THREE FORTUNATE ONES...
...PLEASE COME FORTH?
OH!
YES!
SEE YA LATER!
ONE MORE!
IS THERE ONE MORE WINNER HERE?
IT'S ME...
SHP

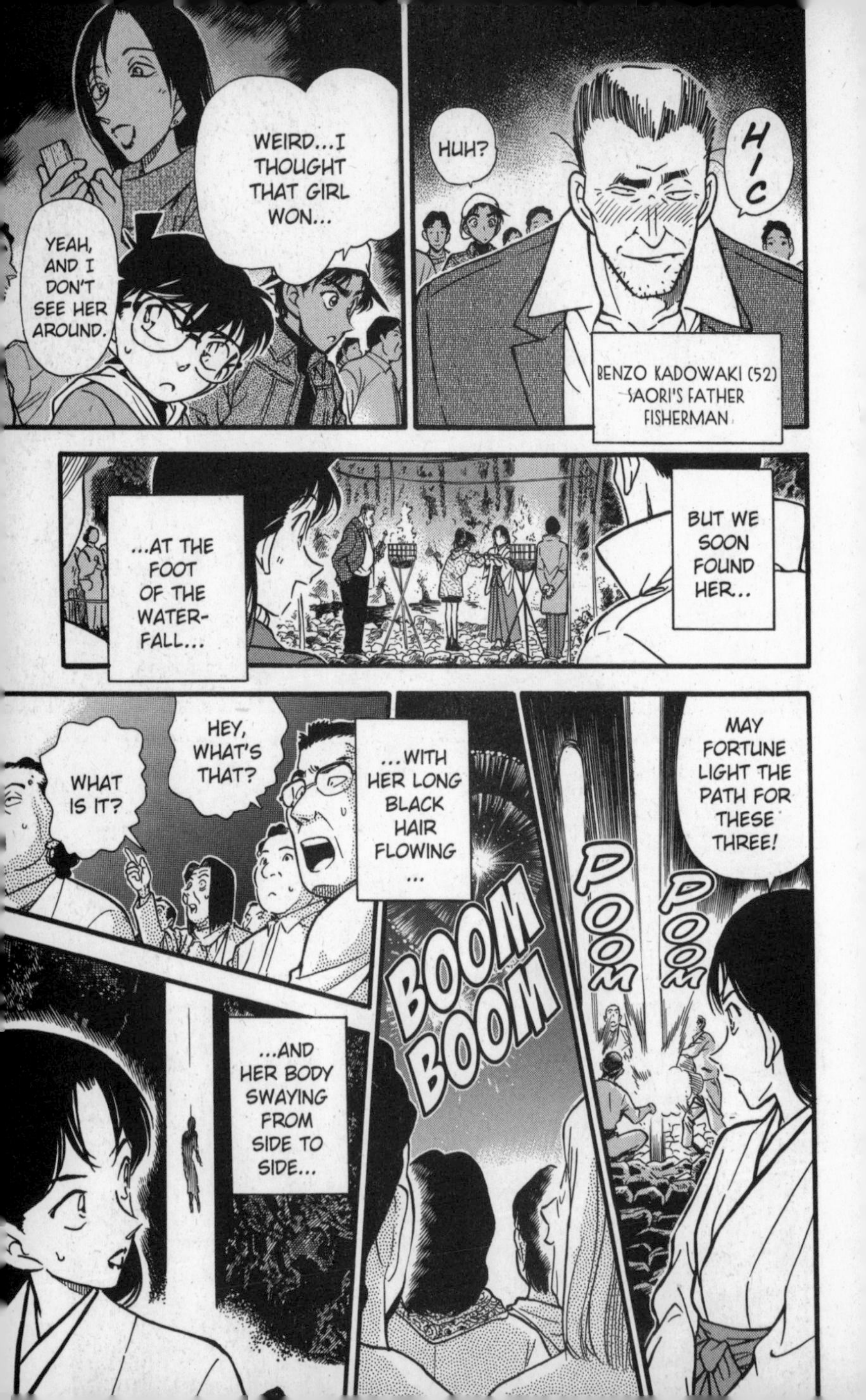
HIC
HUH?
BENZO KADOWAKI (52)
SAORI'S FATHER
FISHERMAN
WEIRD...I THOUGHT THAT GIRL WON...
YEAH, AND I DON'T SEE HER AROUND.
BUT WE SOON FOUND HER...
...AT THE FOOT OF THE WATER-FALL...
MAY FORTUNE LIGHT THE PATH FOR THESE THREE!
POOM POOM
BOOM BOOM
...WITH HER LONG BLACK HAIR FLOWING...
HEY, WHAT'S THAT?
WHAT IS IT?
...AND HER BODY SWAYING FROM SIDE TO SIDE...

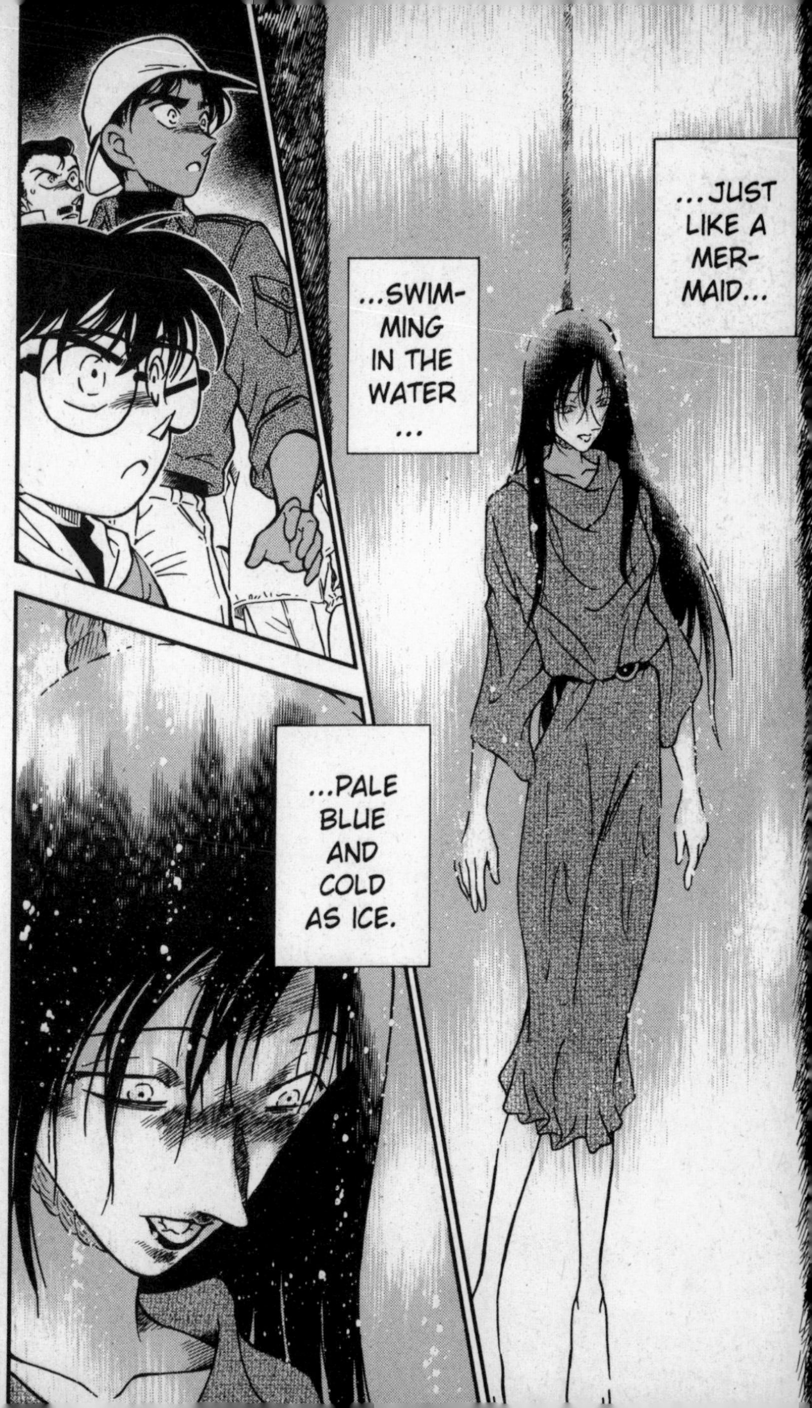
...JUST LIKE A MER-MAID...
...SWIM-MING IN THE WATER ...
...PALE BLUE AND COLD AS ICE.

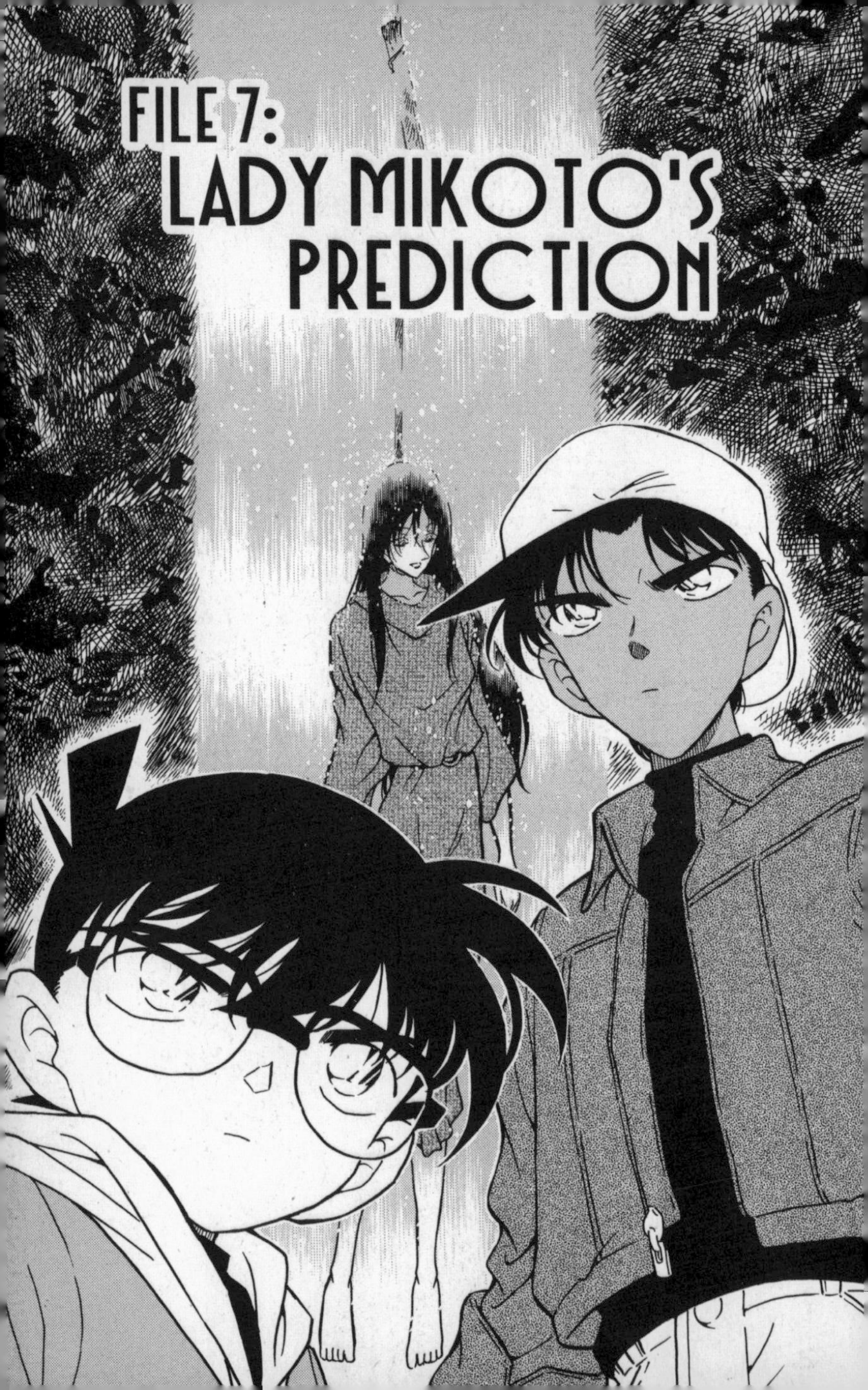
FILE 7:
LADY MIKOTO'S
PREDICTION

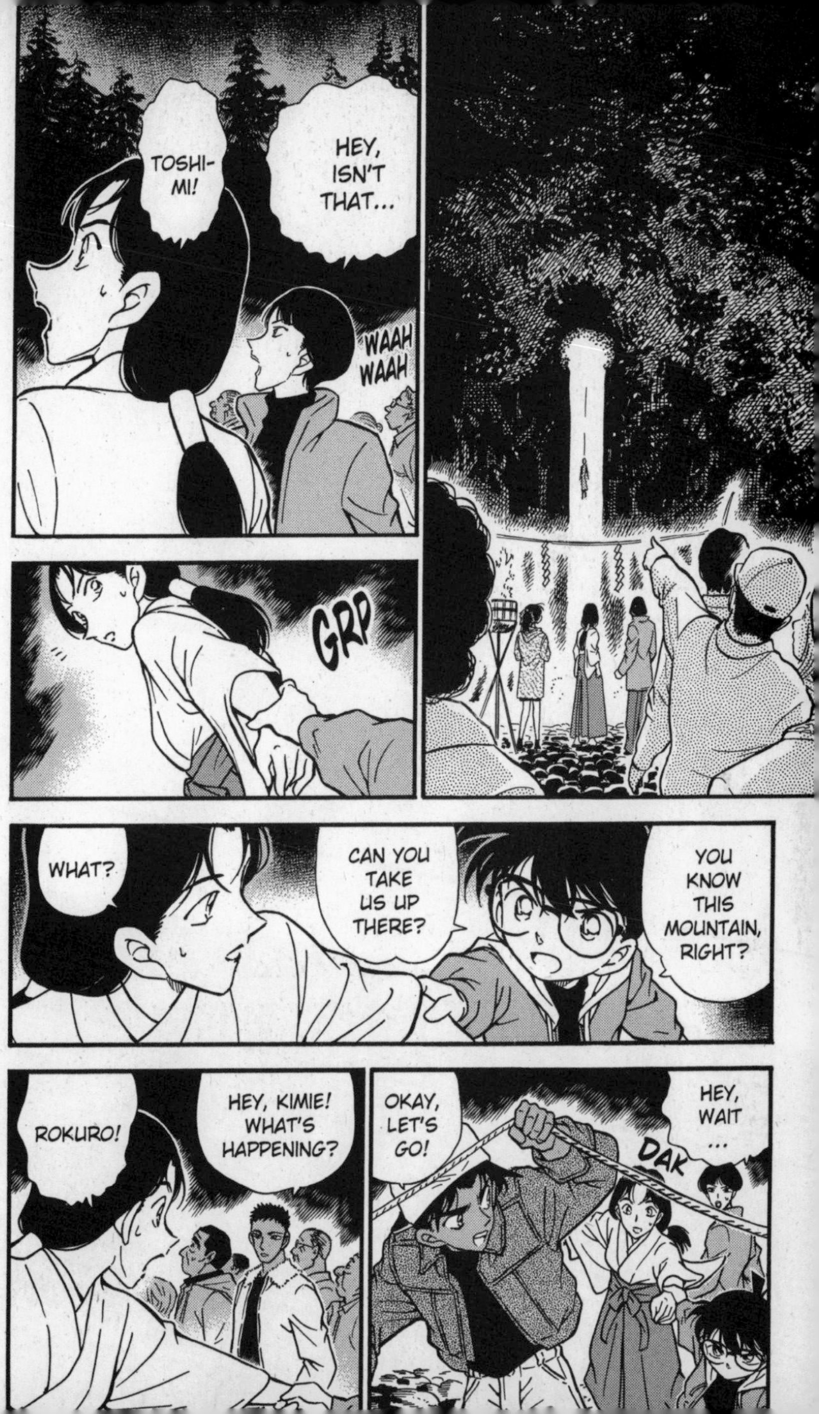
HEY, ISN'T THAT...
TOSHI-MI!
WAAH WAAH
GRP
YOU KNOW THIS MOUNTAIN, RIGHT?
CAN YOU TAKE US UP THERE?
WHAT?
HEY, WAIT ...
DAK
OKAY, LET'S GO!
HEY, KIMIE! WHAT'S HAPPENING?
ROKURO!

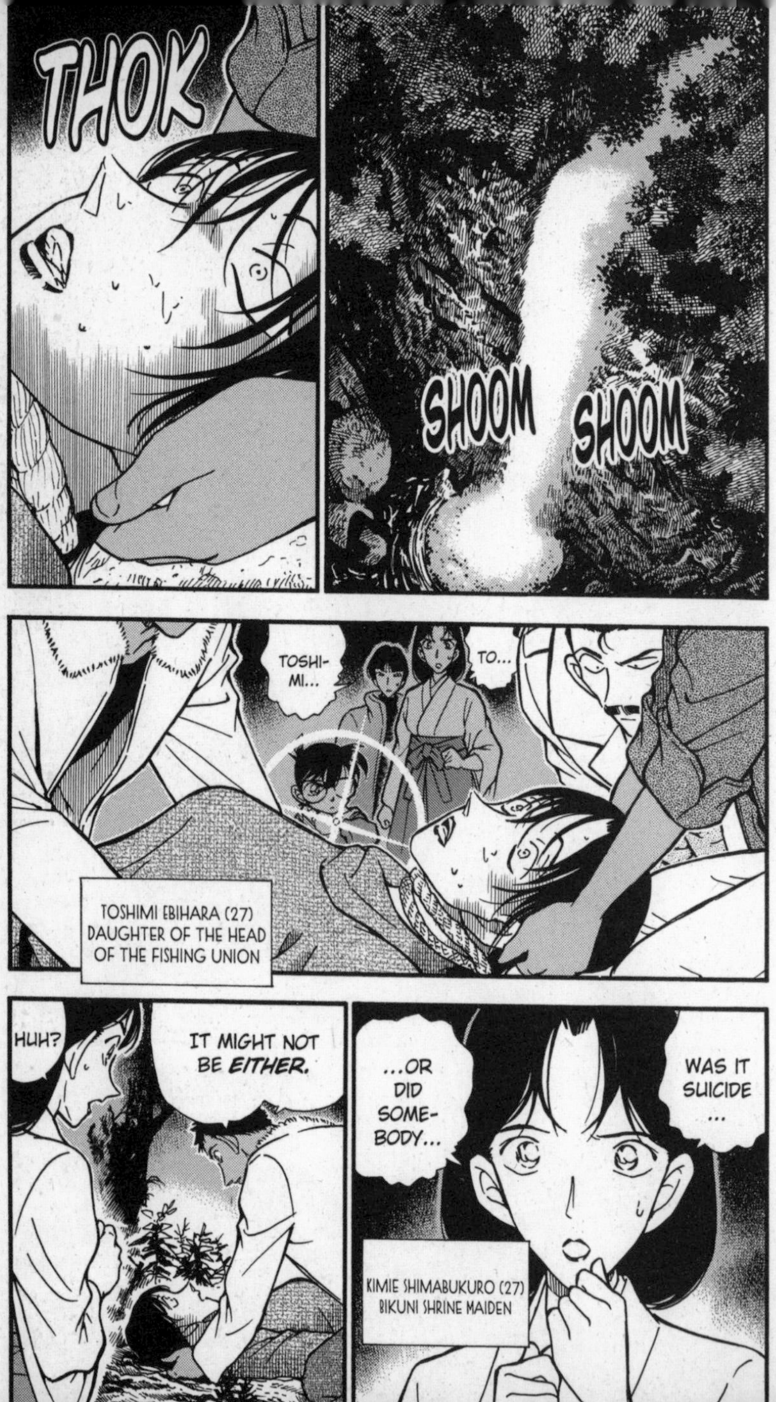
SHOOM
SHOOM
THOK
TO...
TOSHIMI...
TOSHIMI EBIHARA (27) DAUGHTER OF THE HEAD OF THE FISHING UNION
WAS IT SUICIDE...
...OR DID SOMEBODY...
KIMIE SHIMABUKURO (27) BIKUNI SHRINE MAIDEN
IT MIGHT NOT BE *EITHER.*
HUH?

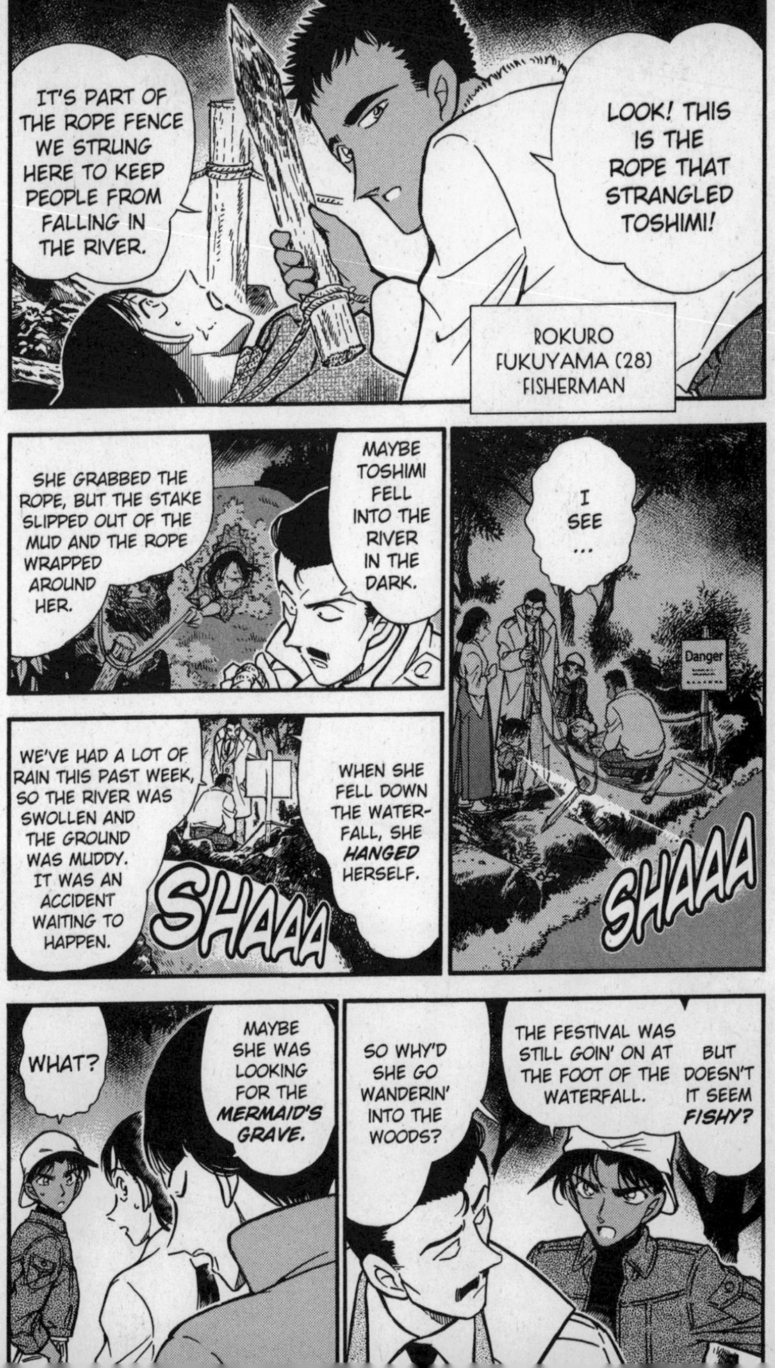
LOOK! THIS IS THE ROPE THAT STRANGLED TOSHIMI!
IT'S PART OF THE ROPE FENCE WE STRUNG HERE TO KEEP PEOPLE FROM FALLING IN THE RIVER.
ROKURO FUKUYAMA (28) FISHERMAN
I SEE ...
Danger
SHAAAA
MAYBE TOSHIMI FELL INTO THE RIVER IN THE DARK.
SHE GRABBED THE ROPE, BUT THE STAKE SLIPPED OUT OF THE MUD AND THE ROPE WRAPPED AROUND HER.
WHEN SHE FELL DOWN THE WATER-FALL, SHE *HANGED* HERSELF.
WE'VE HAD A LOT OF RAIN THIS PAST WEEK, SO THE RIVER WAS SWOLLEN AND THE GROUND WAS MUDDY. IT WAS AN ACCIDENT WAITING TO HAPPEN.
SHAAA
BUT DOESN'T IT SEEM *FISHY?*
THE FESTIVAL WAS STILL GOIN' ON AT THE FOOT OF THE WATERFALL.
SO WHY'D SHE GO WANDERIN' INTO THE WOODS?
MAYBE SHE WAS LOOKING FOR THE *MERMAID'S GRAVE.*
WHAT?

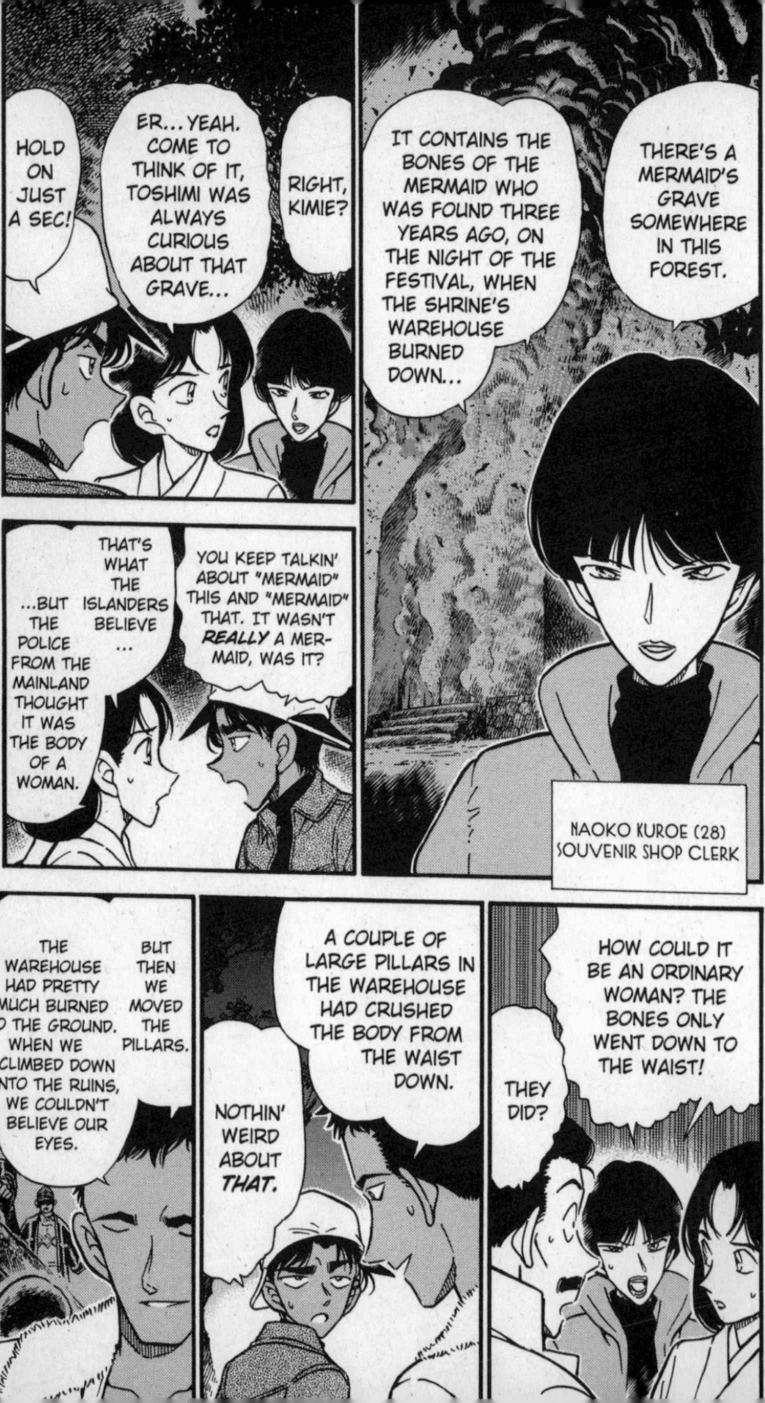
THERE'S A MERMAID'S GRAVE SOMEWHERE IN THIS FOREST.
IT CONTAINS THE BONES OF THE MERMAID WHO WAS FOUND THREE YEARS AGO, ON THE NIGHT OF THE FESTIVAL, WHEN THE SHRINE'S WAREHOUSE BURNED DOWN...
NAOKO KUROE (28) SOUVENIR SHOP CLERK
RIGHT, KIMIE?
ER... YEAH. COME TO THINK OF IT, TOSHIMI WAS ALWAYS CURIOUS ABOUT THAT GRAVE...
HOLD ON JUST A SEC!
YOU KEEP TALKIN' ABOUT "MERMAID" THIS AND "MERMAID" THAT. IT WASN'T REALLY A MERMAID, WAS IT?
THAT'S WHAT THE ISLANDERS BELIEVE...
...BUT THE POLICE FROM THE MAINLAND THOUGHT IT WAS THE BODY OF A WOMAN.
HOW COULD IT BE AN ORDINARY WOMAN? THE BONES ONLY WENT DOWN TO THE WAIST!
THEY DID?
A COUPLE OF LARGE PILLARS IN THE WAREHOUSE HAD CRUSHED THE BODY FROM THE WAIST DOWN.
NOTHIN' WEIRD ABOUT THAT.
BUT THEN WE MOVED THE PILLARS.
THE WAREHOUSE HAD PRETTY MUCH BURNED TO THE GROUND. WHEN WE CLIMBED DOWN INTO THE RUINS, WE COULDN'T BELIEVE OUR EYES.

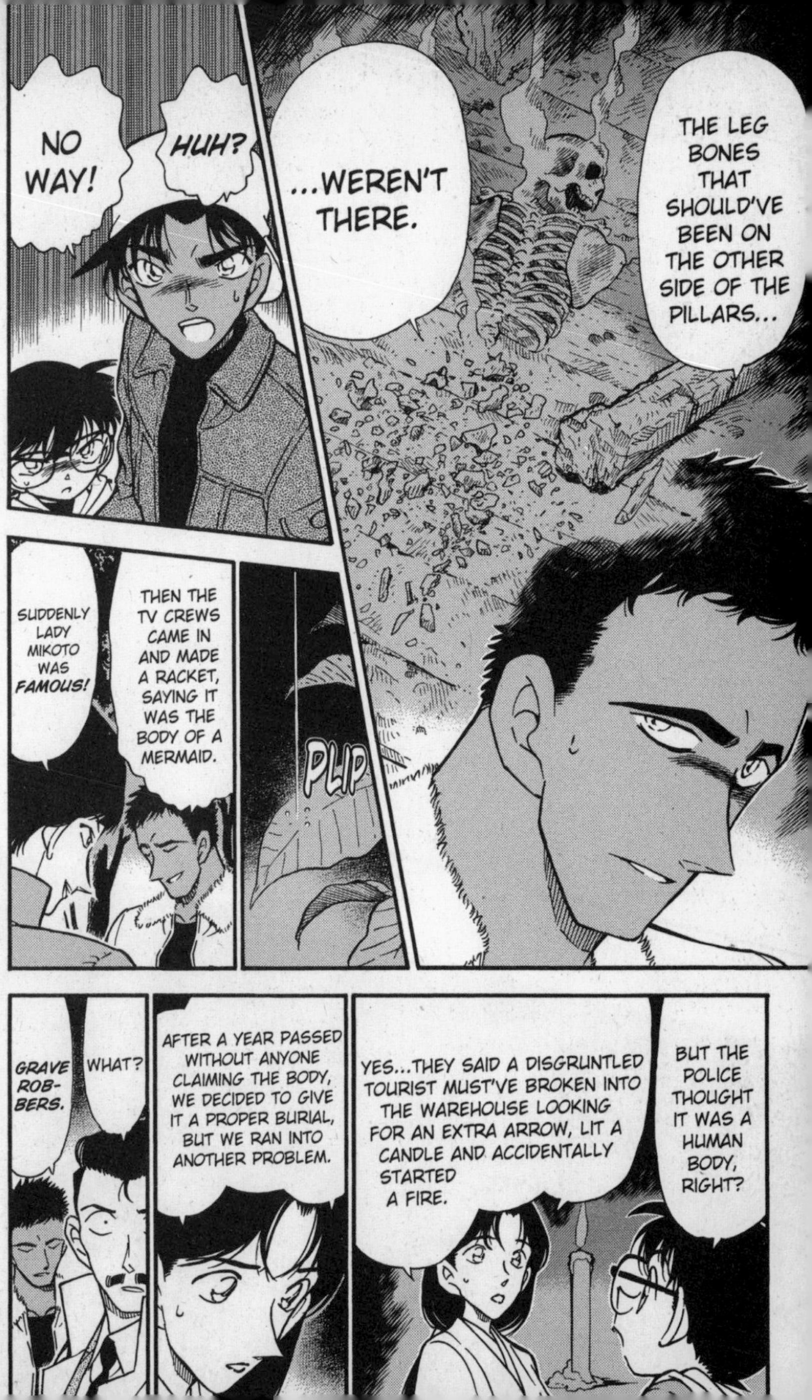
THE LEG BONES THAT SHOULD'VE BEEN ON THE OTHER SIDE OF THE PILLARS...
...WEREN'T THERE.
HUH?
NO WAY!
PLIP
THEN THE TV CREWS CAME IN AND MADE A RACKET, SAYING IT WAS THE BODY OF A MERMAID.
SUDDENLY LADY MIKOTO WAS FAMOUS!
BUT THE POLICE THOUGHT IT WAS A HUMAN BODY, RIGHT?
YES...THEY SAID A DISGRUNTLED TOURIST MUST'VE BROKEN INTO THE WAREHOUSE LOOKING FOR AN EXTRA ARROW, LIT A CANDLE AND ACCIDENTALLY STARTED A FIRE.
AFTER A YEAR PASSED WITHOUT ANYONE CLAIMING THE BODY, WE DECIDED TO GIVE IT A PROPER BURIAL, BUT WE RAN INTO ANOTHER PROBLEM.
WHAT?
GRAVE ROB-BERS.

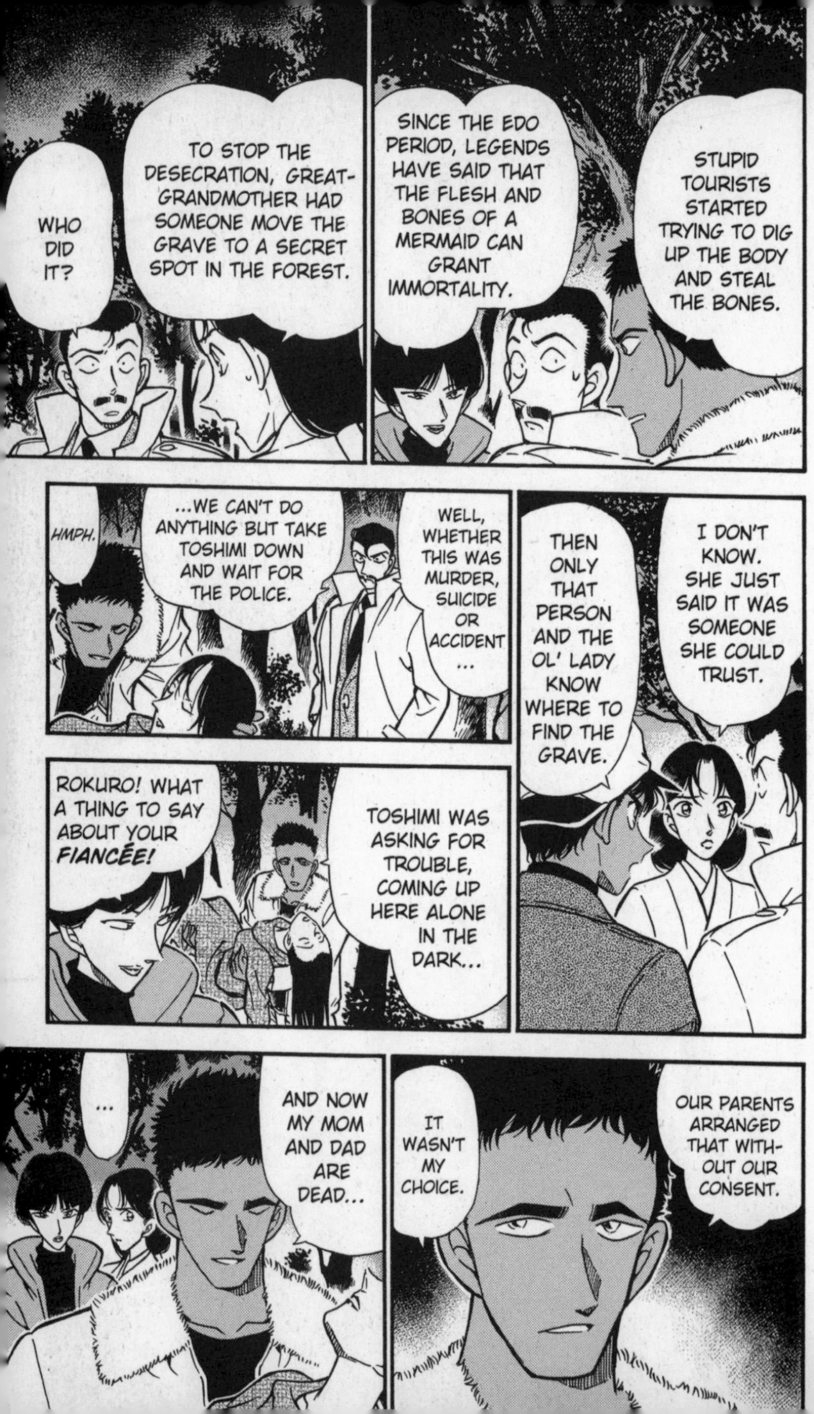
STUPID TOURISTS STARTED TRYING TO DIG UP THE BODY AND STEAL THE BONES.
SINCE THE EDO PERIOD, LEGENDS HAVE SAID THAT THE FLESH AND BONES OF A MERMAID CAN GRANT IMMORTALITY.
TO STOP THE DESECRATION, GREAT-GRANDMOTHER HAD SOMEONE MOVE THE GRAVE TO A SECRET SPOT IN THE FOREST.
WHO DID IT?
I DON'T KNOW. SHE JUST SAID IT WAS SOMEONE SHE COULD TRUST.
THEN ONLY THAT PERSON AND THE OL' LADY KNOW WHERE TO FIND THE GRAVE.
WELL, WHETHER THIS WAS MURDER, SUICIDE OR ACCIDENT...
...WE CAN'T DO ANYTHING BUT TAKE TOSHIMI DOWN AND WAIT FOR THE POLICE.
HMPH.
TOSHIMI WAS ASKING FOR TROUBLE, COMING UP HERE ALONE IN THE DARK...
ROKURO! WHAT A THING TO SAY ABOUT YOUR FIANCÉE!
OUR PARENTS ARRANGED THAT WITHOUT OUR CONSENT.
IT WASN'T MY CHOICE.
AND NOW MY MOM AND DAD ARE DEAD...
...

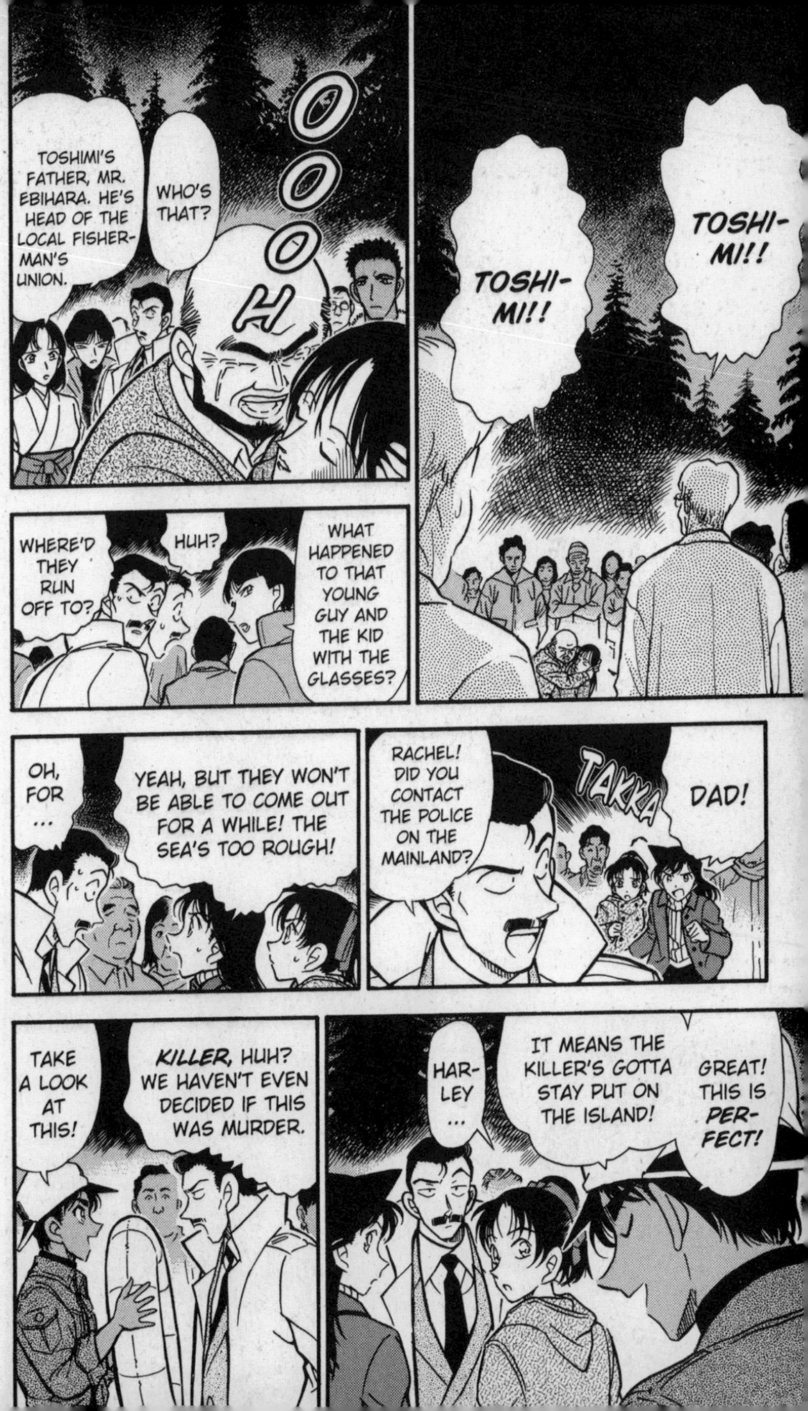
TOSHI-MI!!
TOSHI-MI!!
OOOOH
WHO'S THAT?
TOSHIMI'S FATHER, MR. EBIHARA. HE'S HEAD OF THE LOCAL FISHER-MAN'S UNION.
WHAT HAPPENED TO THAT YOUNG GUY AND THE KID WITH THE GLASSES?
HUH?
WHERE'D THEY RUN OFF TO?
DAD!
TAKKA
RACHEL! DID YOU CONTACT THE POLICE ON THE MAINLAND?
YEAH, BUT THEY WON'T BE ABLE TO COME OUT FOR A WHILE! THE SEA'S TOO ROUGH!
OH, FOR ...
GREAT! THIS IS PER-FECT!
IT MEANS THE KILLER'S GOTTA STAY PUT ON THE ISLAND!
HAR-LEY ...
KILLER, HUH? WE HAVEN'T EVEN DECIDED IF THIS WAS MURDER.
TAKE A LOOK AT THIS!

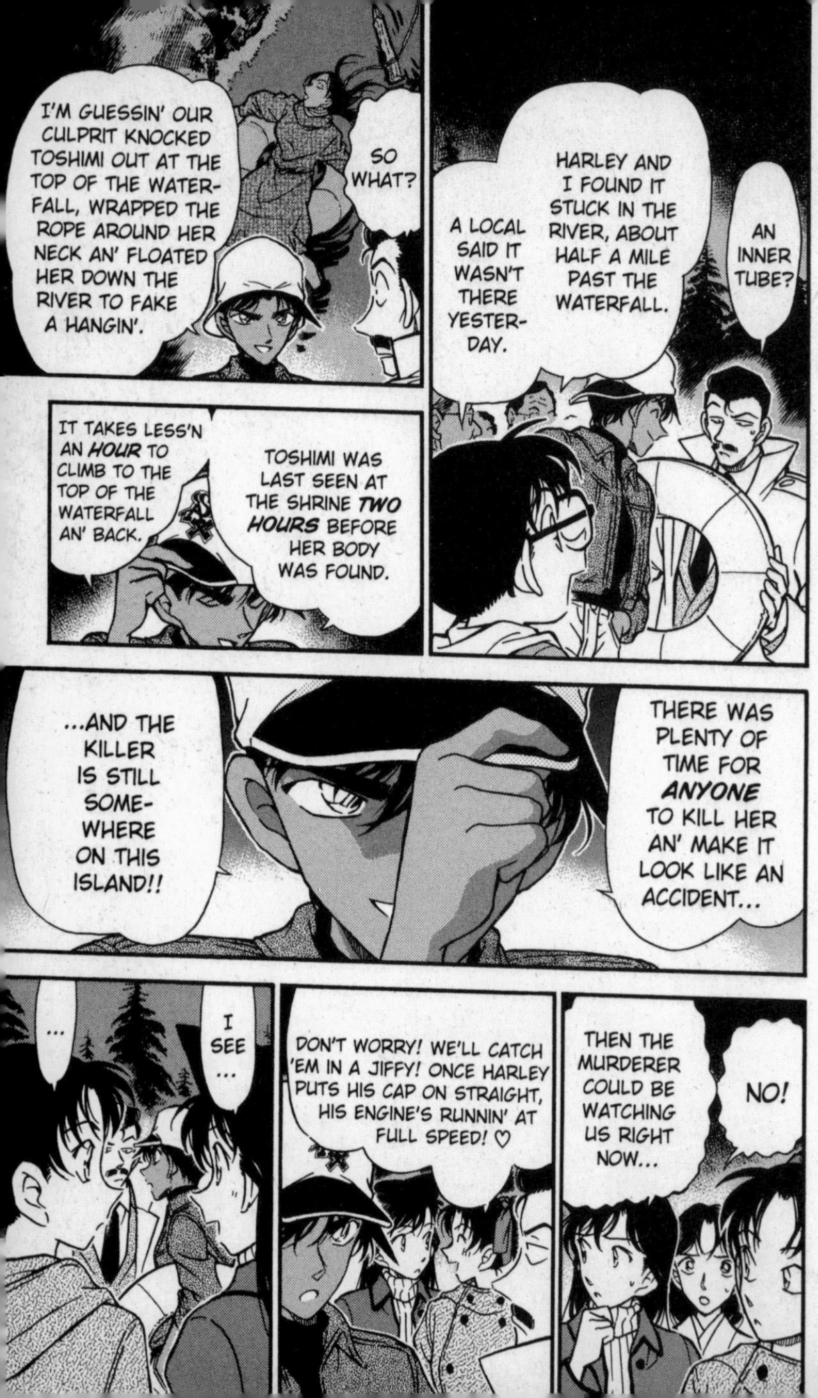
AN INNER TUBE?
HARLEY AND I FOUND IT STUCK IN THE RIVER, ABOUT HALF A MILE PAST THE WATERFALL.
A LOCAL SAID IT WASN'T THERE YESTERDAY.
SO WHAT?
I'M GUESSIN' OUR CULPRIT KNOCKED TOSHIMI OUT AT THE TOP OF THE WATERFALL, WRAPPED THE ROPE AROUND HER NECK AN' FLOATED HER DOWN THE RIVER TO FAKE A HANGIN'.
TOSHIMI WAS LAST SEEN AT THE SHRINE *TWO HOURS* BEFORE HER BODY WAS FOUND.
IT TAKES LESS'N AN *HOUR* TO CLIMB TO THE TOP OF THE WATERFALL AN' BACK.
THERE WAS PLENTY OF TIME FOR *ANYONE* TO KILL HER AN' MAKE IT LOOK LIKE AN ACCIDENT...
...AND THE KILLER IS STILL SOMEWHERE ON THIS ISLAND!!
NO!
THEN THE MURDERER COULD BE WATCHING US RIGHT NOW...
DON'T WORRY! WE'LL CATCH 'EM IN A JIFFY! ONCE HARLEY PUTS HIS CAP ON STRAIGHT, HIS ENGINE'S RUNNIN' AT FULL SPEED! ♡
I SEE...
...

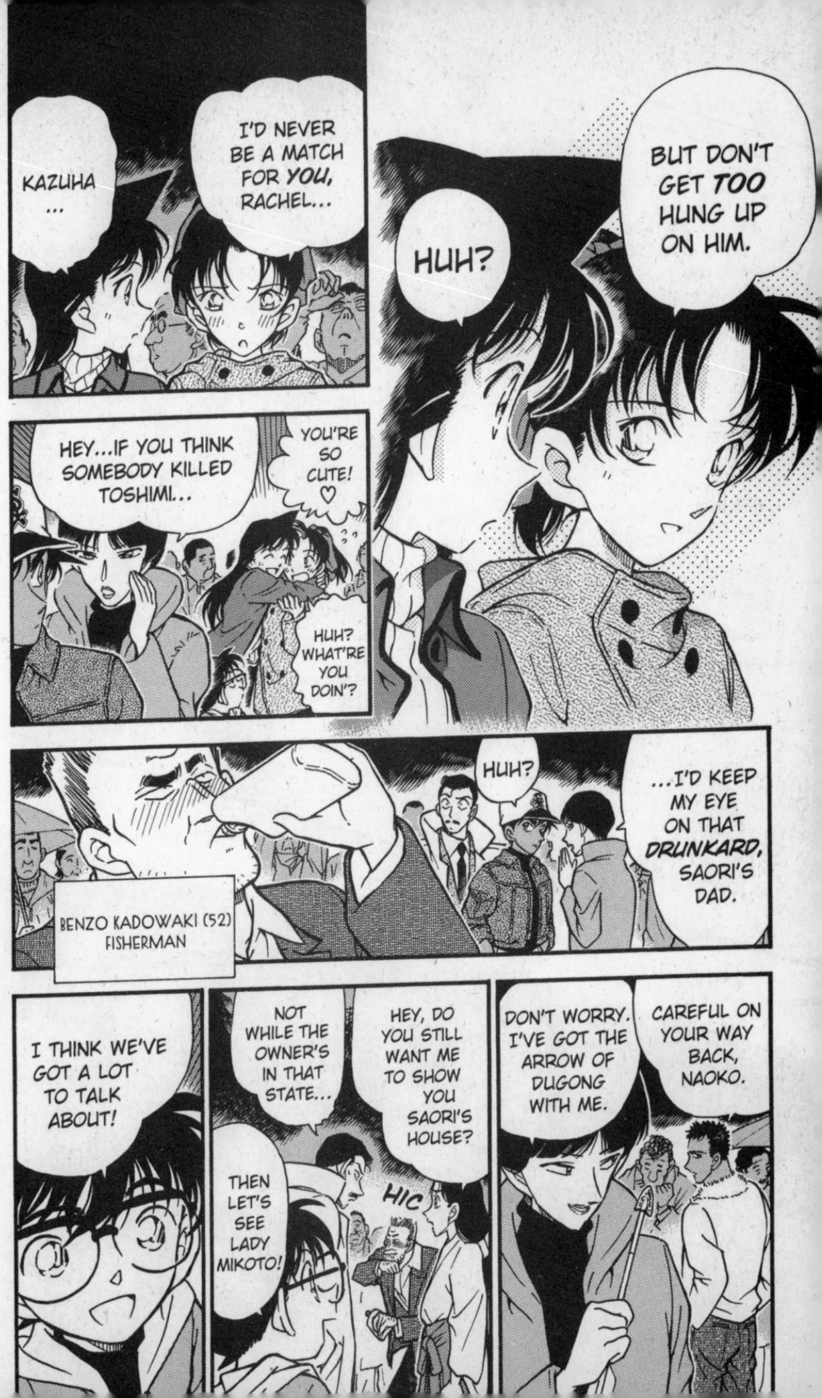
BUT DON'T GET *TOO* HUNG UP ON HIM.
HUH?
I'D NEVER BE A MATCH FOR *YOU*, RACHEL...
KAZUHA ...
HEY...IF YOU THINK SOMEBODY KILLED TOSHIMI...
YOU'RE SO CUTE! ♡
HUH? WHAT'RE YOU DOIN'?
...I'D KEEP MY EYE ON THAT *DRUNKARD*, SAORI'S DAD.
HUH?
BENZO KADOWAKI (52) FISHERMAN
CAREFUL ON YOUR WAY BACK, NAOKO.
DON'T WORRY. I'VE GOT THE ARROW OF DUGONG WITH ME.
HEY, DO YOU STILL WANT ME TO SHOW YOU SAORI'S HOUSE?
NOT WHILE THE OWNER'S IN THAT STATE...
HIC
THEN LET'S SEE LADY MIKOTO!
I THINK WE'VE GOT A LOT TO TALK ABOUT!

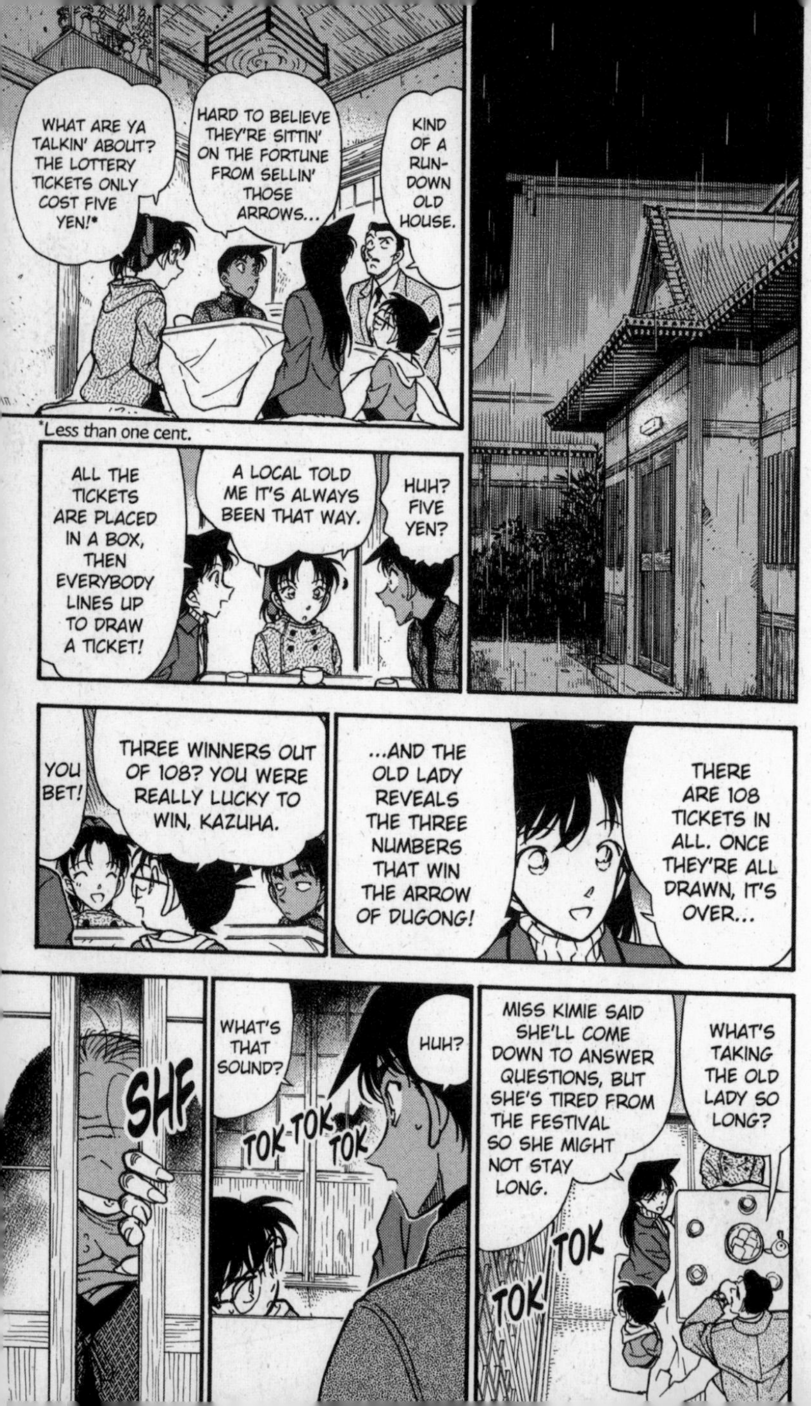
KIND OF A RUN-DOWN OLD HOUSE.
HARD TO BELIEVE THEY'RE SITTIN' ON THE FORTUNE FROM SELLIN' THOSE ARROWS...
WHAT ARE YA TALKIN' ABOUT? THE LOTTERY TICKETS ONLY COST FIVE YEN!*
HUH? FIVE YEN?
A LOCAL TOLD ME IT'S ALWAYS BEEN THAT WAY.
ALL THE TICKETS ARE PLACED IN A BOX, THEN EVERYBODY LINES UP TO DRAW A TICKET!
THERE ARE 108 TICKETS IN ALL. ONCE THEY'RE ALL DRAWN, IT'S OVER...
...AND THE OLD LADY REVEALS THE THREE NUMBERS THAT WIN THE ARROW OF DUGONG!
THREE WINNERS OUT OF 108? YOU WERE REALLY LUCKY TO WIN, KAZUHA.
YOU BET!
WHAT'S TAKING THE OLD LADY SO LONG?
MISS KIMIE SAID SHE'LL COME DOWN TO ANSWER QUESTIONS, BUT SHE'S TIRED FROM THE FESTIVAL SO SHE MIGHT NOT STAY LONG.
TOK
TOK
HUH?
WHAT'S THAT SOUND?
TOK-TOK
TOK
SHF
*Less than one cent.

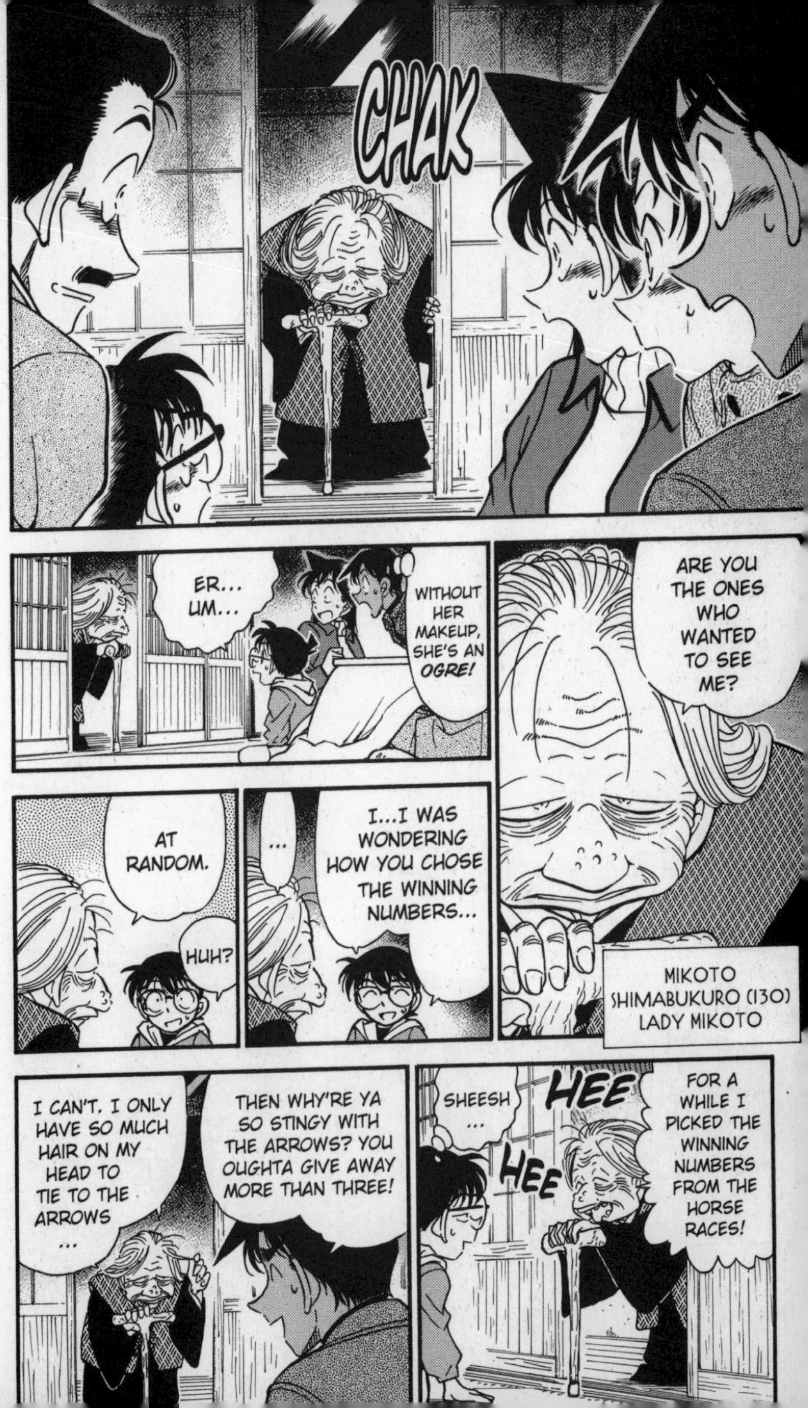
CHAK
ARE YOU THE ONES WHO WANTED TO SEE ME?
MIKOTO SHIMABUKURO (130) LADY MIKOTO
WITHOUT HER MAKEUP, SHE'S AN *OGRE!*
ER... UM...
I...I WAS WONDERING HOW YOU CHOSE THE WINNING NUMBERS...
...
AT RANDOM.
HUH?
FOR A WHILE I PICKED THE WINNING NUMBERS FROM THE HORSE RACES!
HEE
HEE
SHEESH ...
THEN WHY'RE YA SO STINGY WITH THE ARROWS? YOU OUGHTA GIVE AWAY MORE THAN THREE!
I CAN'T. I ONLY HAVE SO MUCH HAIR ON MY HEAD TO TIE TO THE ARROWS ...

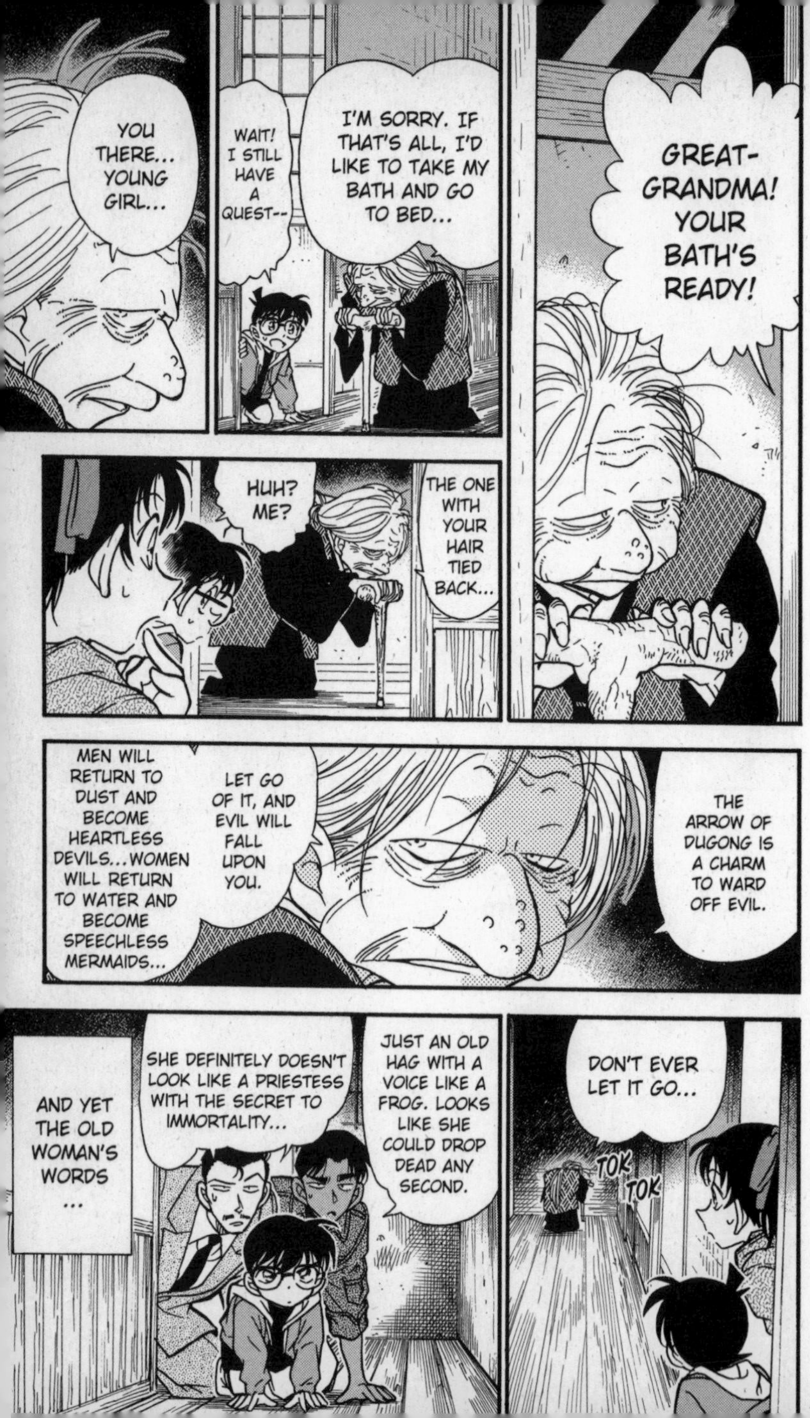
GREAT-GRANDMA! YOUR BATH'S READY!
I'M SORRY. IF THAT'S ALL, I'D LIKE TO TAKE MY BATH AND GO TO BED...
WAIT! I STILL HAVE A QUEST--
YOU THERE... YOUNG GIRL...
HUH? ME?
THE ONE WITH YOUR HAIR TIED BACK...
THE ARROW OF DUGONG IS A CHARM TO WARD OFF EVIL.
LET GO OF IT, AND EVIL WILL FALL UPON YOU.
MEN WILL RETURN TO DUST AND BECOME HEARTLESS DEVILS...WOMEN WILL RETURN TO WATER AND BECOME SPEECHLESS MERMAIDS...
DON'T EVER LET IT GO...
TOK
TOK
JUST AN OLD HAG WITH A VOICE LIKE A FROG. LOOKS LIKE SHE COULD DROP DEAD ANY SECOND.
SHE DEFINITELY DOESN'T LOOK LIKE A PRIESTESS WITH THE SECRET TO IMMORTALITY...
AND YET THE OLD WOMAN'S WORDS ...

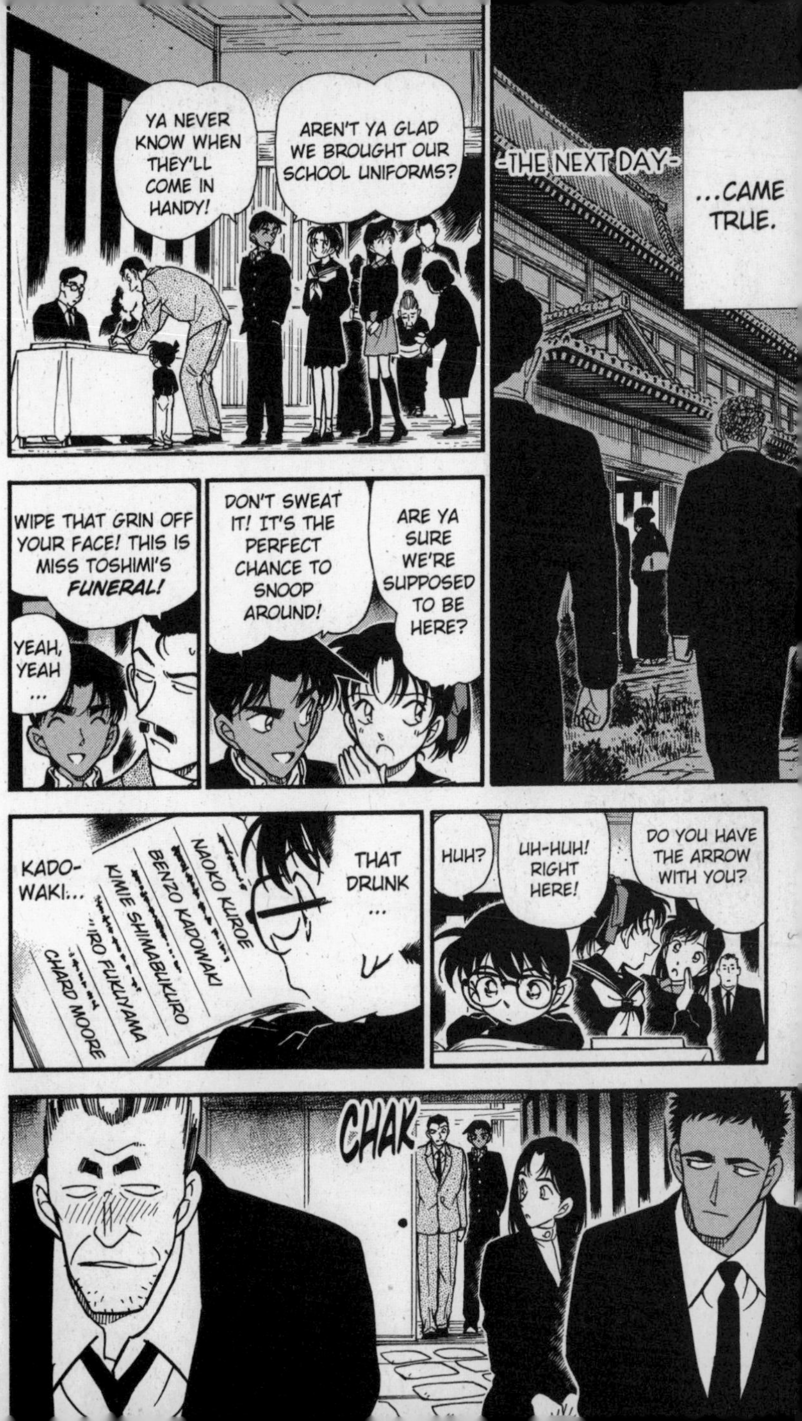
-THE NEXT DAY-
...CAME TRUE.
AREN'T YA GLAD WE BROUGHT OUR SCHOOL UNIFORMS?
YA NEVER KNOW WHEN THEY'LL COME IN HANDY!
ARE YA SURE WE'RE SUPPOSED TO BE HERE?
DON'T SWEAT IT! IT'S THE PERFECT CHANCE TO SNOOP AROUND!
WIPE THAT GRIN OFF YOUR FACE! THIS IS MISS TOSHIMI'S FUNERAL!
YEAH, YEAH ...
DO YOU HAVE THE ARROW WITH YOU?
UH-HUH! RIGHT HERE!
HUH?
THAT DRUNK ...
NAOKO KUROE
BENZO KADOWAKI
KIMIE SHIMABUKURO
...IRO FUKUYAMA
CHARD MOORE
KADO-WAKI...
CHAK

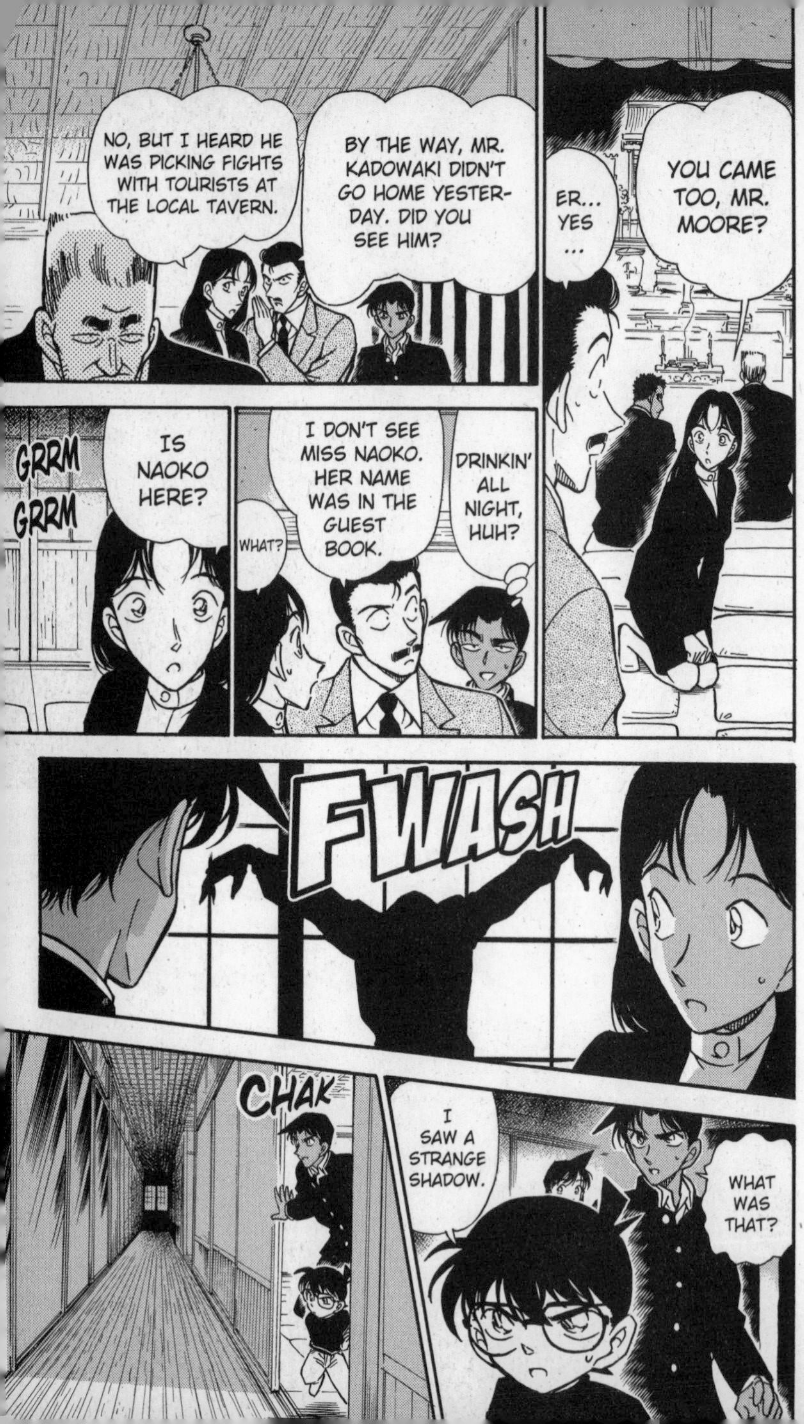
YOU CAME TOO, MR. MOORE?
ER... YES ...
BY THE WAY, MR. KADOWAKI DIDN'T GO HOME YESTERDAY. DID YOU SEE HIM?
NO, BUT I HEARD HE WAS PICKING FIGHTS WITH TOURISTS AT THE LOCAL TAVERN.
I DON'T SEE MISS NAOKO. HER NAME WAS IN THE GUEST BOOK.
DRINKIN' ALL NIGHT, HUH?
WHAT?
IS NAOKO HERE?
GRRM GRRM
FWASH
WHAT WAS THAT?
I SAW A STRANGE SHADOW.
CHAK

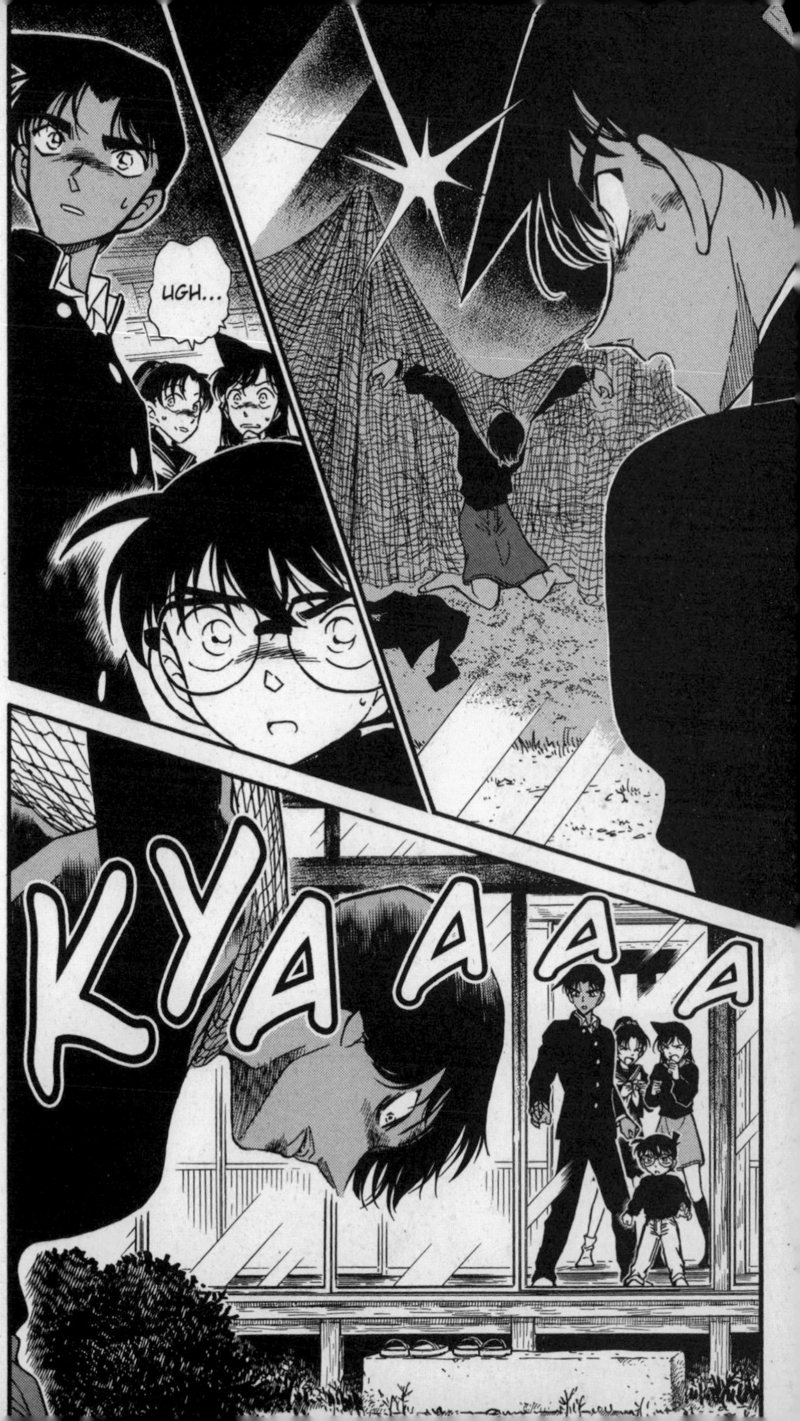
UGH...
KYAAAA

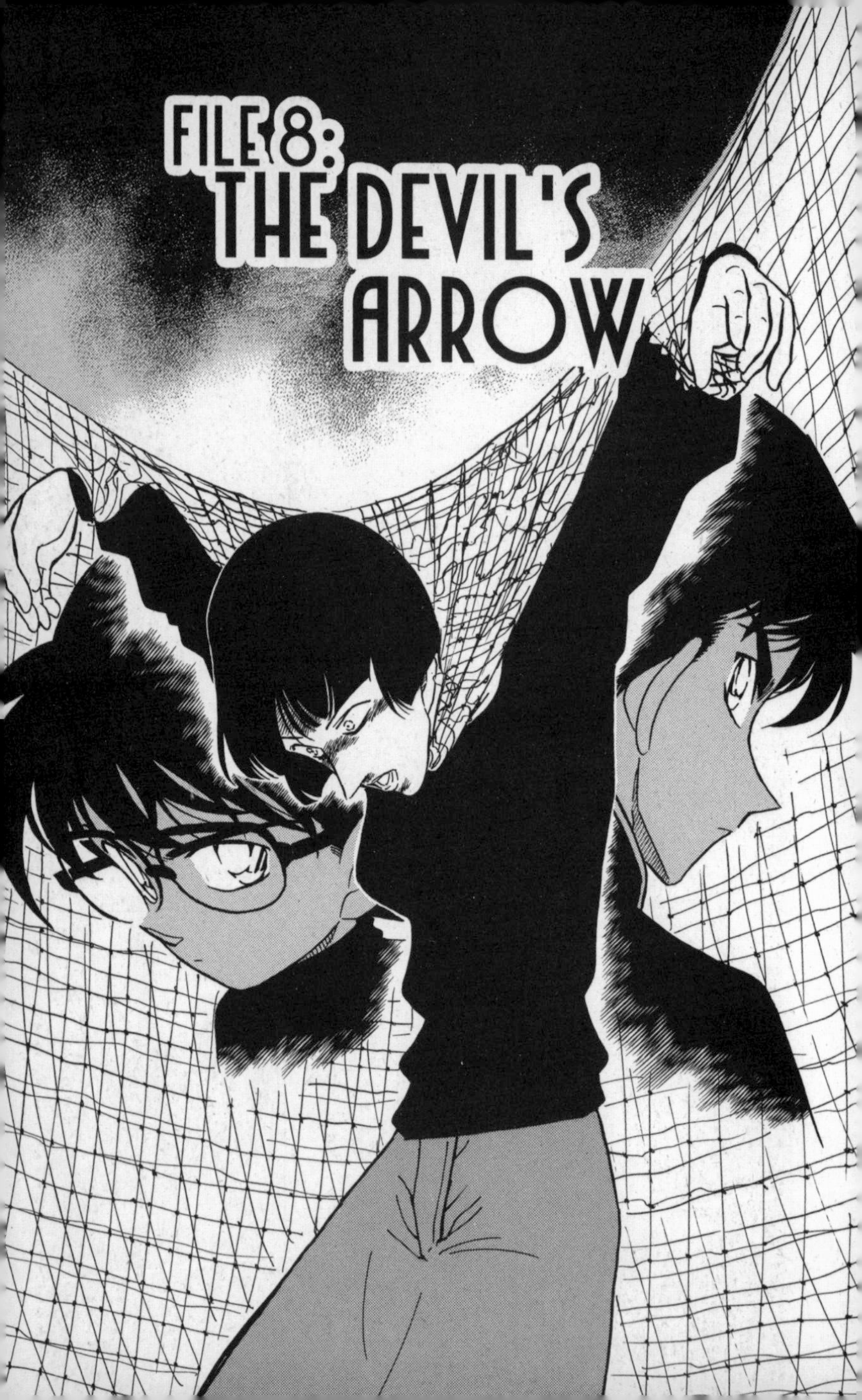
FILE 8:
THE DEVIL'S ARROW

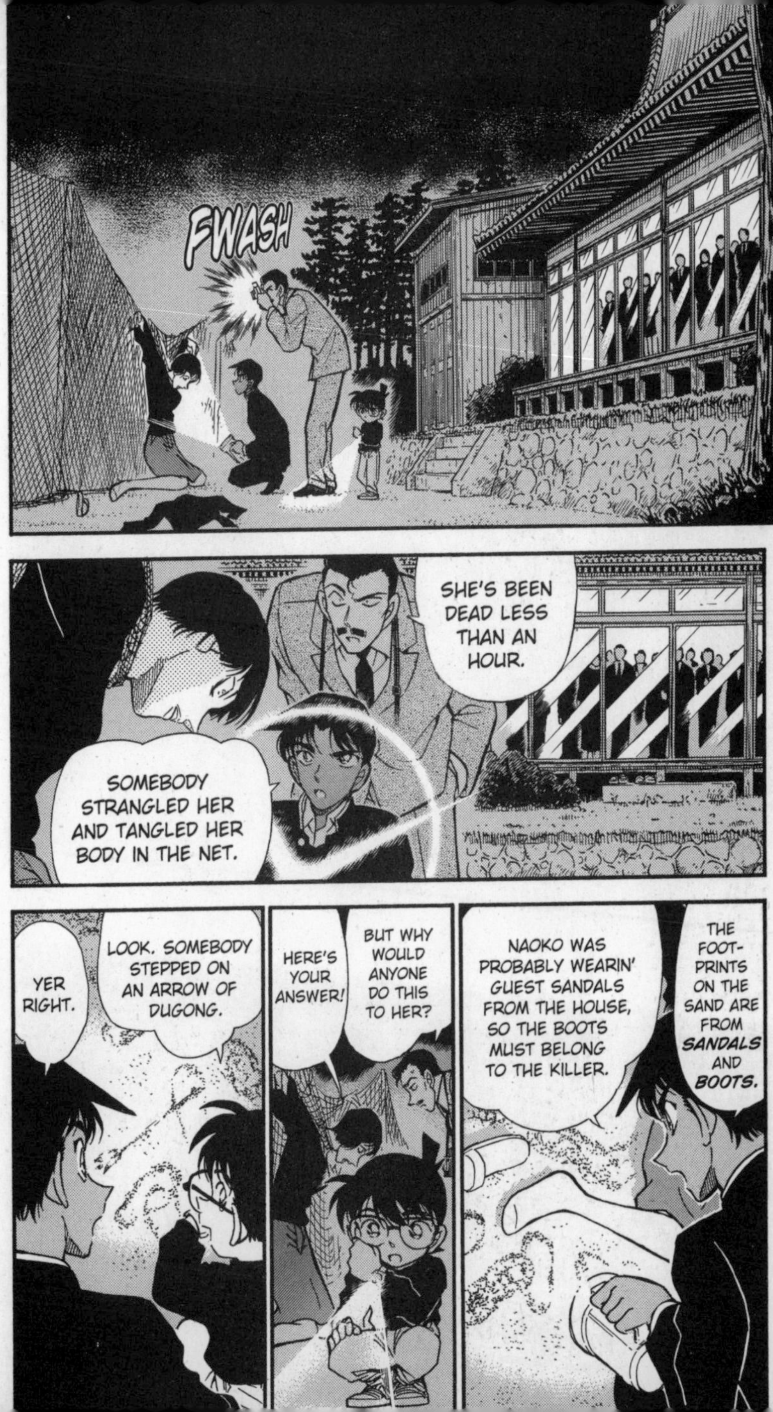
FWASH
SHE'S BEEN DEAD LESS THAN AN HOUR.
SOMEBODY STRANGLED HER AND TANGLED HER BODY IN THE NET.
THE FOOT-PRINTS ON THE SAND ARE FROM SANDALS AND BOOTS.
NAOKO WAS PROBABLY WEARIN' GUEST SANDALS FROM THE HOUSE, SO THE BOOTS MUST BELONG TO THE KILLER.
BUT WHY WOULD ANYONE DO THIS TO HER?
HERE'S YOUR ANSWER!
LOOK. SOMEBODY STEPPED ON AN ARROW OF DUGONG.
YER RIGHT.

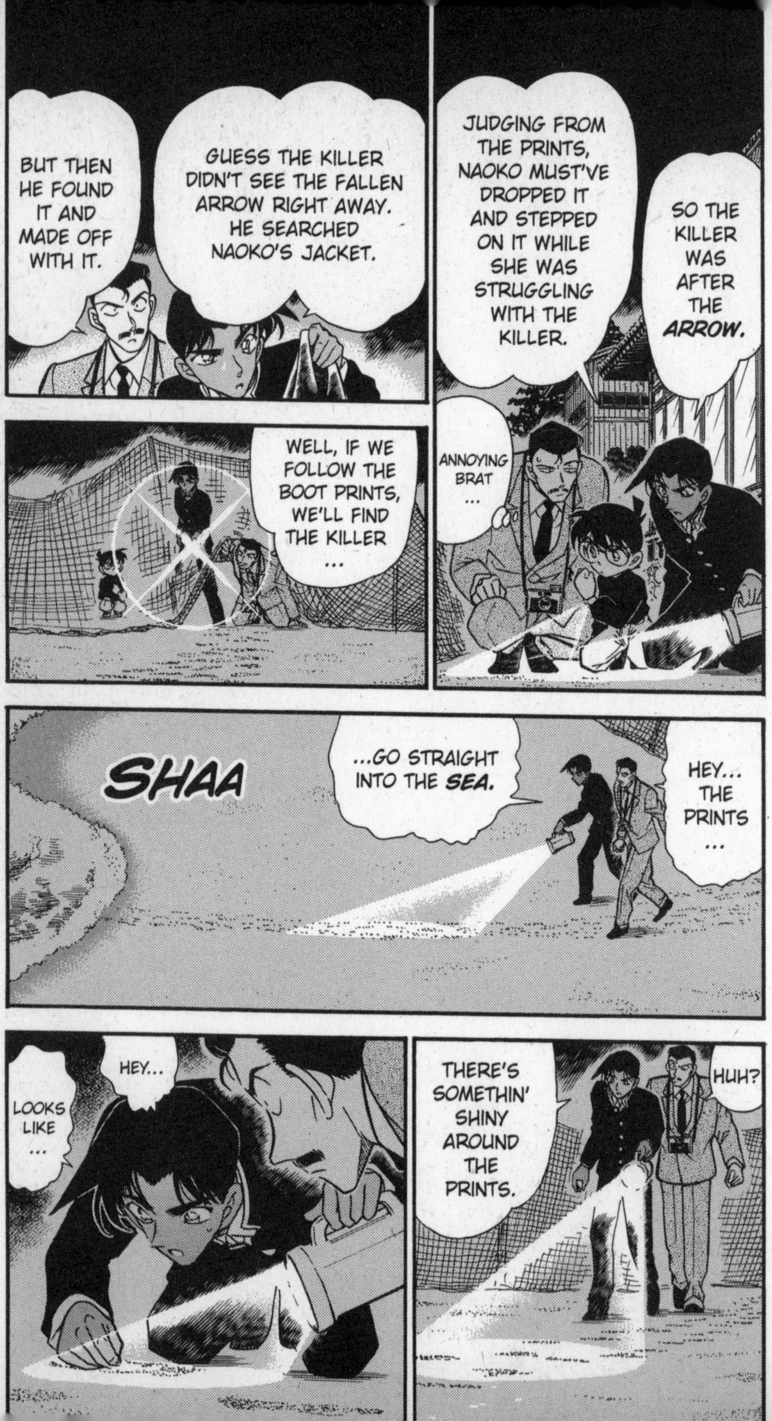
SO THE KILLER WAS AFTER THE *ARROW.*
JUDGING FROM THE PRINTS, NAOKO MUST'VE DROPPED IT AND STEPPED ON IT WHILE SHE WAS STRUGGLING WITH THE KILLER.
GUESS THE KILLER DIDN'T SEE THE FALLEN ARROW RIGHT AWAY. HE SEARCHED NAOKO'S JACKET.
BUT THEN HE FOUND IT AND MADE OFF WITH IT.
ANNOYING BRAT ...
WELL, IF WE FOLLOW THE BOOT PRINTS, WE'LL FIND THE KILLER ...
HEY... THE PRINTS ...
...GO STRAIGHT INTO THE *SEA.*
SHAA
HUH?
THERE'S SOMETHIN' SHINY AROUND THE PRINTS.
HEY...
LOOKS LIKE ...

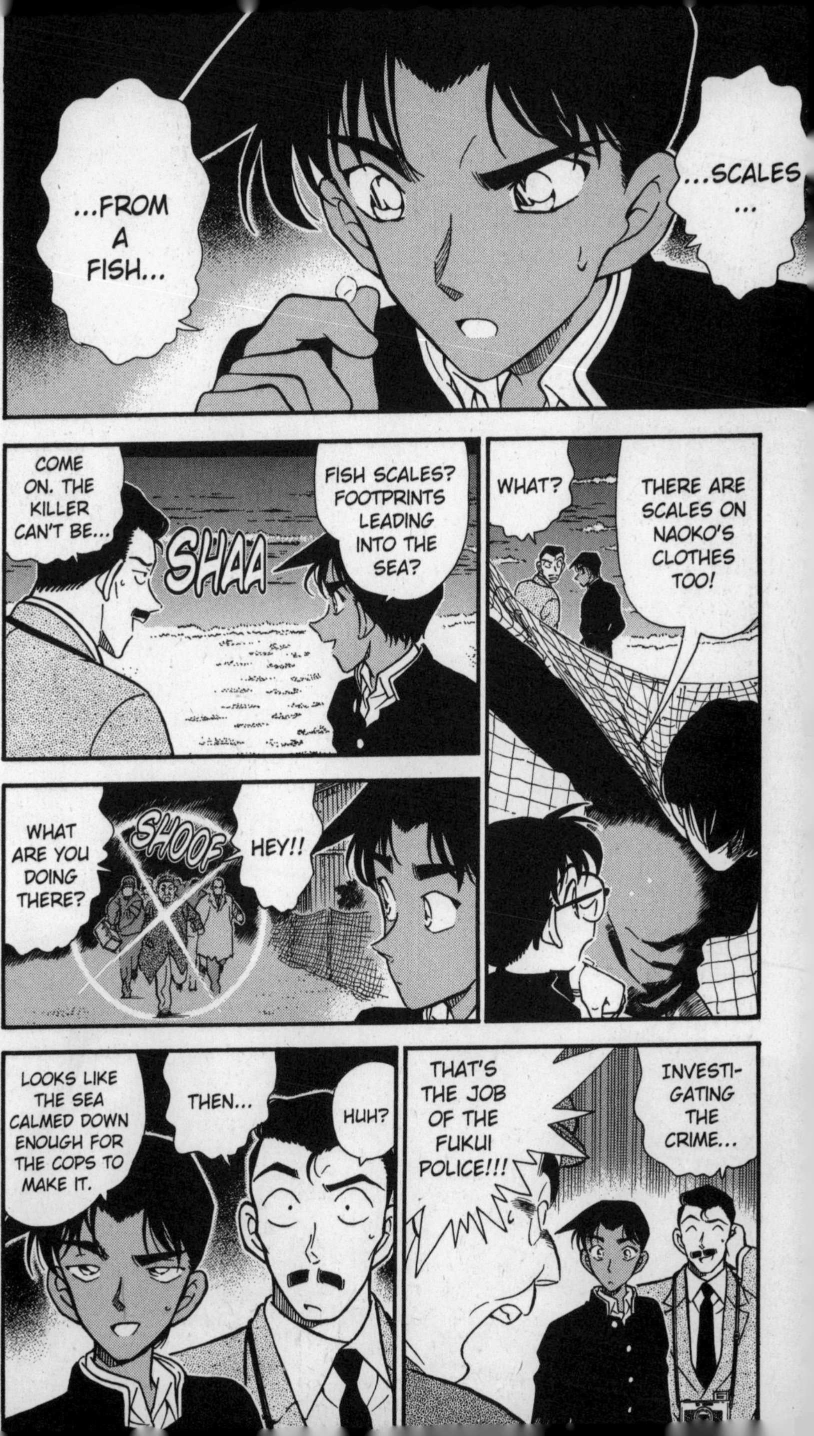
...SCALES ...
...FROM A FISH...
THERE ARE SCALES ON NAOKO'S CLOTHES TOO!
WHAT?
FISH SCALES? FOOTPRINTS LEADING INTO THE SEA?
SHAA
COME ON. THE KILLER CAN'T BE...
HEY!!
SHOOF
WHAT ARE YOU DOING THERE?
INVESTI-GATING THE CRIME...
THAT'S THE JOB OF THE FUKUI POLICE!!!
HUH?
THEN...
LOOKS LIKE THE SEA CALMED DOWN ENOUGH FOR THE COPS TO MAKE IT.

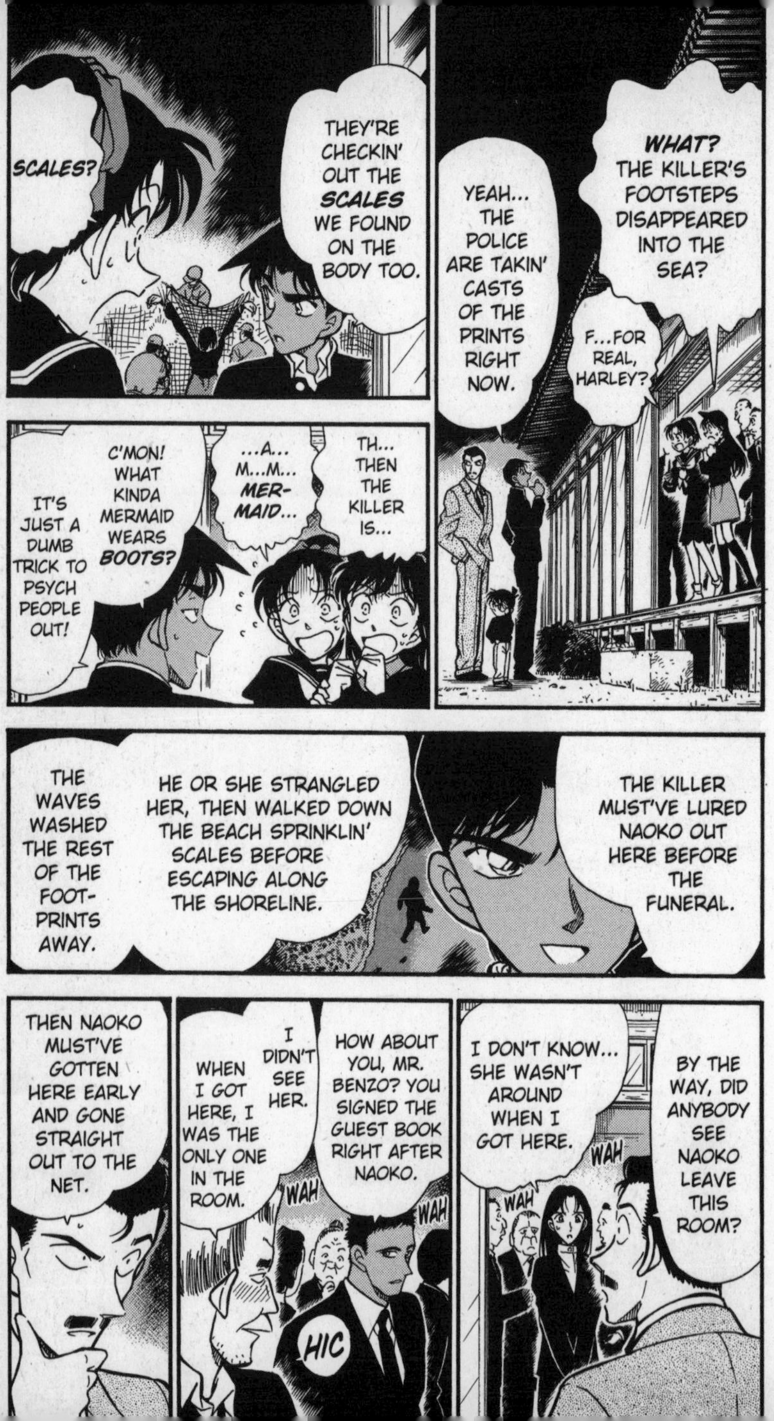
WHAT? THE KILLER'S FOOTSTEPS DISAPPEARED INTO THE SEA?
F...FOR REAL, HARLEY?
YEAH... THE POLICE ARE TAKIN' CASTS OF THE PRINTS RIGHT NOW.
THEY'RE CHECKIN' OUT THE SCALES WE FOUND ON THE BODY TOO.
SCALES?
TH... THEN THE KILLER IS...
...A... M...M... MER-MAID...
C'MON! WHAT KINDA MERMAID WEARS BOOTS?
IT'S JUST A DUMB TRICK TO PSYCH PEOPLE OUT!
THE KILLER MUST'VE LURED NAOKO OUT HERE BEFORE THE FUNERAL.
HE OR SHE STRANGLED HER, THEN WALKED DOWN THE BEACH SPRINKLIN' SCALES BEFORE ESCAPING ALONG THE SHORELINE.
THE WAVES WASHED THE REST OF THE FOOT-PRINTS AWAY.
BY THE WAY, DID ANYBODY SEE NAOKO LEAVE THIS ROOM?
I DON'T KNOW... SHE WASN'T AROUND WHEN I GOT HERE.
WAH
WAH
HOW ABOUT YOU, MR. BENZO? YOU SIGNED THE GUEST BOOK RIGHT AFTER NAOKO.
I DIDN'T SEE HER.
WHEN I GOT HERE, I WAS THE ONLY ONE IN THE ROOM.
WAH
WAH
HIC
THEN NAOKO MUST'VE GOTTEN HERE EARLY AND GONE STRAIGHT OUT TO THE NET.

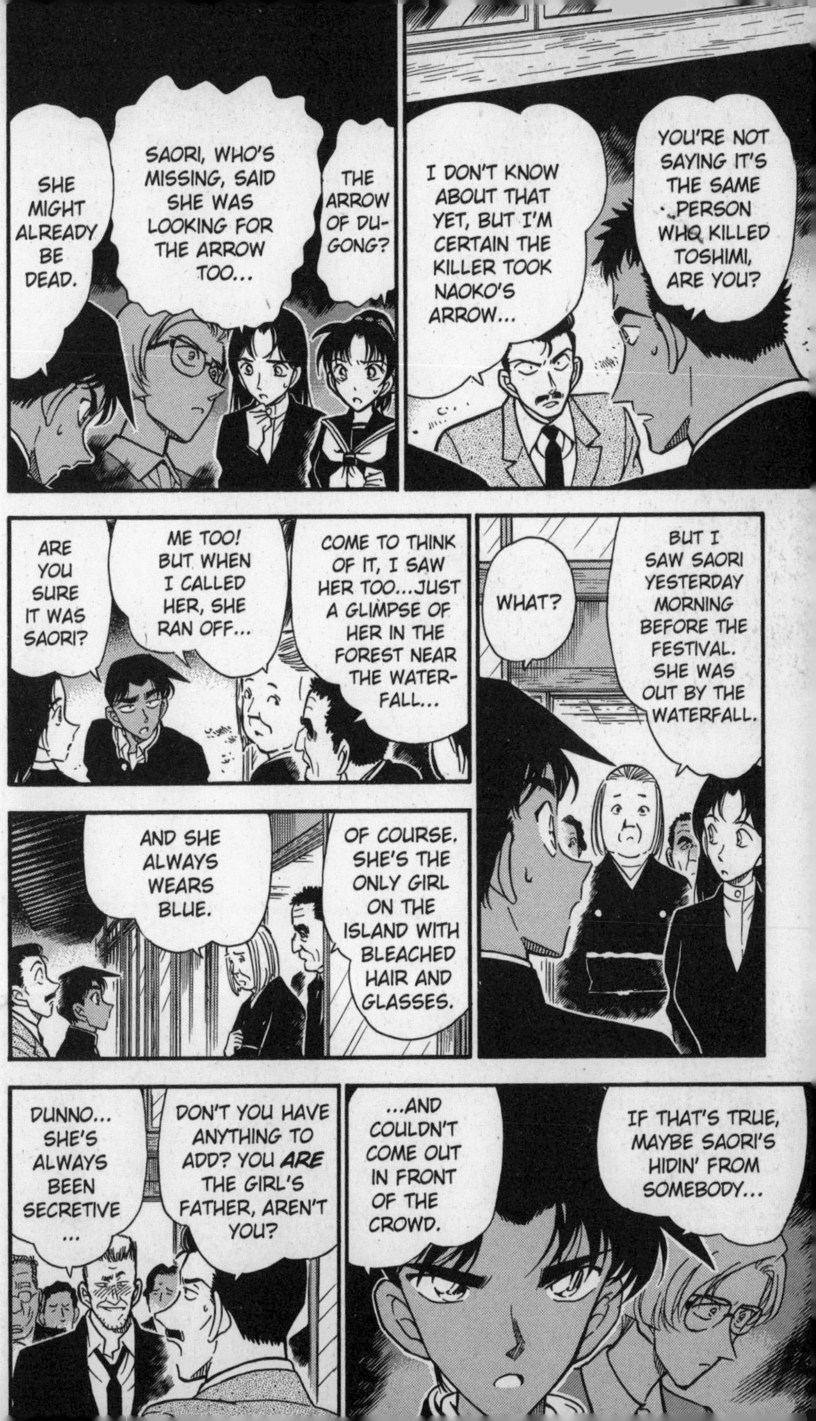
YOU'RE NOT SAYING IT'S THE SAME PERSON WHO KILLED TOSHIMI, ARE YOU?
I DON'T KNOW ABOUT THAT YET, BUT I'M CERTAIN THE KILLER TOOK NAOKO'S ARROW...
THE ARROW OF DU-GONG?
SAORI, WHO'S MISSING, SAID SHE WAS LOOKING FOR THE ARROW TOO...
SHE MIGHT ALREADY BE DEAD.
BUT I SAW SAORI YESTERDAY MORNING BEFORE THE FESTIVAL. SHE WAS OUT BY THE WATERFALL.
WHAT?
COME TO THINK OF IT, I SAW HER TOO...JUST A GLIMPSE OF HER IN THE FOREST NEAR THE WATER-FALL...
ME TOO! BUT WHEN I CALLED HER, SHE RAN OFF...
ARE YOU SURE IT WAS SAORI?
OF COURSE. SHE'S THE ONLY GIRL ON THE ISLAND WITH BLEACHED HAIR AND GLASSES.
AND SHE ALWAYS WEARS BLUE.
IF THAT'S TRUE, MAYBE SAORI'S HIDIN' FROM SOMEBODY...
...AND COULDN'T COME OUT IN FRONT OF THE CROWD.
DON'T YOU HAVE ANYTHING TO ADD? YOU ***ARE*** THE GIRL'S FATHER, AREN'T YOU?
DUNNO... SHE'S ALWAYS BEEN SECRETIVE ...

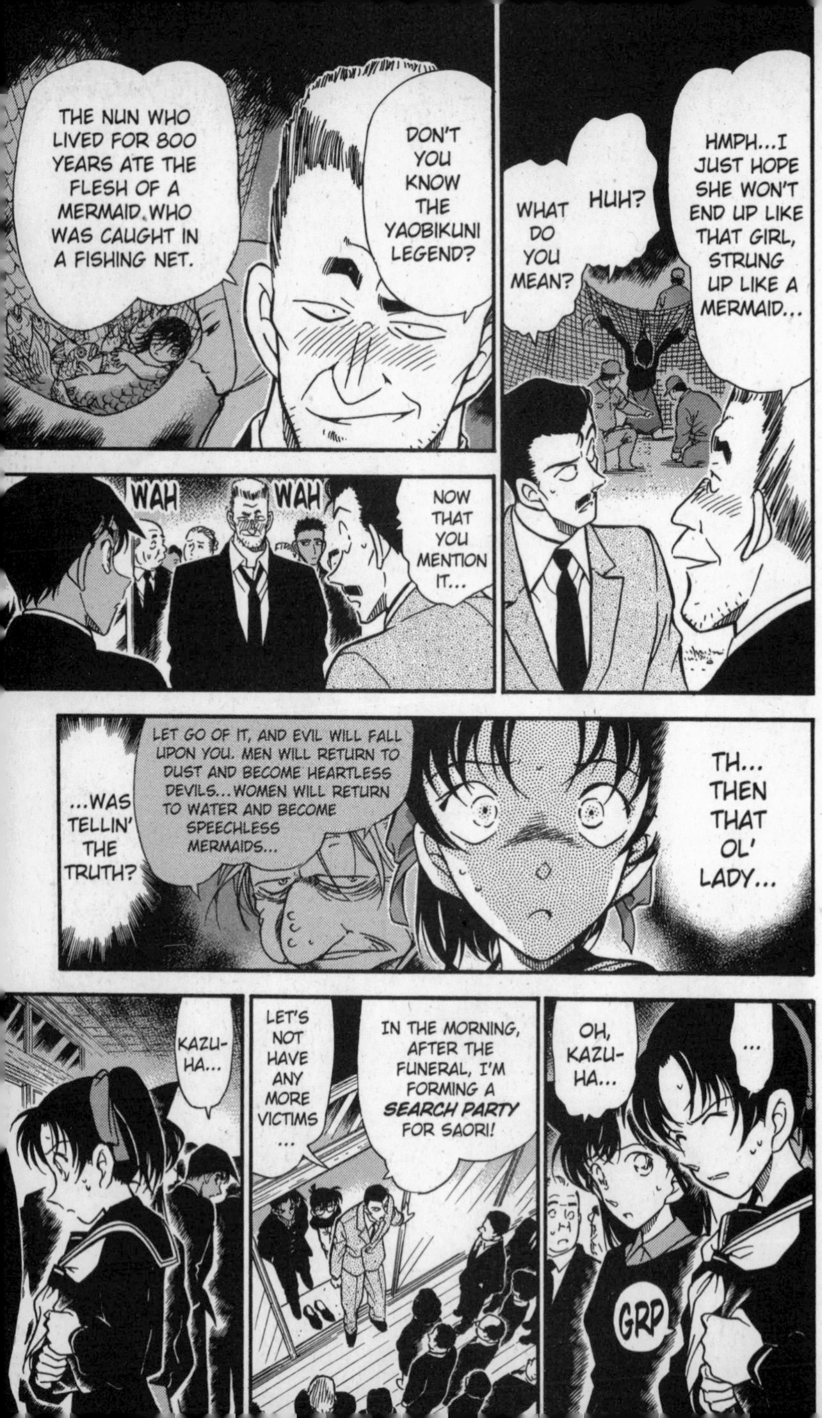

HMPH...I JUST HOPE SHE WON'T END UP LIKE THAT GIRL, STRUNG UP LIKE A MERMAID...
HUH?
WHAT DO YOU MEAN?
DON'T YOU KNOW THE YAOBIKUNI LEGEND?
THE NUN WHO LIVED FOR 800 YEARS ATE THE FLESH OF A MERMAID WHO WAS CAUGHT IN A FISHING NET.
NOW THAT YOU MENTION IT...
WAH
WAH
TH... THEN THAT OL' LADY...
LET GO OF IT, AND EVIL WILL FALL UPON YOU. MEN WILL RETURN TO DUST AND BECOME HEARTLESS DEVILS...WOMEN WILL RETURN TO WATER AND BECOME SPEECHLESS MERMAIDS...
...WAS TELLIN' THE TRUTH?
...
OH, KAZU-HA...
GRP
IN THE MORNING, AFTER THE FUNERAL, I'M FORMING A SEARCH PARTY FOR SAORI!
LET'S NOT HAVE ANY MORE VICTIMS...
KAZU-HA...

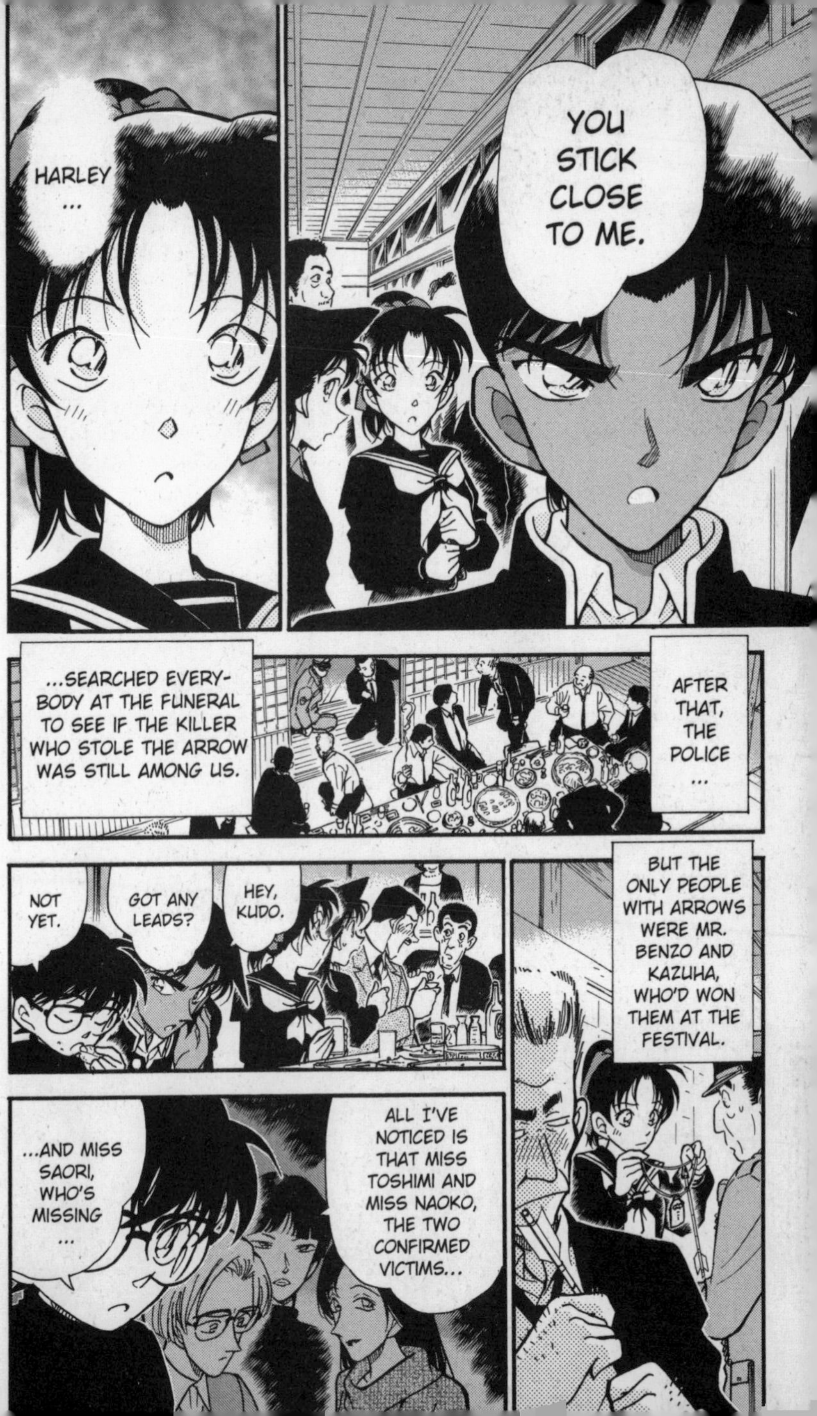
YOU STICK CLOSE TO ME.
HARLEY ...
AFTER THAT, THE POLICE ...
...SEARCHED EVERY-BODY AT THE FUNERAL TO SEE IF THE KILLER WHO STOLE THE ARROW WAS STILL AMONG US.
BUT THE ONLY PEOPLE WITH ARROWS WERE MR. BENZO AND KAZUHA, WHO'D WON THEM AT THE FESTIVAL.
HEY, KUDO.
GOT ANY LEADS?
NOT YET.
ALL I'VE NOTICED IS THAT MISS TOSHIMI AND MISS NAOKO, THE TWO CONFIRMED VICTIMS...
...AND MISS SAORI, WHO'S MISSING ...

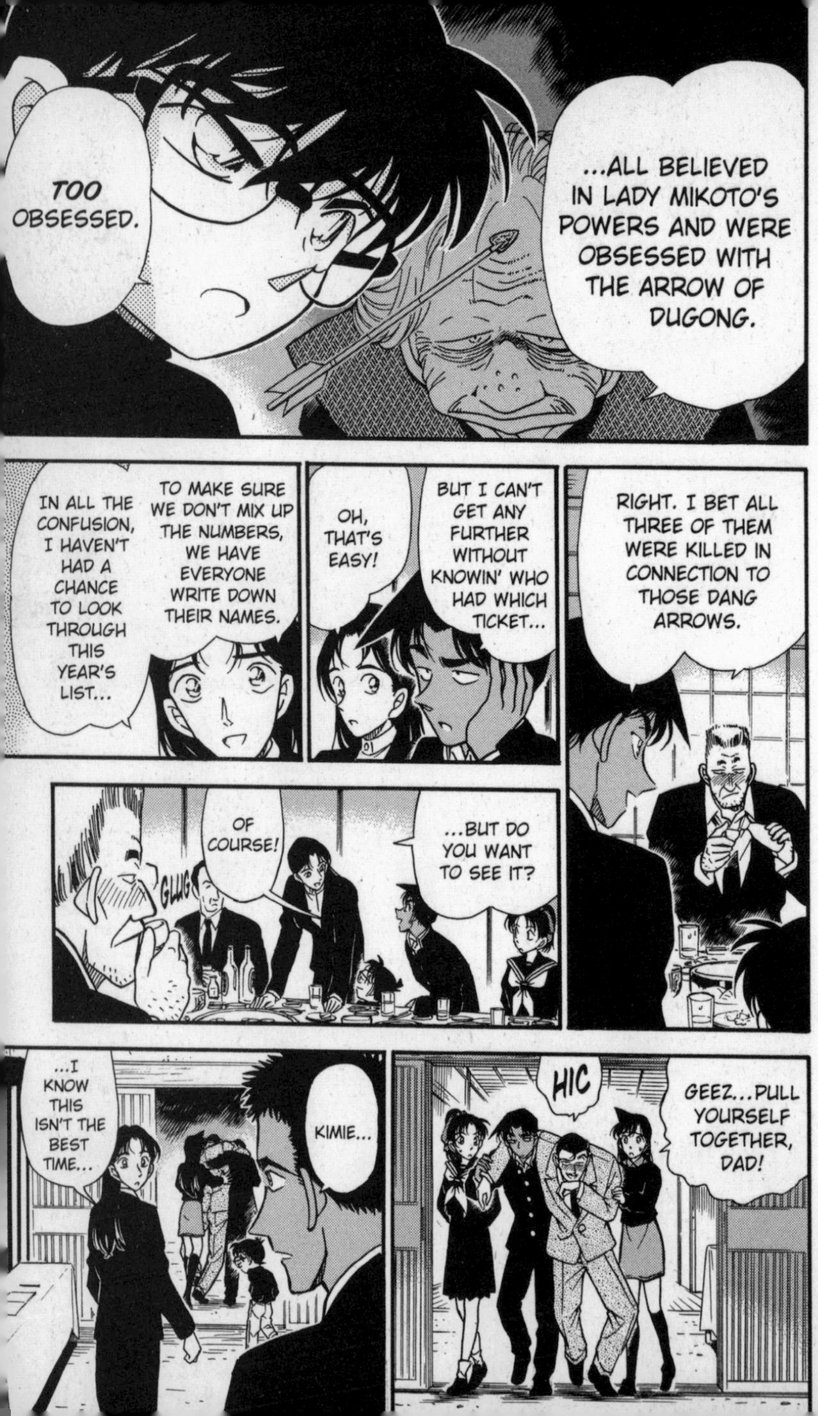
...ALL BELIEVED IN LADY MIKOTO'S POWERS AND WERE OBSESSED WITH THE ARROW OF DUGONG.
TOO OBSESSED.
RIGHT. I BET ALL THREE OF THEM WERE KILLED IN CONNECTION TO THOSE DANG ARROWS.
BUT I CAN'T GET ANY FURTHER WITHOUT KNOWIN' WHO HAD WHICH TICKET...
OH, THAT'S EASY!
TO MAKE SURE WE DON'T MIX UP THE NUMBERS, WE HAVE EVERYONE WRITE DOWN THEIR NAMES.
IN ALL THE CONFUSION, I HAVEN'T HAD A CHANCE TO LOOK THROUGH THIS YEAR'S LIST...
...BUT DO YOU WANT TO SEE IT?
OF COURSE!
GLUG
GEEZ...PULL YOURSELF TOGETHER, DAD!
HIC
KIMIE...
...I KNOW THIS ISN'T THE BEST TIME...

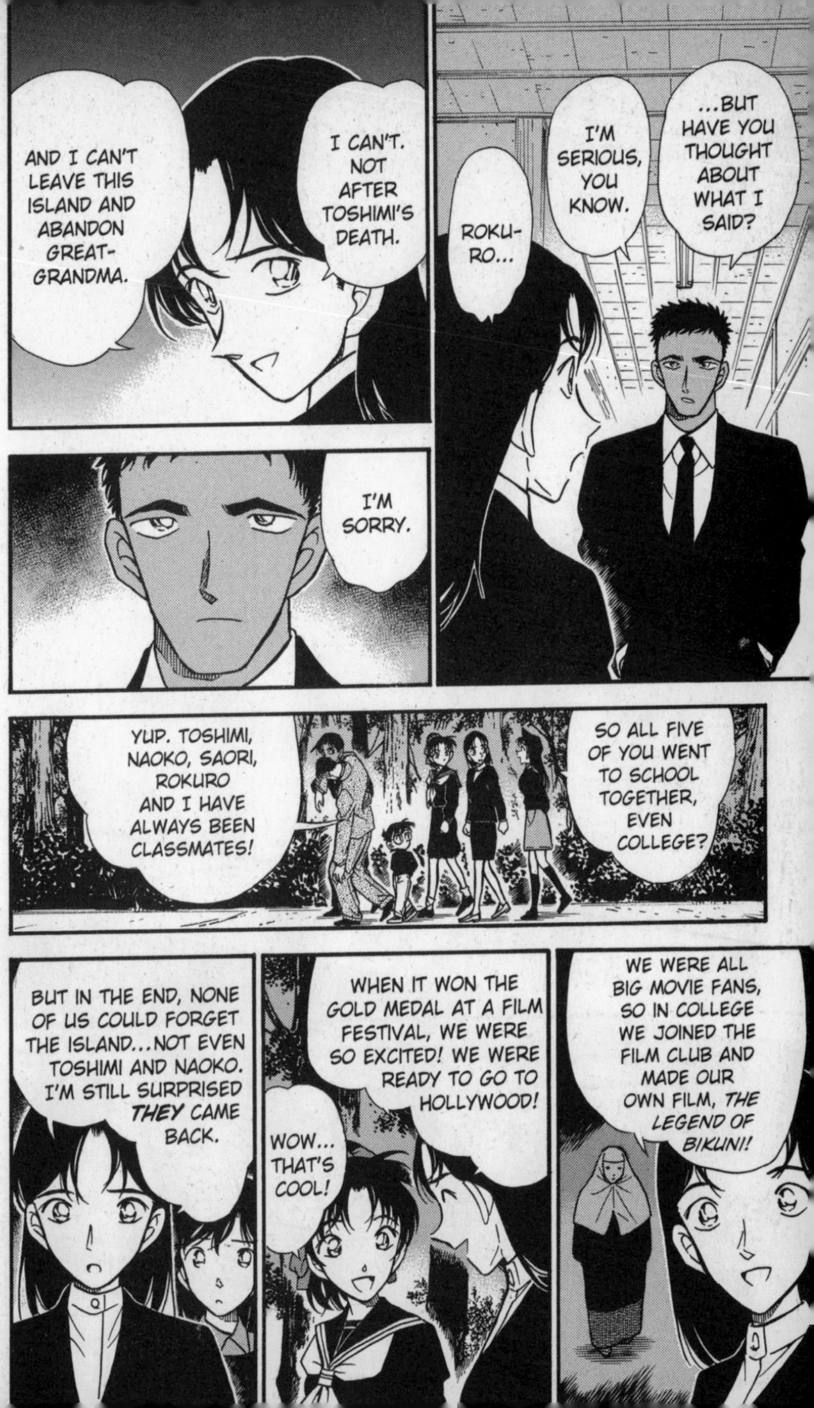
...BUT HAVE YOU THOUGHT ABOUT WHAT I SAID?
I'M SERIOUS, YOU KNOW.
ROKU-RO...
I CAN'T. NOT AFTER TOSHIMI'S DEATH.
AND I CAN'T LEAVE THIS ISLAND AND ABANDON GREAT-GRANDMA.
I'M SORRY.
SO ALL FIVE OF YOU WENT TO SCHOOL TOGETHER, EVEN COLLEGE?
YUP. TOSHIMI, NAOKO, SAORI, ROKURO AND I HAVE ALWAYS BEEN CLASSMATES!
WE WERE ALL BIG MOVIE FANS, SO IN COLLEGE WE JOINED THE FILM CLUB AND MADE OUR OWN FILM, *THE LEGEND OF BIKUNI!*
WHEN IT WON THE GOLD MEDAL AT A FILM FESTIVAL, WE WERE SO EXCITED! WE WERE READY TO GO TO HOLLYWOOD!
WOW... THAT'S COOL!
BUT IN THE END, NONE OF US COULD FORGET THE ISLAND...NOT EVEN TOSHIMI AND NAOKO. I'M STILL SURPRISED ***THEY*** CAME BACK.

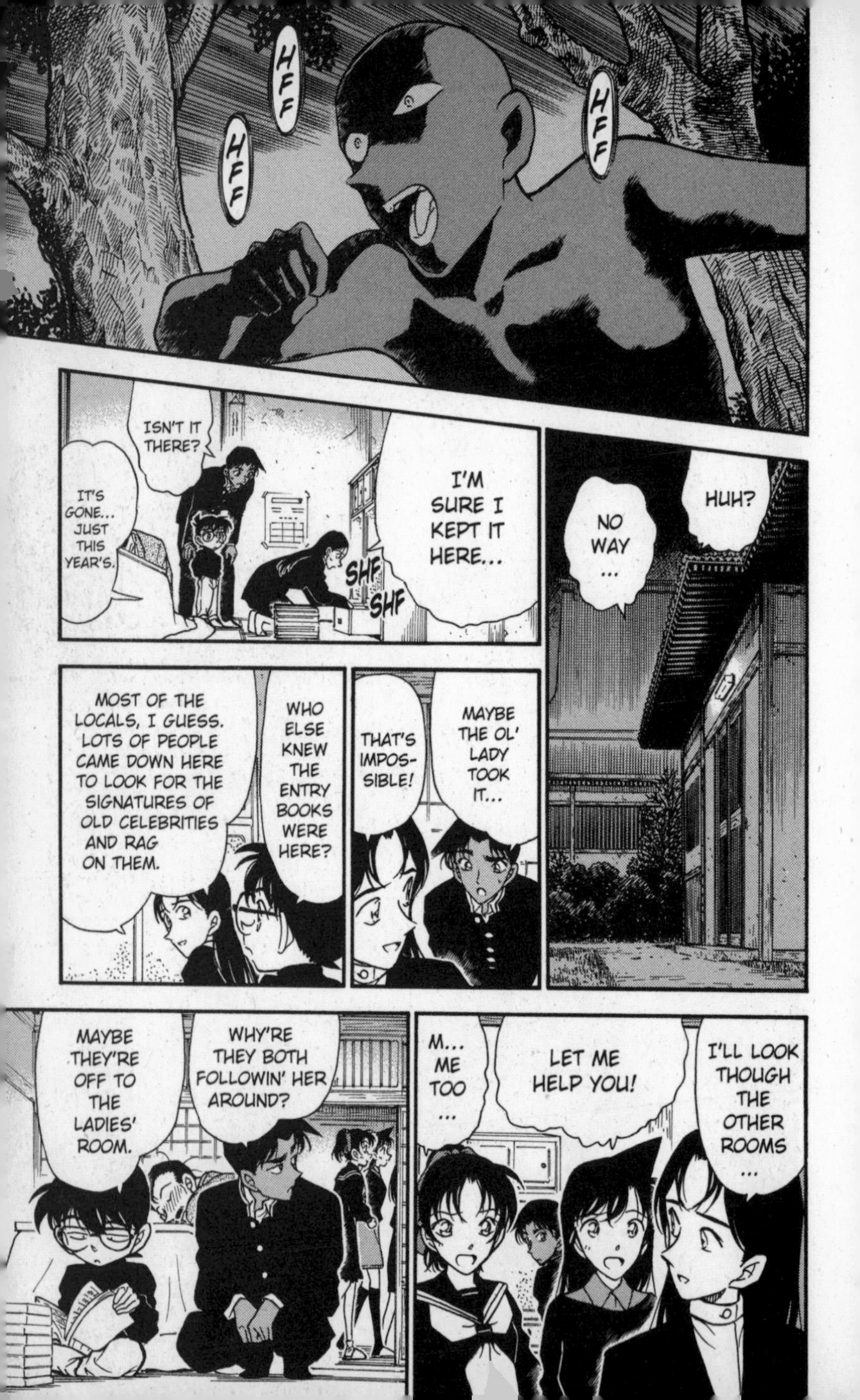
HFF
HFF
HFF
HUH?
NO WAY ...
I'M SURE I KEPT IT HERE...
SHF
SHF
ISN'T IT THERE?
IT'S GONE... JUST THIS YEAR'S.
MAYBE THE OL' LADY TOOK IT...
THAT'S IMPOSSIBLE!
WHO ELSE KNEW THE ENTRY BOOKS WERE HERE?
MOST OF THE LOCALS, I GUESS. LOTS OF PEOPLE CAME DOWN HERE TO LOOK FOR THE SIGNATURES OF OLD CELEBRITIES AND RAG ON THEM.
I'LL LOOK THOUGH THE OTHER ROOMS ...
LET ME HELP YOU!
M... ME TOO ...
WHY'RE THEY BOTH FOLLOWIN' HER AROUND?
MAYBE THEY'RE OFF TO THE LADIES' ROOM.

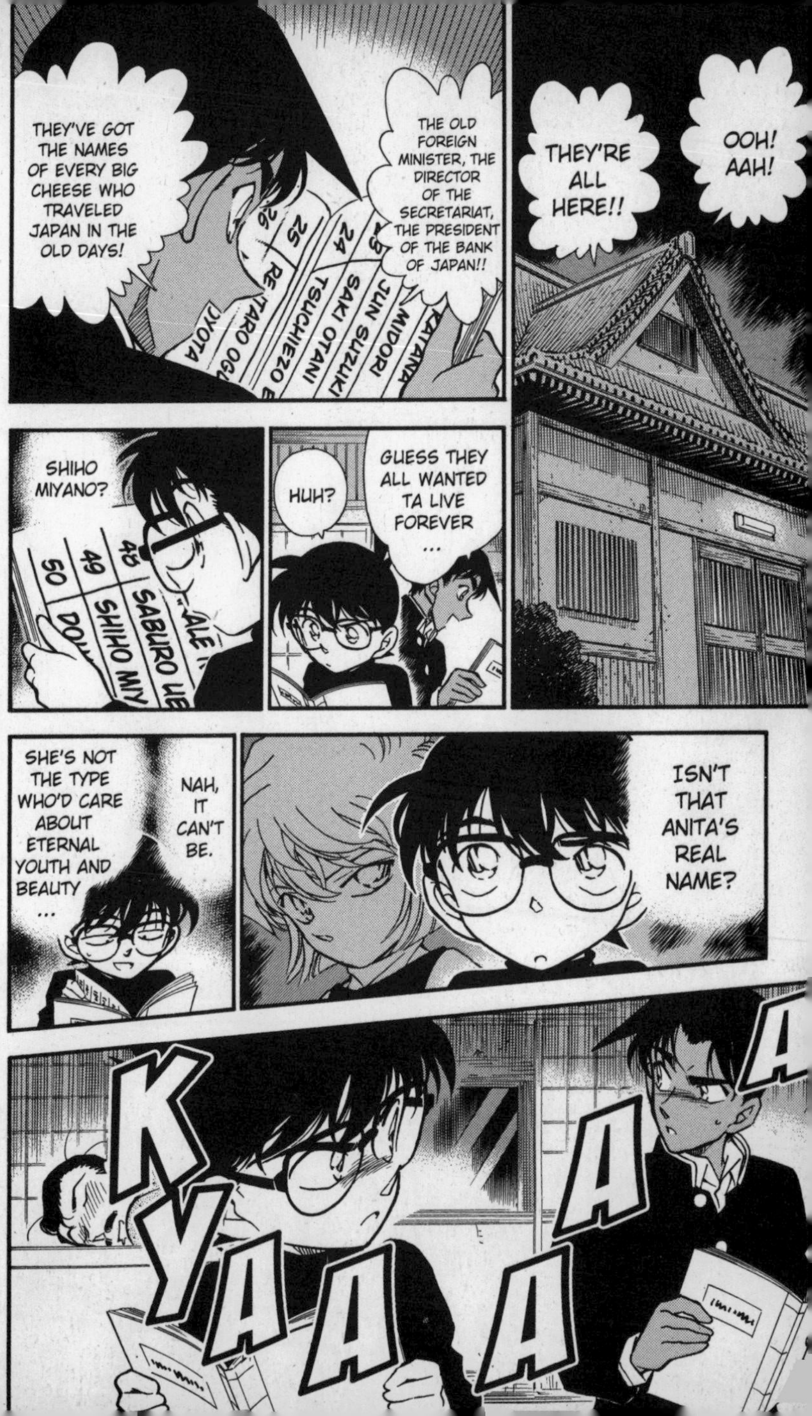
OOH! AAH!
THEY'RE ALL HERE!!
THE OLD FOREIGN MINISTER, THE DIRECTOR OF THE SECRETARIAT, THE PRESIDENT OF THE BANK OF JAPAN!!
THEY'VE GOT THE NAMES OF EVERY BIG CHEESE WHO TRAVELED JAPAN IN THE OLD DAYS!
GUESS THEY ALL WANTED TA LIVE FOREVER ...
HUH?
SHIHO MIYANO?
ISN'T THAT ANITA'S REAL NAME?
NAH, IT CAN'T BE.
SHE'S NOT THE TYPE WHO'D CARE ABOUT ETERNAL YOUTH AND BEAUTY ...
KYAAAAAAA

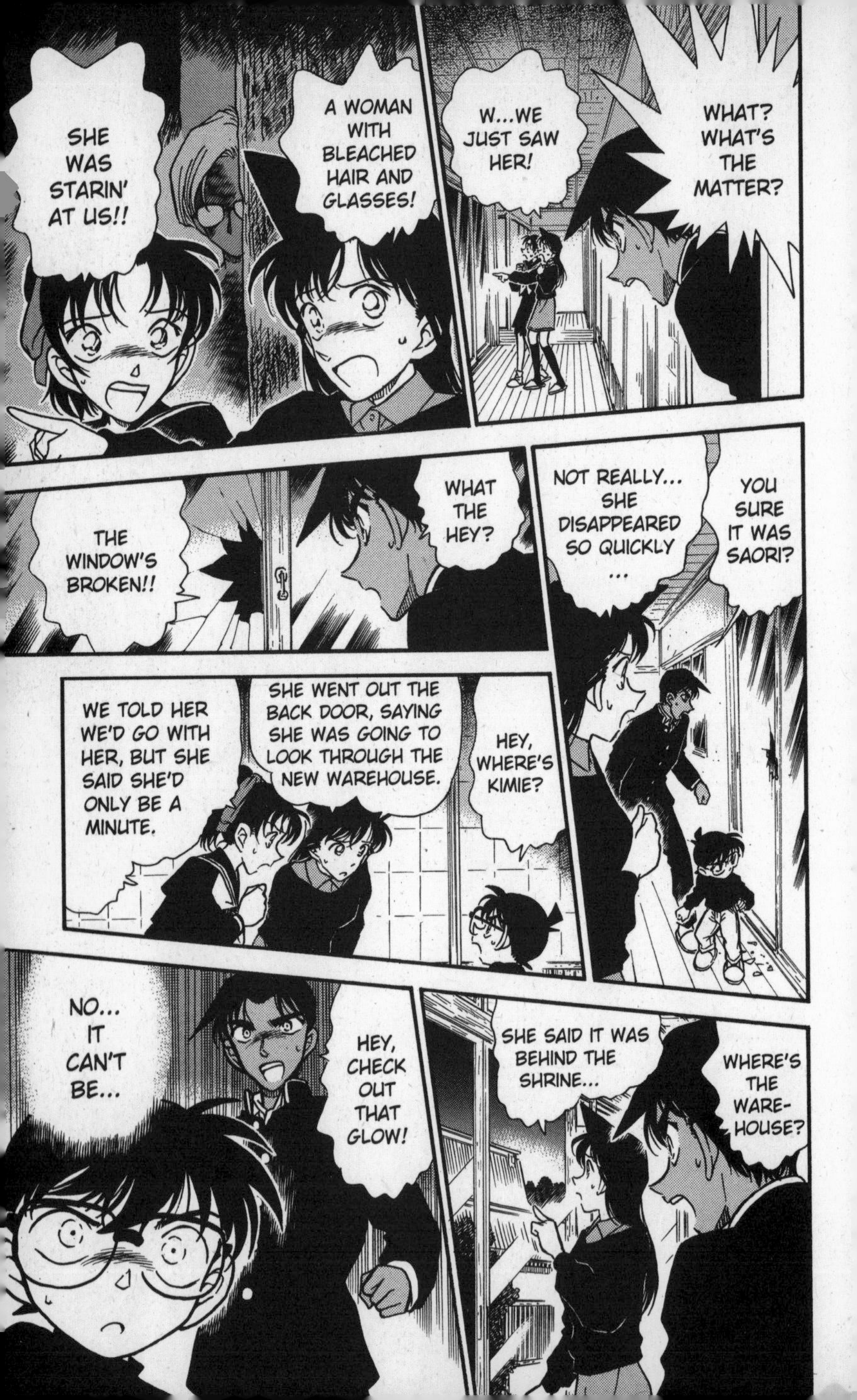
WHAT? WHAT'S THE MATTER?
W...WE JUST SAW HER!
A WOMAN WITH BLEACHED HAIR AND GLASSES!
SHE WAS STARIN' AT US!!
YOU SURE IT WAS SAORI?
NOT REALLY... SHE DISAPPEARED SO QUICKLY ...
WHAT THE HEY?
THE WINDOW'S BROKEN!!
HEY, WHERE'S KIMIE?
SHE WENT OUT THE BACK DOOR, SAYING SHE WAS GOING TO LOOK THROUGH THE NEW WAREHOUSE.
WE TOLD HER WE'D GO WITH HER, BUT SHE SAID SHE'D ONLY BE A MINUTE.
WHERE'S THE WARE-HOUSE?
SHE SAID IT WAS BEHIND THE SHRINE...
HEY, CHECK OUT THAT GLOW!
NO... IT CAN'T BE...

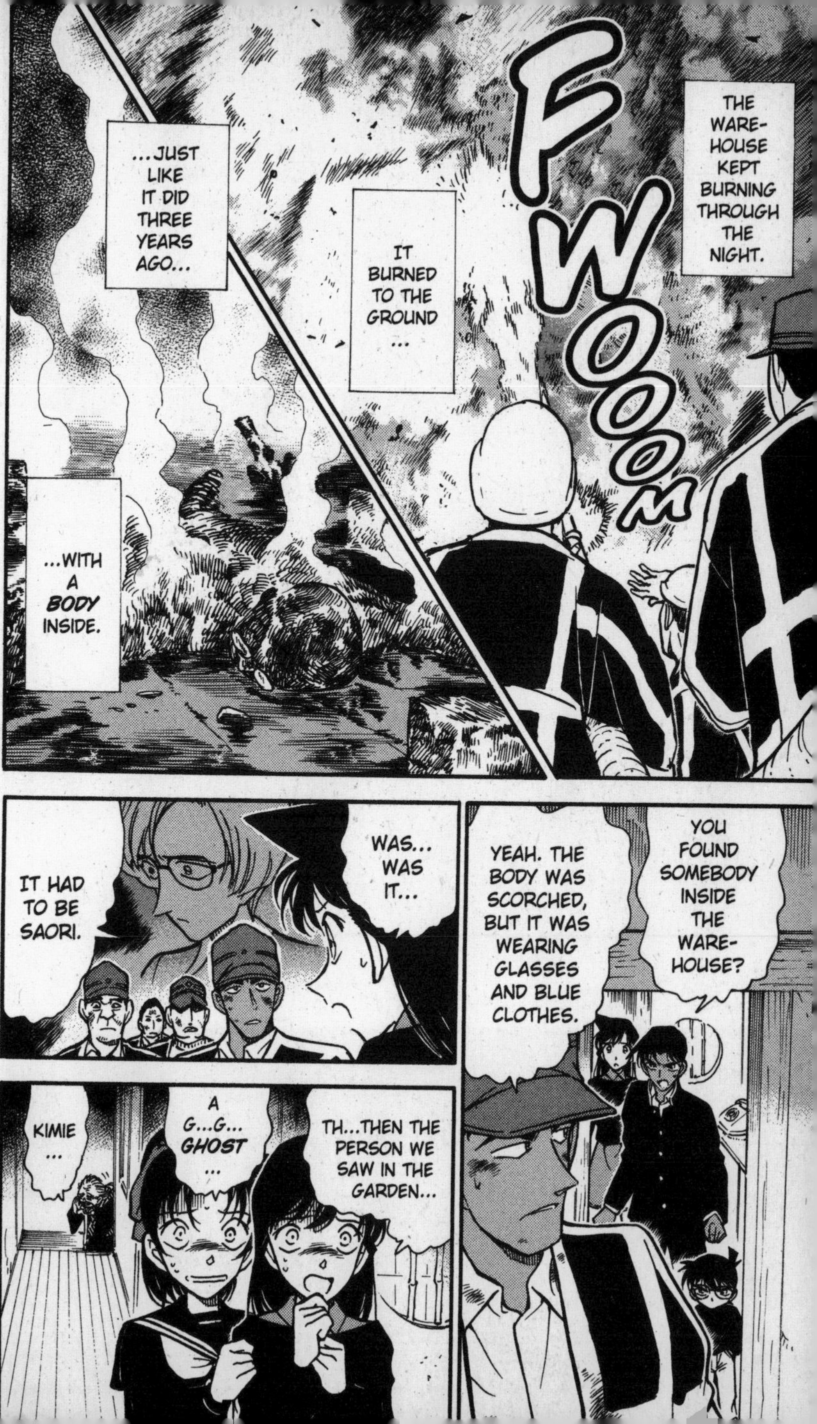
THE WARE-HOUSE KEPT BURNING THROUGH THE NIGHT.
FWOOOOM
IT BURNED TO THE GROUND ...
...JUST LIKE IT DID THREE YEARS AGO...
...WITH A BODY INSIDE.
YOU FOUND SOMEBODY INSIDE THE WARE-HOUSE?
YEAH. THE BODY WAS SCORCHED, BUT IT WAS WEARING GLASSES AND BLUE CLOTHES.
WAS... WAS IT...
IT HAD TO BE SAORI.
TH...THEN THE PERSON WE SAW IN THE GARDEN...
A G...G... GHOST ...
KIMIE ...

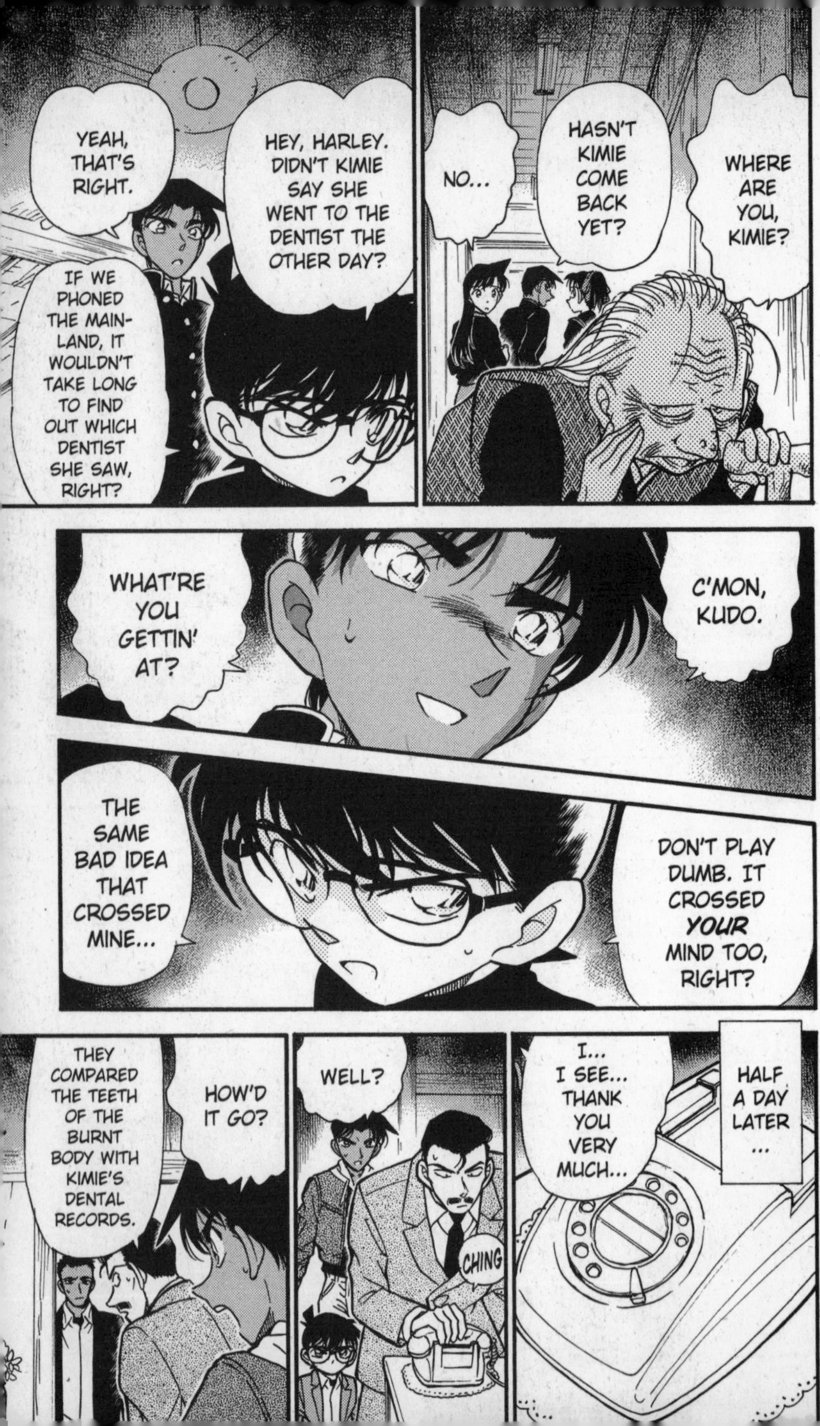
WHERE ARE YOU, KIMIE?
HASN'T KIMIE COME BACK YET?
NO...
HEY, HARLEY. DIDN'T KIMIE SAY SHE WENT TO THE DENTIST THE OTHER DAY?
YEAH, THAT'S RIGHT.
IF WE PHONED THE MAIN-LAND, IT WOULDN'T TAKE LONG TO FIND OUT WHICH DENTIST SHE SAW, RIGHT?
C'MON, KUDO.
WHAT'RE YOU GETTIN' AT?
DON'T PLAY DUMB. IT CROSSED YOUR MIND TOO, RIGHT?
THE SAME BAD IDEA THAT CROSSED MINE...
HALF A DAY LATER...
I... I SEE... THANK YOU VERY MUCH...
CHING
WELL?
HOW'D IT GO?
THEY COMPARED THE TEETH OF THE BURNT BODY WITH KIMIE'S DENTAL RECORDS.

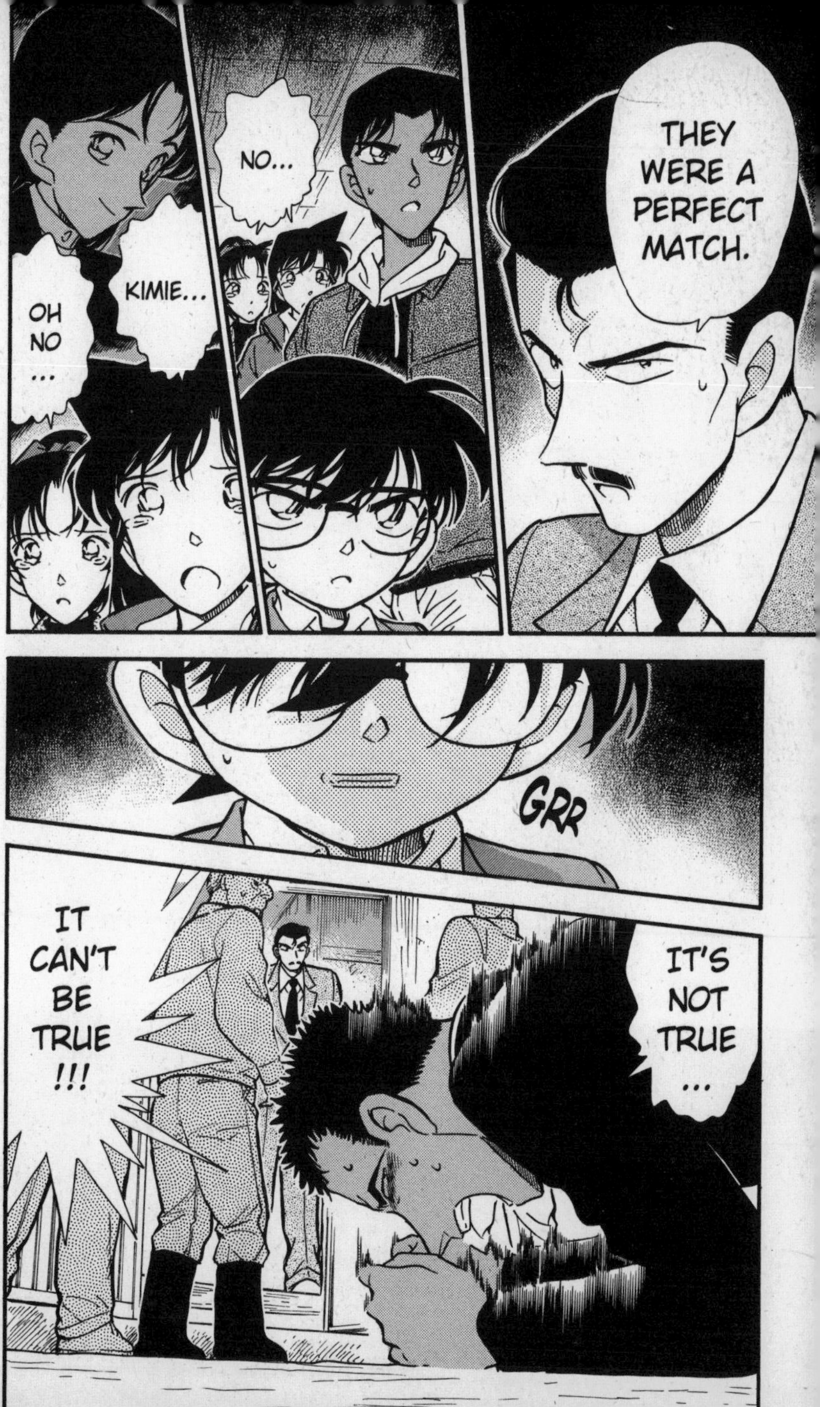
THEY WERE A PERFECT MATCH.
NO...
KIMIE...
OH NO ...
GRR
IT'S NOT TRUE ...
IT CAN'T BE TRUE!!!

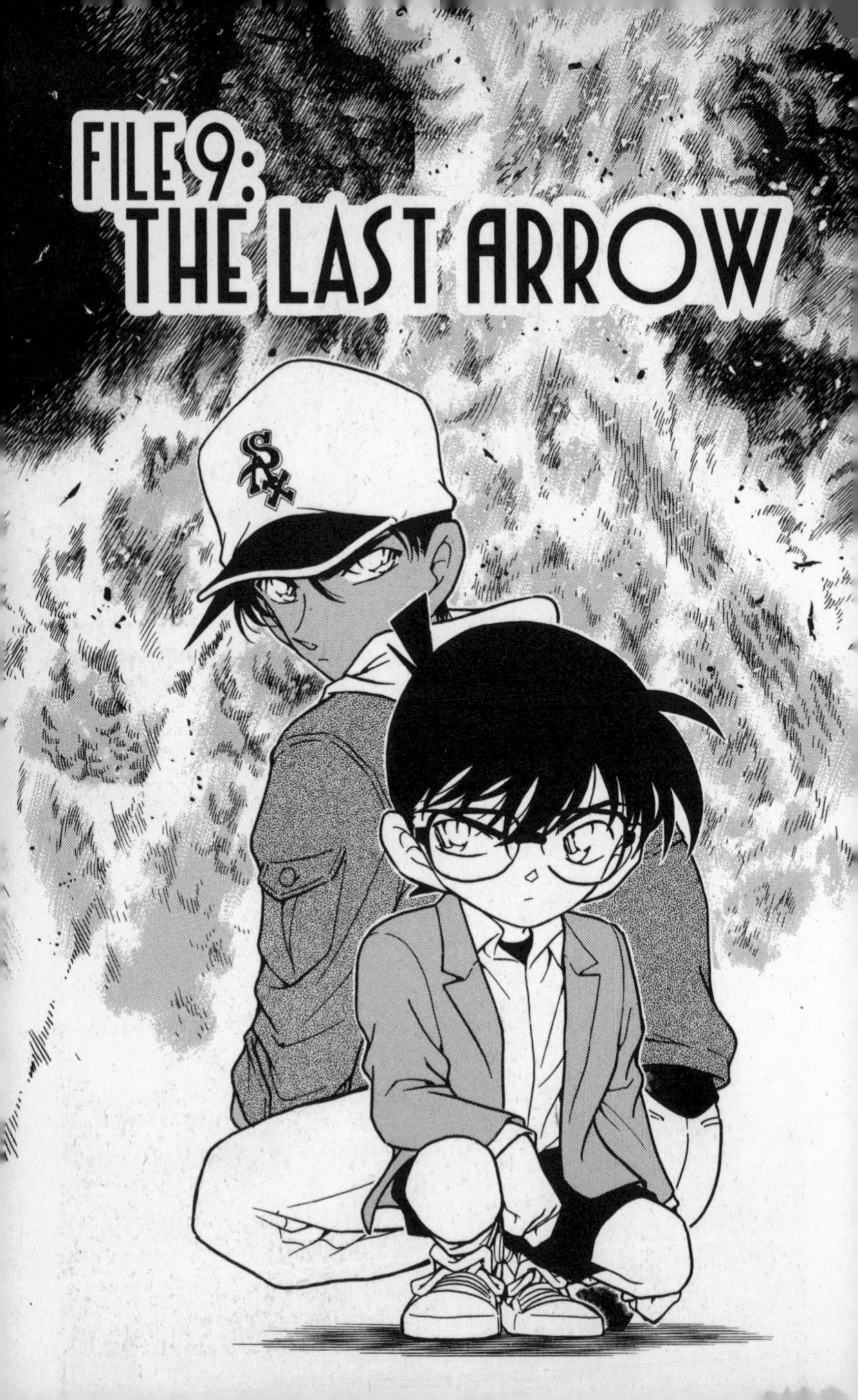
FILE 9:
THE LAST ARROW

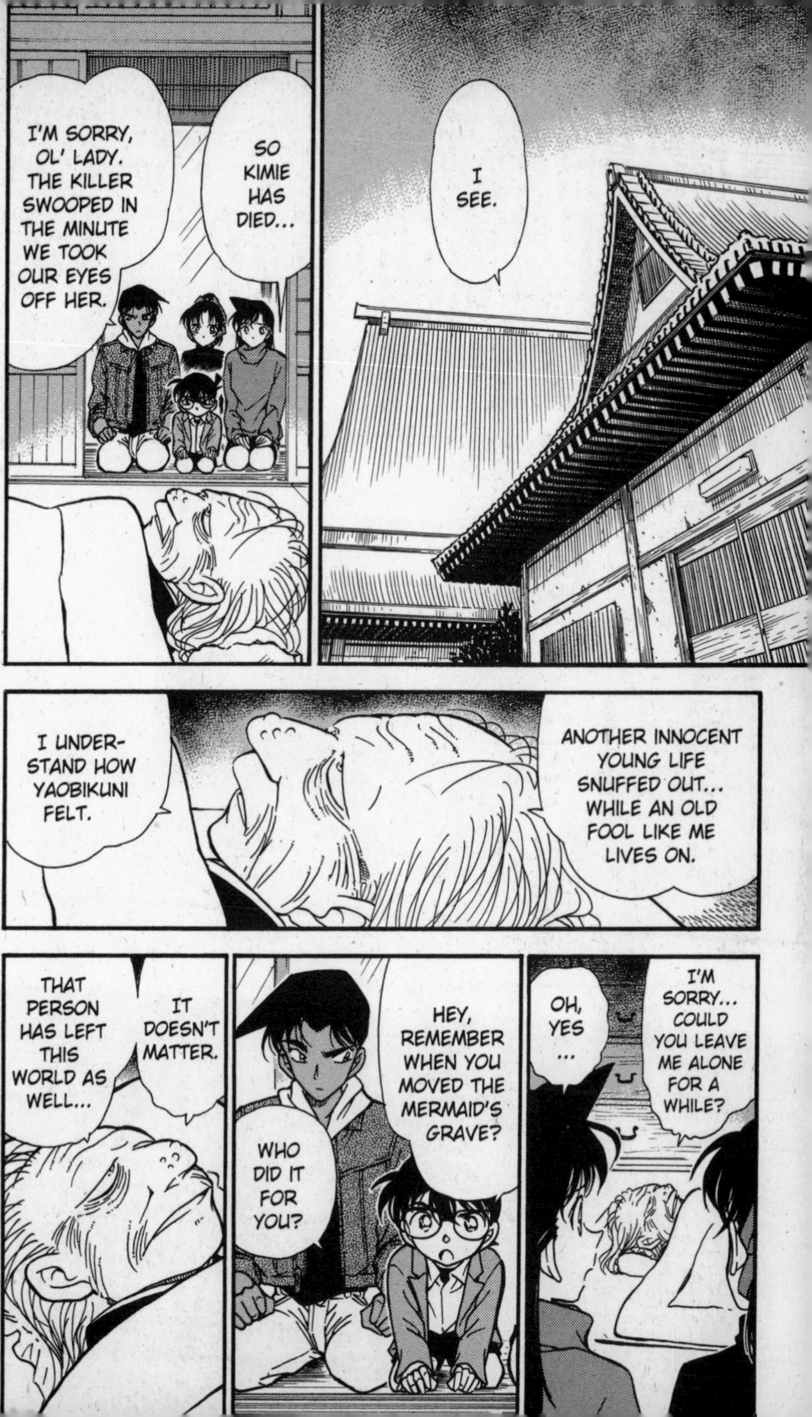
I SEE.
SO KIMIE HAS DIED...
I'M SORRY, OL' LADY. THE KILLER SWOOPED IN THE MINUTE WE TOOK OUR EYES OFF HER.
ANOTHER INNOCENT YOUNG LIFE SNUFFED OUT... WHILE AN OLD FOOL LIKE ME LIVES ON.
I UNDER-STAND HOW YAOBIKUNI FELT.
I'M SORRY... COULD YOU LEAVE ME ALONE FOR A WHILE?
OH, YES...
HEY, REMEMBER WHEN YOU MOVED THE MERMAID'S GRAVE?
WHO DID IT FOR YOU?
IT DOESN'T MATTER.
THAT PERSON HAS LEFT THIS WORLD AS WELL...

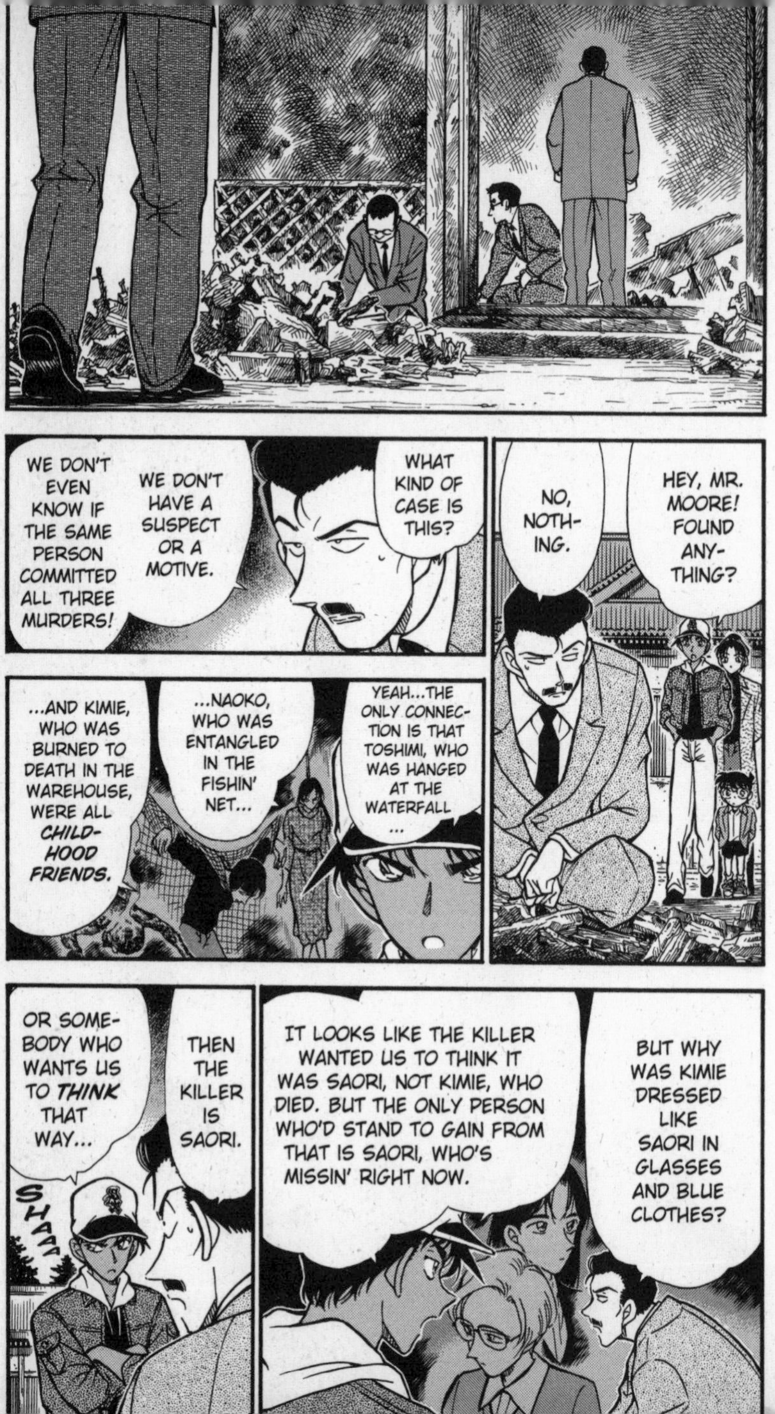
HEY, MR. MOORE! FOUND ANYTHING?
NO, NOTHING.
WHAT KIND OF CASE IS THIS?
WE DON'T HAVE A SUSPECT OR A MOTIVE.
WE DON'T EVEN KNOW IF THE SAME PERSON COMMITTED ALL THREE MURDERS!
YEAH...THE ONLY CONNECTION IS THAT TOSHIMI, WHO WAS HANGED AT THE WATERFALL...
...NAOKO, WHO WAS ENTANGLED IN THE FISHIN' NET...
...AND KIMIE, WHO WAS BURNED TO DEATH IN THE WAREHOUSE, WERE ALL CHILDHOOD FRIENDS.
BUT WHY WAS KIMIE DRESSED LIKE SAORI IN GLASSES AND BLUE CLOTHES?
IT LOOKS LIKE THE KILLER WANTED US TO THINK IT WAS SAORI, NOT KIMIE, WHO DIED. BUT THE ONLY PERSON WHO'D STAND TO GAIN FROM THAT IS SAORI, WHO'S MISSIN' RIGHT NOW.
THEN THE KILLER IS SAORI.
OR SOMEBODY WHO WANTS US TO THINK THAT WAY...
SHAAA

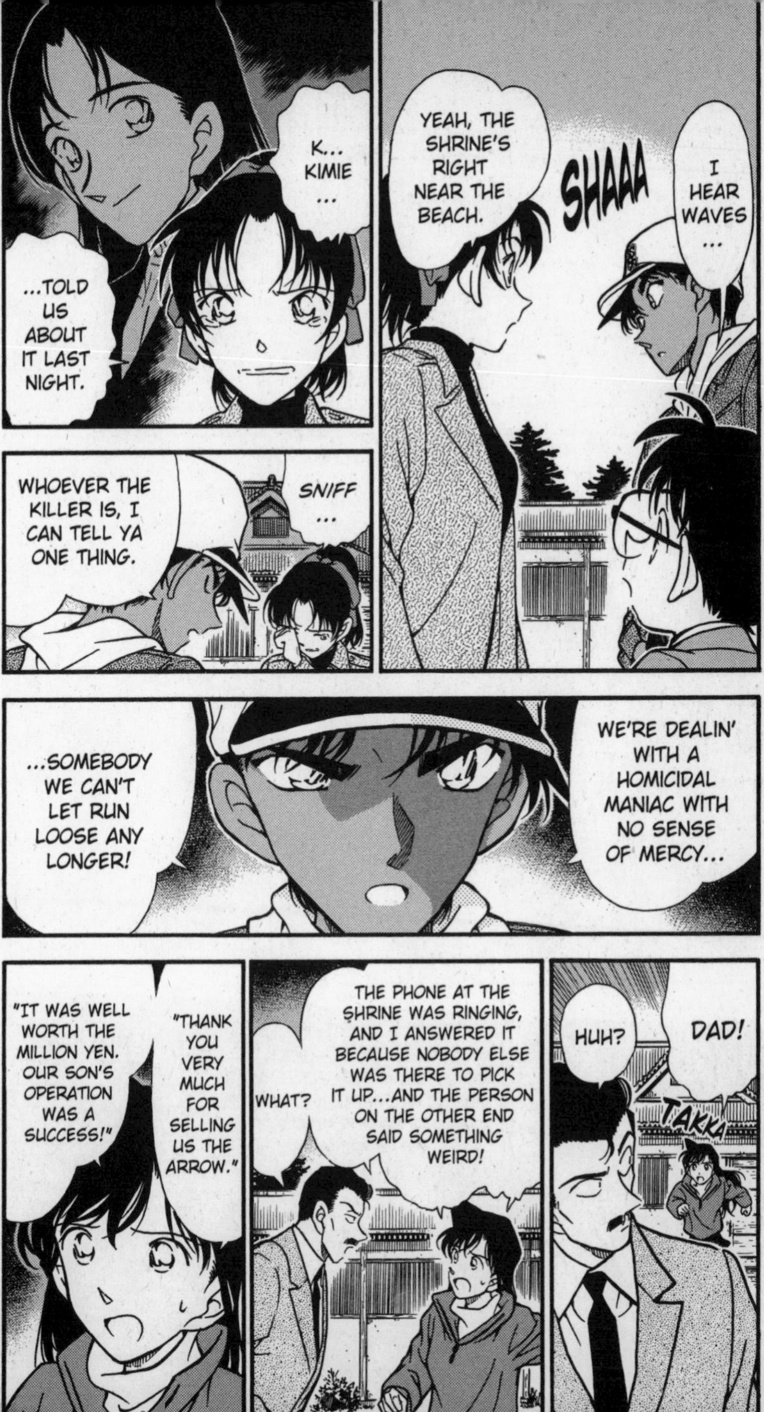
I HEAR WAVES...
SHAAA
YEAH, THE SHRINE'S RIGHT NEAR THE BEACH.
K... KIMIE...
...TOLD US ABOUT IT LAST NIGHT.
SNIFF...
WHOEVER THE KILLER IS, I CAN TELL YA ONE THING.
WE'RE DEALIN' WITH A HOMICIDAL MANIAC WITH NO SENSE OF MERCY...
...SOMEBODY WE CAN'T LET RUN LOOSE ANY LONGER!
DAD!
TAKKA
HUH?
THE PHONE AT THE SHRINE WAS RINGING, AND I ANSWERED IT BECAUSE NOBODY ELSE WAS THERE TO PICK IT UP...AND THE PERSON ON THE OTHER END SAID SOMETHING WEIRD!
WHAT?
"THANK YOU VERY MUCH FOR SELLING US THE ARROW."
"IT WAS WELL WORTH THE MILLION YEN. OUR SON'S OPERATION WAS A SUCCESS!"

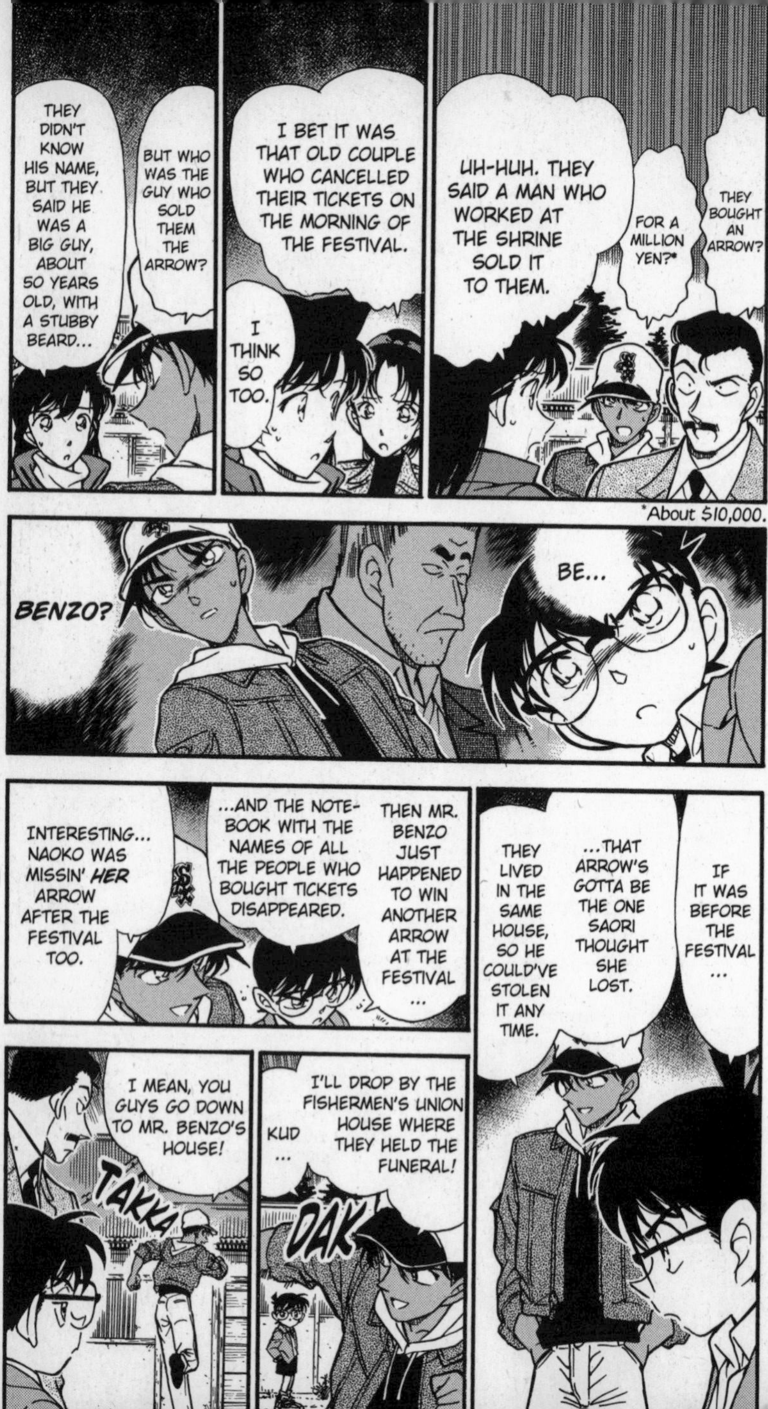
THEY BOUGHT AN ARROW?
FOR A MILLION YEN?*
UH-HUH. THEY SAID A MAN WHO WORKED AT THE SHRINE SOLD IT TO THEM.
I BET IT WAS THAT OLD COUPLE WHO CANCELLED THEIR TICKETS ON THE MORNING OF THE FESTIVAL.
I THINK SO TOO.
BUT WHO WAS THE GUY WHO SOLD THEM THE ARROW?
THEY DIDN'T KNOW HIS NAME, BUT THEY SAID HE WAS A BIG GUY, ABOUT 50 YEARS OLD, WITH A STUBBY BEARD...
BE...
BENZO?
IF IT WAS BEFORE THE FESTIVAL...
...THAT ARROW'S GOTTA BE THE ONE SAORI THOUGHT SHE LOST.
THEY LIVED IN THE SAME HOUSE, SO HE COULD'VE STOLEN IT ANY TIME.
THEN MR. BENZO JUST HAPPENED TO WIN ANOTHER ARROW AT THE FESTIVAL...
...AND THE NOTE-BOOK WITH THE NAMES OF ALL THE PEOPLE WHO BOUGHT TICKETS DISAPPEARED.
INTERESTING... NAOKO WAS MISSIN' *HER* ARROW AFTER THE FESTIVAL TOO.
I'LL DROP BY THE FISHERMEN'S UNION HOUSE WHERE THEY HELD THE FUNERAL!
KUD...
DAK
I MEAN, YOU GUYS GO DOWN TO MR. BENZO'S HOUSE!
TAKKA

*About $10,000.

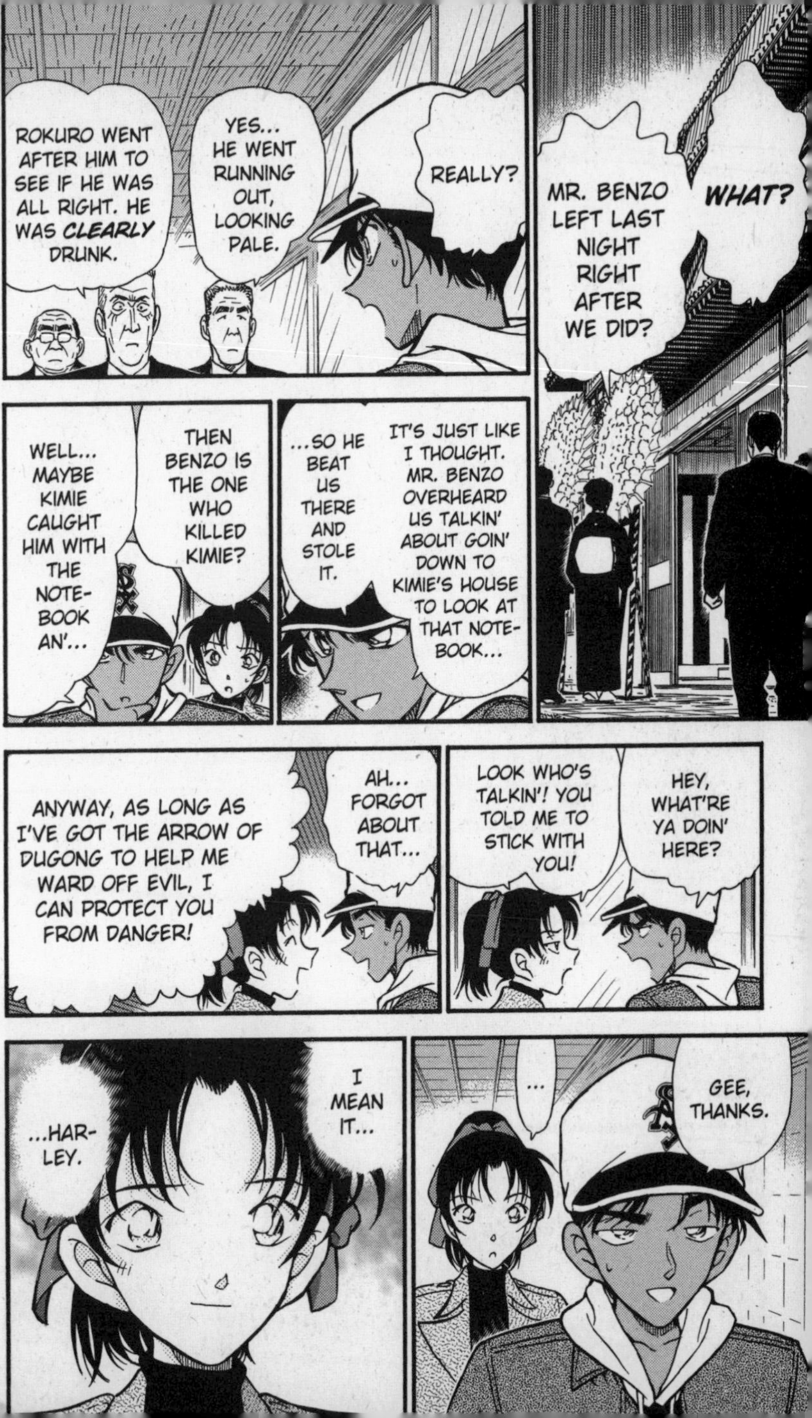
WHAT?
MR. BENZO LEFT LAST NIGHT RIGHT AFTER WE DID?
REALLY?
YES... HE WENT RUNNING OUT, LOOKING PALE.
ROKURO WENT AFTER HIM TO SEE IF HE WAS ALL RIGHT. HE WAS *CLEARLY* DRUNK.
IT'S JUST LIKE I THOUGHT. MR. BENZO OVERHEARD US TALKIN' ABOUT GOIN' DOWN TO KIMIE'S HOUSE TO LOOK AT THAT NOTE-BOOK...
...SO HE BEAT US THERE AND STOLE IT.
THEN BENZO IS THE ONE WHO KILLED KIMIE?
WELL... MAYBE KIMIE CAUGHT HIM WITH THE NOTE-BOOK AN'...
HEY, WHAT'RE YA DOIN' HERE?
LOOK WHO'S TALKIN'! YOU TOLD ME TO STICK WITH YOU!
AH... FORGOT ABOUT THAT...
ANYWAY, AS LONG AS I'VE GOT THE ARROW OF DUGONG TO HELP ME WARD OFF EVIL, I CAN PROTECT YOU FROM DANGER!
GEE, THANKS.
...
I MEAN IT...
...HAR-LEY.

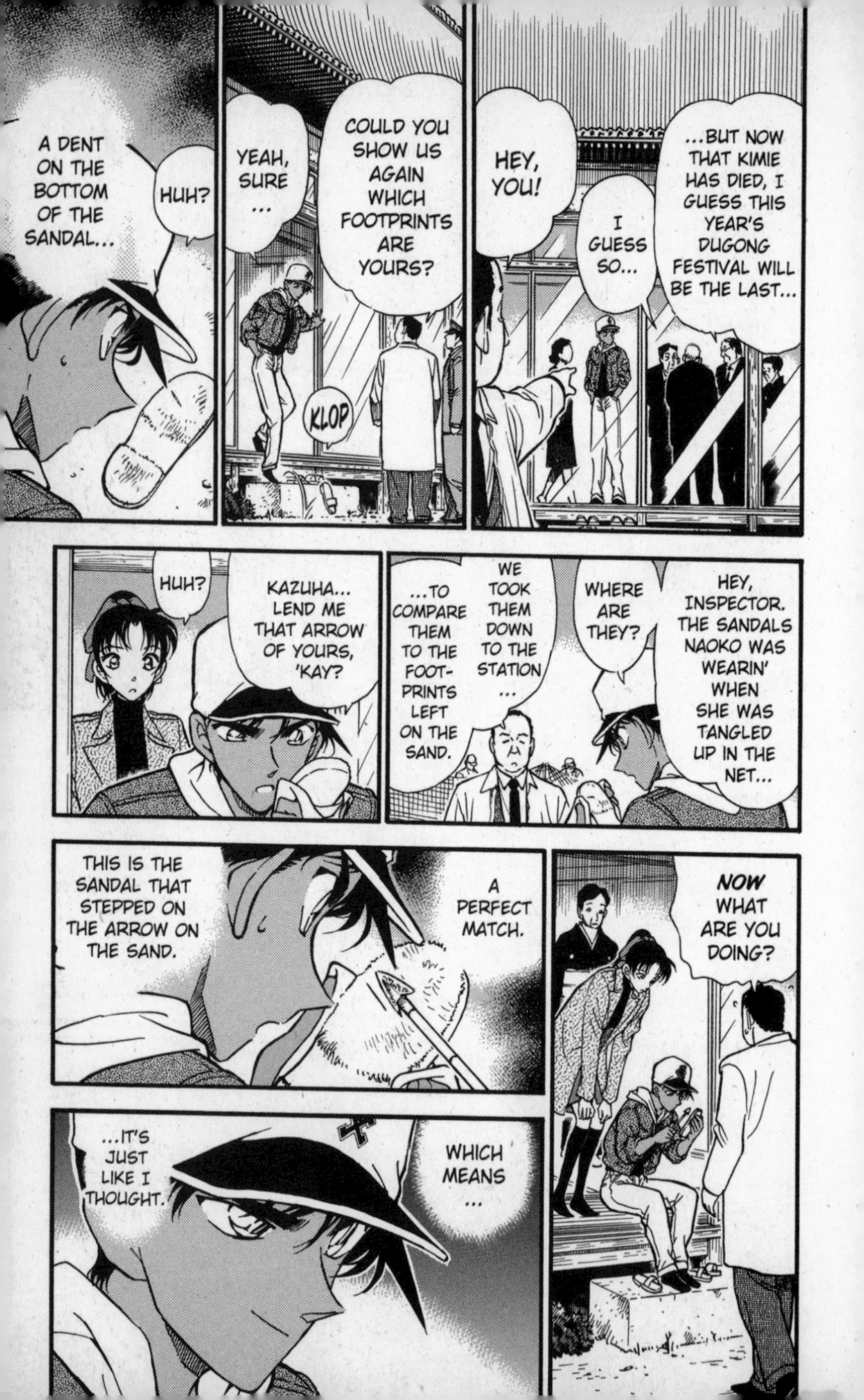
...BUT NOW THAT KIMIE HAS DIED, I GUESS THIS YEAR'S DUGONG FESTIVAL WILL BE THE LAST...
I GUESS SO...
HEY, YOU!
COULD YOU SHOW US AGAIN WHICH FOOTPRINTS ARE YOURS?
YEAH, SURE...
KLOP
HUH?
A DENT ON THE BOTTOM OF THE SANDAL...
HEY, INSPECTOR. THE SANDALS NAOKO WAS WEARIN' WHEN SHE WAS TANGLED UP IN THE NET...
WHERE ARE THEY?
WE TOOK THEM DOWN TO THE STATION...
...TO COMPARE THEM TO THE FOOT-PRINTS LEFT ON THE SAND.
KAZUHA... LEND ME THAT ARROW OF YOURS, 'KAY?
HUH?
NOW WHAT ARE YOU DOING?
A PERFECT MATCH.
THIS IS THE SANDAL THAT STEPPED ON THE ARROW ON THE SAND.
WHICH MEANS...
...IT'S JUST LIKE I THOUGHT.

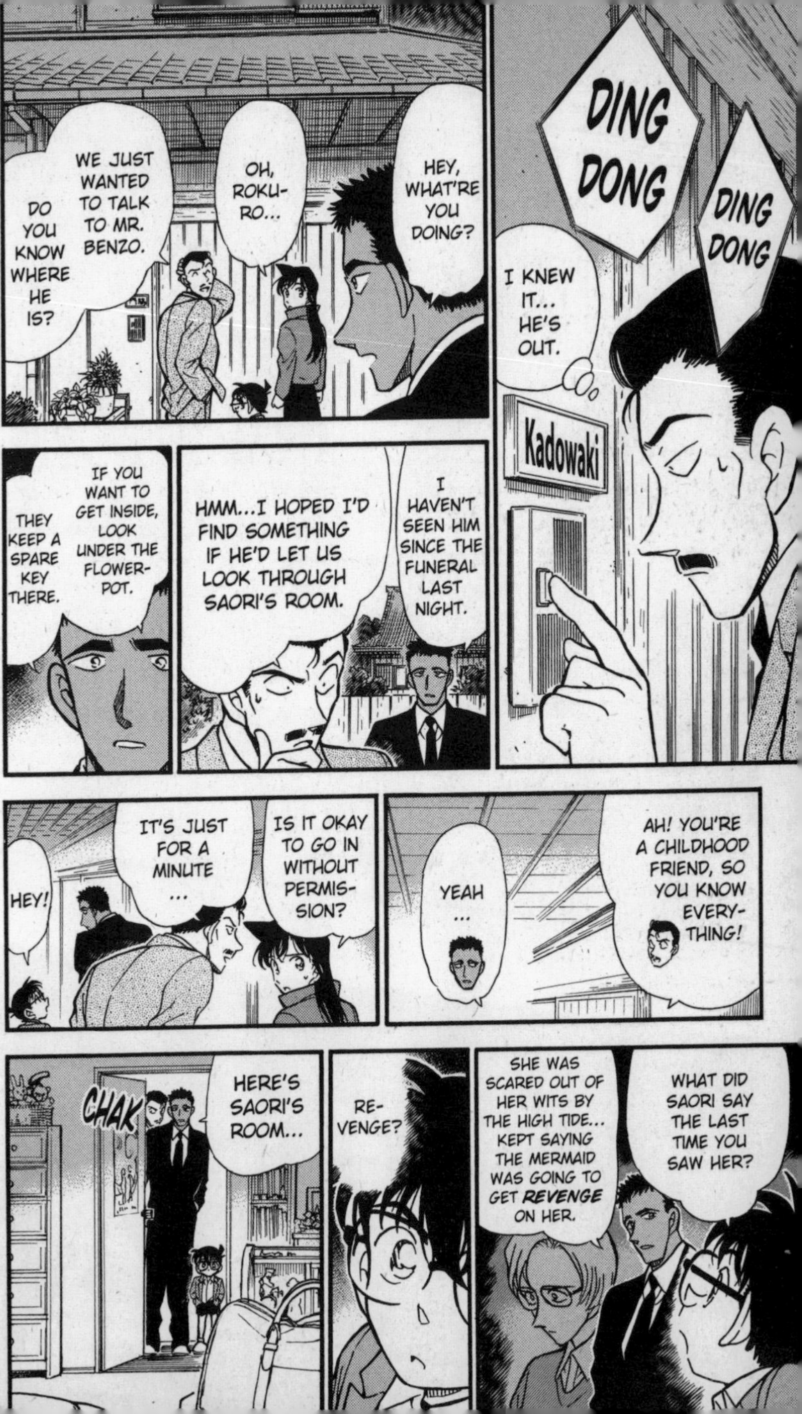
DING DONG
DING DONG
I KNEW IT... HE'S OUT.
Kadowaki
HEY, WHAT'RE YOU DOING?
OH, ROKURO...
WE JUST WANTED TO TALK TO MR. BENZO.
DO YOU KNOW WHERE HE IS?
I HAVEN'T SEEN HIM SINCE THE FUNERAL LAST NIGHT.
HMM...I HOPED I'D FIND SOMETHING IF HE'D LET US LOOK THROUGH SAORI'S ROOM.
IF YOU WANT TO GET INSIDE, LOOK UNDER THE FLOWER-POT.
THEY KEEP A SPARE KEY THERE.
AH! YOU'RE A CHILDHOOD FRIEND, SO YOU KNOW EVERY-THING!
YEAH...
IS IT OKAY TO GO IN WITHOUT PERMIS-SION?
IT'S JUST FOR A MINUTE...
HEY!
WHAT DID SAORI SAY THE LAST TIME YOU SAW HER?
SHE WAS SCARED OUT OF HER WITS BY THE HIGH TIDE... KEPT SAYING THE MERMAID WAS GOING TO GET ***REVENGE*** ON HER.
RE-VENGE?
HERE'S SAORI'S ROOM...
CHAK

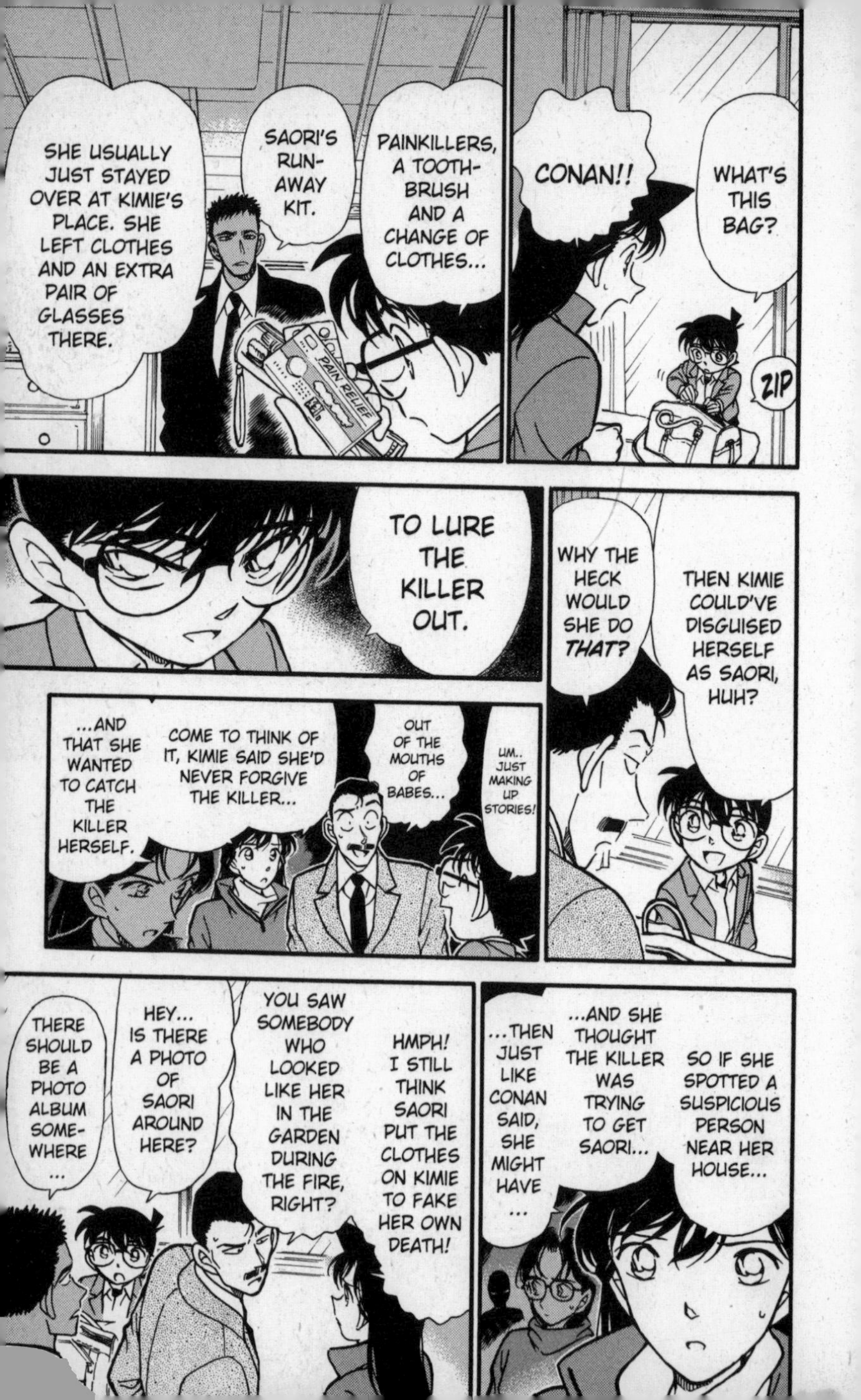
WHAT'S THIS BAG?
ZIP
CONAN!!
PAINKILLERS, A TOOTH-BRUSH AND A CHANGE OF CLOTHES...
SAORI'S RUN-AWAY KIT.
PAIN RELIEF
SHE USUALLY JUST STAYED OVER AT KIMIE'S PLACE. SHE LEFT CLOTHES AND AN EXTRA PAIR OF GLASSES THERE.
THEN KIMIE COULD'VE DISGUISED HERSELF AS SAORI, HUH?
WHY THE HECK WOULD SHE DO *THAT*?
TO LURE THE KILLER OUT.
UM.. JUST MAKING UP STORIES!
OUT OF THE MOUTHS OF BABES...
COME TO THINK OF IT, KIMIE SAID SHE'D NEVER FORGIVE THE KILLER...
...AND THAT SHE WANTED TO CATCH THE KILLER HERSELF.
SO IF SHE SPOTTED A SUSPICIOUS PERSON NEAR HER HOUSE...
...AND SHE THOUGHT THE KILLER WAS TRYING TO GET SAORI...
...THEN JUST LIKE CONAN SAID, SHE MIGHT HAVE ...
HMPH! I STILL THINK SAORI PUT THE CLOTHES ON KIMIE TO FAKE HER OWN DEATH!
YOU SAW SOMEBODY WHO LOOKED LIKE HER IN THE GARDEN DURING THE FIRE, RIGHT?
HEY... IS THERE A PHOTO OF SAORI AROUND HERE?
THERE SHOULD BE A PHOTO ALBUM SOME-WHERE ...

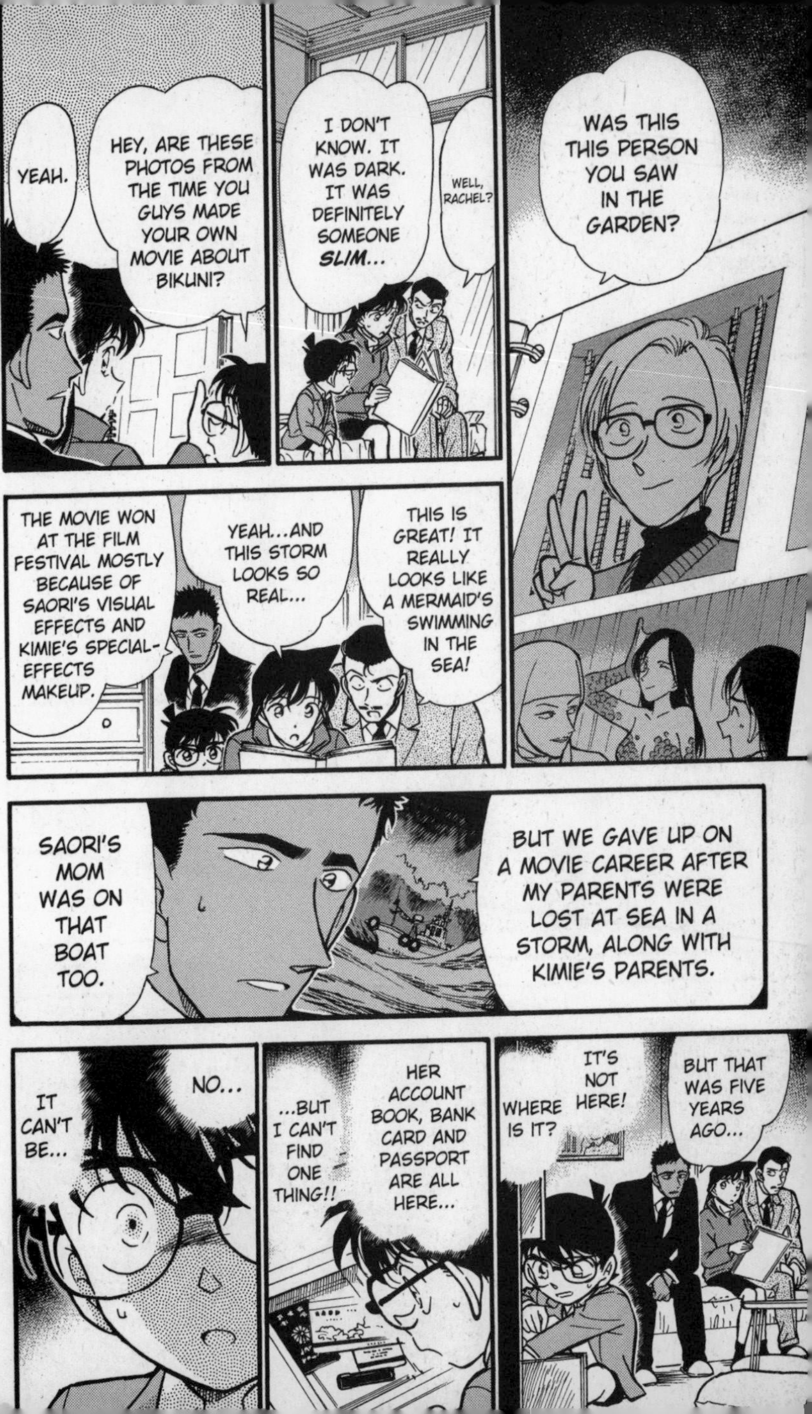
WAS THIS THIS PERSON YOU SAW IN THE GARDEN?
WELL, RACHEL?
I DON'T KNOW. IT WAS DARK. IT WAS DEFINITELY SOMEONE *SLIM*...
HEY, ARE THESE PHOTOS FROM THE TIME YOU GUYS MADE YOUR OWN MOVIE ABOUT BIKUNI?
YEAH.
THIS IS GREAT! IT REALLY LOOKS LIKE A MERMAID'S SWIMMING IN THE SEA!
YEAH...AND THIS STORM LOOKS SO REAL...
THE MOVIE WON AT THE FILM FESTIVAL MOSTLY BECAUSE OF SAORI'S VISUAL EFFECTS AND KIMIE'S SPECIAL-EFFECTS MAKEUP.
BUT WE GAVE UP ON A MOVIE CAREER AFTER MY PARENTS WERE LOST AT SEA IN A STORM, ALONG WITH KIMIE'S PARENTS.
SAORI'S MOM WAS ON THAT BOAT TOO.
BUT THAT WAS FIVE YEARS AGO...
IT'S NOT HERE!
WHERE IS IT?
HER ACCOUNT BOOK, BANK CARD AND PASSPORT ARE ALL HERE...
...BUT I CAN'T FIND ONE THING!!
NO...
IT CAN'T BE...

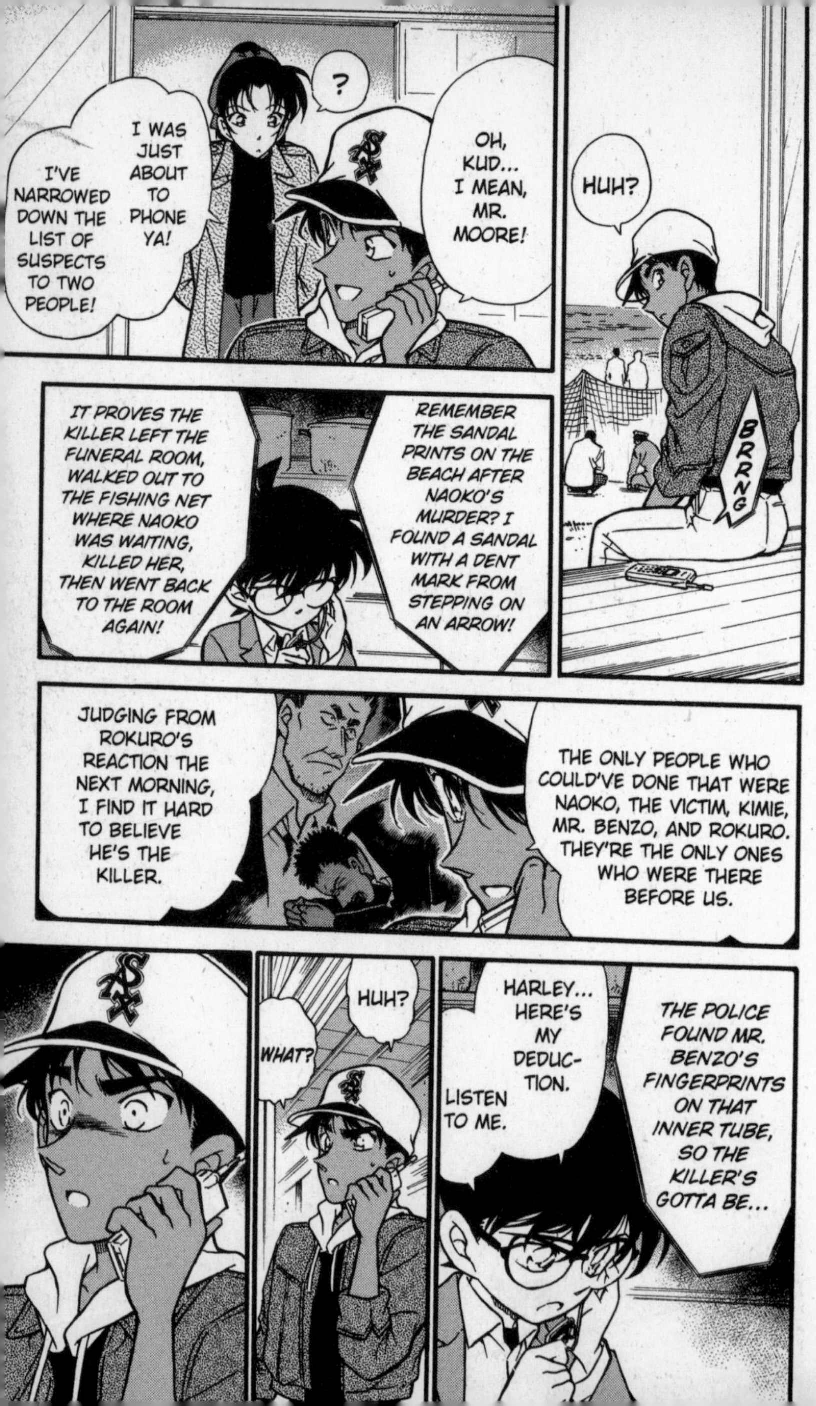
HUH?
BRRNG
OH, KUD... I MEAN, MR. MOORE!
?
I WAS JUST ABOUT TO PHONE YA!
I'VE NARROWED DOWN THE LIST OF SUSPECTS TO TWO PEOPLE!
REMEMBER THE SANDAL PRINTS ON THE BEACH AFTER NAOKO'S MURDER? I FOUND A SANDAL WITH A DENT MARK FROM STEPPING ON AN ARROW!
IT PROVES THE KILLER LEFT THE FUNERAL ROOM, WALKED OUT TO THE FISHING NET WHERE NAOKO WAS WAITING, KILLED HER, THEN WENT BACK TO THE ROOM AGAIN!
THE ONLY PEOPLE WHO COULD'VE DONE THAT WERE NAOKO, THE VICTIM, KIMIE, MR. BENZO, AND ROKURO. THEY'RE THE ONLY ONES WHO WERE THERE BEFORE US.
JUDGING FROM ROKURO'S REACTION THE NEXT MORNING, I FIND IT HARD TO BELIEVE HE'S THE KILLER.
THE POLICE FOUND MR. BENZO'S FINGERPRINTS ON THAT INNER TUBE, SO THE KILLER'S GOTTA BE...
HARLEY... HERE'S MY DEDUC-TION.
LISTEN TO ME.
HUH?
WHAT?

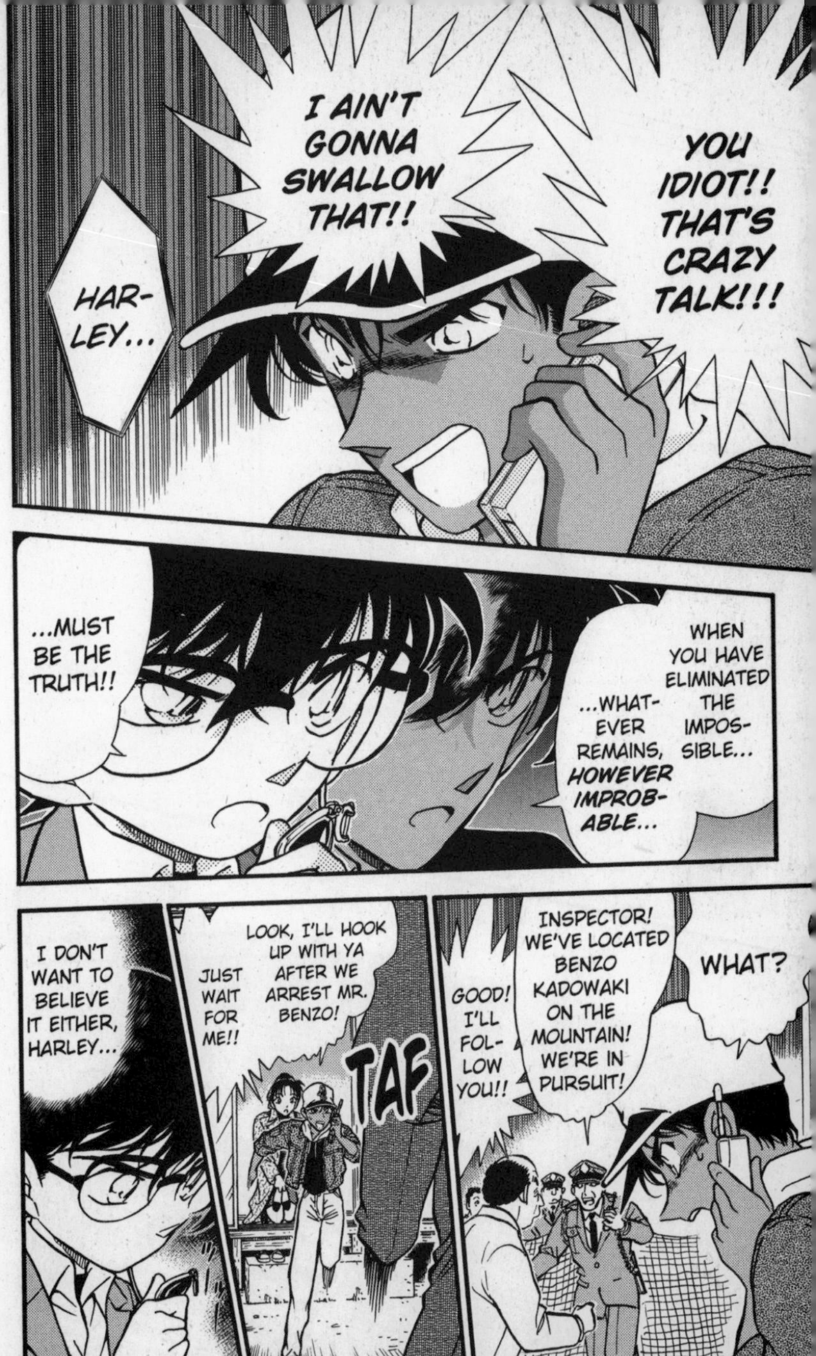

YOU IDIOT!! THAT'S CRAZY TALK!!!
I AIN'T GONNA SWALLOW THAT!!
HAR-LEY...
WHEN YOU HAVE ELIMINATED THE IMPOSSIBLE...
...WHAT-EVER REMAINS, *HOWEVER IMPROB-ABLE...*
...MUST BE THE TRUTH!!
WHAT?
INSPECTOR! WE'VE LOCATED BENZO KADOWAKI ON THE MOUNTAIN! WE'RE IN PURSUIT!
GOOD! I'LL FOL-LOW YOU!!
LOOK, I'LL HOOK UP WITH YA AFTER WE ARREST MR. BENZO!
JUST WAIT FOR ME!!
TAF
I DON'T WANT TO BELIEVE IT EITHER, HARLEY...

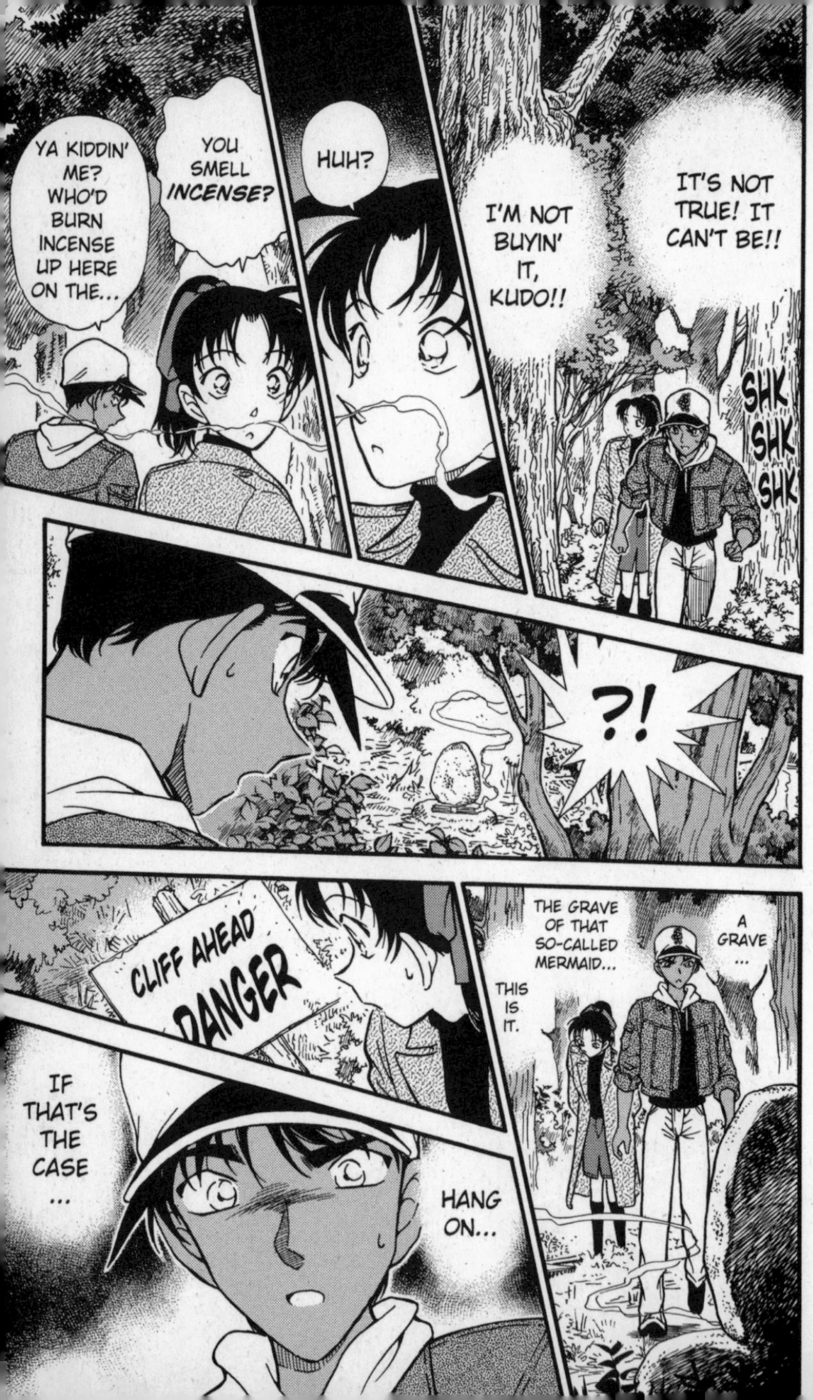

IT'S NOT TRUE! IT CAN'T BE!!
I'M NOT BUYIN' IT, KUDO!!
SHK SHK SHK
HUH?
YOU SMELL INCENSE?
YA KIDDIN' ME? WHO'D BURN INCENSE UP HERE ON THE...
?!
A GRAVE...
THE GRAVE OF THAT SO-CALLED MERMAID...
THIS IS IT.
CLIFF AHEAD
DANGER
HANG ON...
IF THAT'S THE CASE...

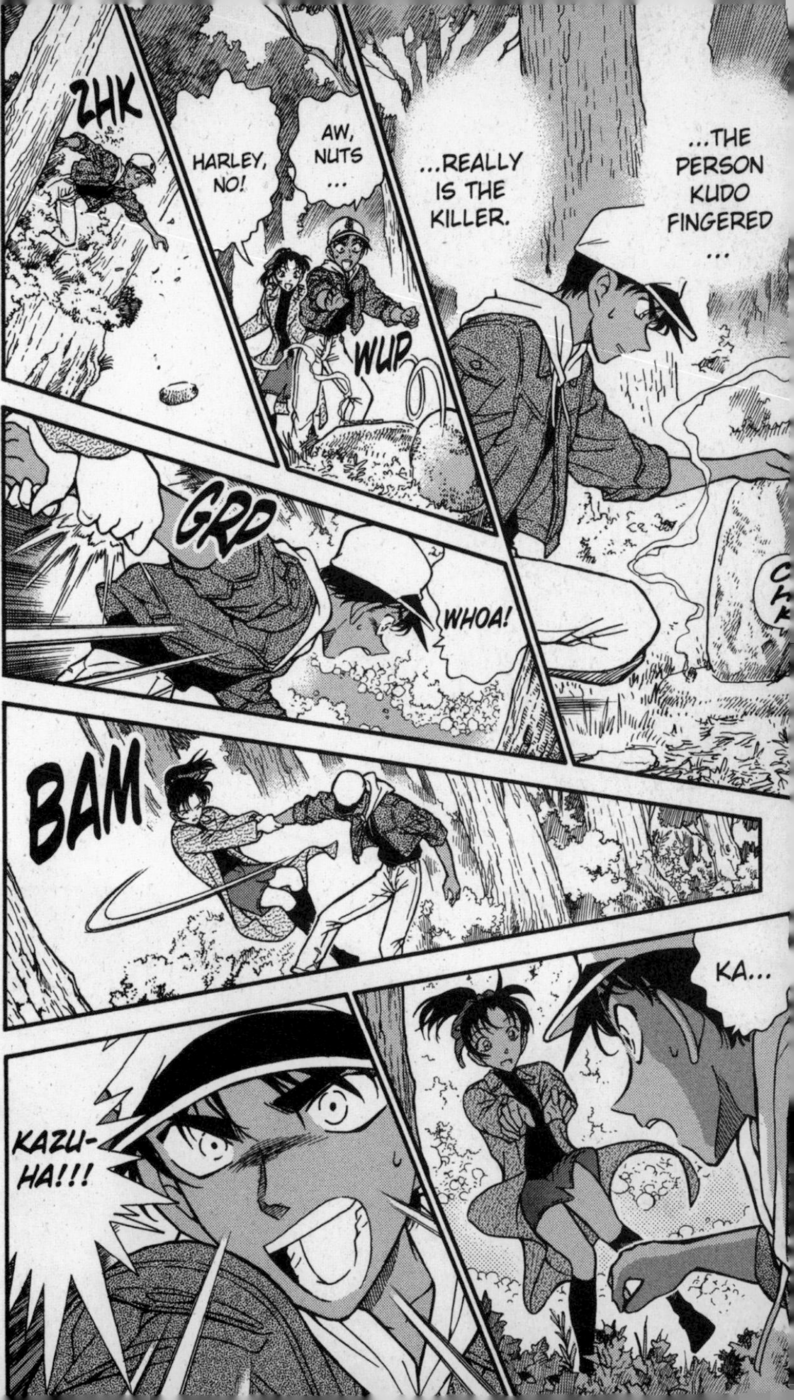
...THE PERSON KUDO FINGERED ...
...REALLY IS THE KILLER.
CHK
AW, NUTS ...
HARLEY, NO!
WUP
ZHK
WHOA!
GRD
BAM
KA...
KAZU-HA!!!

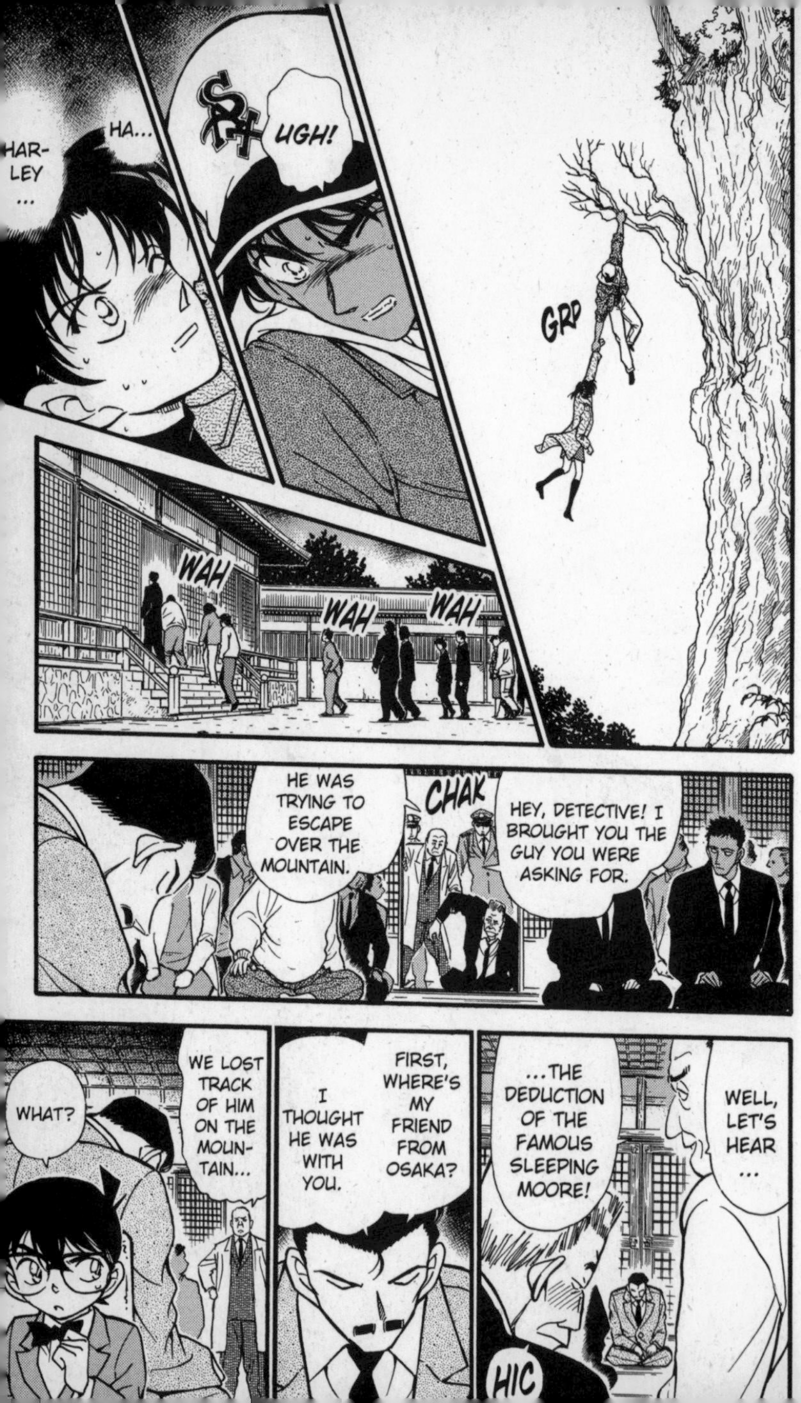
GRP
UGH!
HA...
HAR-LEY ...
WAH
WAH
WAH
HEY, DETECTIVE! I BROUGHT YOU THE GUY YOU WERE ASKING FOR.
CHAK
HE WAS TRYING TO ESCAPE OVER THE MOUNTAIN.
WELL, LET'S HEAR ...
...THE DEDUCTION OF THE FAMOUS SLEEPING MOORE!
HIC
FIRST, WHERE'S MY FRIEND FROM OSAKA?
I THOUGHT HE WAS WITH YOU.
WE LOST TRACK OF HIM ON THE MOUN-TAIN...
WHAT?

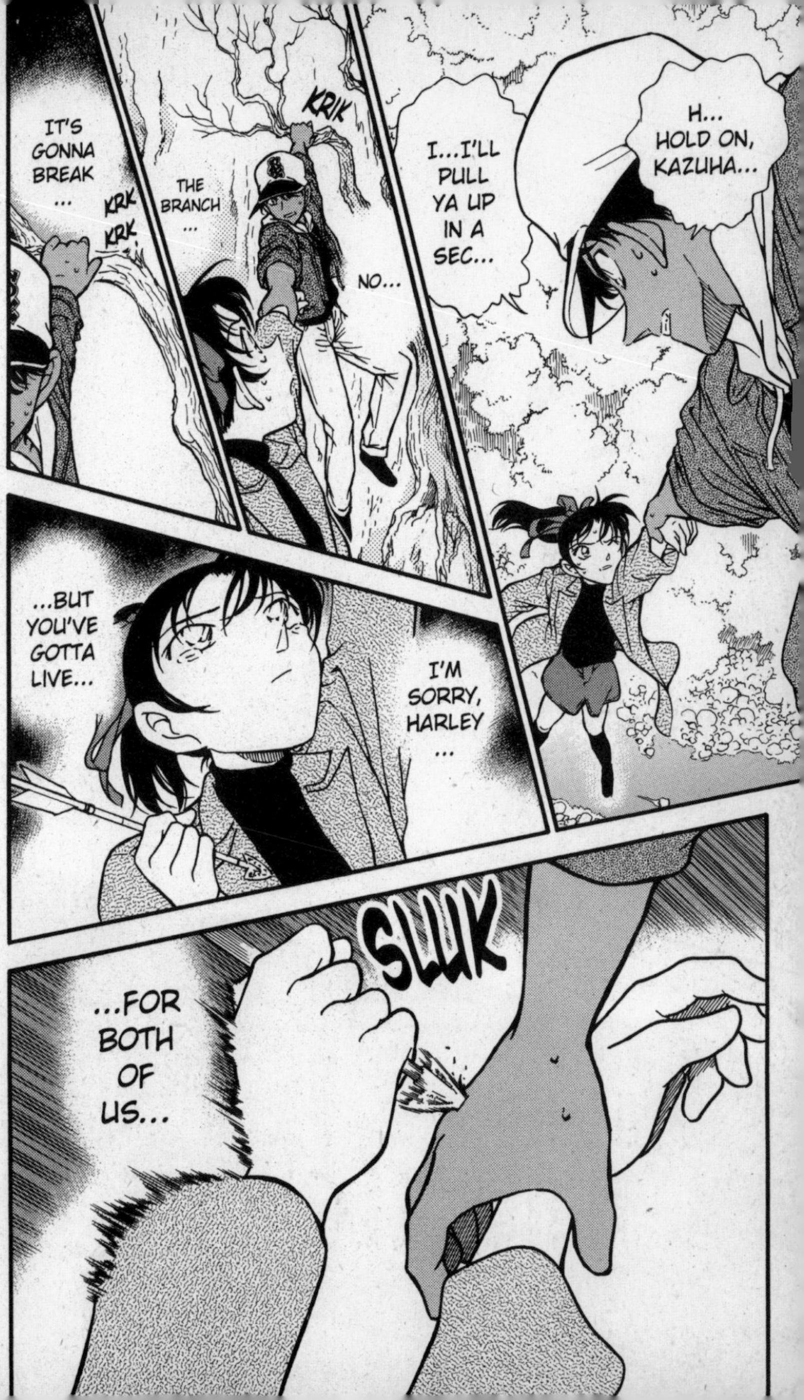
H... HOLD ON, KAZUHA...
I...I'LL PULL YA UP IN A SEC...
KRIK
THE BRANCH ...
NO...
IT'S GONNA BREAK ...
KRK KRK
I'M SORRY, HARLEY ...
...BUT YOU'VE GOTTA LIVE...
SLIIK
...FOR BOTH OF US...

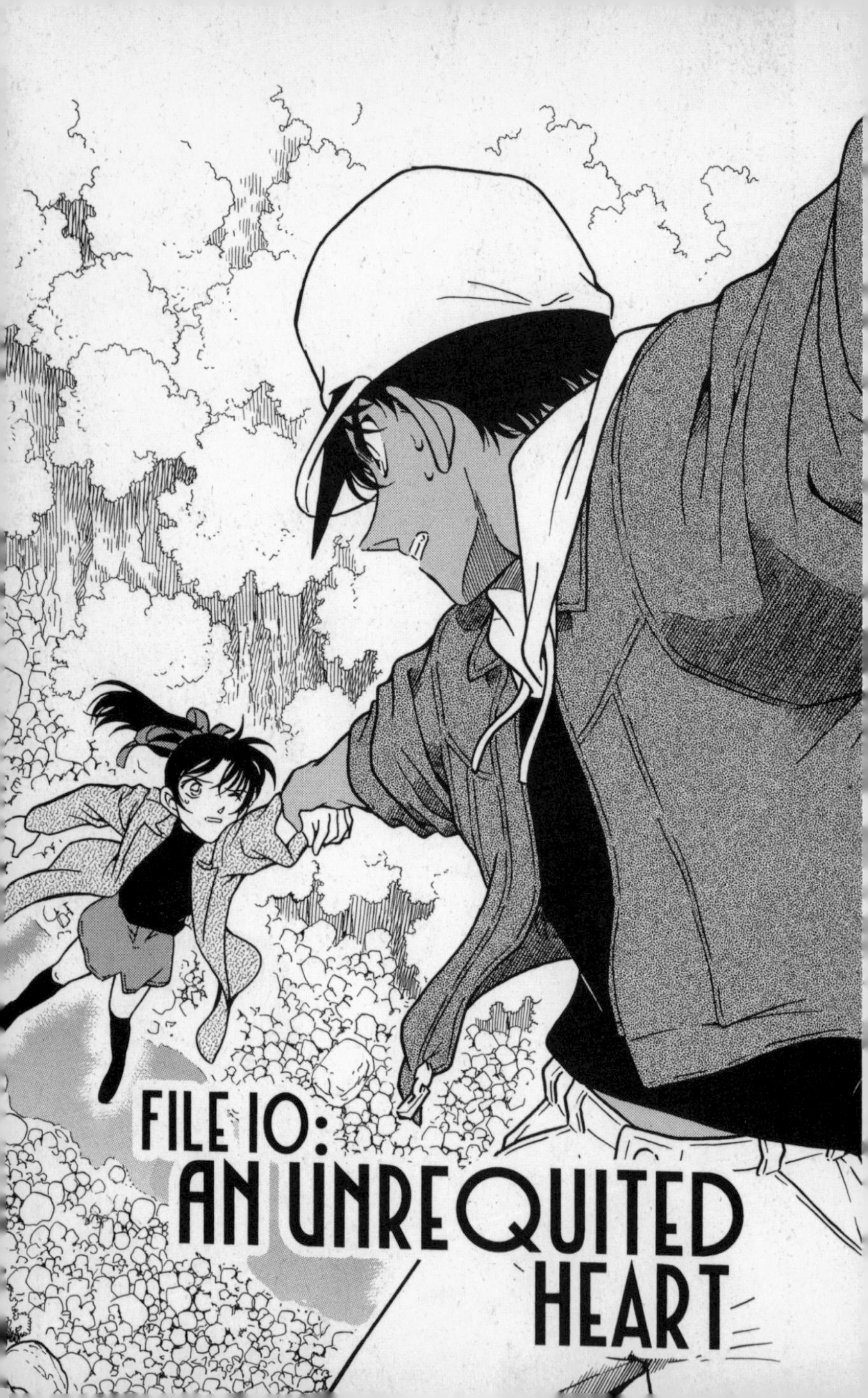
FILE 10:
AN UNREQUITED HEART

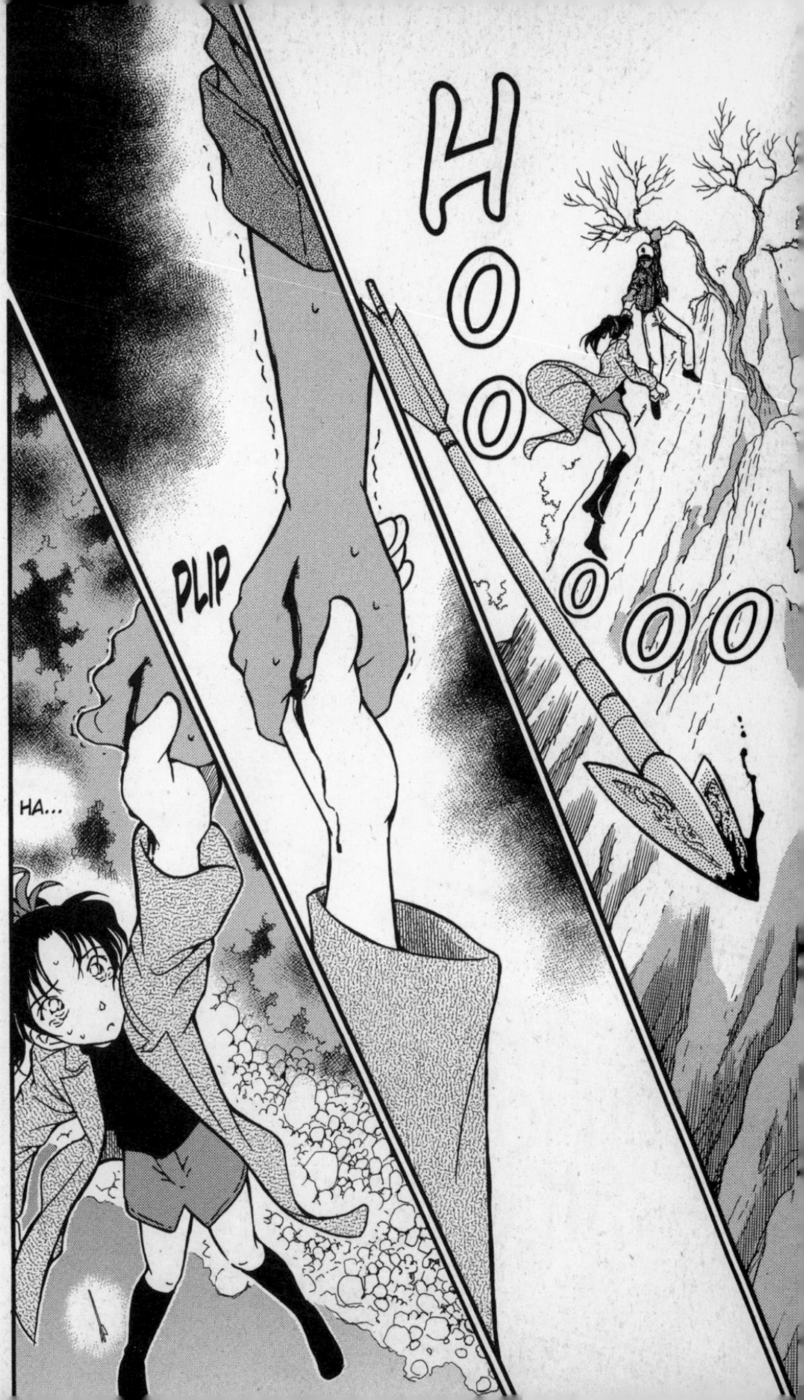
HOOOOOOO
PLIP
HA...

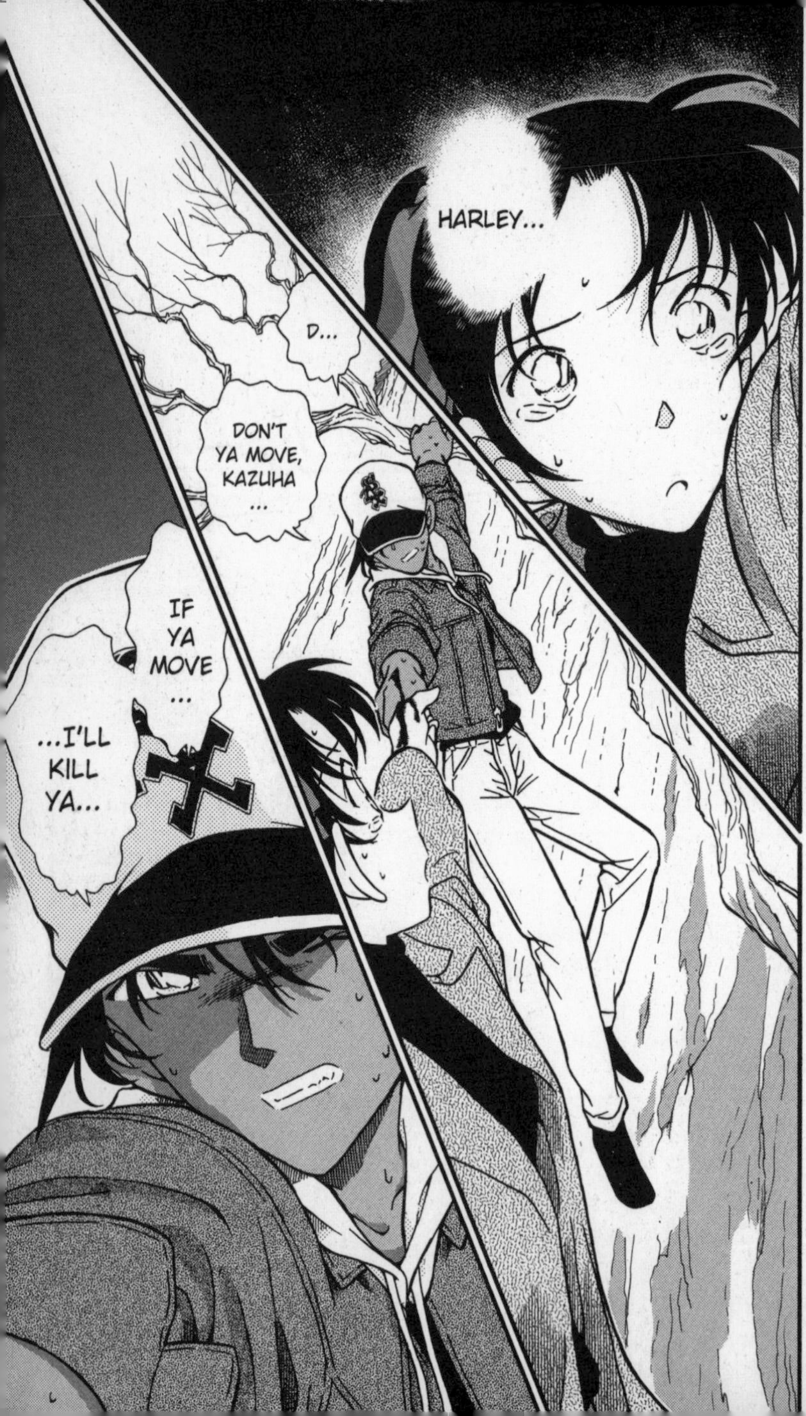
HARLEY...
D...
DON'T YA MOVE, KAZUHA ...
IF YA MOVE ...
...I'LL KILL YA...

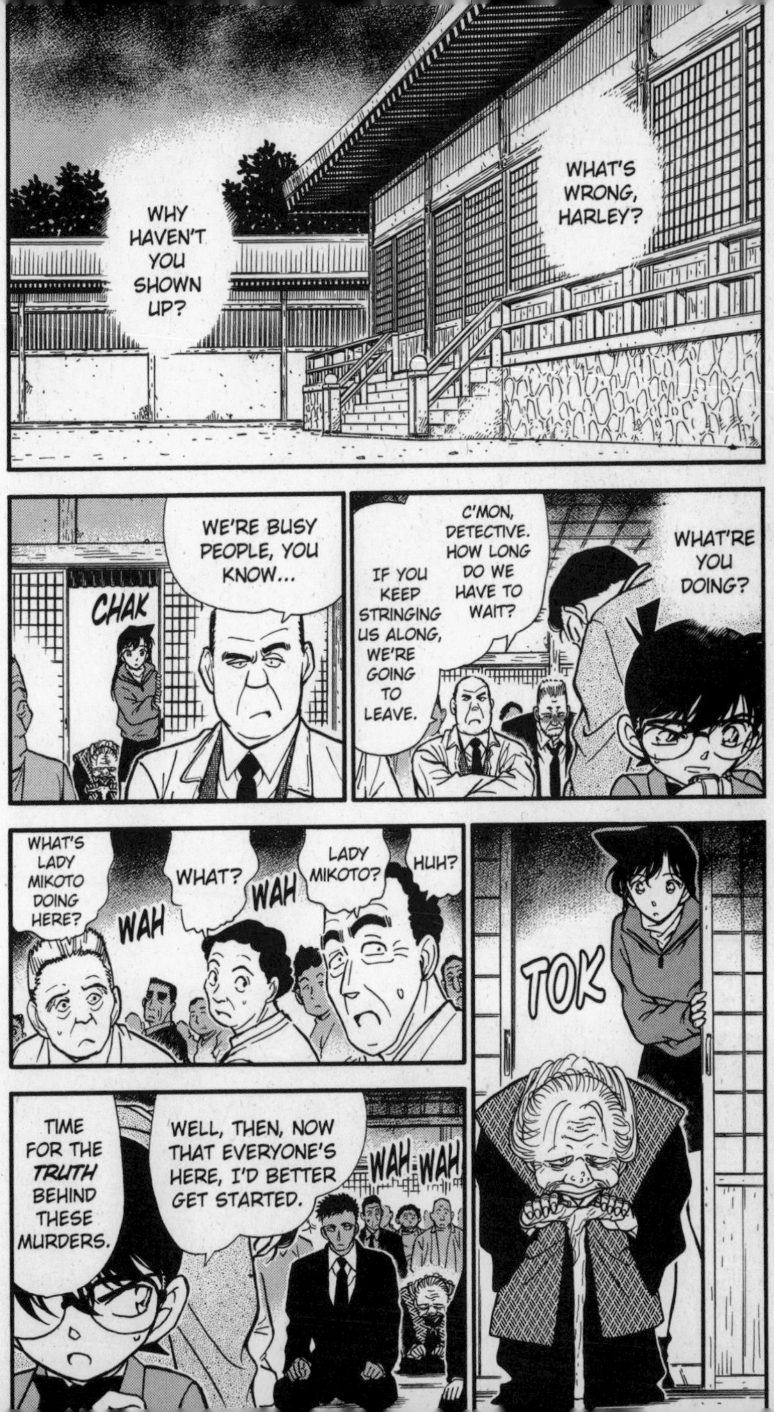
WHAT'S WRONG, HARLEY?
WHY HAVEN'T YOU SHOWN UP?
WHAT'RE YOU DOING?
C'MON, DETECTIVE. HOW LONG DO WE HAVE TO WAIT?
IF YOU KEEP STRINGING US ALONG, WE'RE GOING TO LEAVE.
WE'RE BUSY PEOPLE, YOU KNOW...
CHAK
TOK
HUH?
LADY MIKOTO?
WAH
WHAT?
WAH
WHAT'S LADY MIKOTO DOING HERE?
WAH WAH
WELL, THEN, NOW THAT EVERYONE'S HERE, I'D BETTER GET STARTED.
TIME FOR THE TRUTH BEHIND THESE MURDERS.

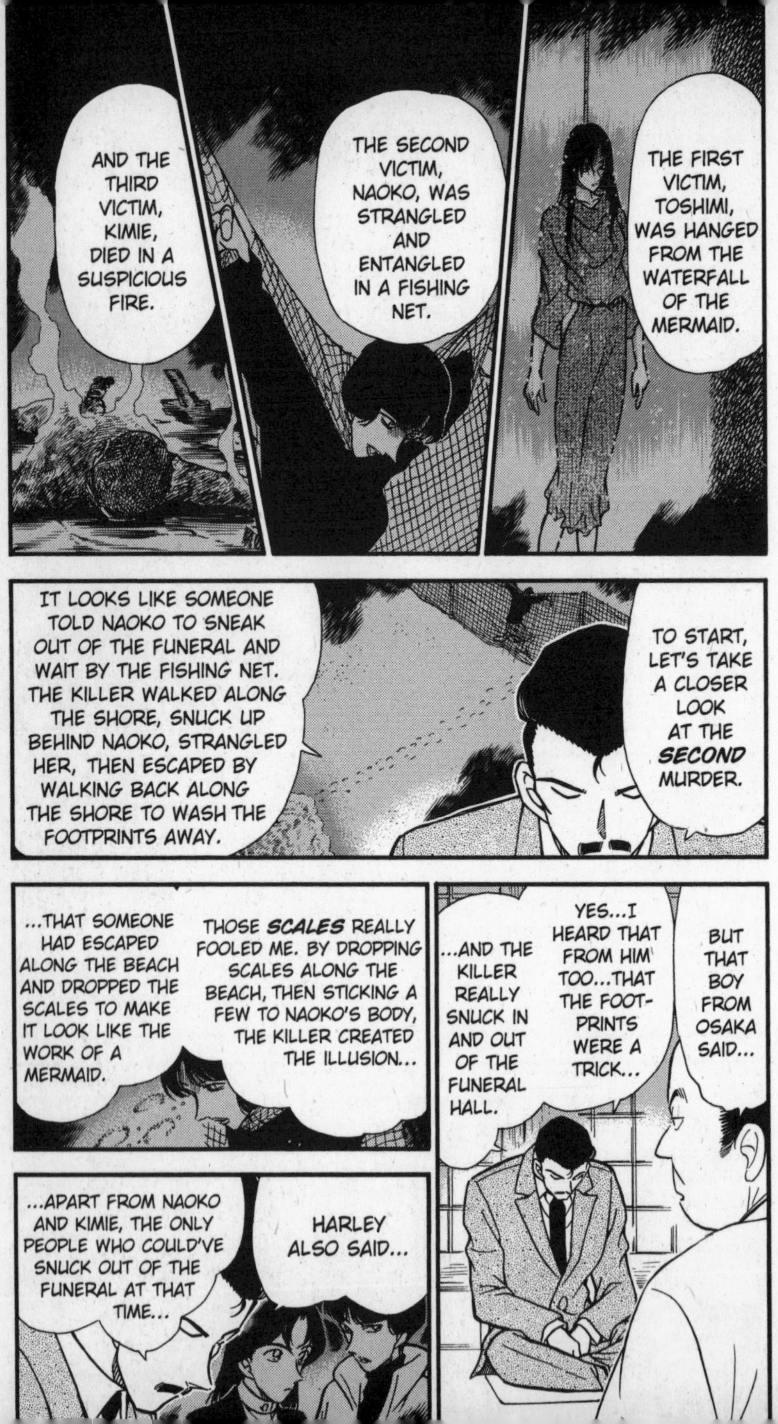
THE FIRST VICTIM, TOSHIMI, WAS HANGED FROM THE WATERFALL OF THE MERMAID.
THE SECOND VICTIM, NAOKO, WAS STRANGLED AND ENTANGLED IN A FISHING NET.
AND THE THIRD VICTIM, KIMIE, DIED IN A SUSPICIOUS FIRE.
TO START, LET'S TAKE A CLOSER LOOK AT THE *SECOND* MURDER.
IT LOOKS LIKE SOMEONE TOLD NAOKO TO SNEAK OUT OF THE FUNERAL AND WAIT BY THE FISHING NET. THE KILLER WALKED ALONG THE SHORE, SNUCK UP BEHIND NAOKO, STRANGLED HER, THEN ESCAPED BY WALKING BACK ALONG THE SHORE TO WASH THE FOOTPRINTS AWAY.
BUT THAT BOY FROM OSAKA SAID...
YES...I HEARD THAT FROM HIM TOO...THAT THE FOOT-PRINTS WERE A TRICK...
...AND THE KILLER REALLY SNUCK IN AND OUT OF THE FUNERAL HALL.
THOSE *SCALES* REALLY FOOLED ME. BY DROPPING SCALES ALONG THE BEACH, THEN STICKING A FEW TO NAOKO'S BODY, THE KILLER CREATED THE ILLUSION...
...THAT SOMEONE HAD ESCAPED ALONG THE BEACH AND DROPPED THE SCALES TO MAKE IT LOOK LIKE THE WORK OF A MERMAID.
HARLEY ALSO SAID...
...APART FROM NAOKO AND KIMIE, THE ONLY PEOPLE WHO COULD'VE SNUCK OUT OF THE FUNERAL AT THAT TIME...

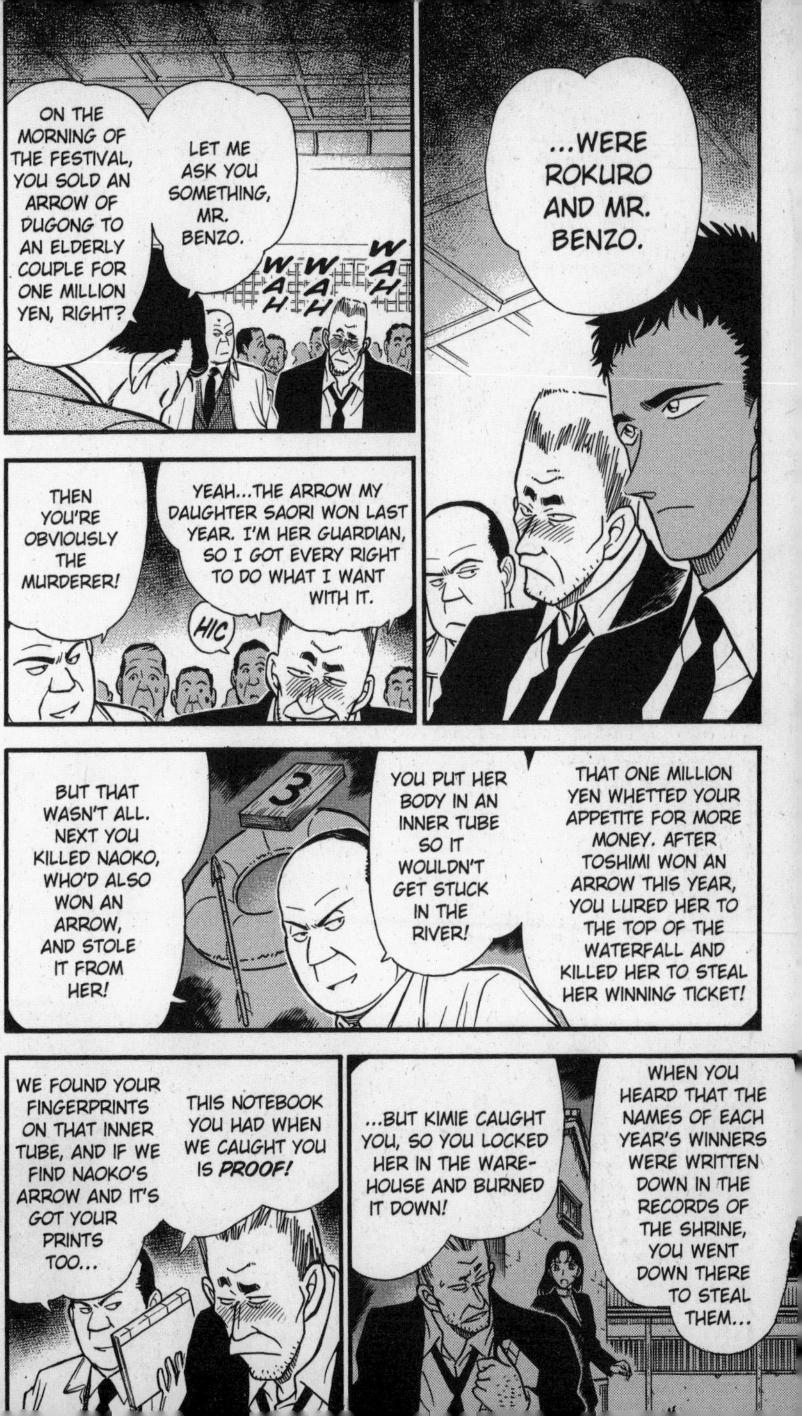
...WERE ROKURO AND MR. BENZO.
LET ME ASK YOU SOMETHING, MR. BENZO.
WAH WAH WAH
ON THE MORNING OF THE FESTIVAL, YOU SOLD AN ARROW OF DUGONG TO AN ELDERLY COUPLE FOR ONE MILLION YEN, RIGHT?
YEAH...THE ARROW MY DAUGHTER SAORI WON LAST YEAR. I'M HER GUARDIAN, SO I GOT EVERY RIGHT TO DO WHAT I WANT WITH IT.
HIC
THEN YOU'RE OBVIOUSLY THE MURDERER!
THAT ONE MILLION YEN WHETTED YOUR APPETITE FOR MORE MONEY. AFTER TOSHIMI WON AN ARROW THIS YEAR, YOU LURED HER TO THE TOP OF THE WATERFALL AND KILLED HER TO STEAL HER WINNING TICKET!
YOU PUT HER BODY IN AN INNER TUBE SO IT WOULDN'T GET STUCK IN THE RIVER!
3
BUT THAT WASN'T ALL. NEXT YOU KILLED NAOKO, WHO'D ALSO WON AN ARROW, AND STOLE IT FROM HER!
WHEN YOU HEARD THAT THE NAMES OF EACH YEAR'S WINNERS WERE WRITTEN DOWN IN THE RECORDS OF THE SHRINE, YOU WENT DOWN THERE TO STEAL THEM...
...BUT KIMIE CAUGHT YOU, SO YOU LOCKED HER IN THE WARE-HOUSE AND BURNED IT DOWN!
THIS NOTEBOOK YOU HAD WHEN WE CAUGHT YOU IS PROOF!
WE FOUND YOUR FINGERPRINTS ON THAT INNER TUBE, AND IF WE FIND NAOKO'S ARROW AND IT'S GOT YOUR PRINTS TOO...

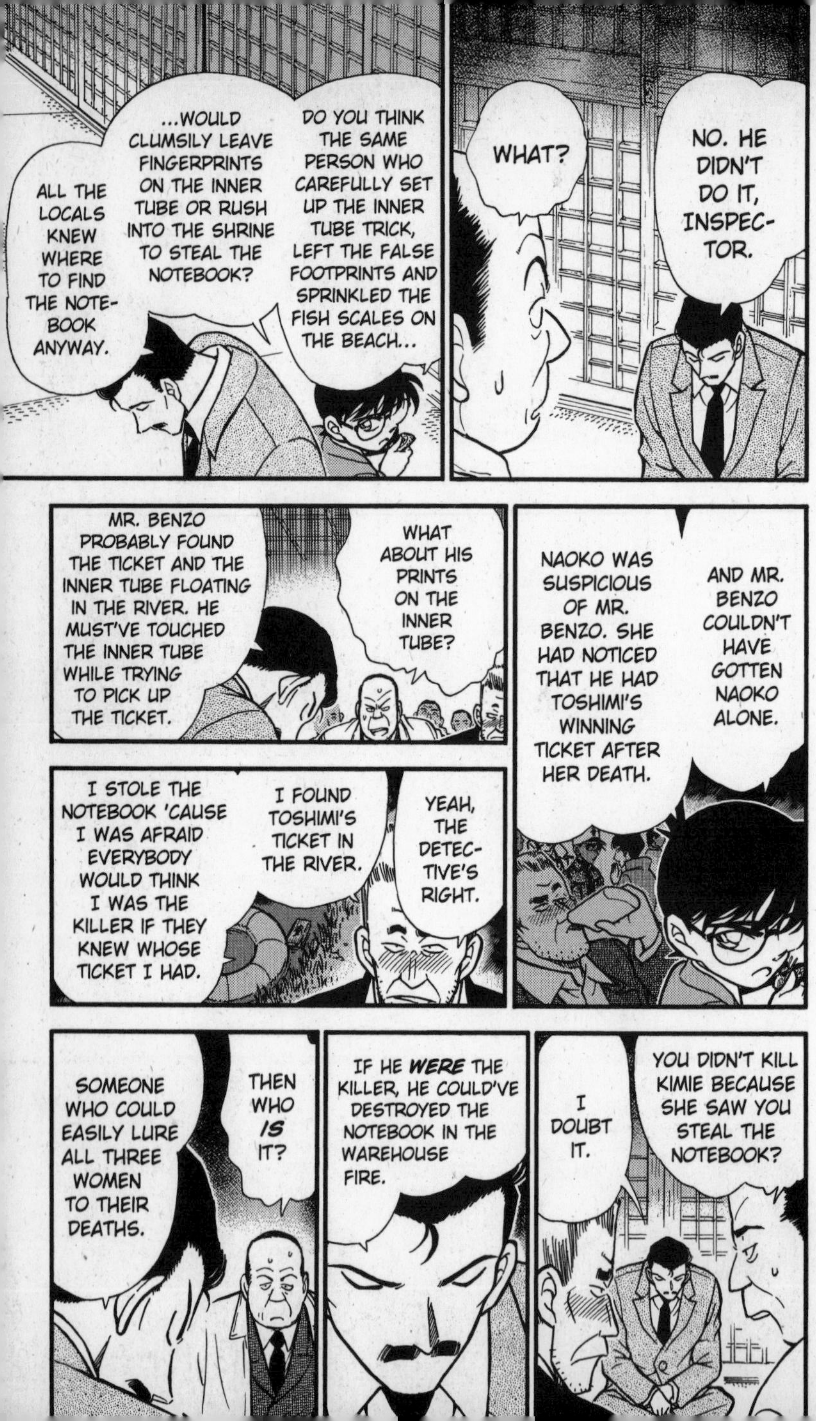
NO. HE DIDN'T DO IT, INSPECTOR.
WHAT?
DO YOU THINK THE SAME PERSON WHO CAREFULLY SET UP THE INNER TUBE TRICK, LEFT THE FALSE FOOTPRINTS AND SPRINKLED THE FISH SCALES ON THE BEACH...
...WOULD CLUMSILY LEAVE FINGERPRINTS ON THE INNER TUBE OR RUSH INTO THE SHRINE TO STEAL THE NOTEBOOK?
ALL THE LOCALS KNEW WHERE TO FIND THE NOTE-BOOK ANYWAY.
NAOKO WAS SUSPICIOUS OF MR. BENZO. SHE HAD NOTICED THAT HE HAD TOSHIMI'S WINNING TICKET AFTER HER DEATH.
AND MR. BENZO COULDN'T HAVE GOTTEN NAOKO ALONE.
WHAT ABOUT HIS PRINTS ON THE INNER TUBE?
MR. BENZO PROBABLY FOUND THE TICKET AND THE INNER TUBE FLOATING IN THE RIVER. HE MUST'VE TOUCHED THE INNER TUBE WHILE TRYING TO PICK UP THE TICKET.
YEAH, THE DETEC-TIVE'S RIGHT.
I FOUND TOSHIMI'S TICKET IN THE RIVER.
I STOLE THE NOTEBOOK 'CAUSE I WAS AFRAID EVERYBODY WOULD THINK I WAS THE KILLER IF THEY KNEW WHOSE TICKET I HAD.
YOU DIDN'T KILL KIMIE BECAUSE SHE SAW YOU STEAL THE NOTEBOOK?
I DOUBT IT.
IF HE *WERE* THE KILLER, HE COULD'VE DESTROYED THE NOTEBOOK IN THE WAREHOUSE FIRE.
THEN WHO *IS* IT?
SOMEONE WHO COULD EASILY LURE ALL THREE WOMEN TO THEIR DEATHS.

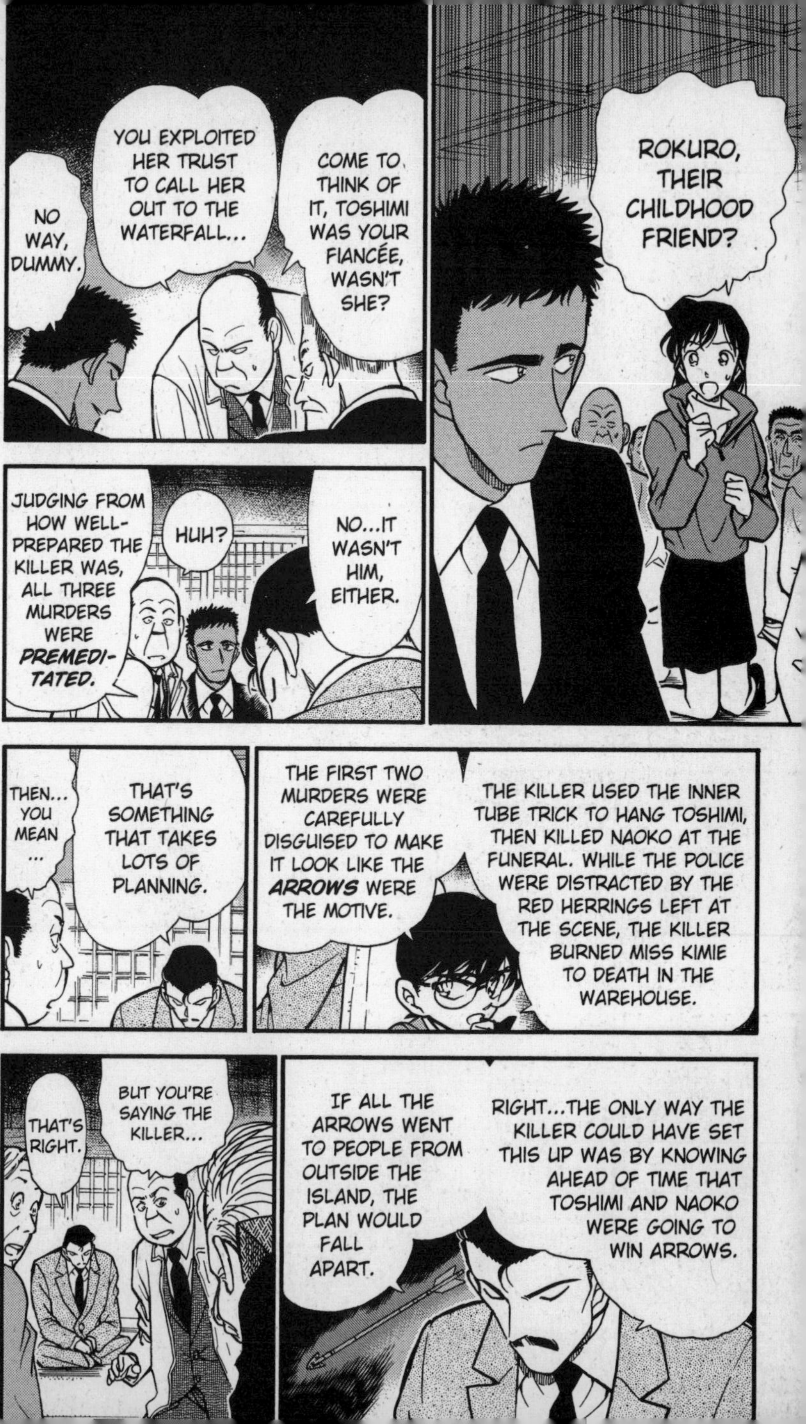
ROKURO, THEIR CHILDHOOD FRIEND?
COME TO THINK OF IT, TOSHIMI WAS YOUR FIANCÉE, WASN'T SHE?
YOU EXPLOITED HER TRUST TO CALL HER OUT TO THE WATERFALL...
NO WAY, DUMMY.
NO...IT WASN'T HIM, EITHER.
HUH?
JUDGING FROM HOW WELL-PREPARED THE KILLER WAS, ALL THREE MURDERS WERE *PREMEDITATED.*
THE KILLER USED THE INNER TUBE TRICK TO HANG TOSHIMI, THEN KILLED NAOKO AT THE FUNERAL. WHILE THE POLICE WERE DISTRACTED BY THE RED HERRINGS LEFT AT THE SCENE, THE KILLER BURNED MISS KIMIE TO DEATH IN THE WAREHOUSE.
THE FIRST TWO MURDERS WERE CAREFULLY DISGUISED TO MAKE IT LOOK LIKE THE *ARROWS* WERE THE MOTIVE.
THAT'S SOMETHING THAT TAKES LOTS OF PLANNING.
THEN... YOU MEAN ...
RIGHT...THE ONLY WAY THE KILLER COULD HAVE SET THIS UP WAS BY KNOWING AHEAD OF TIME THAT TOSHIMI AND NAOKO WERE GOING TO WIN ARROWS.
IF ALL THE ARROWS WENT TO PEOPLE FROM OUTSIDE THE ISLAND, THE PLAN WOULD FALL APART.
BUT YOU'RE SAYING THE KILLER...
THAT'S RIGHT.

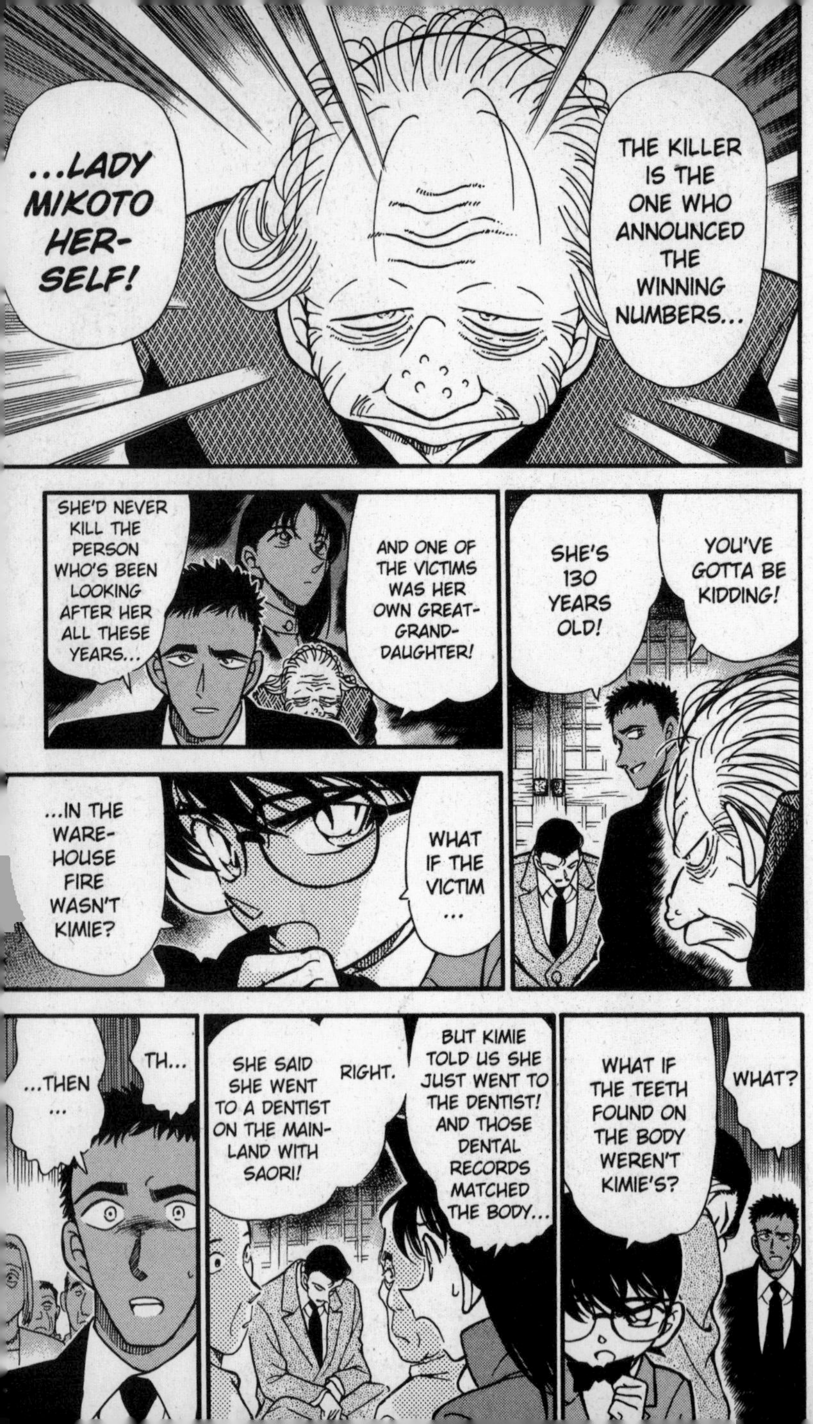
THE KILLER IS THE ONE WHO ANNOUNCED THE WINNING NUMBERS...
...LADY MIKOTO HERSELF!
YOU'VE GOTTA BE KIDDING!
SHE'S 130 YEARS OLD!
AND ONE OF THE VICTIMS WAS HER OWN GREAT-GRANDDAUGHTER!
SHE'D NEVER KILL THE PERSON WHO'S BEEN LOOKING AFTER HER ALL THESE YEARS...
WHAT IF THE VICTIM...
...IN THE WAREHOUSE FIRE WASN'T KIMIE?
WHAT?
WHAT IF THE TEETH FOUND ON THE BODY WEREN'T KIMIE'S?
BUT KIMIE TOLD US SHE JUST WENT TO THE DENTIST! AND THOSE DENTAL RECORDS MATCHED THE BODY...
RIGHT.
SHE SAID SHE WENT TO A DENTIST ON THE MAINLAND WITH SAORI!
TH...
...THEN...

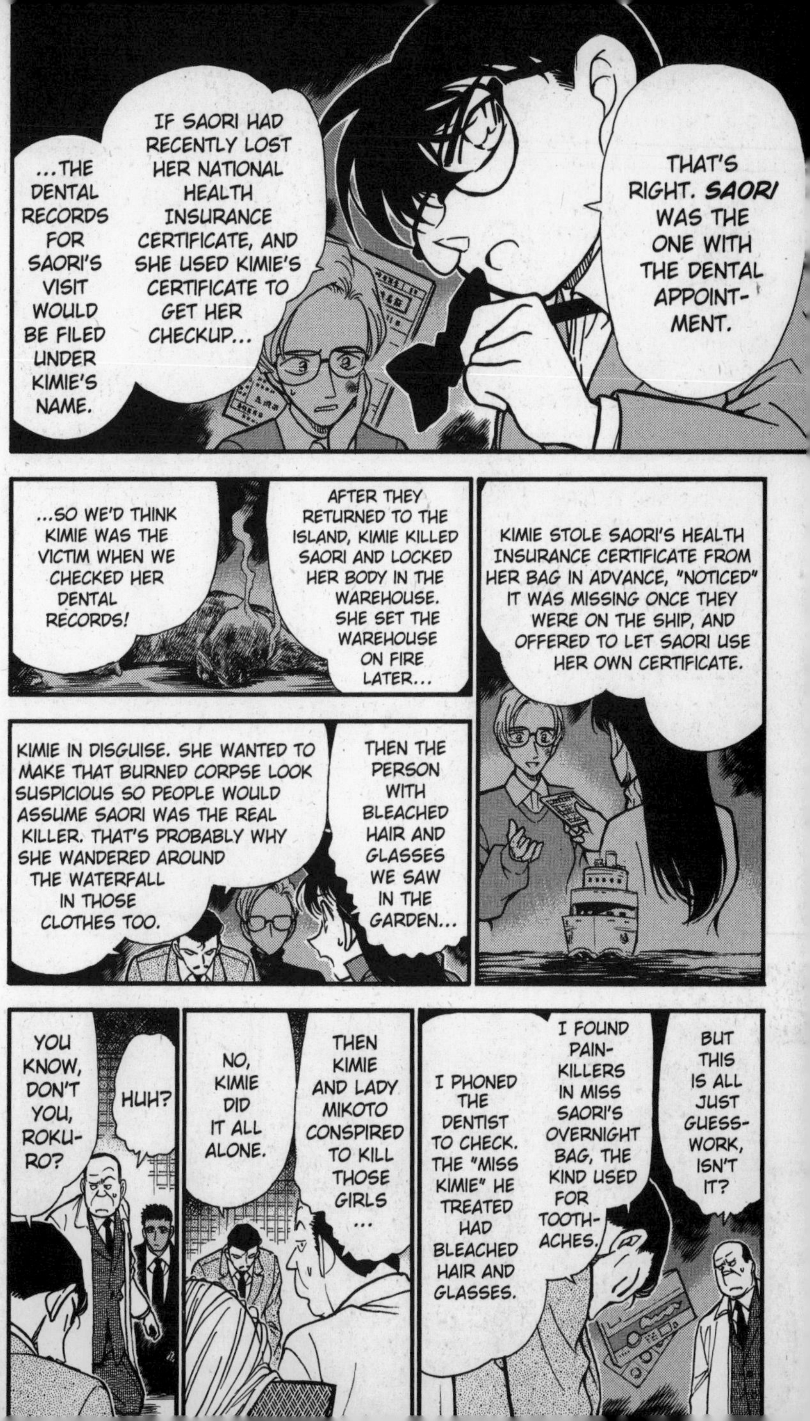
THAT'S RIGHT. *SAORI* WAS THE ONE WITH THE DENTAL APPOINTMENT.
IF SAORI HAD RECENTLY LOST HER NATIONAL HEALTH INSURANCE CERTIFICATE, AND SHE USED KIMIE'S CERTIFICATE TO GET HER CHECKUP...
...THE DENTAL RECORDS FOR SAORI'S VISIT WOULD BE FILED UNDER KIMIE'S NAME.
KIMIE STOLE SAORI'S HEALTH INSURANCE CERTIFICATE FROM HER BAG IN ADVANCE, "NOTICED" IT WAS MISSING ONCE THEY WERE ON THE SHIP, AND OFFERED TO LET SAORI USE HER OWN CERTIFICATE.
AFTER THEY RETURNED TO THE ISLAND, KIMIE KILLED SAORI AND LOCKED HER BODY IN THE WAREHOUSE. SHE SET THE WAREHOUSE ON FIRE LATER...
...SO WE'D THINK KIMIE WAS THE VICTIM WHEN WE CHECKED HER DENTAL RECORDS!
THEN THE PERSON WITH BLEACHED HAIR AND GLASSES WE SAW IN THE GARDEN...
KIMIE IN DISGUISE. SHE WANTED TO MAKE THAT BURNED CORPSE LOOK SUSPICIOUS SO PEOPLE WOULD ASSUME SAORI WAS THE REAL KILLER. THAT'S PROBABLY WHY SHE WANDERED AROUND THE WATERFALL IN THOSE CLOTHES TOO.
BUT THIS IS ALL JUST GUESS-WORK, ISN'T IT?
I FOUND PAIN-KILLERS IN MISS SAORI'S OVERNIGHT BAG, THE KIND USED FOR TOOTH-ACHES.
I PHONED THE DENTIST TO CHECK. THE "MISS KIMIE" HE TREATED HAD BLEACHED HAIR AND GLASSES.
THEN KIMIE AND LADY MIKOTO CONSPIRED TO KILL THOSE GIRLS...
NO, KIMIE DID IT ALL ALONE.
HUH?
YOU KNOW, DON'T YOU, ROKU-RO?

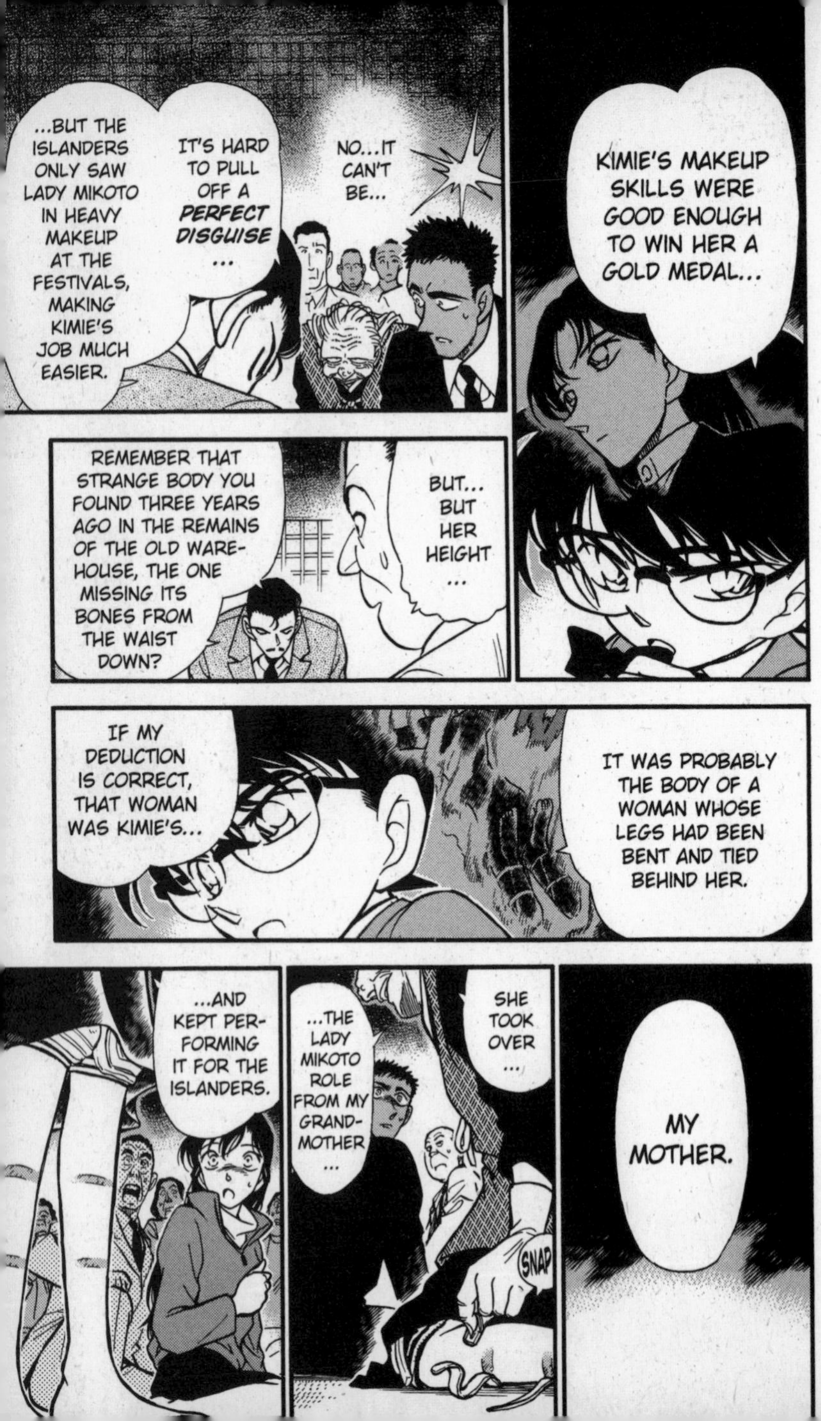
KIMIE'S MAKEUP SKILLS WERE GOOD ENOUGH TO WIN HER A GOLD MEDAL...
NO...IT CAN'T BE...
IT'S HARD TO PULL OFF A PERFECT DISGUISE...
...BUT THE ISLANDERS ONLY SAW LADY MIKOTO IN HEAVY MAKEUP AT THE FESTIVALS, MAKING KIMIE'S JOB MUCH EASIER.
BUT... BUT HER HEIGHT...
REMEMBER THAT STRANGE BODY YOU FOUND THREE YEARS AGO IN THE REMAINS OF THE OLD WARE-HOUSE, THE ONE MISSING ITS BONES FROM THE WAIST DOWN?
IT WAS PROBABLY THE BODY OF A WOMAN WHOSE LEGS HAD BEEN BENT AND TIED BEHIND HER.
IF MY DEDUCTION IS CORRECT, THAT WOMAN WAS KIMIE'S...
MY MOTHER.
SHE TOOK OVER...
...THE LADY MIKOTO ROLE FROM MY GRAND-MOTHER...
SNAP
...AND KEPT PER-FORMING IT FOR THE ISLANDERS.

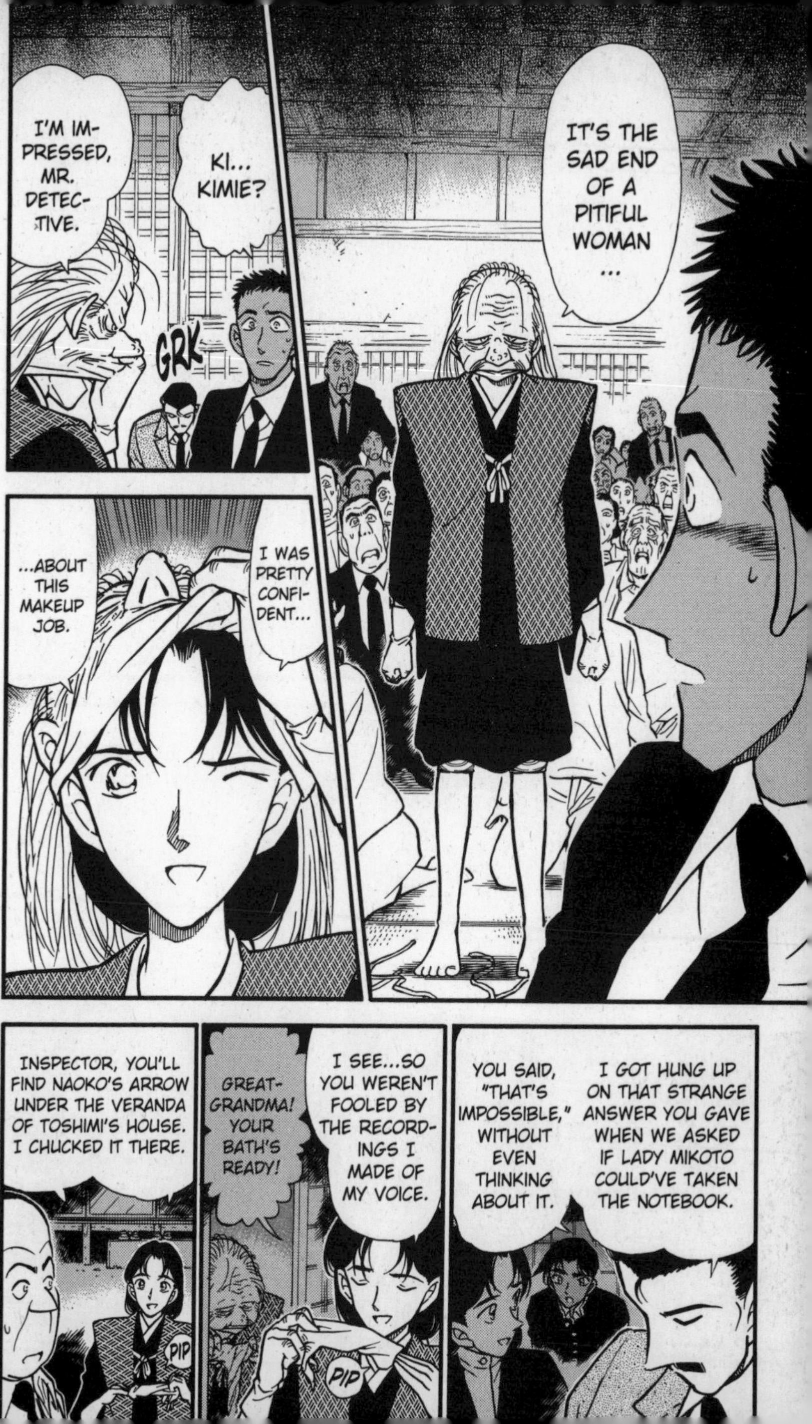
IT'S THE SAD END OF A PITIFUL WOMAN ...
KI... KIMIE?
I'M IM-PRESSED, MR. DETEC-TIVE.
GRK
I WAS PRETTY CONFI-DENT...
...ABOUT THIS MAKEUP JOB.
I GOT HUNG UP ON THAT STRANGE ANSWER YOU GAVE WHEN WE ASKED IF LADY MIKOTO COULD'VE TAKEN THE NOTEBOOK.
YOU SAID, "THAT'S IMPOSSIBLE," WITHOUT EVEN THINKING ABOUT IT.
I SEE...SO YOU WEREN'T FOOLED BY THE RECORD-INGS I MADE OF MY VOICE.
GREAT-GRANDMA! YOUR BATH'S READY!
PIP
INSPECTOR, YOU'LL FIND NAOKO'S ARROW UNDER THE VERANDA OF TOSHIMI'S HOUSE. I CHUCKED IT THERE.
PIP

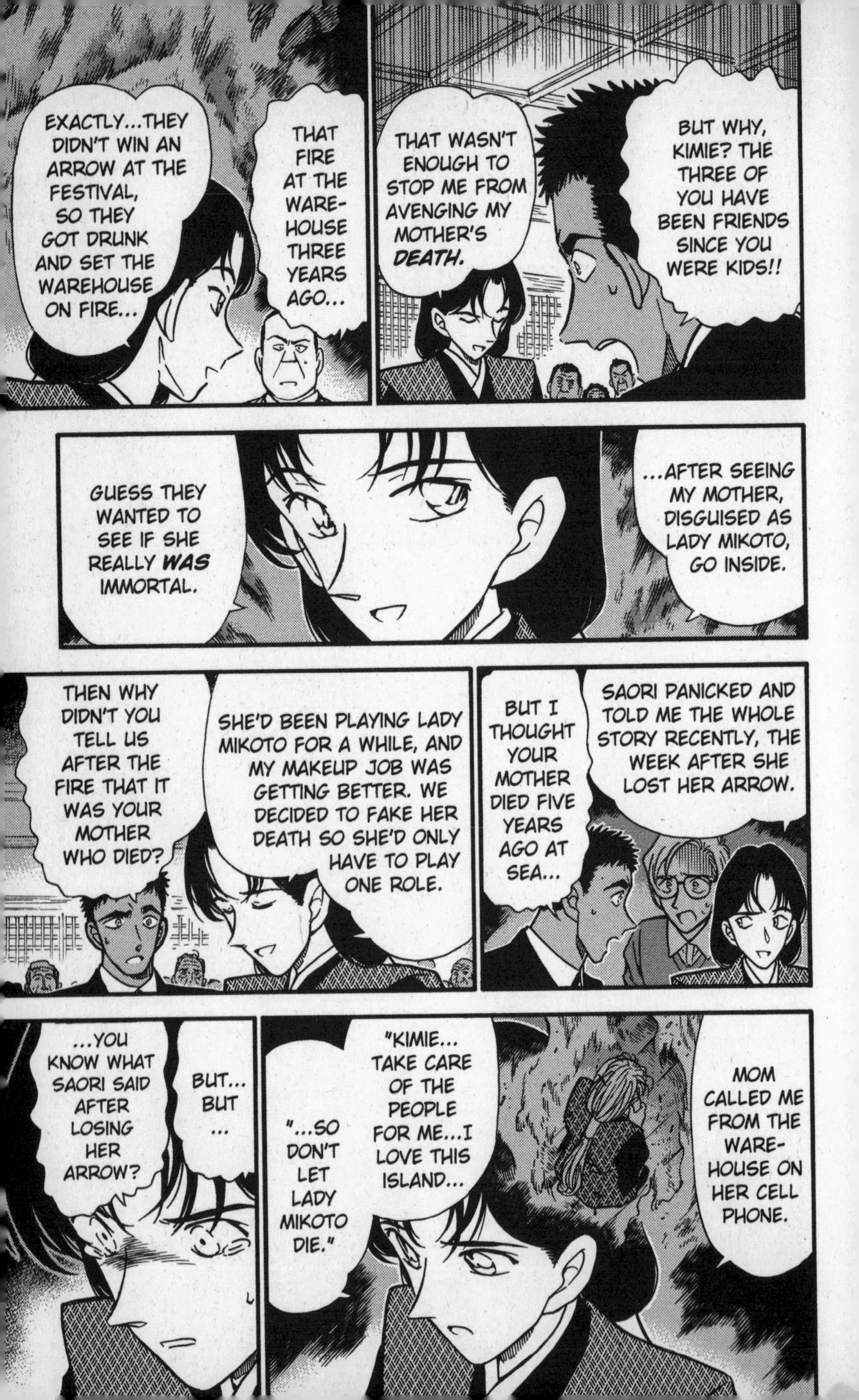
BUT WHY, KIMIE? THE THREE OF YOU HAVE BEEN FRIENDS SINCE YOU WERE KIDS!!
THAT WASN'T ENOUGH TO STOP ME FROM AVENGING MY MOTHER'S DEATH.
THAT FIRE AT THE WAREHOUSE THREE YEARS AGO...
EXACTLY...THEY DIDN'T WIN AN ARROW AT THE FESTIVAL, SO THEY GOT DRUNK AND SET THE WAREHOUSE ON FIRE...
...AFTER SEEING MY MOTHER, DISGUISED AS LADY MIKOTO, GO INSIDE.
GUESS THEY WANTED TO SEE IF SHE REALLY WAS IMMORTAL.
SAORI PANICKED AND TOLD ME THE WHOLE STORY RECENTLY, THE WEEK AFTER SHE LOST HER ARROW.
BUT I THOUGHT YOUR MOTHER DIED FIVE YEARS AGO AT SEA...
THEN WHY DIDN'T YOU TELL US AFTER THE FIRE THAT IT WAS YOUR MOTHER WHO DIED?
SHE'D BEEN PLAYING LADY MIKOTO FOR A WHILE, AND MY MAKEUP JOB WAS GETTING BETTER. WE DECIDED TO FAKE HER DEATH SO SHE'D ONLY HAVE TO PLAY ONE ROLE.
MOM CALLED ME FROM THE WAREHOUSE ON HER CELL PHONE.
"KIMIE... TAKE CARE OF THE PEOPLE FOR ME...I LOVE THIS ISLAND...
"...SO DON'T LET LADY MIKOTO DIE."
BUT... BUT ...
...YOU KNOW WHAT SAORI SAID AFTER LOSING HER ARROW?

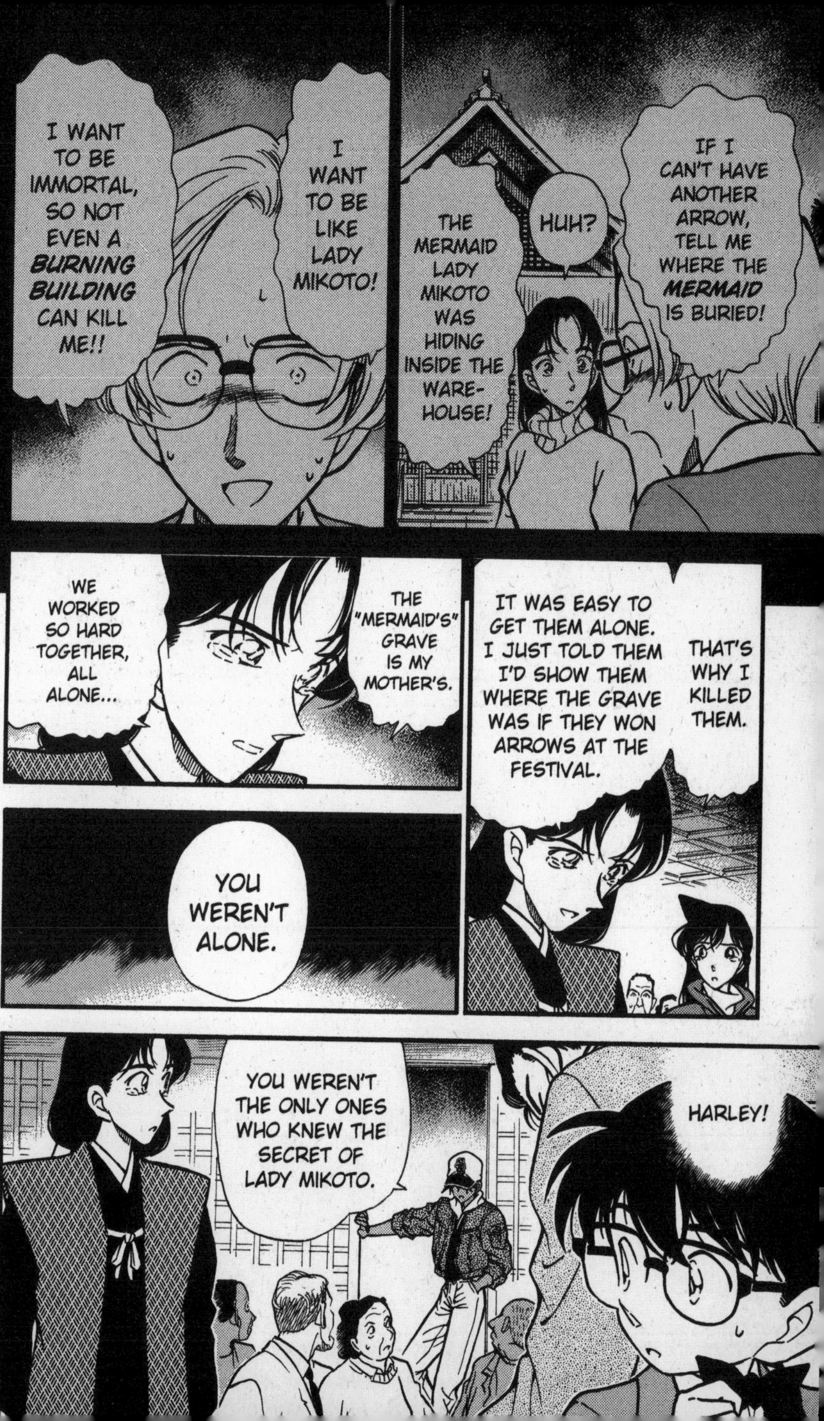
IF I CAN'T HAVE ANOTHER ARROW, TELL ME WHERE THE MERMAID IS BURIED!
HUH?
THE MERMAID LADY MIKOTO WAS HIDING INSIDE THE WARE-HOUSE!
I WANT TO BE LIKE LADY MIKOTO!
I WANT TO BE IMMORTAL, SO NOT EVEN A BURNING BUILDING CAN KILL ME!!
THAT'S WHY I KILLED THEM.
IT WAS EASY TO GET THEM ALONE. I JUST TOLD THEM I'D SHOW THEM WHERE THE GRAVE WAS IF THEY WON ARROWS AT THE FESTIVAL.
THE "MERMAID'S" GRAVE IS MY MOTHER'S.
WE WORKED SO HARD TOGETHER, ALL ALONE...
YOU WEREN'T ALONE.
HARLEY!
YOU WEREN'T THE ONLY ONES WHO KNEW THE SECRET OF LADY MIKOTO.

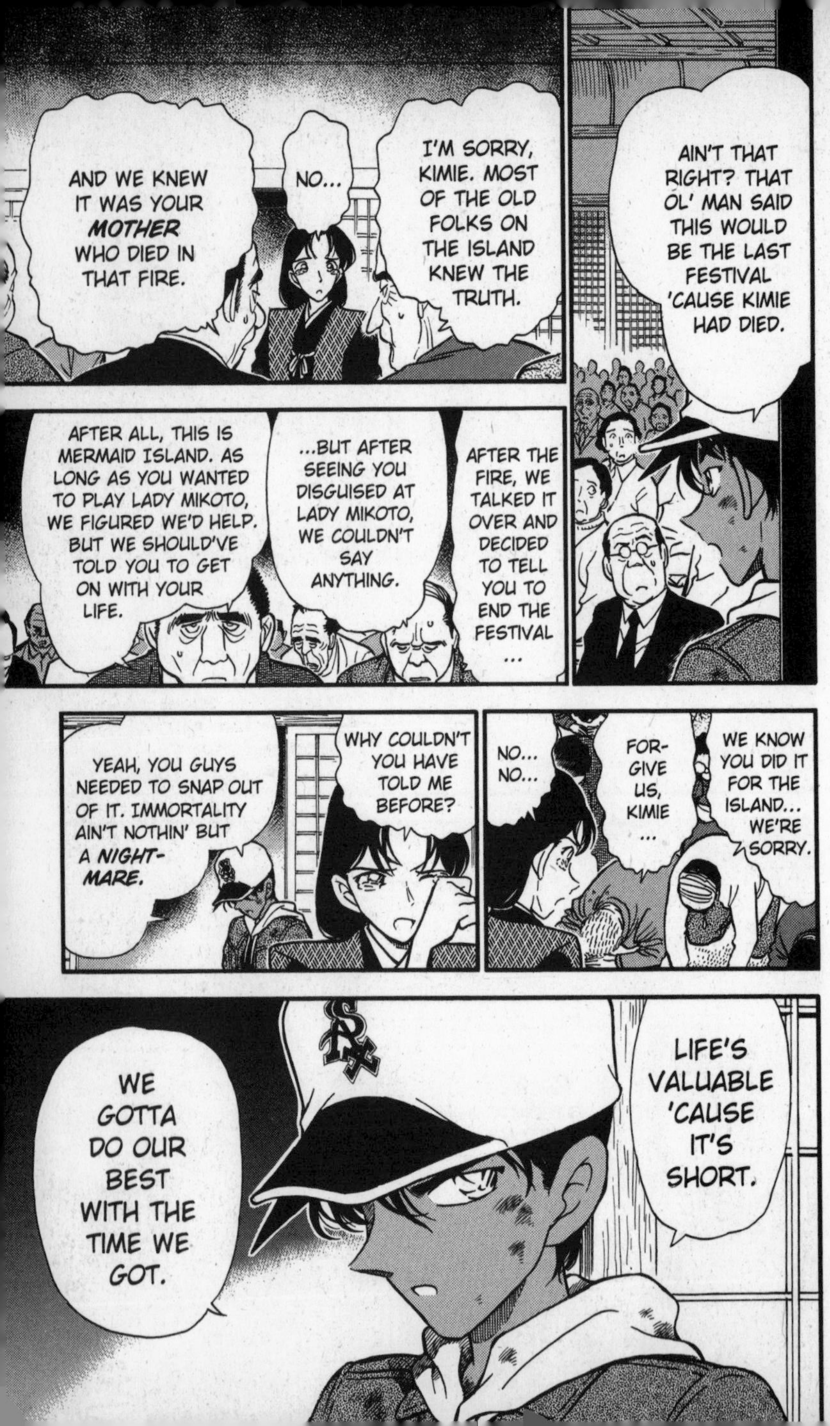
AIN'T THAT RIGHT? THAT OL' MAN SAID THIS WOULD BE THE LAST FESTIVAL 'CAUSE KIMIE HAD DIED.
I'M SORRY, KIMIE. MOST OF THE OLD FOLKS ON THE ISLAND KNEW THE TRUTH.
NO...
AND WE KNEW IT WAS YOUR ***MOTHER*** WHO DIED IN THAT FIRE.
AFTER THE FIRE, WE TALKED IT OVER AND DECIDED TO TELL YOU TO END THE FESTIVAL ...
...BUT AFTER SEEING YOU DISGUISED AT LADY MIKOTO, WE COULDN'T SAY ANYTHING.
AFTER ALL, THIS IS MERMAID ISLAND. AS LONG AS YOU WANTED TO PLAY LADY MIKOTO, WE FIGURED WE'D HELP. BUT WE SHOULD'VE TOLD YOU TO GET ON WITH YOUR LIFE.
WE KNOW YOU DID IT FOR THE ISLAND... WE'RE SORRY.
FOR-GIVE US, KIMIE ...
NO... NO...
WHY COULDN'T YOU HAVE TOLD ME BEFORE?
YEAH, YOU GUYS NEEDED TO SNAP OUT OF IT. IMMORTALITY AIN'T NOTHIN' BUT A ***NIGHT-MARE.***
LIFE'S VALUABLE 'CAUSE IT'S SHORT.
WE GOTTA DO OUR BEST WITH THE TIME WE GOT.

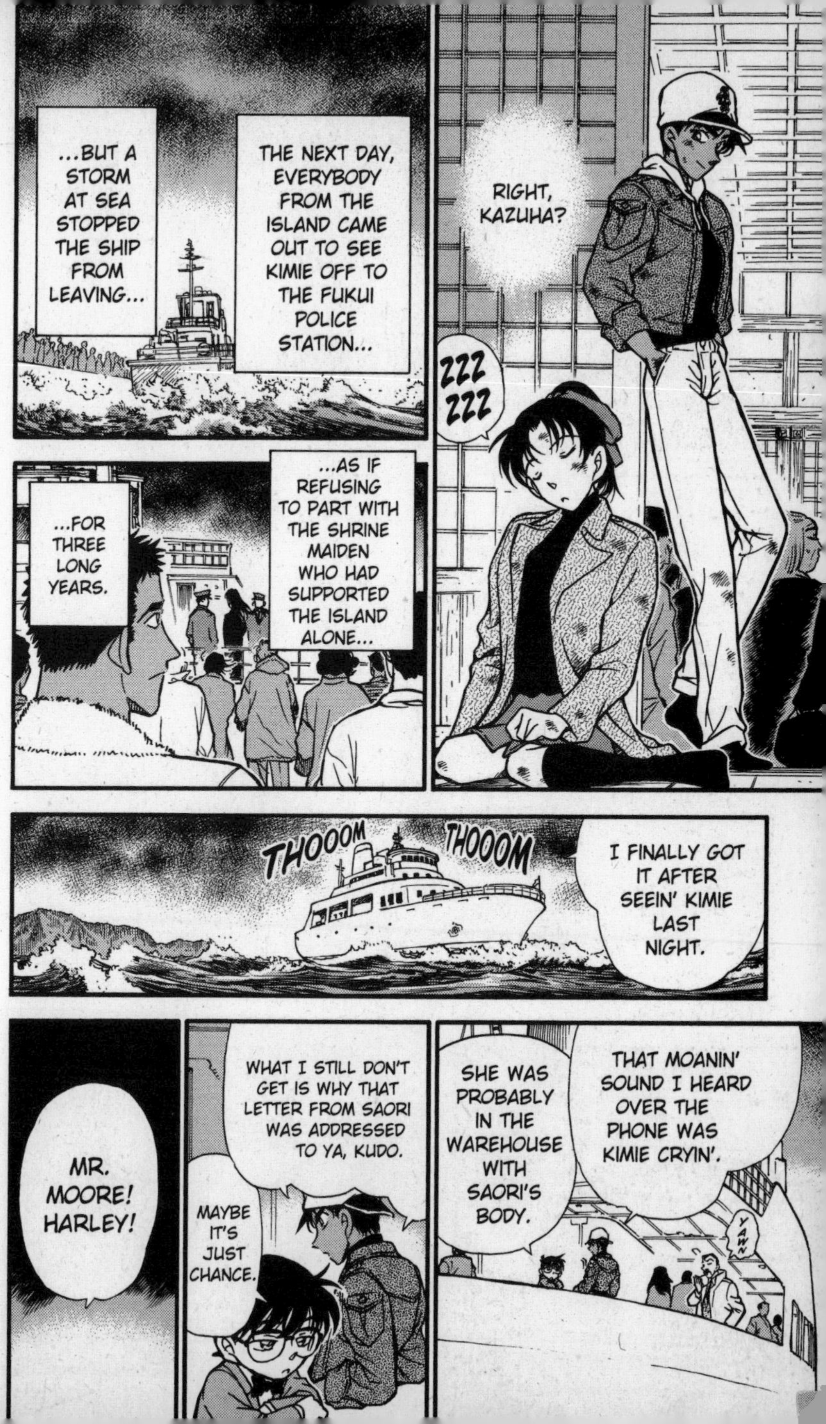
RIGHT, KAZUHA?
ZZZ ZZZ
THE NEXT DAY, EVERYBODY FROM THE ISLAND CAME OUT TO SEE KIMIE OFF TO THE FUKUI POLICE STATION...
...BUT A STORM AT SEA STOPPED THE SHIP FROM LEAVING...
...AS IF REFUSING TO PART WITH THE SHRINE MAIDEN WHO HAD SUPPORTED THE ISLAND ALONE...
...FOR THREE LONG YEARS.
I FINALLY GOT IT AFTER SEEIN' KIMIE LAST NIGHT.
THOOOM
THOOOM
THAT MOANIN' SOUND I HEARD OVER THE PHONE WAS KIMIE CRYIN'.
SHE WAS PROBABLY IN THE WAREHOUSE WITH SAORI'S BODY.
YAWN
WHAT I STILL DON'T GET IS WHY THAT LETTER FROM SAORI WAS ADDRESSED TO YA, KUDO.
MAYBE IT'S JUST CHANCE.
MR. MOORE! HARLEY!

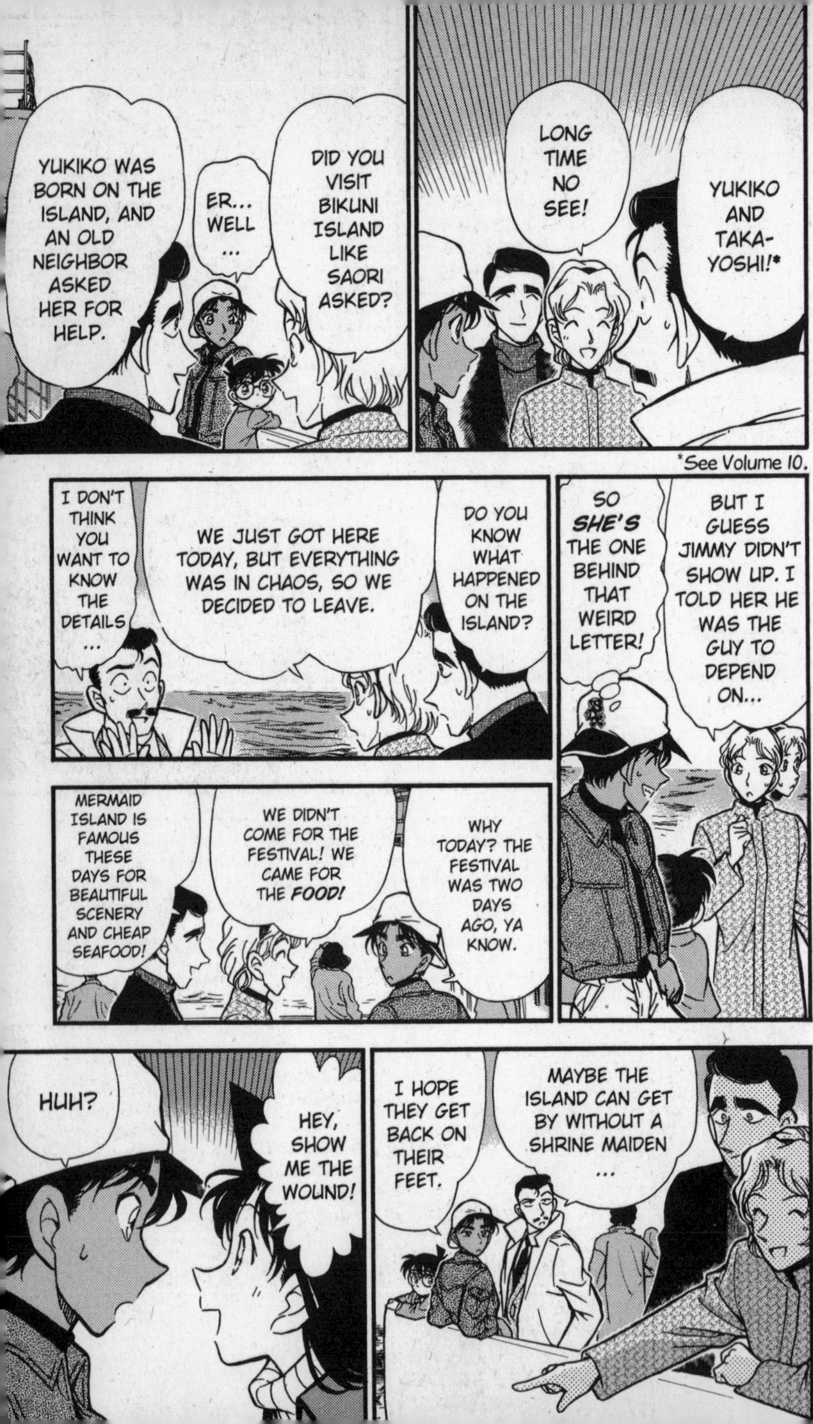
YUKIKO AND TAKA-YOSHI!*
LONG TIME NO SEE!
DID YOU VISIT BIKUNI ISLAND LIKE SAORI ASKED?
ER... WELL ...
YUKIKO WAS BORN ON THE ISLAND, AND AN OLD NEIGHBOR ASKED HER FOR HELP.
BUT I GUESS JIMMY DIDN'T SHOW UP. I TOLD HER HE WAS THE GUY TO DEPEND ON...
SO *SHE'S* THE ONE BEHIND THAT WEIRD LETTER!
DO YOU KNOW WHAT HAPPENED ON THE ISLAND?
WE JUST GOT HERE TODAY, BUT EVERYTHING WAS IN CHAOS, SO WE DECIDED TO LEAVE.
I DON'T THINK YOU WANT TO KNOW THE DETAILS ...
WHY TODAY? THE FESTIVAL WAS TWO DAYS AGO, YA KNOW.
WE DIDN'T COME FOR THE FESTIVAL! WE CAME FOR THE *FOOD!*
MERMAID ISLAND IS FAMOUS THESE DAYS FOR BEAUTIFUL SCENERY AND CHEAP SEAFOOD!
MAYBE THE ISLAND CAN GET BY WITHOUT A SHRINE MAIDEN ...
I HOPE THEY GET BACK ON THEIR FEET.
HEY, SHOW ME THE WOUND!
HUH?

*See Volume 10.

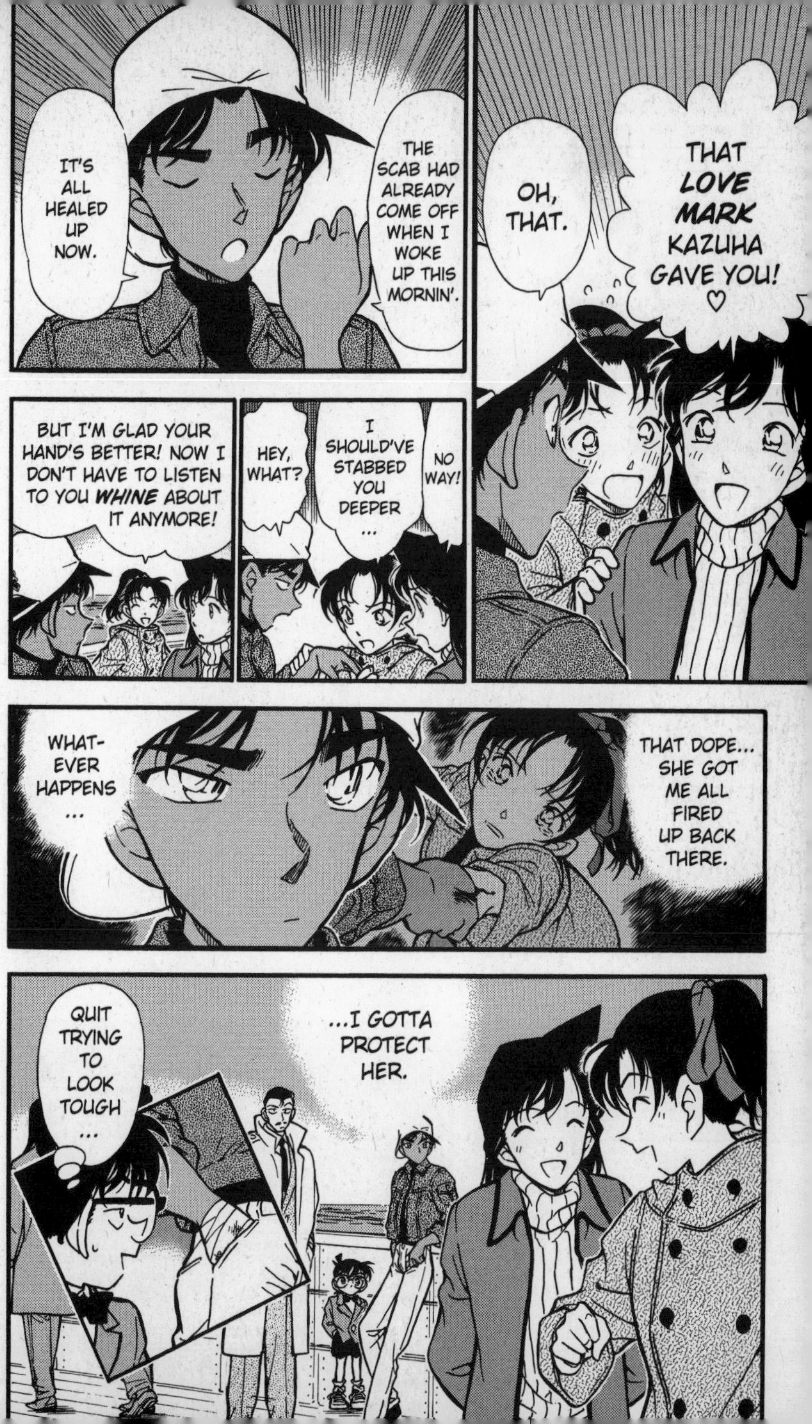
THAT *LOVE MARK* KAZUHA GAVE YOU! ♡
OH, THAT.
THE SCAB HAD ALREADY COME OFF WHEN I WOKE UP THIS MORNIN'.
IT'S ALL HEALED UP NOW.
NO WAY!
I SHOULD'VE STABBED YOU DEEPER ...
HEY, WHAT?
BUT I'M GLAD YOUR HAND'S BETTER! NOW I DON'T HAVE TO LISTEN TO YOU *WHINE* ABOUT IT ANYMORE!
THAT DOPE... SHE GOT ME ALL FIRED UP BACK THERE.
WHAT-EVER HAPPENS ...
...I GOTTA PROTECT HER.
QUIT TRYING TO LOOK TOUGH ...

FILE 11: A SECRET ENCLOSED

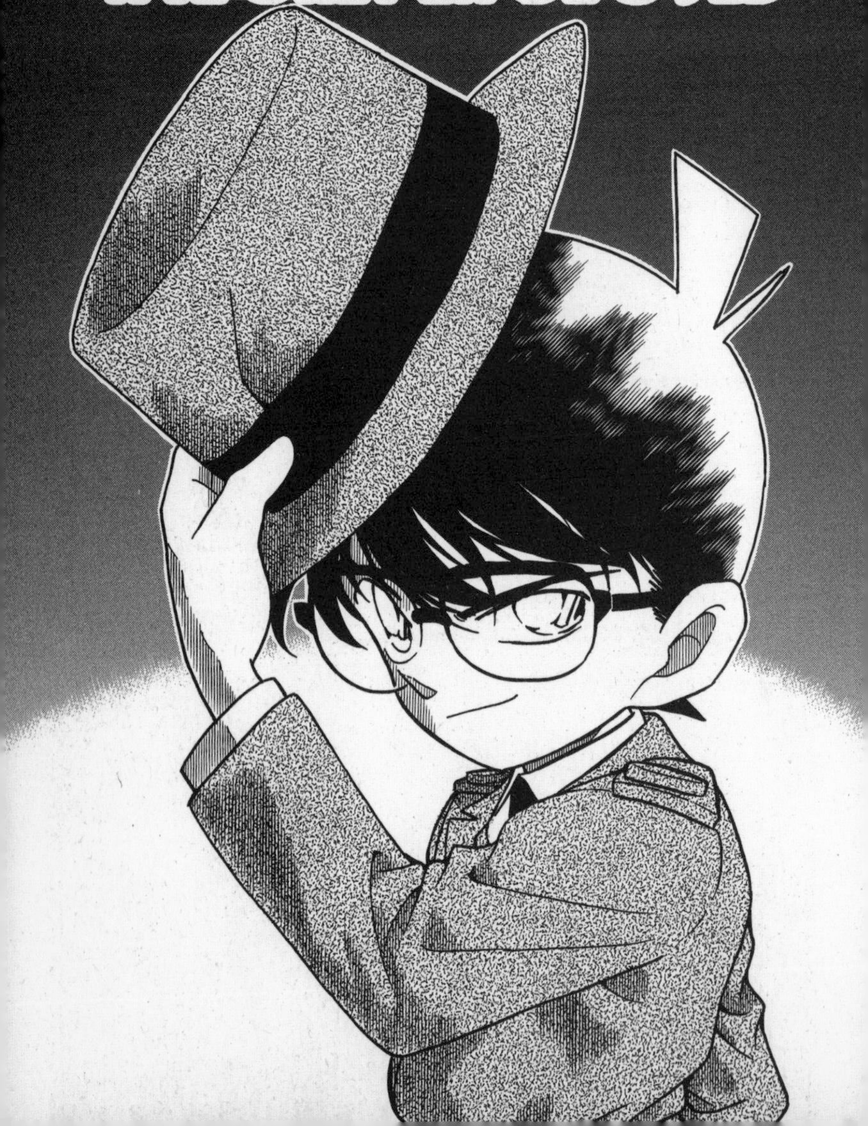

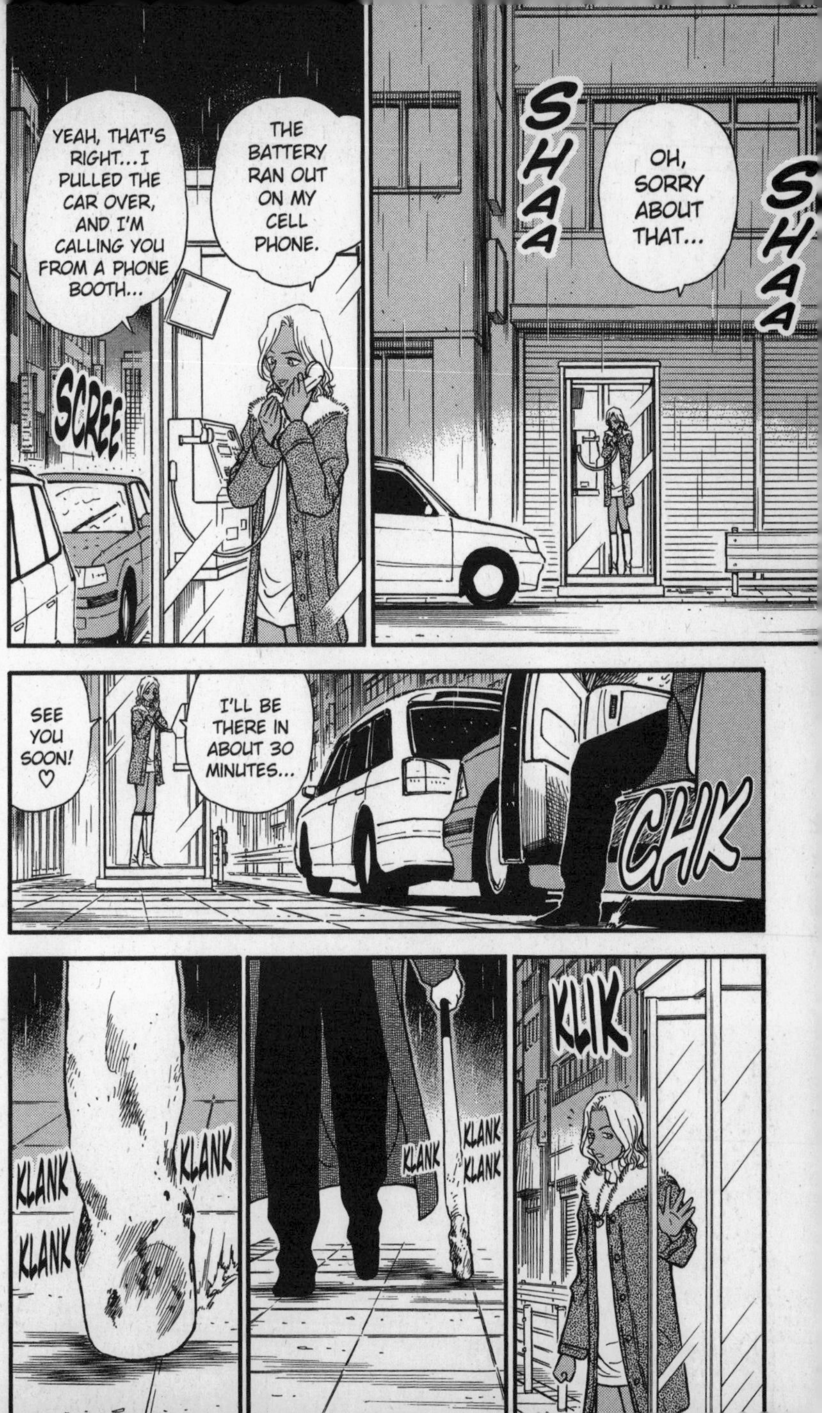
SHAA
SHAA
OH, SORRY ABOUT THAT...
THE BATTERY RAN OUT ON MY CELL PHONE.
YEAH, THAT'S RIGHT...I PULLED THE CAR OVER, AND I'M CALLING YOU FROM A PHONE BOOTH...
SCREE
CHK
I'LL BE THERE IN ABOUT 30 MINUTES...
SEE YOU SOON! ♡
KLIK
KLANK KLANK
KLANK
KLANK
KLANK
KLANK

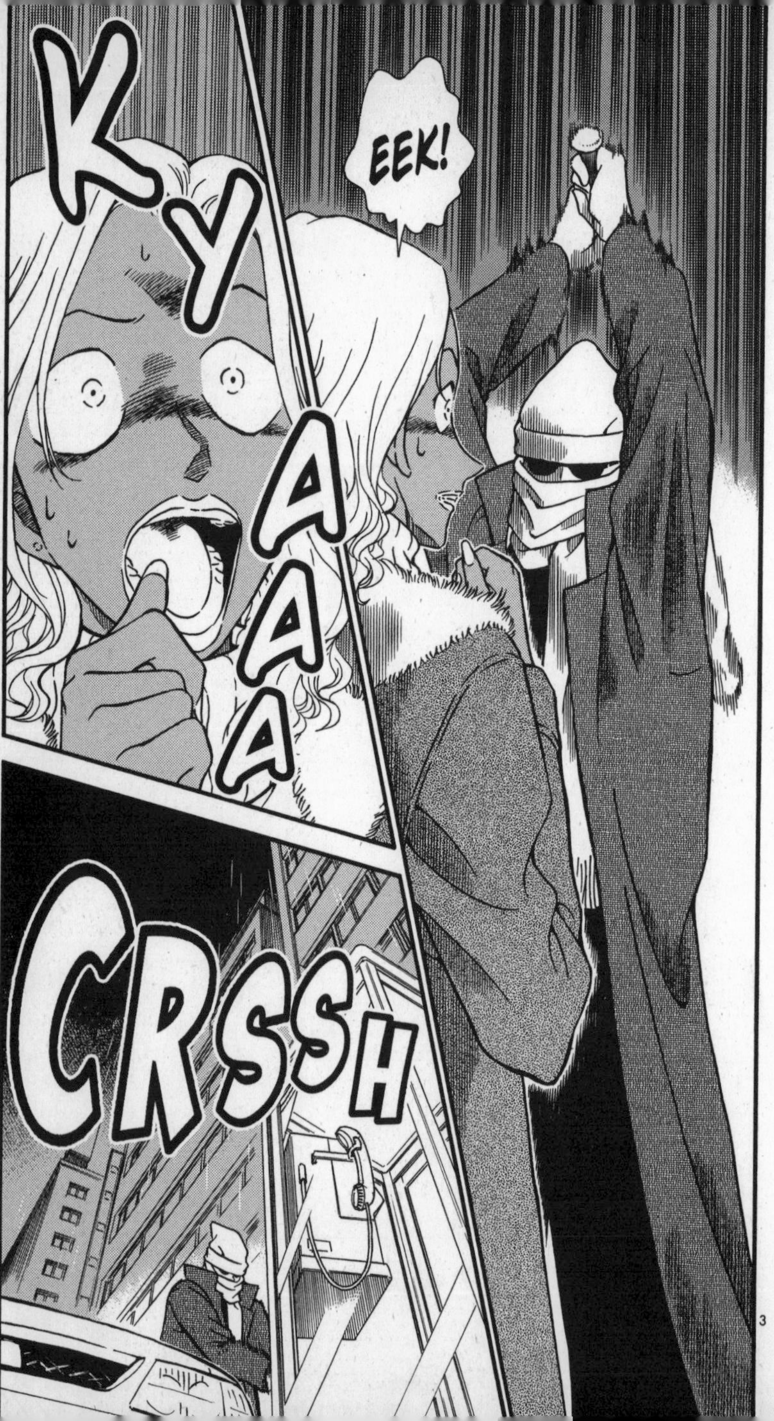
EEK!
KYAAAA
CRSSH

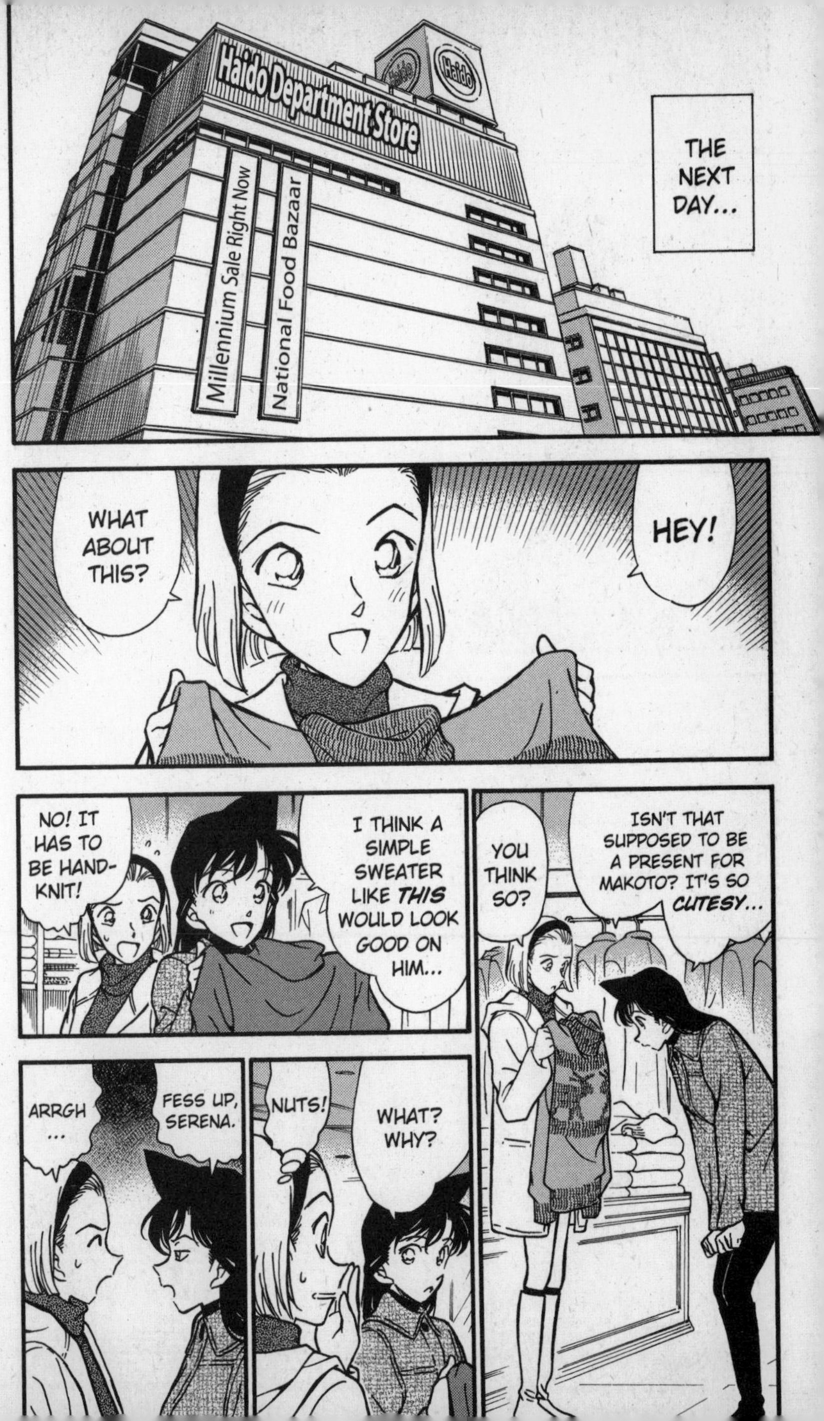
Haido Department Store
Haido
Millennium Sale Right Now
National Food Bazaar
THE NEXT DAY...
HEY!
WHAT ABOUT THIS?
ISN'T THAT SUPPOSED TO BE A PRESENT FOR MAKOTO? IT'S SO *CUTESY*...
YOU THINK SO?
I THINK A SIMPLE SWEATER LIKE *THIS* WOULD LOOK GOOD ON HIM...
NO! IT HAS TO BE HAND-KNIT!
WHAT? WHY?
NUTS!
FESS UP, SERENA.
ARRGH ...

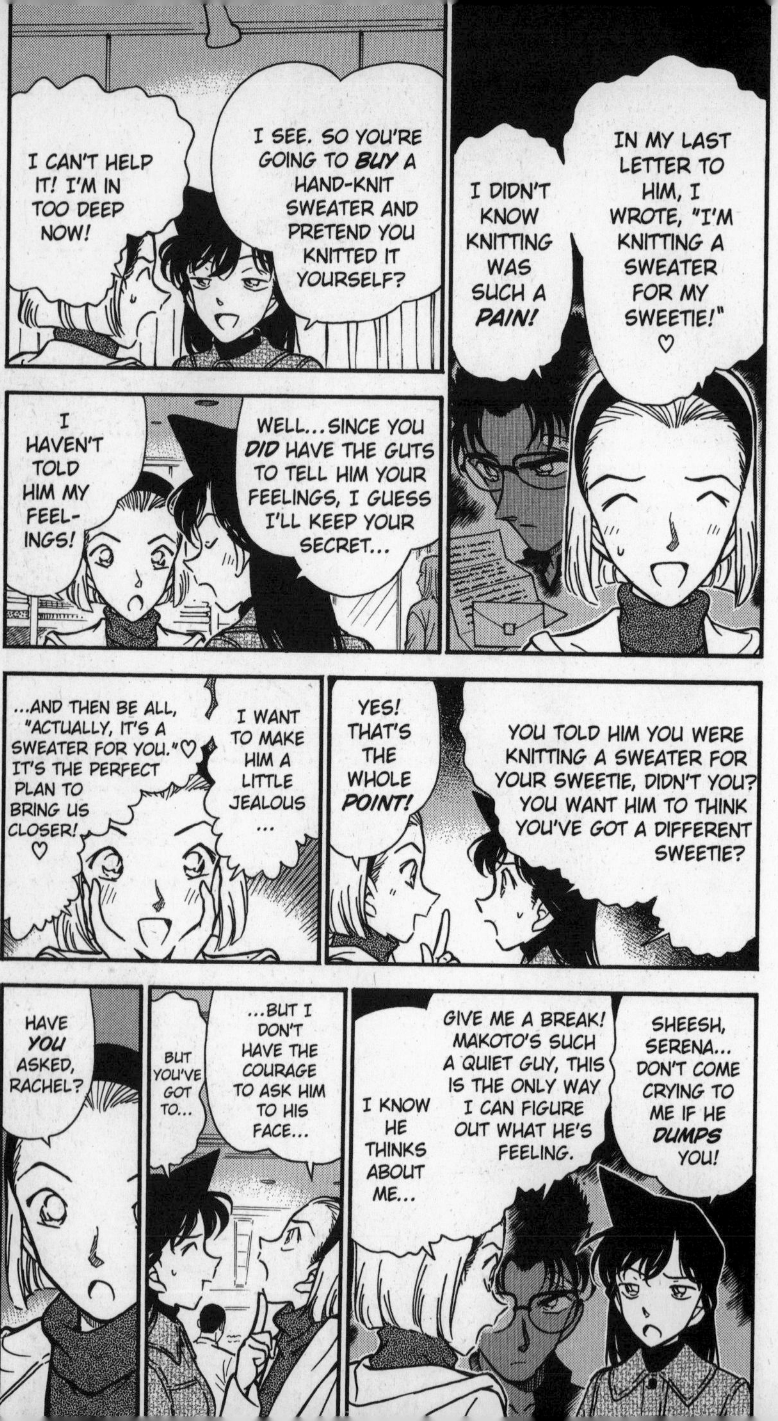
IN MY LAST LETTER TO HIM, I WROTE, "I'M KNITTING A SWEATER FOR MY SWEETIE!" ♡
I DIDN'T KNOW KNITTING WAS SUCH A PAIN!
I SEE. SO YOU'RE GOING TO BUY A HAND-KNIT SWEATER AND PRETEND YOU KNITTED IT YOURSELF?
I CAN'T HELP IT! I'M IN TOO DEEP NOW!
WELL...SINCE YOU DID HAVE THE GUTS TO TELL HIM YOUR FEELINGS, I GUESS I'LL KEEP YOUR SECRET...
I HAVEN'T TOLD HIM MY FEEL-INGS!
YOU TOLD HIM YOU WERE KNITTING A SWEATER FOR YOUR SWEETIE, DIDN'T YOU? YOU WANT HIM TO THINK YOU'VE GOT A DIFFERENT SWEETIE?
YES! THAT'S THE WHOLE POINT!
I WANT TO MAKE HIM A LITTLE JEALOUS...
...AND THEN BE ALL, "ACTUALLY, IT'S A SWEATER FOR YOU."♡ IT'S THE PERFECT PLAN TO BRING US CLOSER! ♡
SHEESH, SERENA... DON'T COME CRYING TO ME IF HE DUMPS YOU!
GIVE ME A BREAK! MAKOTO'S SUCH A QUIET GUY, THIS IS THE ONLY WAY I CAN FIGURE OUT WHAT HE'S FEELING.
I KNOW HE THINKS ABOUT ME...
...BUT I DON'T HAVE THE COURAGE TO ASK HIM TO HIS FACE...
BUT YOU'VE GOT TO...
HAVE YOU ASKED, RACHEL?

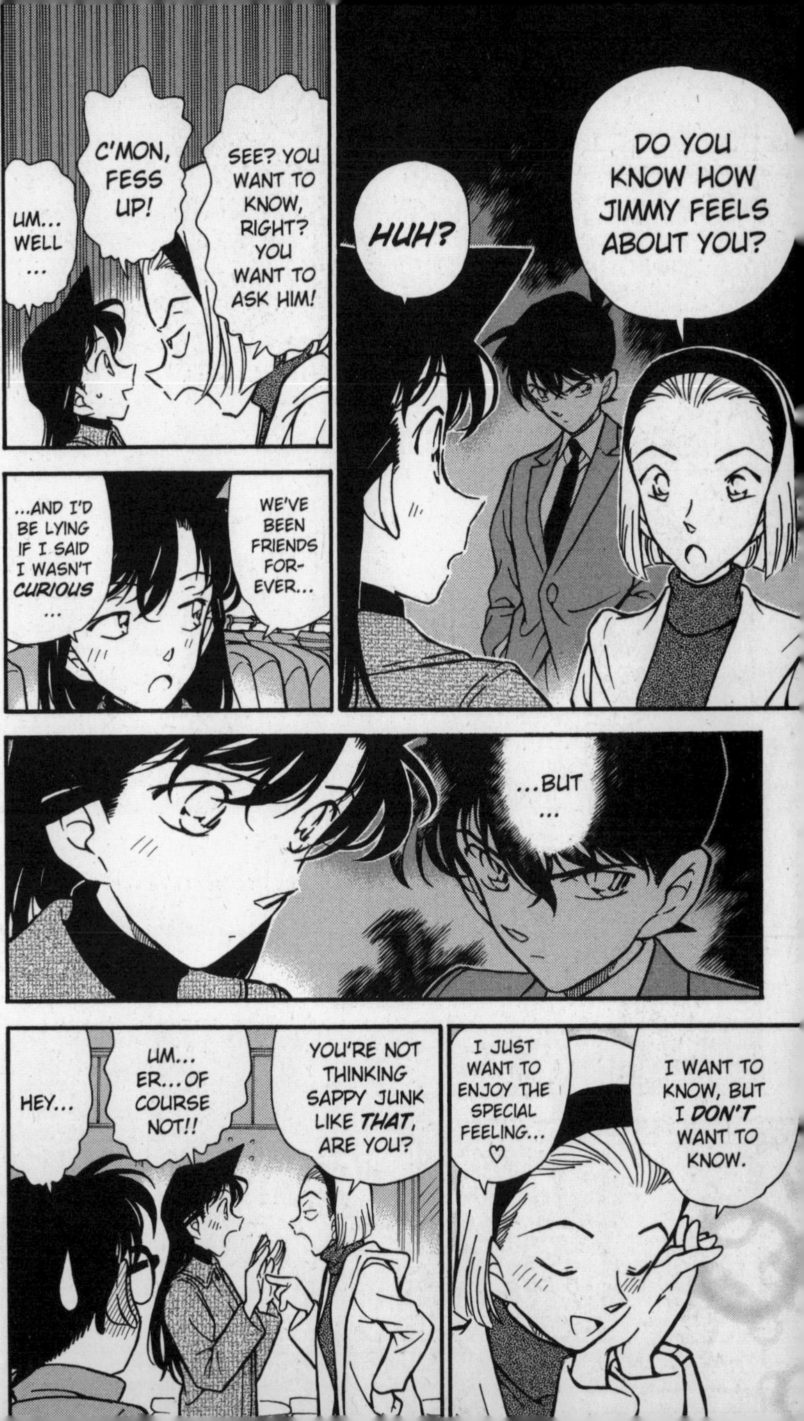
DO YOU KNOW HOW JIMMY FEELS ABOUT YOU?
HUH?
SEE? YOU WANT TO KNOW, RIGHT? YOU WANT TO ASK HIM!
C'MON, FESS UP!
UM... WELL ...
WE'VE BEEN FRIENDS FOR-EVER...
...AND I'D BE LYING IF I SAID I WASN'T *CURIOUS* ...
...BUT ...
I WANT TO KNOW, BUT I *DON'T* WANT TO KNOW.
I JUST WANT TO ENJOY THE SPECIAL FEELING... ♡
YOU'RE NOT THINKING SAPPY JUNK LIKE *THAT*, ARE YOU?
UM... ER...OF COURSE NOT!!
HEY...

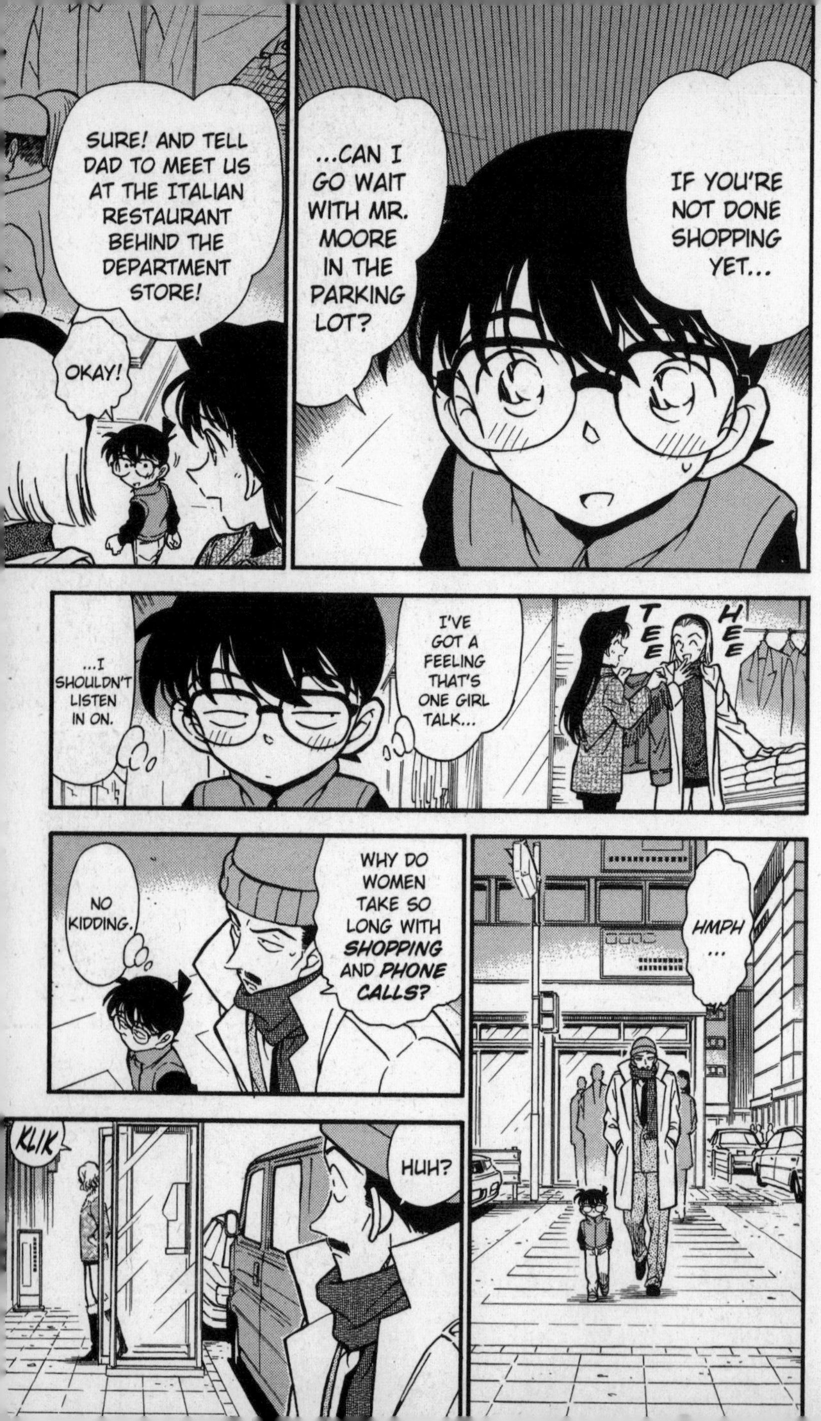
IF YOU'RE NOT DONE SHOPPING YET...
...CAN I GO WAIT WITH MR. MOORE IN THE PARKING LOT?
SURE! AND TELL DAD TO MEET US AT THE ITALIAN RESTAURANT BEHIND THE DEPARTMENT STORE!
OKAY!
TEE HEE
I'VE GOT A FEELING THAT'S ONE GIRL TALK...
...I SHOULDN'T LISTEN IN ON.
HMPH ...
WHY DO WOMEN TAKE SO LONG WITH **SHOPPING** AND **PHONE CALLS?**
NO KIDDING.
KLIK
HUH?

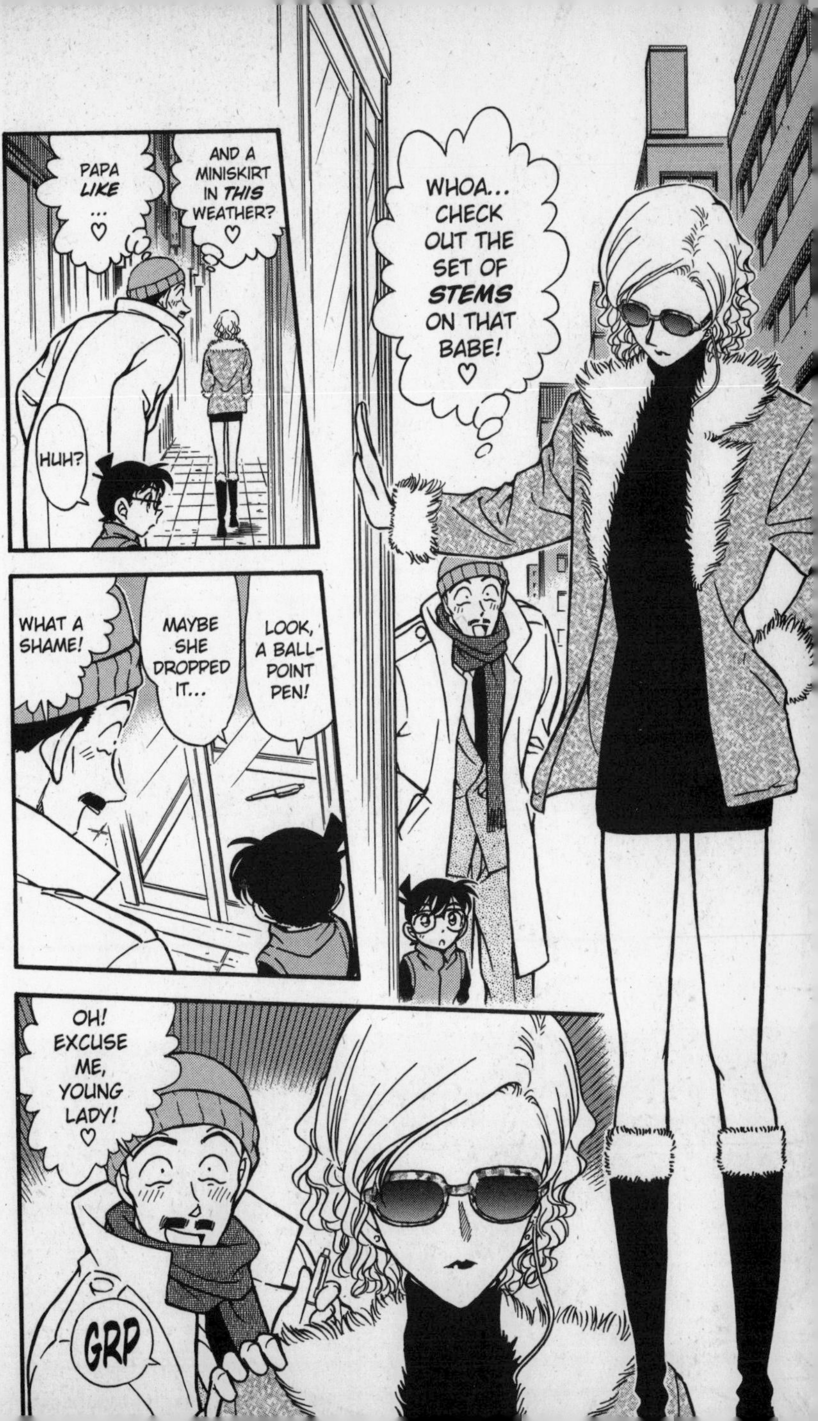
WHOA... CHECK OUT THE SET OF **STEMS** ON THAT BABE! ♡
AND A MINISKIRT IN ***THIS*** WEATHER? ♡
PAPA ***LIKE*** ... ♡
HUH?
LOOK, A BALL-POINT PEN!
MAYBE SHE DROPPED IT...
WHAT A SHAME!
OH! EXCUSE ME, YOUNG LADY! ♡
GRP

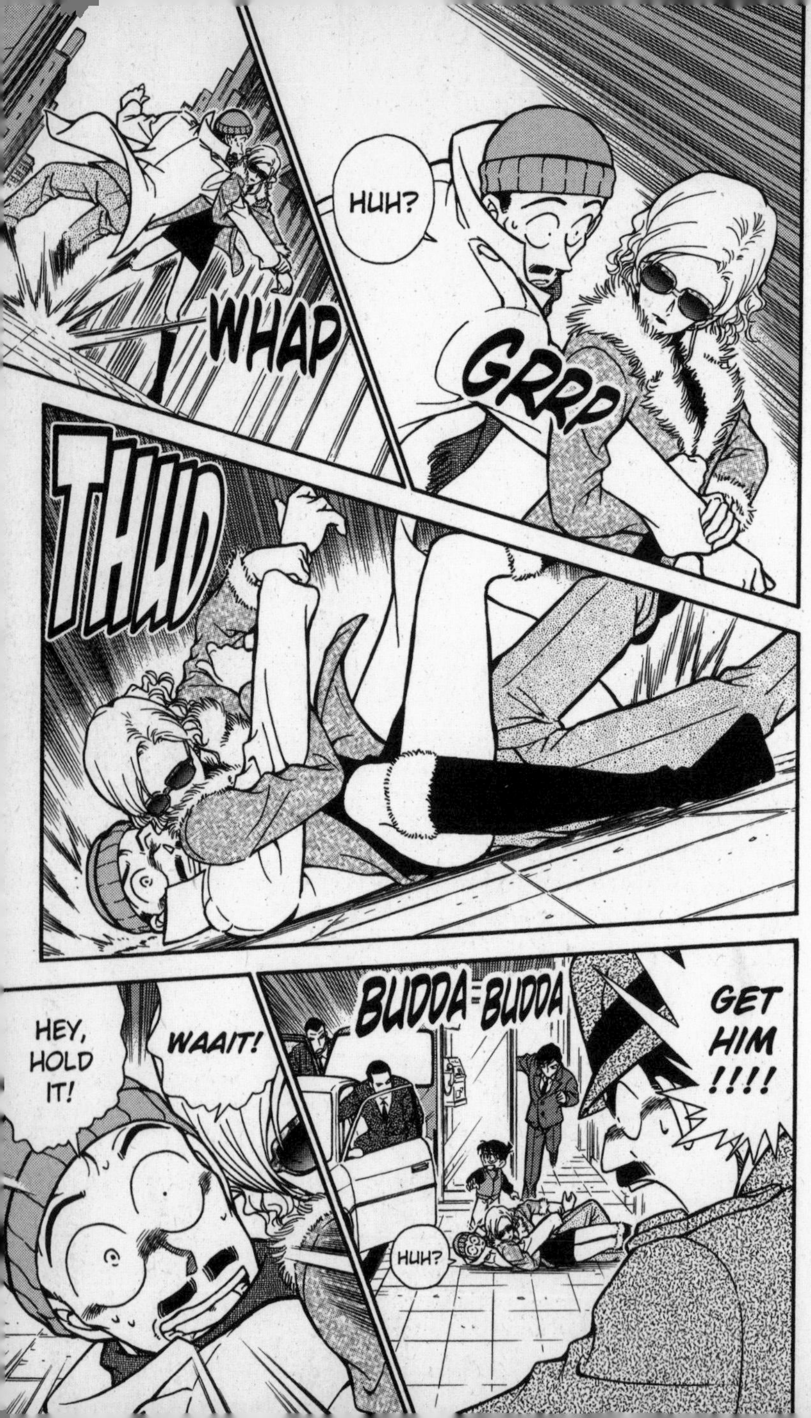
HUH?
GRRP
WHAP
THUD
GET HIM !!!!
BUDDA-BUDDA
HUH?
WAAIT!
HEY, HOLD IT!

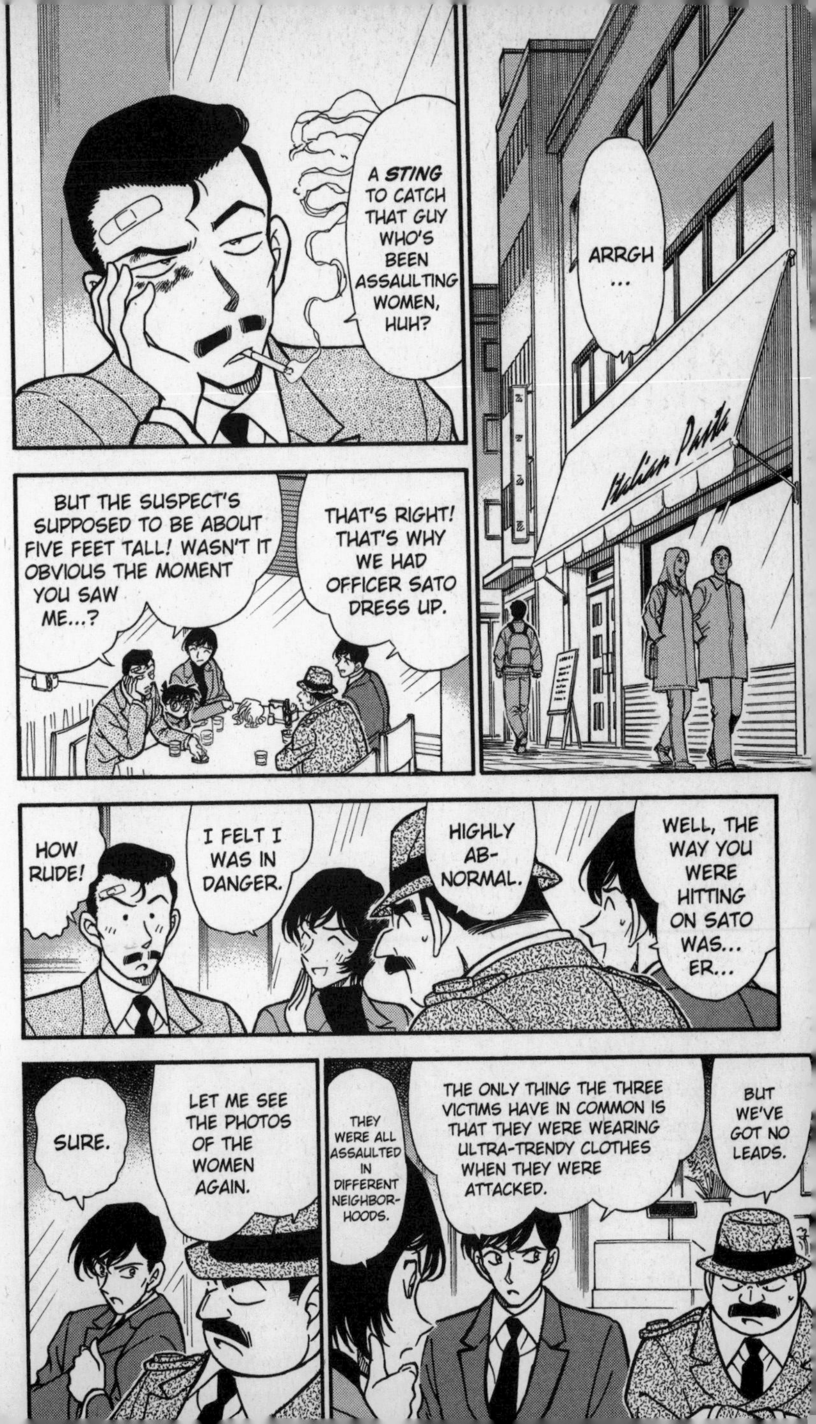
ARRGH...
A STING TO CATCH THAT GUY WHO'S BEEN ASSAULTING WOMEN, HUH?
THAT'S RIGHT! THAT'S WHY WE HAD OFFICER SATO DRESS UP.
BUT THE SUSPECT'S SUPPOSED TO BE ABOUT FIVE FEET TALL! WASN'T IT OBVIOUS THE MOMENT YOU SAW ME...?
WELL, THE WAY YOU WERE HITTING ON SATO WAS... ER...
HIGHLY AB-NORMAL.
I FELT I WAS IN DANGER.
HOW RUDE!
BUT WE'VE GOT NO LEADS.
THE ONLY THING THE THREE VICTIMS HAVE IN COMMON IS THAT THEY WERE WEARING ULTRA-TRENDY CLOTHES WHEN THEY WERE ATTACKED.
THEY WERE ALL ASSAULTED IN DIFFERENT NEIGHBOR-HOODS.
LET ME SEE THE PHOTOS OF THE WOMEN AGAIN.
SURE.

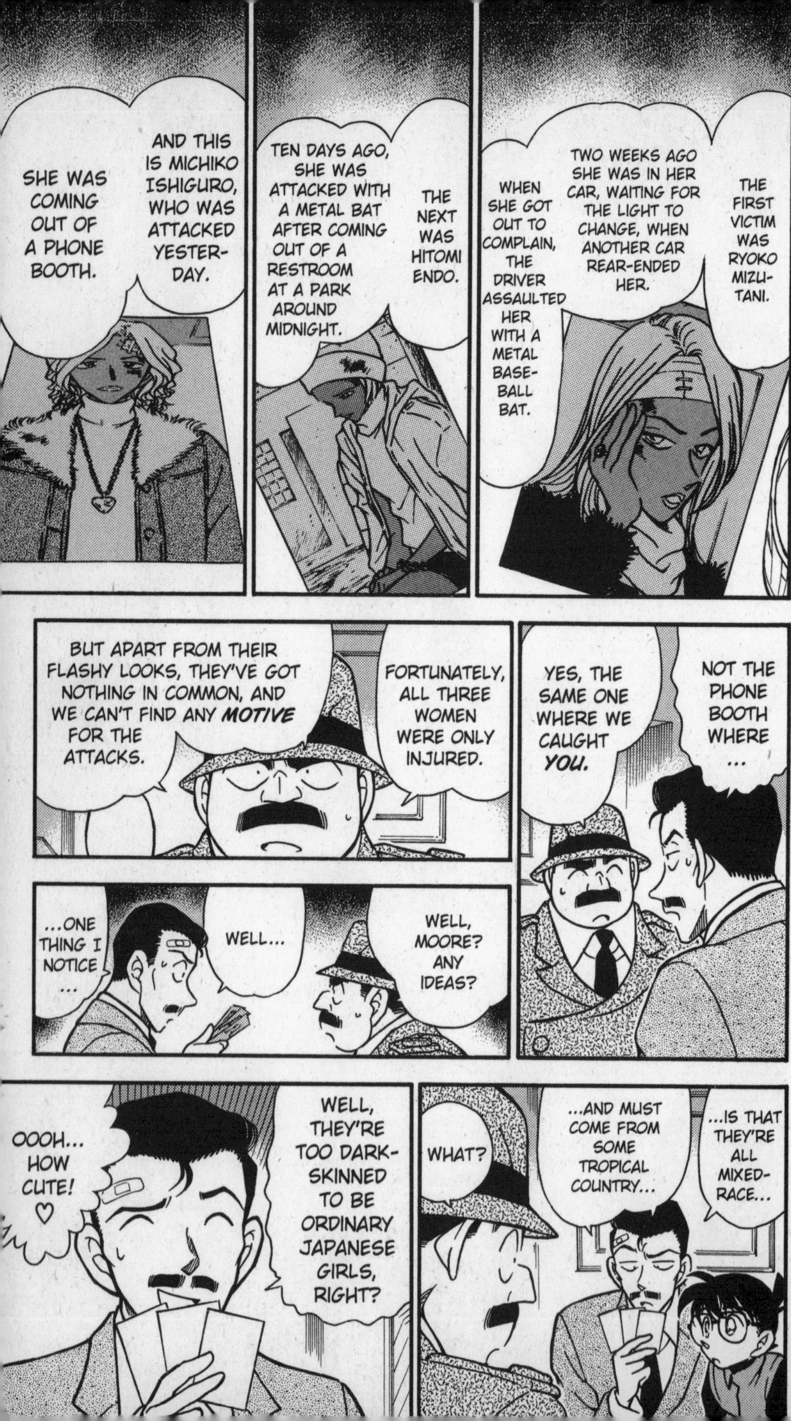
THE FIRST VICTIM WAS RYOKO MIZUTANI.
TWO WEEKS AGO SHE WAS IN HER CAR, WAITING FOR THE LIGHT TO CHANGE, WHEN ANOTHER CAR REAR-ENDED HER.
WHEN SHE GOT OUT TO COMPLAIN, THE DRIVER ASSAULTED HER WITH A METAL BASE-BALL BAT.
THE NEXT WAS HITOMI ENDO.
TEN DAYS AGO, SHE WAS ATTACKED WITH A METAL BAT AFTER COMING OUT OF A RESTROOM AT A PARK AROUND MIDNIGHT.
AND THIS IS MICHIKO ISHIGURO, WHO WAS ATTACKED YESTER-DAY.
SHE WAS COMING OUT OF A PHONE BOOTH.
NOT THE PHONE BOOTH WHERE ...
YES, THE SAME ONE WHERE WE CAUGHT ***YOU.***
FORTUNATELY, ALL THREE WOMEN WERE ONLY INJURED.
BUT APART FROM THEIR FLASHY LOOKS, THEY'VE GOT NOTHING IN COMMON, AND WE CAN'T FIND ANY ***MOTIVE*** FOR THE ATTACKS.
WELL, MOORE? ANY IDEAS?
WELL...
...ONE THING I NOTICE ...
...IS THAT THEY'RE ALL MIXED-RACE...
...AND MUST COME FROM SOME TROPICAL COUNTRY...
WHAT?
WELL, THEY'RE TOO DARK-SKINNED TO BE ORDINARY JAPANESE GIRLS, RIGHT?
OOOH... HOW CUTE! ♡

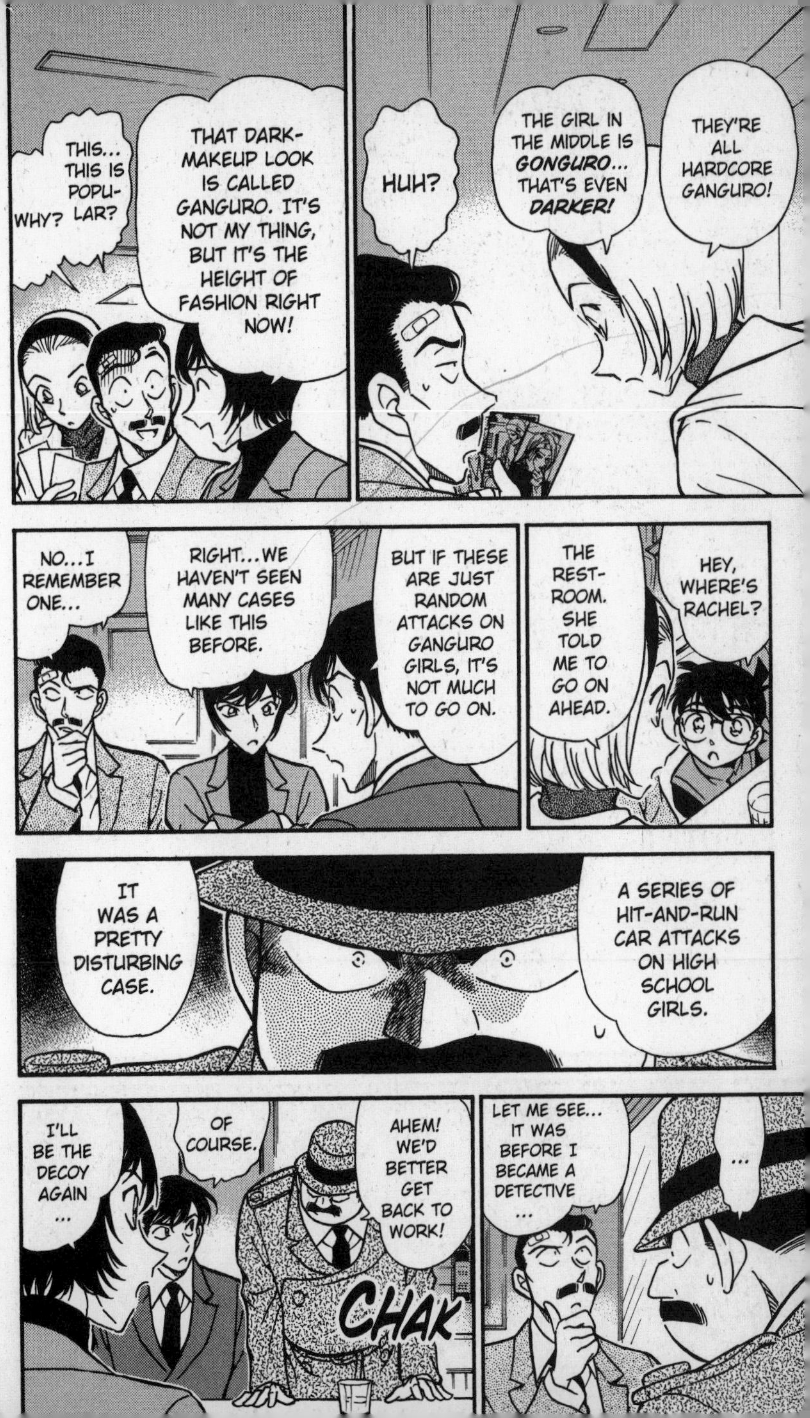
THEY'RE ALL HARDCORE GANGURO!
THE GIRL IN THE MIDDLE IS *GONGURO*... THAT'S EVEN *DARKER!*
HUH?
THAT DARK-MAKEUP LOOK IS CALLED GANGURO. IT'S NOT MY THING, BUT IT'S THE HEIGHT OF FASHION RIGHT NOW!
THIS... THIS IS POPULAR?
WHY?
HEY, WHERE'S RACHEL?
THE RESTROOM. SHE TOLD ME TO GO ON AHEAD.
BUT IF THESE ARE JUST RANDOM ATTACKS ON GANGURO GIRLS, IT'S NOT MUCH TO GO ON.
RIGHT...WE HAVEN'T SEEN MANY CASES LIKE THIS BEFORE.
NO...I REMEMBER ONE...
A SERIES OF HIT-AND-RUN CAR ATTACKS ON HIGH SCHOOL GIRLS.
IT WAS A PRETTY DISTURBING CASE.
...
LET ME SEE... IT WAS BEFORE I BECAME A DETECTIVE ...
AHEM! WE'D BETTER GET BACK TO WORK!
CHAK
OF COURSE.
I'LL BE THE DECOY AGAIN ...

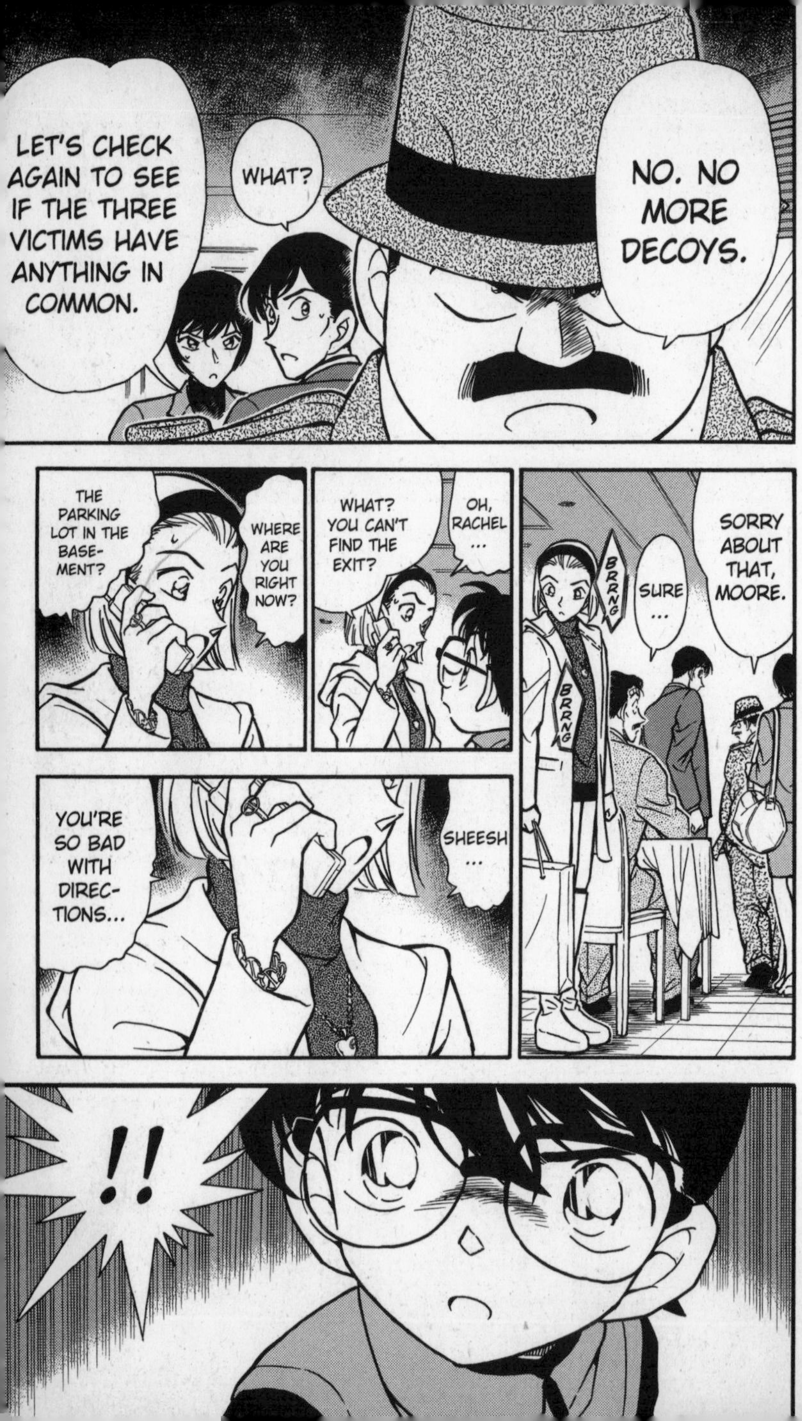
NO. NO MORE DECOYS.
WHAT?
LET'S CHECK AGAIN TO SEE IF THE THREE VICTIMS HAVE ANYTHING IN COMMON.
SORRY ABOUT THAT, MOORE.
SURE...
BRRNG
BRRNG
OH, RACHEL...
WHAT? YOU CAN'T FIND THE EXIT?
WHERE ARE YOU RIGHT NOW?
THE PARKING LOT IN THE BASEMENT?
SHEESH...
YOU'RE SO BAD WITH DIRECTIONS...
!!

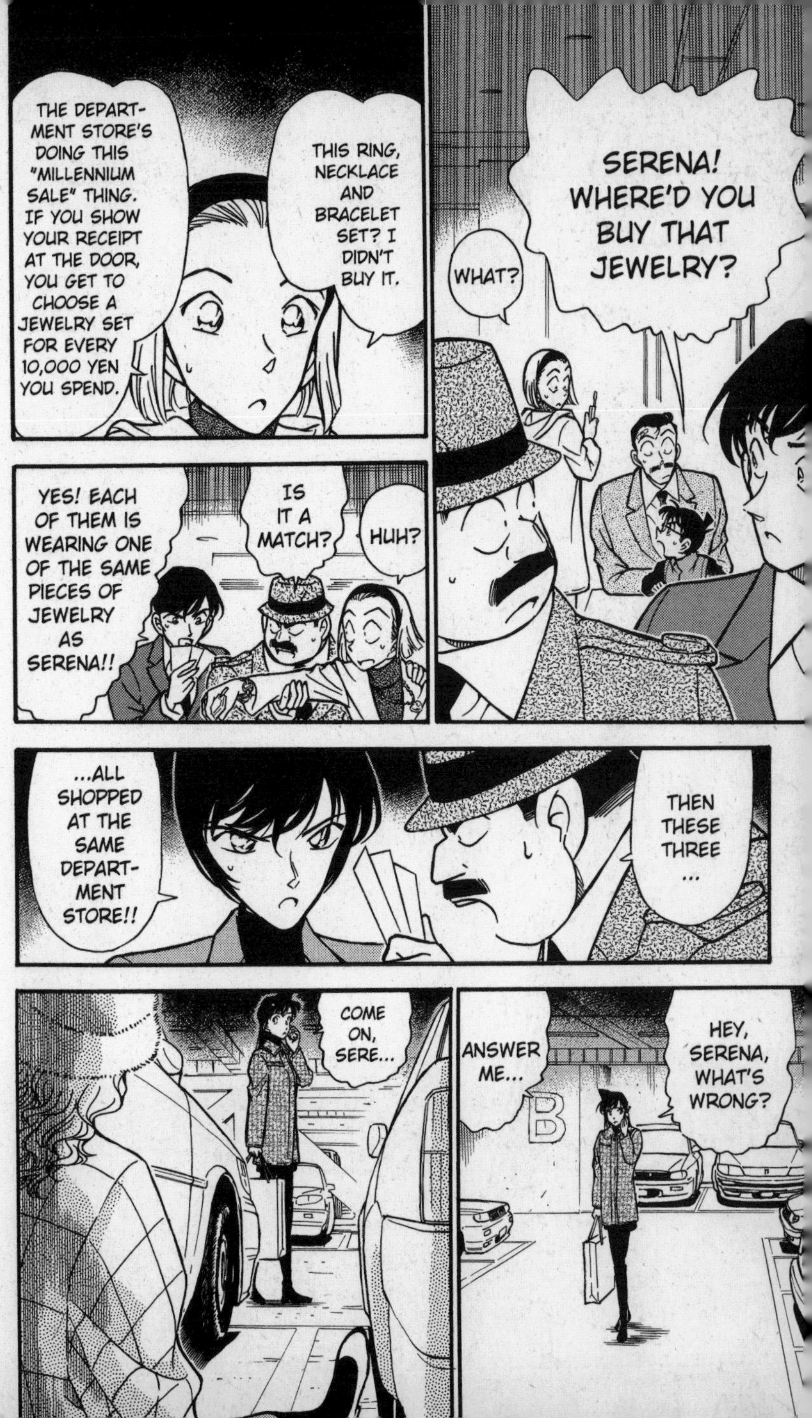
SERENA! WHERE'D YOU BUY THAT JEWELRY?
WHAT?
THIS RING, NECKLACE AND BRACELET SET? I DIDN'T BUY IT.
THE DEPART-MENT STORE'S DOING THIS "MILLENNIUM SALE" THING. IF YOU SHOW YOUR RECEIPT AT THE DOOR, YOU GET TO CHOOSE A JEWELRY SET FOR EVERY 10,000 YEN YOU SPEND.
HUH?
IS IT A MATCH?
YES! EACH OF THEM IS WEARING ONE OF THE SAME PIECES OF JEWELRY AS SERENA!!
THEN THESE THREE ...
...ALL SHOPPED AT THE SAME DEPART-MENT STORE!!
HEY, SERENA, WHAT'S WRONG?
ANSWER ME...
B
COME ON, SERE...

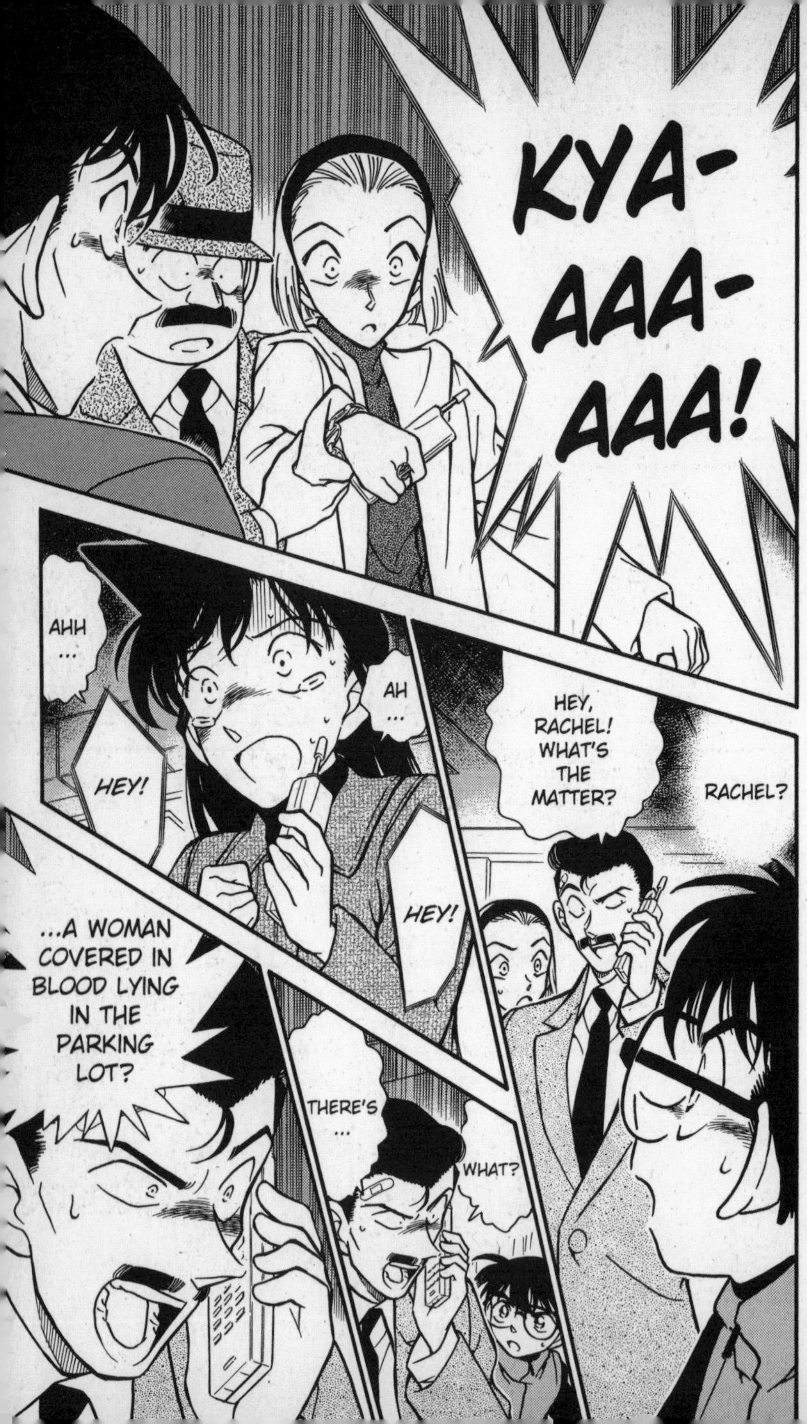
KYA-
AAA-
AAA!
RACHEL?
HEY, RACHEL! WHAT'S THE MATTER?
AH ...
AHH ...
HEY!
HEY!
THERE'S ...
WHAT?
...A WOMAN COVERED IN BLOOD LYING IN THE PARKING LOT?

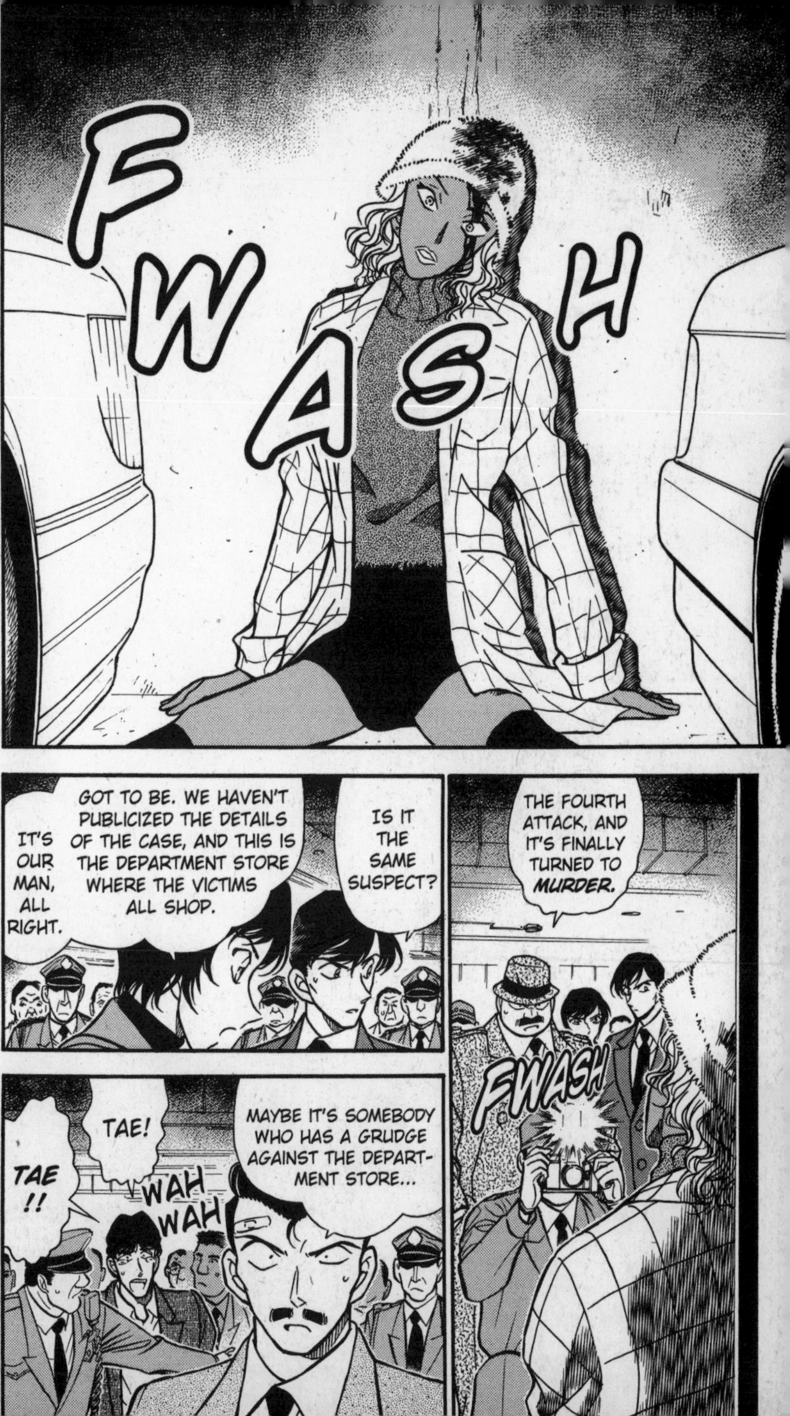
FWASH
THE FOURTH ATTACK, AND IT'S FINALLY TURNED TO *MURDER.*
FWASH
IS IT THE SAME SUSPECT?
GOT TO BE. WE HAVEN'T PUBLICIZED THE DETAILS OF THE CASE, AND THIS IS THE DEPARTMENT STORE WHERE THE VICTIMS ALL SHOP.
IT'S OUR MAN, ALL RIGHT.
MAYBE IT'S SOMEBODY WHO HAS A GRUDGE AGAINST THE DEPARTMENT STORE...
TAE!
WAH WAH
TAE !!

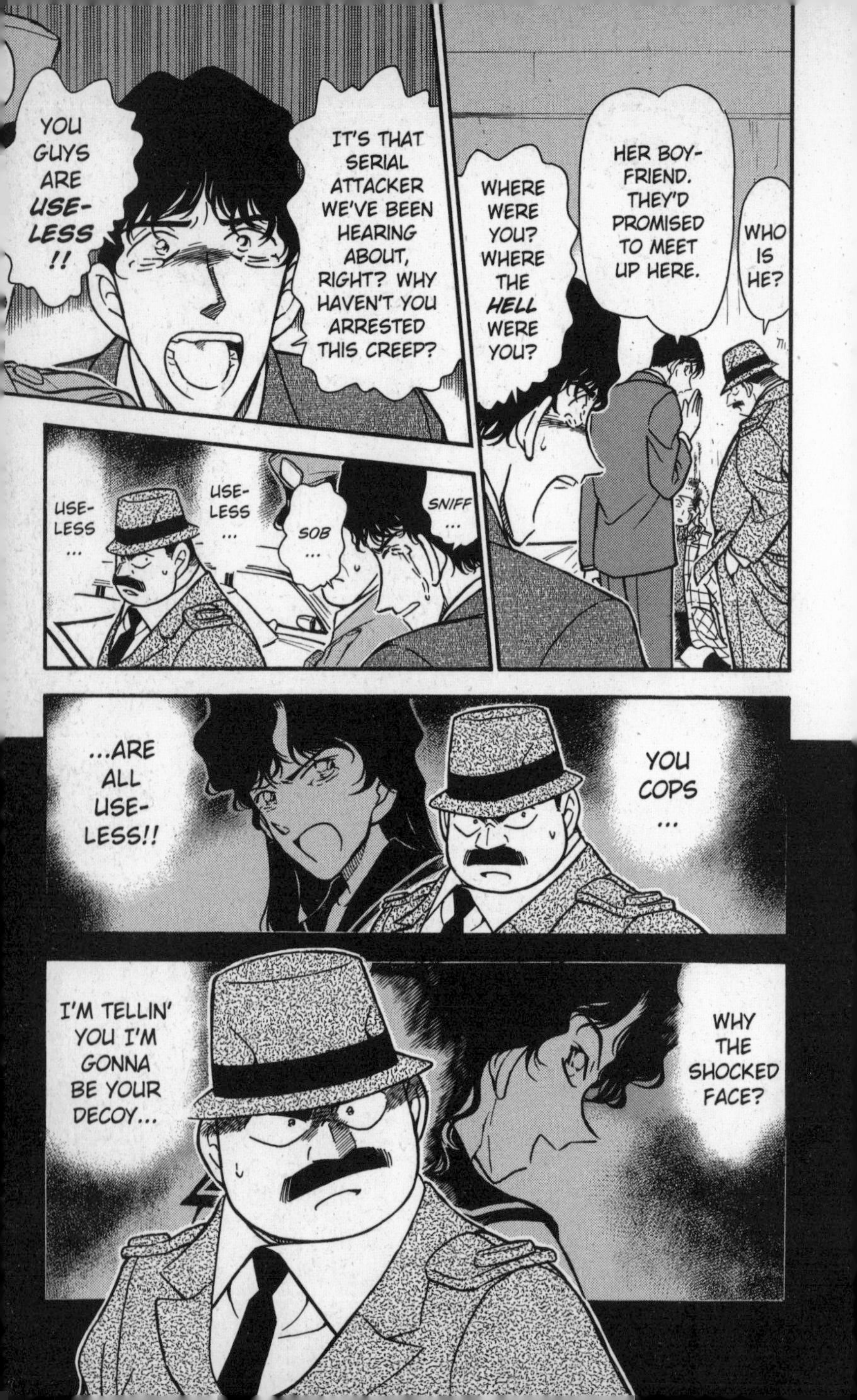
WHO IS HE?
HER BOY-FRIEND. THEY'D PROMISED TO MEET UP HERE.
WHERE WERE YOU? WHERE THE *HELL* WERE YOU?
IT'S THAT SERIAL ATTACKER WE'VE BEEN HEARING ABOUT, RIGHT? WHY HAVEN'T YOU ARRESTED THIS CREEP?
YOU GUYS ARE *USE-LESS* !!
SNIFF ...
SOB ...
USE-LESS ...
USE-LESS ...
YOU COPS ...
...ARE ALL USE-LESS!!
WHY THE SHOCKED FACE?
I'M TELLIN' YOU I'M GONNA BE YOUR DECOY...

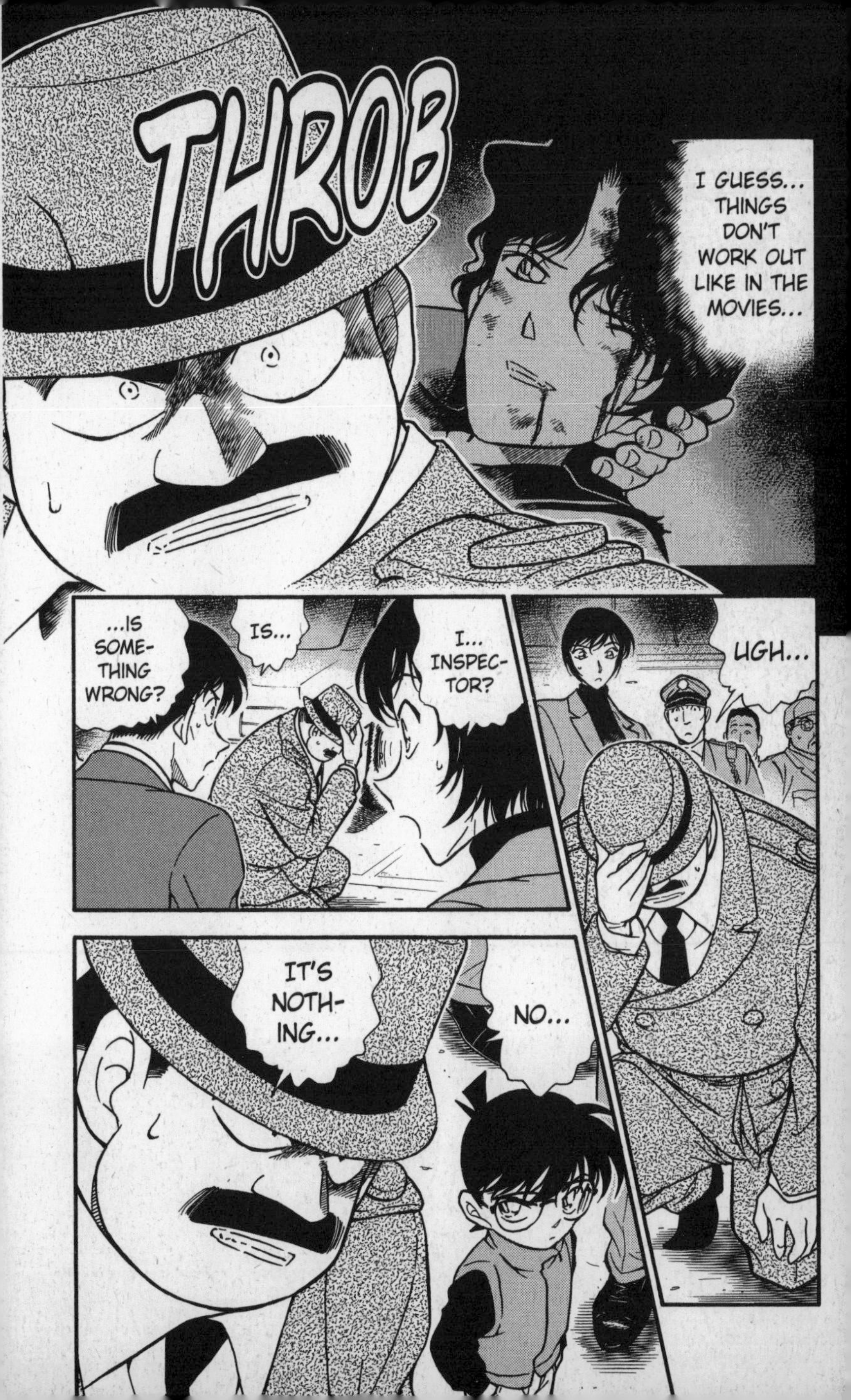
I GUESS... THINGS DON'T WORK OUT LIKE IN THE MOVIES...
THROB
UGH...
I... INSPECTOR?
IS...
...IS SOMETHING WRONG?
NO...
IT'S NOTHING...

Hello, Aoyama here.

Guess what? Conan has landed in Italy, the land of soccer!

I haven't taken a vacation in two years, but I finally got a chance to go to Venice, where the chef at a restaurant called Corte Sconta asked me to draw a sketch of Conan and autograph it. If you ever get the chance to go there, you may be able to see the slapdash drawing of Conan I did when I was drunk...

Gosho Aoyama's
Mystery Library

28

KYOSUKE KAMIZU

Although there are many master sleuths in Japan, only Kyosuke Kamizu deserves to be called a genius. He received a doctorate for a mathematical dissertation he wrote in high school, and by age 19 he had mastered six languages and was majoring in forensic medicine at college. It's been said of him, "There was no Kamizu before Kamizu, and there will never be another Kamizu after him!"

Kamizu puts his intellect to full use in criminal investigations. Sometimes he can figure out a case just by hearing the essential points from his partner, Kenzo Matsushita. He's a tall, slim, handsome man, with a wide brow and clear eyes. He's a smart dresser and a concert-level pianist...as you can imagine, women fall all over him, but he hates women. He won't touch tobacco or alcohol either. His creator, Akimitsu Takagi, was told to become a writer by a fortune-teller. The very first novel he wrote got published. I'd love to meet that fortune-teller and ask about this year's pennant race.

I recommend *Ningyo Wa Naze Korosareru?* (Why Was the Doll Killed?).

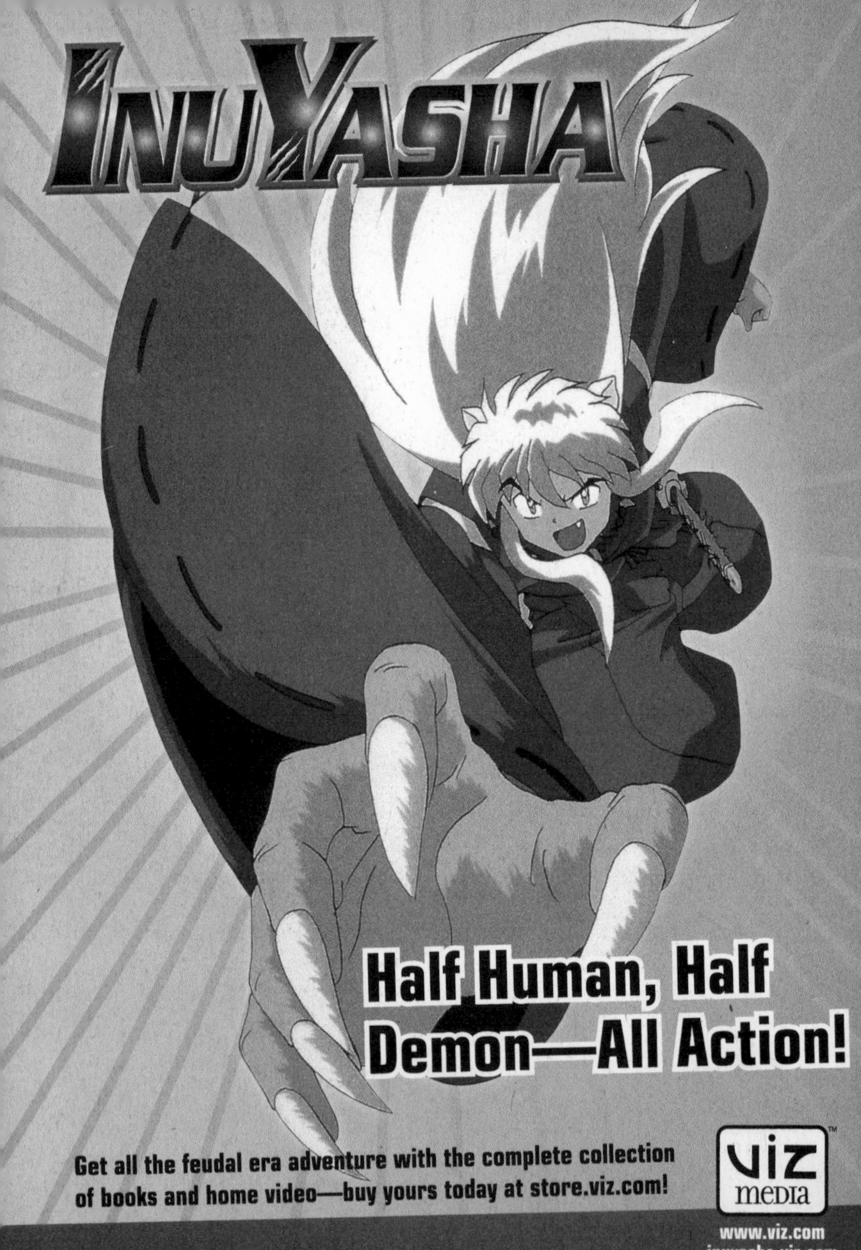

INUYASHA
Half Human, Half Demon—All Action!
Get all the feudal era adventure with the complete collection of books and home video—buy yours today at store.viz.com!
viz media
www.viz.com
inuyasha.viz.com
© 2001 Rumiko TAKAHASHI/Shogakukan Inc.

INUYASHA

Read the action from the start with the original manga series

Full color adaptation of the popular TV series

The Art of INUYASHA

Original illustrations by
Rumiko Takahashi

Art book with cel art, paintings, character profiles and more

TV SERIES & MOVIES ON DVD!

See more of the action in *Inuyasha* full-length movies

www.viz.com
inuyasha.viz.com

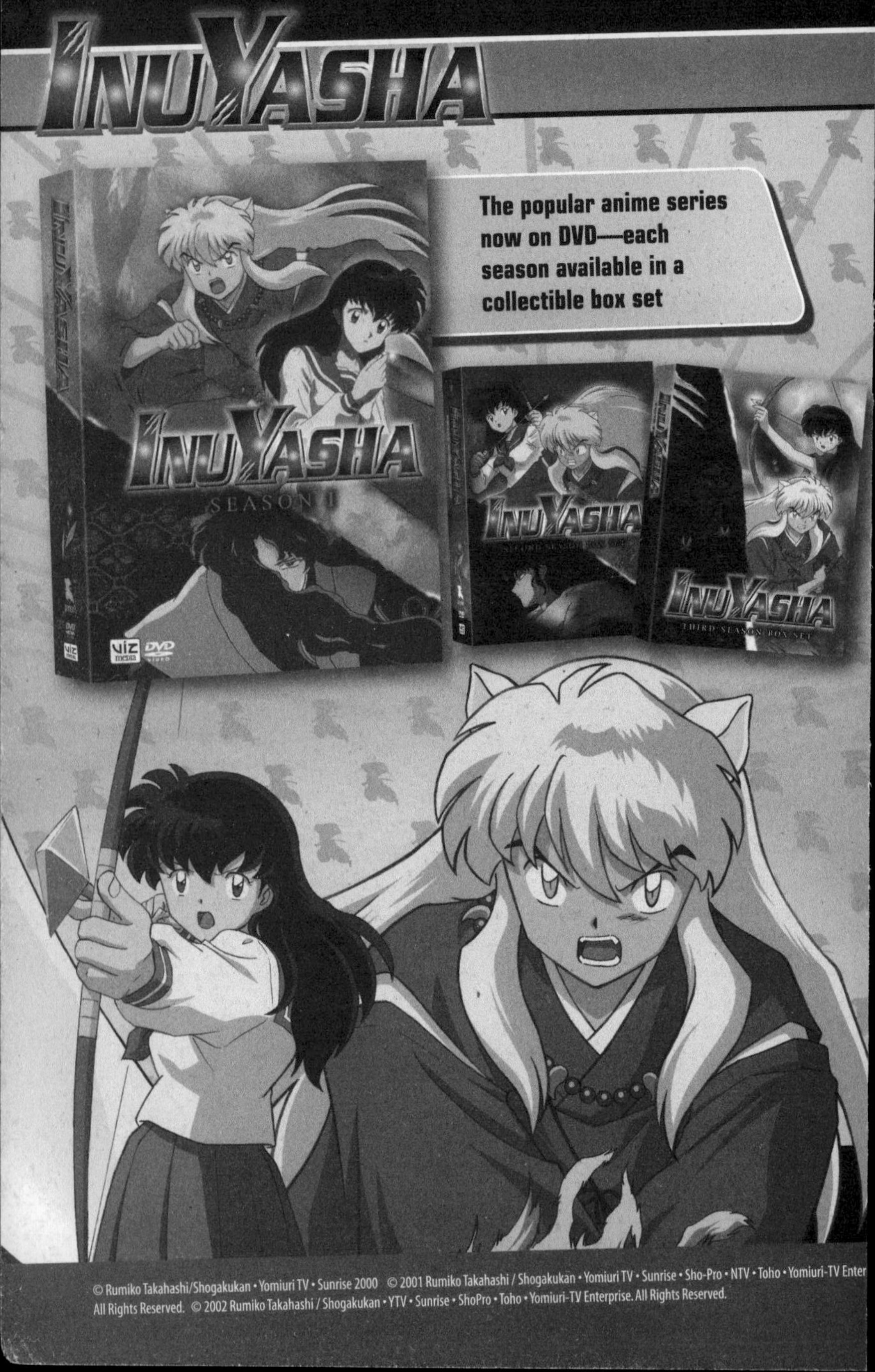
InuYasha
The popular anime series now on DVD—each season available in a collectible box set
InuYasha
SEASON 1
InuYasha
InuYasha
THIRD SEASON BOX SET

LOVE MANGA?

LET U̶S̶ [...] THINK!

...S NOW
...ASE VISIT:
...RVEY

HELP US MAKE THE MANGA
YOU LOVE BETTER!